Material Practice

Binder Practice

ISBN: 9798397421256

Percent

1. Which of the following best represents 48% of 1060?

    (A) A little more than 630.
    (B) A little less than 550.
    (C) A little less than 530.
    (D) A little more than 530.

2. A bag contains 80 marbles that are either red, white or blue. If 25% are red and there are four times as many white marbles as blue marbles, what percent are blue?

    (A) 60% (B) 50% (C) 25% (D) 15%

3. In Newton High School, 28% of all students listed math as their favorite subject, and 75% of those students are in the math club. What percent of all students are in the math club?

    (A) 103%   (B) 79%
    (C) 47%   (D) 21%

4. In Montgomery Middle School, 30% of all students play a musical instrument, and 80% of those students are in the marching band. What percent of all students are in the marching band?

    (A) 110%   (B) 50%
    (C) 24%   (D) 18%

5. Khalid guides groups on nature walks through the local park. He is paid $20 for the short trail and $25 for the long trail. If 60% of the groups take the short trail, then how many groups must he guide to earn a total of $220?

    (A) 6   (B) 8   (C) 9   (D) 10

6. Last year there were 1,020 students at Deaconville Middle School. This year there are 20% more students than last year. How many students go to Deaconville this year?

    (A) 204   (B) 1,224
    (C) 1,280   (D) 1,356

7. Ms. Saunders is a saleswoman. She receives a weekly base salary plus 12% of her weekly sales. In one week, after making $2,000 in sales, she received $500. What is Ms. Saunders's base salary?

    (A) $180.00   (B) $240.00
    (C) $260.00   (D) $740.00

8. A shirt which was originally sold for $60, was marked down 25%. How much was the sale price?

    (A) $35 (B) $45 (C) $48 (D) $80

9. During the first basketball game of the season, Vince scored $\frac{5}{50}$ of the points. During the second basketball game, he scored $\frac{27}{72}$ of the points. By what percentage did Vince improve the fraction of points he scored between the first and seconds games?

    (A) 10%   (B) 22%
    (C) 27.5%   (D) 37.5%

10. McDohl and Eli are co-editing a small novel. McDohl has so far edited 12% of the book, while Eli has edited $\frac{1}{3}$ of the story. To the nearest percent, how much of the novel is left to edit?

    (A) 45% (B) 55% (C) 58% (D) 70%

11. Two–thirds of a bus is full. What percent of the bus is **empty**?

    (A) 67% (B) 25% (C) 33% (D) $\frac{2}{3}$%

12. Amit had to run for 4 minutes in order to complete one lap. He ran for 3 minutes. About what percentage of the lap did Amit complete?

    (A) 25% (B) 55% (C) 75% (D) 80%

13. A study showed that 3 out of every 25 rabbits do not like carrots. Express this as a percentage.

    (A) 0.12%   (B) 3.25%
    (C) 12%   (D) 32.5%

14. Express $\frac{3}{5}$ as a percentage.

    (A) 30%   (B) 50%
    (C) 60%   (D) 166%

15. To help pay for recent renovations, a college is increasing tuition by 5%. If tuition was $45,000 a year before the 5% increase, what will the new tuition be?

    (A) $2,250   (B) $47,250
    (C) $52,500   (D) $67,500

16. What percent is represented by the picture?

    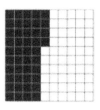

    (A) 0.44%   (B) 0.54%
    (C) 44%   (D) 54%

17. A baseball player earned a raise of 35% of his last year's salary. His salary was $30,000 last year. What is his new salary?

    (A) $4,500   (B) $10,500
    (C) $40,500   (D) $50,000

18. A book that originally costs $22.50 is at a 16% discount. How much is the book's sale price?

    (A) $1.41   (B) $3.60
    (C) $18.90   (D) $21.09

19. What is 0.1% of 1000?

    (A) 0.1 (B) 1   (C) 10   (D) 100

20. A large company took a survey of its 2,700 employees. 17% responded that they would like better management. How many employees dislike the company management?

    (A) 46   (B) 459
    (C) 1700   (D) 2241

21. Kristen bought a skirt. The original price was $27. The store, however, had a 20% sale, and then had to pay a 7.25% tax on the reduced price. How much did Kristen end up paying? Round your answer to the nearest 10 cents.

    (A) $19.75 (B) $21.60
    (C) $23.20 (D) $24.55

22. In the town of Carwell, all sales tax is 7%. Harry's Hardware's cash register does not compute the sales tax, however. What amount of tax should Harry add on to a purchase of $21.75?

    (A) $0.07 (B) $0.75
    (C) $1.34 (D) $1.52

23. A football stadium was $\frac{7}{11}$ full. What percent of the football stadium was full?

    (A) 7% (B) 11% (C) 36% (D) 64%

24. On a test, Bess got 85% of the questions correct. There were 160 question. How many did she get right?

    (A) 136 (B) 188 (C) 245 (D) 296

25. George said that 300% of 6 is 1.8. Without solving, explain why you think this is wrong.

26. How does 60% of a number less than zero compare with that number?

    (A) It is equal to that number.
    (B) It is less than that number.
    (C) It is greater than that number.
    (D) It depends on the number.

27. Base your answer to the following question on the graph below.

    ### Number of Student Failures

    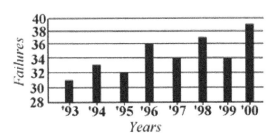

    There were 250 students in the class in 1997. What percentage of the class failed that year?

    (A) 12.9% (B) 13.6%
    (C) 15%   (D) 25%

Lunch Sales

[Bar chart showing Number Sold by Day: Mon. ~200, Tue. ~100, Wed. ~75, Thu. ~175, Fri. ~125]

28. What percentage of the total lunches sold during the week was sold on Tuesday (to the nearest percent)?

    (A) 11% (B) 15% (C) 22% (D) 24%

29. Mr. Putter, a salesperson, earned $503.00 at the end of one week. He receives a weekly base salary of $404.00 in addition to 11% of his weekly sales. What is the amount of Mr. Putter's sales?

    (A) $44.40   (B) $99.00
    (C) $900.00   (D) $907.00

30. Shari bought a car for $5300. The car's value depreciates each year. If the car is worth $1630 after 5 years, what is the rate of depreciation?

    (A) 9% (B) 13% (C) 15% (D) 21%

31. Maggie said that 45% of 10 is 45. Explain why you think this is wrong without solving.

32. The chart below represents the amount of liquid purchased by the staff Rondell High School.

Drink	Amount of Bottles
Soda	150
Water	250
Iced Tea	100
Lemonade	125

    To the nearest percent, what percentage of liquid purchased was soda?

    (A) 12% (B) 24% (C) 48% (D) 75%

33. Christoph collected pens. He owned 10,000 pens. 10% of his pens ran out of ink every week. After 4 weeks, how many pens did he have left?

    (A) 1,000   (B) 6,000
    (C) 6,561   (D) 9,960

34. Jim sold candies on Thursday and Friday. On Thursday, he sold $\frac{1}{5}$ of the candies. On Friday, he sold 50% of the remaining candies. What percent of the candies did Jim sell in total?

    (A) 30% (B) 40% (C) 60% (D) 70%

35. What is 25% of 180?

36. A car manufacturer rejects 5% of the cars it makes. If 285 cars pass, how many cars were there to begin with?

37. Express 0.54% as a decimal
    (A) 5.4
    (B) 0.54
    (C) 0.054
    (D) 0.0054

38. You bought a winter jacket at 30% off the regular price, which is $136.31. Sales tax is 8.5% of the discount price. To the nearest dollar, what is the total cost of the winter jacket?
    (A) $95
    (B) $100
    (C) $103
    (D) $104

39. Which of the following is true about 110% of 57?
    (A) It is less than 57.
    (B) It is greater than 57.
    (C) It is equal to 57.
    (D) It can't be determined.

40. A school auditorium is $\frac{3}{5}$ full. After half the students leave the auditorium, what percentage of the school auditorium is full?
    (A) 4% (B) 15% (C) 30% (D) 50%

41. Denise bought a toaster that was on sale for 30% off the original price. The original price of the toaster was $80.00. If there is an 8% sales tax, how much did Denise pay for the toaster?
    (A) $24.34
    (B) $25.92
    (C) $56.68
    (D) $60.48

42. A bag of candy was $\frac{3}{16}$ full. What percent of the bag of candy was full?
    (A) 3.16%
    (B) 6.25%
    (C) 18.75%
    (D) 81.25%

43. Using a calculator, solve for how much a $50 bank account will be worth after 2 years with 7% compound interest.

44. What is 15% of 30?
    (A) 0.45 (B) 4.5 (C) 45 (D) 450

45. Margot got 18 questions correct on a test with 20 questions. What was her percentage grade?
    (A) 95% (B) 90% (C) 85% (D) 80%

46. Jimi knows that his daily commute to work is 25 minutes long. He looks at a clock and notes that he has been driving for 9 minutes. About what percentage of his commute has he completed?
    (A) 9% (B) 25% (C) 36% (D) 50%

47. Juanita wanted to buy $80 shoes but only had $64. Every hour the price was reduced by 10% from the previous hour's price. In how many hours was Juanita able to buy the shoes?
    (A) 1 (B) 2 (C) 3 (D) 16

48. Sandy purchased a used car for $2,500. After doing some body work on it, she sold it later for $3,000. How much is her percentage of profit?

    (A) 5%   (B) 20%
    (C) 25%   (D) 500%

49. Using a calculator, solve for how much a $250 account will be worth after ten years if it has 6% simple interest.

50. Expressed as a percentage, 0.001 is

    (A) 0.001%.   (B) 0.01%.
    (C) 0.1%.   (D) 1%.

51. Joe wanted to buy a house, but couldn't afford it. He went to the bank and borrowed $9,000 at a fixed interest of 24% per year. How much interest will he pay when he pays the loan in total at the end of two years?

    (A) $2,160   (B) $4,320
    (C) $11,160   (D) $13,320

52. What is 23% of 30?

    (A) 1.9   (B) 5.8   (C) 6.9   (D) 14.2

53. A tennis racket normally costs $145. Arnold bought the racket for $108.75. What percent discount did he receive?

    (A) 25%   (B) 30%   (C) 45%   (D) 50%

54. Kathy goes to a special store that lets the customer figure out his or her own sales tax. The cashier tells her that the sales tax on her $18.50 blouse is 7%. What will Kathy need to pay in total, to the nearest cent, with the tax included?

    (A) $1.30   (B) $2.60
    (C) $18.50   (D) $19.80

55. The ratio of baseball cards to football cards in Jordan's collection is 3:5. What percent of the cards are football cards?

    (A) 166.66%   (B) 87.5%
    (C) 70%   (D) 62.5%

56. The 6% tax on a certain item is exactly $3. How much does the item cost?

57. Andrea spent $4.50 out of an allowance of $15.00. What percent of her allowance did she spend?

    (A) 0.3%   (B) 3.3%
    (C) 30%   (D) 33%

58. Rafael wanted to buy a $120 jacket but only had $100. Every hour the price was reduced by 5% from the previous hour's price. In how many hours was Rafael able to buy the jacket?

    (A) 3   (B) 4   (C) 5   (D) 15

59. Trever scored a $\frac{22}{30}$ on his first math test. On his second math test, he scored a $\frac{50}{60}$. By what percentage did his score improve from his first to his second math test?

    (A) 10% (B) 15% (C) 20% (D) 25%

60. Sabrina is taking a history test on the Spanish Inquisition and the Protestant Reformation. She answered 16 out of 20 questions correctly on the Spanish Inquisition and 26 out of 30 questions correct on the Reformation. What percentage of total question did she answer correctly?

    (A) 80% (B) 84% (C) 87% (D) 90%

61. For parties larger than 10 people, a restaurant adds a 15% gratuity charge to the bill. How much would each person in a 15 person party pay if the bill before the gratuity charge is $638.40, assuming each person pays an equal amount?

    (A) $44.41   (B) $46.82
    (C) $48.94   (D) $52.56

62. Chad bought a boxed set DVD series for 25% off the original price and the total, without tax, came to $87. What was the original price?

    (A) $75   (B) $90
    (C) $99   (D) $116

63. The clothes store in the Blue Mall is having a 35% off sale. The clothes store in the Green Mall is taking three–eighths off of purchases. In which store would it cost more to buy a $15 shirt?

64. Solve using mental math.

    30% of 300.

    (A) 60 (B) 90 (C) 600 (D) 900

65. What is 25% of 18.64?

    (A) 4.66   (B) 46.6
    (C) 466   (D) 4,660

66. Claud made a purchase at 25% off of the regular $138.67 price tag. Sales tax is 8.5% of the discount price. To the nearest dollar, what is the total cost of Claud's purchase?

    (A) $95   (B) $104
    (C) $112   (D) $113

67. In Anytown, 55% of the 20,000 inhabitants live in houses, 25% of the inhabitants live in apartments, and the rest of the inhabitants live in condominiums. How many Anytownians live in condominiums?

68. A store sold 500 milk containers in 2 days. If 75 of those were sour, what percentage of the milk cartons sold were normal?

    (A) 15% (B) 25% (C) 75% (D) 85%

69. Pants were on sale for 15% off of the original price. Peter bought a pair of pants on sale that had an original price of $46.00. The sales tax was 8.75%. How much did Peter pay for the pants?

    Show your work.

8

70. Gasoline prices increased from $3.00 a gallon to $4.00 a gallon. What is the approximate percent increase in the price of gasoline?

    (A) 1%   (B) 10%   (C) 33%   (D) 50%

71. Last season, Carl and Doug together won 40 tennis matches. Carl won 35% of these matches. How many matches did Doug win?

    (A) 14   (B) 16   (C) 24   (D) 26

72. A class of 35 students is taking a trip by train to the zoo. The price of a standard ticket for one person round trip is $15.00. If the students get a 35% discount for their tickets, how much does a student's ticket cost?

    (A) $5.25   (B) $9.75
    (C) $11.25   (D) $12.75

73. Last week, 200 people went on a flight to California. The plane was filled to 85% of its capacity. About how many people can the plane hold?

    (A) 170   (B) 235   (C) 240   (D) 285

74. Benito bought a T-shirt for $12.50. The sales tax is 7%. How much did Benito pay for the shirt, including tax?

    (A) $11.63   (B) $12.50
    (C) $13.38   (D) $21.25

75. A computer originally cost $500. Now it costs $600. Which of the following may have taken place?

    (A) An increase of $20
    (B) An increase of 20%
    (C) A decrease of $20
    (D) A decrease of 20%

76. Diane's credit card company charges a 2.5% monthly interest rate on each monthly balance. How much interest was she charged on her end-of-month balance if she spent $400 last month?

    (A) $2.50   (B) $10.00
    (C) $25.00   (D) $100.00

77. Walt got 70 out of 100 points on his last math test. The test had 50 questions. How many questions did Walt get wrong?

    (A) 15   (B) 35   (C) 50   (D) 70

78. What is 60% of 90?

    (A) 30   (B) 54   (C) 60   (D) 66

79. What is 54% of 50?

80. The number of Hope Middle School students that donated money to the United Fund increased 115% this year compared to last year. Which of the following correctly describes this situation?

    (A) The amount of money raised this year is greater than the amount of money raised last year.
    (B) There were 15 more Hope Middle School students who donated this year compared to last year.
    (C) The number of students who donated this year increased from the number of students who donated last year.
    (D) The number of students who donated this year decreased from the number of students who donated last year.

81. Cameras were on sale for 20% off of the original price. Ulga bought a camera on sale that had an original price of $256.00. The sales tax was 6.75%. How much did Ulga pay for the camera?

    Show your work.

82. Dave ate $\frac{3}{5}$ of his sandwich. What is this represented as a percent?

    (A) 0.6%   (B) 3.5%
    (C) 20%   (D) 60%

83. Ethan was at school for basketball practice. He made 80% of his free throws that he tried. He made 120 successful free throws. How many attempts did he make?

    (A) 66   (B) 96   (C) 150   (D) 216

84. Anna ate $\frac{3}{4}$ of her sandwich. What is this represented as a percent?

    (A) 0.75%   (B) 3.4%
    (C) 25%   (D) 75%

85. A rental car service had 139 cars to rent. 79 of the cars were rented out. Approximately what percent of the cars were rented?

    (A) 42.1%   (B) 53.5%
    (C) 56.8%   (D) 79.5%

86. Adam answered 38% of a 50 question test incorrectly. How many questions did he answer correctly?

    (A) 38   (B) 31   (C) 19   (D) 12

87. During a recent election, Bob received 60% of the 3,800 votes. Gary received the remainder of the votes. How many more votes did Bob get than Gary?

    (A) 760   (B) 1,520
    (C) 2,000   (D) 2,280

88. Stereos were on sale for 10% off of the original price. Tavia bought a stereo on sale that had an original price of $99.95. The sales tax was 8.25%. How much did Tavia pay for the stereo?

    Show your work.

89. Bill claimed that 30% of 150 is 450. Without solving, explain why you think this is wrong.

90. A baseball which cost $4 was then signed by Homer Run, a famous baseball player. It is now worth $40. Which of the following represents the increase in value?

    (A) A 9% increase
    (B) A 90% increase
    (C) A 900% increase
    (D) A 9,000% increase

Base your answers to questions **91** and **92** on the table below which shows the kind of fruit preferred for the 8th grade at Central Middle School, separated by gender.

	Male	Female
Apple	56	74
Orange	44	26

91. What percent of those who prefer apples are female?

    (A) 56% (B) 57% (C) 65% (D) 74%

92. What percent of students prefer oranges?

    (A) 26 %   (B) 35 %
    (C) 44 %   (D) 70 %

93. Solve for x rounded to the nearest whole number.
    $6 \div x = 54.54\%$

    (A) 9   (B) 10   (C) 11   (D) 12

94. John is purchasing a video game console. When the console came out, it originally cost $300.00. It now costs 20% off its original price. How much does the console cost now, before sales tax?

    (A) $60   (B) $120
    (C) $240   (D) $360

95. Dr. Julius bought 5 lab coats for $60 each but ended up paying $322.50 after tax. What is the tax rate?

    (A) 7.5%   (B) 9.5%
    (C) 17%   (D) 22.5%

96. Leana and Brett went out to a fancy restaurant together for dinner. Their dinner amounted to $125.00 before their tip. They decided to leave a tip that equaled 20% of their bill total. What is the total cost of the bill including the tip?

    (A) $25.00   (B) $55.00
    (C) $150.00   (D) $175.00

97. Melanie and Matthew sold lemonade on Saturday. Melanie sold $\frac{1}{3}$ of the lemonade and Matthew sold $\frac{1}{4}$ of the lemonade. What percent (to the nearest whole number) of the lemonade did they sell?

    (A) 42% (B) 50% (C) 58% (D) 68%

98. Enrique had 45 marbles total. He used 11 of them. Approximately what percent of his marbles did he use?

    (A) 2.4%   (B) 11%
    (C) 24%   (D) 45%

99. What is $\frac{3}{2}$ expressed as a percent?

    (A) 1.5%   (B) 15%
    (C) 150%   (D) 1,500%

100. Base your answer to the following question on A store is having a sale on pianos that have a retail price of $3900 each. Starting on May 9th, the price of these pianos will be lowered by 20%. Every day after May 9th, the remaining pianos will be reduced by another 20% off. Mr. Thomas can only afford to spend $2200 on a piano.

    What is the first day Mr. Thomas can afford a piano?

    (A) May 10th   (B) May 11th
    (C) May 12th   (D) May 13th

RP and Fractions

1. Three–fifths of the students in a class are boys. If 5 girls and 5 boys are added to the class, which of the following statements is true?

    (A) There are more boys than girls.
    (B) There are more girls than boys.
    (C) There are an equal number of boys and girls.
    (D) It is impossible to determine whether there are more boys or girls.

2. The sonar system of a submarine receives an echo back from a ship that is known to be 1,000 meters away in 4.5 seconds. It then receives an echo back from a second ship that is 3,500 meters away. Which of the following proportions could be used to find how long it took to receive the echo from the second ship?

    (A) $\dfrac{4.5}{1,000} = \dfrac{x}{3,500}$
    (B) $\dfrac{1,000}{4.5} = \dfrac{x}{3,500}$
    (C) $\dfrac{4.5}{x} = \dfrac{3,500}{1,000}$
    (D) $\dfrac{3,500}{4.5} = \dfrac{1,000}{x}$

3. Rob is looking at a map to see how far it is from his house to a state fair in Albany. The scale on the map is 1 inch = 75 miles. If the distance on the map between his home and the state fair is $2\frac{1}{2}$ inches, then what is the actual distance?

    (A) $187\frac{1}{2}$ miles
    (B) 200 miles
    (C) 225 miles
    (D) $250\frac{1}{2}$ miles

4. In Clarence's homeroom, $\frac{1}{3}$ of the students walk to school and $\frac{1}{5}$ come by school bus. The remaining 14 students come by car. How many students are in Clarence's homeroom?

    (A) 26 (B) 30 (C) 36 (D) 40

5. In the first race of the season, Donovan biked his event in 8 minutes and 15 seconds. By his last race, he wants to complete the event in $\frac{2}{3}$ his original time. If Donovan completes his goal, how long will it take him to complete the race?

    (A) 2 minutes 45 seconds
    (B) 3 minutes 17 seconds
    (C) 5 minutes 30 seconds
    (D) 5 minutes 43 seconds

6. What is the ratio of the circumference of a circle to its radius?

    (A) π^2 (B) π (C) $\frac{3}{2}\pi$ (D) 2π

7. What is the ratio of the circumference of a circle to its diameter?

    (A) π^2 (B) 3 (C) π (D) 2π

8. There are 25 blue marbles and 70 green marbles in a bag. What is the ratio of green marbles to blue marbles?

    (A) 5 to 14
    (B) 5 to 7
    (C) 14:5
    (D) 5:21

9. The bodies of an adult and a child are proportional. If an adult is 72 inches tall and has a armspan of 54 inches, a child 48 inches tall will have a armspan of how many inches?

    (A) 28 (B) 30 (C) 33 (D) 36

RP and Fractions

10. At Mrs. Wang's sports camp, $\frac{3}{8}$ of the kids play basketball. If 128 kids come to camp, how many play sports other than basketball?

    (A) 24   (B) 48   (C) 60   (D) 80

11. The ratio of students who play sports to those who don't is 3 to 9. Which of the following represents this in decimal form?

    (A) 0.23   (B) 0.30   (C) 0.31   (D) 0.33

12. 5 out of every 8 people in Educity went for ice cream on a hot summer day. Which percentage represents this amount?

    (A) 62.5%   (B) 65%
    (C) 67.5%   (D) 69%

13. In Tito's family, 4 out of every 5 people went to college. Which decimal represents this ratio?

    (A) 0.7   (B) 0.75   (C) 0.8   (D) 0.85

14. If Claire walked into a video store and saw a sign that said 30% off everything, what proportion of the original price of a video would Claire pay?

    (A) $\frac{3}{10}$ (B) $\frac{4}{10}$ (C) $\frac{7}{10}$ (D) $\frac{8}{10}$

15. What is the following ratio in simplest form: 39 to 48

    (A) 16 to 13   (B) $\frac{39}{48}$
    (C) 3 to 4   (D) $\frac{13}{16}$

16. What is the following ratio in simplest form: $\frac{18}{42}$

    (A) $\frac{3}{7}$ (B) $\frac{7}{9}$ (C) $\frac{9}{21}$ (D) $\frac{3}{11}$

17. What is the simplest form of the ratio 60:28

    (A) 7:15   (B) 20:9   (C) 15:7   (D) 2:1

18. Waldo was walking by a pet store and saw a sign that said, "20% off everything." Which of the following is another way to say the same thing?

    (A) 0.25 off everything
    (B) $\frac{1}{4}$ off everything
    (C) $\frac{1}{5}$ off everything
    (D) 0.15 off everything

19. Which is smaller, one–fifth of 55 or a third of 36?

    (A) one–fifth of 55   (B) one–third of 36
    (C) both are the same

20. Brown Middle School had a good football team last year. On average, they outscored their opponents by a ratio of 3:1 in every game they played. If their average score was 24 points per game, then what was the average number of points scored by their opponents each game?

    (A) 6   (B) 8   (C) 12   (D) 16

21. Which is bigger: a third of 48 or one–fourth of 72?

    (A) one–third of 48   (B) one–forth of 72
    (C) both are the same

RP and Fractions

22. Victoria always takes exactly 6 minutes to run a mile. If she is running at her normal pace, and 2 minutes have passed, about what fraction of the mile has she run?

    (A) $\frac{2}{5}$ (B) $\frac{1}{3}$ (C) $\frac{1}{2}$ (D) $\frac{2}{3}$

Base your answers to questions **23** and **24** on the following information. Isabella saw a sign in a storefront window that said:

"$\frac{1}{5}$ off everything!"

23. What percent of the original price of an item would Isabella pay?

    (A) 20% (B) 40% (C) 60% (D) 80%

24. What percent discount would Isabella receive if she bought something in that store?

    (A) 10% (B) 15% (C) 20% (D) 25%

---

25. A special new snowboard costs $249.99. Which of the following sale prices would result in the lowest price for the snowboard?

    (A) $\frac{1}{5}$ reduction on the regular price
    (B) 90% of the regular price
    (C) 15% discount on the regular price
    (D) $35.00 less than the regular price

26. Victor knows that his daily commute to work is 25 minutes long. He looks at a clock and notes that he has been driving for 12 minutes. About what fraction of his commute has he completed?

    (A) $\frac{1}{4}$ (B) $\frac{1}{3}$ (C) $\frac{1}{2}$ (D) $\frac{3}{5}$

27. In Kenny's family, 6 people out of 8 can roll their tongue. Which number represents the same amount?

    (A) 0.075 (B) 0.75
    (C) 6.8   (D) 7.5

28. In Dale's family, $\frac{3}{5}$ of the people have blonde hair. Which number represents the same amount?

    (A) 0.60 (B) 3.5 (C) 6.0 (D) 60

29. On Mrs. Math's last test, $\frac{3}{4}$ of her students passed. Express this in decimal form.

    (A) 0.75 (B) 3.4 (C) 12 (D) 75

30. A glass is half full with water. Ingrid pours some amount of vinegar into the glass. She then pours an equal amount of orange juice into the glass and $\frac{2}{3}$ of the orange juice spills over the glass. What fraction of a glass of vinegar did she pour in?

    (A) $\frac{1}{4}$ (B) $\frac{3}{8}$ (C) $\frac{1}{2}$ (D) $\frac{2}{3}$

31. What portion of the rectangle below is shaded?

    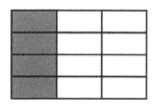

    (A) $\frac{1}{4}$ (B) $\frac{1}{3}$ (C) $\frac{3}{10}$ (D) 30%

RP and Fractions

32. If a total of 400 students eat lunch, about how many go home for lunch?

    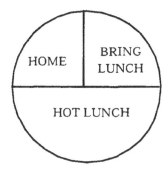

    (A) 25   (B) 100   (C) 200   (D) 300

33. The regular price of a computer game is $49.95. Which of the following sale prices would result in the lowest price for the computer game?

    (A) $8 less than the regular price
    (B) 20% discount on the regular price
    (C) $\frac{1}{4}$ reduction on the regular price
    (D) 85% of the regular price

34. A detective solves 5 out of every 6 cases. He solved 460 cases last year. How many cases did he probably have in total? Explain your answer.

35. Eric and his friends are going to Europe. They are getting ready to exchange their American dollars for Euros. Eric wants to have 500. If the exchange rate is $.87 for every 1, how many American dollars will Eric need in order to have 500?

    (A) $587.00   (B) $574.71
    (C) $435.00   (D) $413.13

36. The ratio of quarts of water to bags of cement mix is 12 : 9. If a construction site needs 2700 bags of cement, how many quarts of water need to be added?

    (A) 2025 quarts   (B) 2400 quarts
    (C) 3000 quarts   (D) 3600 quarts

37. The quality control group at a company found errors in 5 out of every 1,000 products. How many errors are expected in 35,000 products?

    (A) 7   (B) 24.5
    (C) 175   (D) 2450

38. Dora traveled 20 miles in one hour. How many miles would she travel in 4 hours at the same rate?

    (A) 4 miles   (B) 5 miles
    (C) 80 miles   (D) 100 miles

39. A soup company sells two sizes of their soup: small and large. It takes 12 minutes to fill a box full of the small cans and 15 minutes for the larger cans. If the manager needs to pack 10 boxes of each size and has 4 hours to finish the job, can he complete it on time? Assume that the company can only pack one box at a time.

    (A) No, it will take him 4.5 hours to finish.
    (B) Yes, he will finish on time in 4 hours.
    (C) No, it will take him 5 hours to finish.
    (D) Yes, he will finish in 3 hours.

RP and Fractions

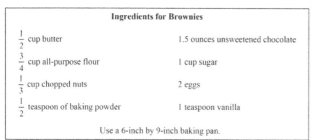

40. If the bakery chef needs to make double the recipe, how many eggs will he need?

    (A) 2   (B) 4   (C) 6   (D) 8

41. At a certain time of the day, Billy's shadow was 2 feet long. At the same time, a nearby building's shadow was 8 feet long. If Bill is 5 feet tall, how tall is the building?

    (A) 3.2 feet   (B) 12 feet
    (C) 16 feet   (D) 20 feet

42. George is using plywood to build props for the school play. He needs $\frac{2}{3}$ of a sheet of plywood for each prop. If the director asks for 6 props, how many sheets of plywood will George need?

    (A) 2   (B) 3   (C) 4   (D) 9

43. The regular price for a shirt is $39. Which of the following sale prices would result in the lowest price for the shirt?

    (A) 25% off the regular price
    (B) $10 off the regular price
    (C) paying $\frac{4}{5}$ of the regular price
    (D) paying 78% of the regular price

44. The New York state flag is rectangular and has a width–to–height ratio of 19:10. Which of the following can be used to find h, the height of a New York state flag with a width of 28 inches?

    (A) $\frac{10}{19} = \frac{h}{28}$ (B) $10h = 19 \times 28$
    (C) $19 + 28 = 10 + h$ (D) $28 \times 10 = h$

45. The ratio of boys to girls in an 8th grade math class is 4:3. If there are 35 students total in the class, how many of them are girls?

    (A) 5   (B) 15   (C) 20   (D) 25

46. At the grocery store, Anna saw a sign that said "A dozen apples for $6.60." If she only wants 4 apples, how much would it cost her to purchase these 4 apples at the same unit rate?

    (A) $1.10   (B) $2.20
    (C) $3.30   (D) $4.40

47. Jim is playing a game with Danielle. For every 2 times that Jim claps his hands, Danielle walks forward 3 steps. If Jim clapped his hands 12 times, how many steps has Danielle taken?

    (A) 12 steps   (B) 8 steps
    (C) 18 steps   (D) 20 steps

48. A mail service charges $3.50 per 7 pounds of mail shipped overnight. Which of the following rates is equivalent?

    (A) Charging $0.50 for a 20 pound package
    (B) Charging $3.50 for a 5 pound package
    (C) Charging $7.50 for a 15 pound package
    (D) Charging $9.50 for a 10 pound package

RP and Fractions

49. To estimate the total number of fish in a lake, the Department of Wildlife catches 300 fish, tags them, and returns them all to the lake. A week later they catch another 300 fish and 12 are tagged. What is the best estimate for the total amount of fish in the lake?

    (A) 3,600 (B) 5,000
    (C) 7,500 (D) 10,000

50. Mr. Daniels is making 25 cups of trail mix to bring for his hiking group. His favorite mix requires 3 parts raisins and 2 parts peanuts. How many cups of raisins does he need for his mix?

    (A) 5 cups (B) 10 cups
    (C) 15 cups (D) 20 cups

51. Mike makes $27 in 6 hours. How long will it take for him to earn $180?

52. Jason built a model aircraft carrier for which the scale was 20 feet to 2 inches. The actual size of the landing strip is 1000 feet. What is the size of the landing strip on Jason's model?

    (A) 20 inches (B) 50 inches
    (C) 100 inches (D) 1000 feet

53. A store sells onions in 5–pound bags for $5.40. Which of the following bags of onions would be the same price per pound?

    (A) A 10 pound bag for $11.00
    (B) A 1 pound bag for $1.80
    (C) A 7 pound bag for $7.56
    (D) A 2 pound bag for 2.15

54. If 20,000 students apply to a certain college, and only 1% of the students are accepted, how many students are accepted?

    (A) 2,000 students (B) 20 students
    (C) 200 students (D) 2 students

55. Brett ran 180 meters in 24 seconds and Elsbeth ran 28 meters in 4 seconds. Based on these rates, which of the following is true?

    (A) Brett's average speed was 7.6 meters per second faster than Elsbeth's average speed.
    (B) Brett's average speed was 1.5 meters per second faster than Elsbeth's average speed.
    (C) Brett's average speed was 0.5 meters per second faster than Elsbeth's average speed.
    (D) Brett's average speed was equal to Elsbeth's average speed.

56. A piece of chocolate cake contains 200 calories. A piece of cheesecake contains 120 calories. How many pieces of cheesecakes are needed to get the amount of calories that is in one piece of chocolate cake?

    (A) $\frac{2}{3}$ (B) $1\frac{2}{3}$ (C) 1.8 (D) 6

57. A can of white paint weighs 24 kilograms. A can of blue paint weighs 18 kilograms. How many cans of blue paint are needed to equal the weight of paint that is in a can of white paint?

    (A) $\frac{1}{3}$ of a can (B) $1\frac{1}{3}$ cans
    (C) 2 cans (D) 6 cans

RP and Fractions

58. There are 27 students in a biology class and 30 students in a chemistry class. If there are 6 students that are in both classes, what is the ratio of students who only take biology to those who only take chemistry?

    (A) $\frac{8}{7}$ (B) $\frac{27}{30}$ (C) $\frac{30}{27}$ (D) $\frac{7}{8}$

59. Anna traveled 55 miles in one hour. She travels at this speed for an additional 3 hours. How many miles did she travel in total?

    (A) 55 miles (B) 58 miles
    (C) 165 miles (D) 220 miles

60. What is the value of x in the following proportion?

    $$\frac{x}{32} = \frac{18}{48}$$

    (A) 9 (B) 12 (C) 16 (D) 24

61. A car that is always traveling at the same speed travels 30 miles every 0.5 hours. How many miles does it travel in 4.5 hours?

    (A) 45 miles (B) 120 miles
    (C) 135 miles (D) 270 miles

62. A recipe for fruit punch uses $4\frac{1}{3}$ ounces of fruit mix to make 6 glasses of punch. How many glasses of this punch can be made from 26 ounces of fruit mix?

    (A) 24 (B) 32 (C) 36 (D) 48

63. Sam took a practice quiz. Out of the 15 questions, he got 2 wrong. At this rate, how many questions will he answer incorrectly if he answers a total of 105 question?

    (A) 6 (B) 7 (C) 12 (D) 14

64. Anita swam 195 meters in 60 seconds and Cam swam 39 meters in 12 seconds. Based on these ratios, which of the following statements is true?

    (A) Anita's average speed was 1.75 meters per second faster than Cam's average speed.
    (B) Anita's average speed was 3.25 meters per second faster than Cam's average speed.
    (C) Cam's average speed was 3 meters per second faster than Anita's average speed.
    (D) Anita's average speed was equal to Cam's average speed.

65. The Plaxis Corporation randomly selected 350 bills going out and found errors on 2 bills. Based upon this information, how many of the 2,800 bills sent out each week can be expected to be incorrect?

    (A) 12 (B) 14 (C) 15 (D) 16

66. A map uses a scale of 1 inch = 3 miles. In the map, the distance between John's house and the library is 1.5 inches. What is the actual distance between John's house and the library?

    (A) 2.0 in. (B) 3.0 in.
    (C) 3.5 in. (D) 4.5 in.

RP and Fractions

67. A 4 foot tall child casts a 12 foot shadow. If, at the same time a 20 foot tall tree casts a shadow, how long is its shadow?

    (A) 6.67 feet (B) 60 feet
    (C) 70 feet   (D) 120 feet

68. The label on a box of cookies reads that 6 cookies contain 75 calories. John ate 18 cookies. How many calories did he have?

    (A) 75 calories   (B) 1,350 calories
    (C) 450 calories (D) 225 calories

69. Frank has collected 28 coins from a series that contains a total of 560 coins. Garrett has collected the same percent of coins as Frank, but he is collecting a different series. The series Garrett is collecting has a total of 260. How many coins from his series does Garrett have?

    Show your work.

70. A dog can run from point *A* to point *B* in 2.5 minutes. How fast is the dog running in miles per hour? (1760 yards = 1 mile) Round your answer to the nearest whole number.

    A   500 yards   B

    (A) 5 mph   (B) 6 mph
    (C) 7 mph   (D) 8 mph

71. An object shot out of a cannon, in space, moves 26 miles in 2 hours. At this rate, about how many miles could the object move in 7 hours?

    (A) 91   (B) 130   (C) 146   (D) 182

72. Approximately every 3 out of 5 coins Mark is holding is a dime. Since Mark is holding 45 coins, which equation would he use to determine how many dimes he has?

    (A) $\frac{3}{45} = \frac{x}{5}$ (B) $\frac{3}{5} = \frac{x}{45}$ (C) $\frac{5}{3} = \frac{x}{45}$ (D) $\frac{3}{45} = \frac{5}{x}$

73. Jane has 120 friends. 2 out of every 5 of Jane's friends said they would be able to attend her party. How many friends were able to attend her party?

    (A) 24   (B) 48   (C) 72   (D) 120

74. Katie's pig had a litter of 24 piglets. The ratio of males to females was 2:1. How many piglets are male?

    (A) 4   (B) 6   (C) 8   (D) 16

75. On a school field trip, 128 students fill up four school buses. How many buses are necessary to transport 288 students?

    (A) 9   (B) 11   (C) 12   (D) 13

RP and Fractions

76. Rolland's dad works for the telephone company and speaks to 54 people a day. On average, only 6 out of 10 people will answer the phone. In order to speak to 54 people, how many calls does Rolland's dad need to make each day?

    (A) 80   (B) 86   (C) 90   (D) 96

77. Last year, there were 1100 students enrolled at a college. The school boasted a student to faculty ratio of 11:2. Based on this ratio, which is the closest to the number of faculty members last year?

    (A) 100   (B) 200
    (C) 400   (D) 6050

78. Rose invests $300 in the bank. A year later, she had earned $65 more. Jon puts $500 in an account with the same interest rate. How much should he expect to earn in a year?

    (A) $65.00   (B) $108.33
    (C) $132.67   (D) $148.93

79. Jenny travels 30 mph in her boat. If the dock is 600 miles away, how many hours will she be sailing for at least?

    (A) 18   (B) 19   (C) 20   (D) 21

80. Katherine reads a particular magazine at a rate of $\frac{1}{2}$ page per minute. At this rate, how long will it take Katherine to finish her 90 page magazine?

    (A) $\frac{1}{2}$ hour   (B) 1 hour
    (C) 2 hours   (D) 3 hours

81. Laura knows that approximately 4 out of every 9 of her 108 friends wear sunglasses. What proportion should she use to determine how many of her friends wear sunglasses?

    (A) $\frac{4}{9} = \frac{x}{108}$ (B) $\frac{4}{108} = \frac{x}{9}$ (C) $\frac{9}{108} = \frac{x}{4}$ (D) $\frac{9}{4} = \frac{x}{108}$

82. Last week, 765 people attended the opening of a movie. The theater was filled to 85% capacity. What is the theater's capacity?

    (A) 650   (B) 680   (C) 850   (D) 900

83. Tuna fish swim across the sea. If the distance across the sea is 135 miles and the tuna travels for 3 hours, what is the speed at which the tuna swims?

    (A) 2.25 miles per hour
    (B) 45 miles per hour
    (C) 135 miles per hour
    (D) 405 miles per hour

84. A 2 pound brisket takes 35 minutes to cook. Mary has a 12 pound brisket that she wants to serve at 5:00 PM. What time should she start cooking the brisket?

    (A) 1:15 PM   (B) 1:30 PM
    (C) 1:45 PM   (D) 2:00 PM

85. Which of the following is closest to 790 out of 1,000?

    (A) $\frac{2}{3}$ (B) $\frac{3}{4}$ (C) $\frac{4}{5}$ (D) $\frac{5}{6}$

RP and Fractions

86. You want to find the missing number in the equation below.

    $\frac{1}{30} = \frac{?}{600}$

    Which of the following operations could be used?

    (A) divide 30 by 600
    (B) divide 600 by 30
    (C) multiply 600 by 30
    (D) subtract 30 from 300

87. It takes Maria and Randy each 5.5 minutes to ride their bikes 1 mile. Maria rode 12.3 miles and Randy rode 2.7 miles. How much longer was Maria riding than Randy?

    (A) 14.85 minutes (B) 52.8 minutes
    (C) 67.65 minutes (D) 82.5 minutes

88. Dave makes 2 out of every 11 three–pointer throws when he practices his basketball skills. Dave attempted 3,560 three–pointers. How many did he make? Round your answer to the nearest whole number.

    (A) 22 (B) 324 (C) 647 (D) 648

RP and Fractions

89. The following is a list of ingredients needed to make 2 loaves of bread.

Bread Recipe	
water	$\frac{1}{2}$ cup
milk	$\frac{1}{2}$ cup
flour	$2\frac{1}{2}$ cups
sugar	2 tablespoons
yeast	$1\frac{3}{4}$ teaspoons

How much flour is needed to make 3 loaves of bread?

(A) 3 cups   (B) $3\frac{3}{4}$ cups   (C) 4 cups   (D) $4\frac{3}{4}$ cups

90. A map uses a scale of 1 centimeter = 2.4 miles. In the map, Josh's house and Mini's house is 2.5 centimeters. How far apart do Josh and Mini live from one another?

(A) 0.960 mi   (B) 1.042 mi
(C) 4.800 mi   (D) 6.000 mi

91. School cooks at Central Middle School know that when pizza is served, 3 out of 5 students eat hot lunch. Pizza is being served for hot lunch today. If 200 students are in school today, about how many students will eat pizza?

(A) about 40 students
(B) about 100 students
(C) about 120 students
(D) about 150 students

92. A man who is 6 feet tall is casting a 3 foot shadow. If the tree next to him is casting a 20 foot shadow, how tall is the tree?

(A) 20 ft   (B) 40 ft   (C) 60 ft   (D) 80 ft

93. At a restaurant, there must be a supervisor for every 4 employees. What is the minimum amount of supervisors needed if the restaurant has 28 employees?

(A) 1   (B) 7   (C) 28   (D) 112

94. In a bag full of red and blue candy, the ratio of red to blue pieces of candy is 3:1. If there are 15 pieces of red candy, how many pieces of blue candy are there?

(A) 1 pieces   (B) 3 pieces
(C) 4 pieces   (D) 5 pieces

RP and Fractions

95. Cayla has a measuring cup with a capacity of $\frac{2}{3}$ cup. How many times will she fill her measuring cup with juice to measure $5\frac{1}{3}$ cups?

    Show your work.

96. The American Sandwich Deli can make between 550 and 600 sandwiches a day. If the restaurant needs to make 3,000 sandwiches for a party, what is the least number of days possible to prepare for the order based on this rate?

    (A) 4   (B) 5   (C) 6   (D) 7

97. Max bought a can of nuts. That contained 7 peanuts for every 11 walnuts. The can contained 108 nuts all together. How many walnuts were in the can?

    (A) 18   (B) 42   (C) 66   (D) 77

98. Mark used to weigh 147 pounds. He now weighs 164 pounds. Which proportion can be used to determine his percent increase in weight?

    (A) $\frac{17}{100} = \frac{x}{147}$ (B) $\frac{x}{100} = \frac{17}{147}$ (C) $\frac{x}{164} = \frac{17}{100}$ (D) $\frac{147}{164} = \frac{x}{100}$

99. An advertisement claims that 4 out of 5 dentists prefer a certain toothpaste. You poll 100 dentists. How many dentists would you expect to *not* prefer the toothpaste?

    (A) 10   (B) 20   (C) 45   (D) 80

100. Chuck ran 75 meters in 15 seconds at practice. If he maintained this constant speed, how long would it take him to run 0.5 kilometers?

    (A) 1 minute
    (B) 1 minute 20 seconds
    (C) 1 minute 40 seconds
    (D) 2 minutes

Number System

1. Which of the following is an irrational number?
   (A) $\sqrt{32}$
   (B) $\frac{5}{3}$
   (C) –2.52
   (D) $\sqrt{81}$

2. Which of the following is an irrational number?
   (A) $\sqrt{24}$
   (B) $\frac{4}{3}$
   (C) $\sqrt{144}$
   (D) –2.37

3. Which number family does –1 belong to?
   (A) Imaginary numbers
   (B) Integers
   (C) Irrational numbers
   (D) Whole numbers

4. Mrs. Dhadwal writes the following four irrational numbers on the blackboard and asks Timmy to choose the one closest to 4. Which irrational number should Timmy choose?
   (A) π
   (B) $\sqrt{13}$
   (C) $\pi - 1$
   (D) $\sqrt{18}$

5. The number $2.4\bar{2}$ belongs in which of the following number family?
   (A) Imaginary numbers
   (B) Irrational numbers
   (C) Rational numbers
   (D) Integers

6. The number –52 belongs to which of the following number families?
   (A) Positive numbers
   (B) Imaginary numbers
   (C) Integers
   (D) Irrational numbers

7. The number $\frac{13}{16}$ belongs to which of the following number families?
   (A) Rational numbers
   (B) Integers
   (C) Irrational numbers
   (D) Imaginary numbers

8. Which of the following numbers is irrational?
   (A) $-\frac{\sqrt{1}}{4}$
   (B) 3.14
   (C) $\frac{\pi}{4}$
   (D) $2.\bar{3}$

9. Find the sum: $3\sqrt{5} + 4\sqrt{5}$
   (A) $6\sqrt{5}$
   (B) $7\sqrt{5}$
   (C) $\sqrt{5}$
   (D) $12\sqrt{5}$

10. Which of the following is a rational number?
    (A) $\sqrt{2}$
    (B) π
    (C) $\sqrt[3]{9}$
    (D) $\frac{2}{9}$

11. Which of the following choices has the greatest value?
    (A) $\frac{1}{4}$
    (B) 0.232
    (C) $|-0.26|$
    (D) –0.5

Number System

12. Order $\frac{1}{3}, \frac{3}{4}, \frac{1}{5}, \frac{1}{2}$ and $\frac{2}{3}$ from greatest to least value.

13. Which of the following fractions is less than 0.412?

    (A) $\frac{4}{7}$ (B) $\frac{2}{5}$ (C) $\frac{1}{2}$ (D) $\frac{3}{5}$

14. What set of numbers is $\sqrt{54}$ a part of?

    (A) Real numbers   (B) Rational numbers
    (C) Integers   (D) Imaginary

15. Which fraction is greater than 0.875?

    (A) $\frac{8}{9}$ (B) $\frac{3}{4}$ (C) $\frac{2}{5}$ (D) $\frac{2}{3}$

16. Marie's teacher asked her to pick the largest of the following numbers:

    $3\pi, \sqrt{78}, \frac{64}{7}, 8$

    Which number should Marie choose?

    (A) 3π (B) $\sqrt{78}$ (C) $\frac{64}{7}$ (D) 8

17. What is the absolute value of 15?

    (A) –15   (B) 0   (C) 1   (D) 15

18. Which of the following integers is a perfect square?

    (A) 300   (B) 490   (C) 625   (D) 800

19. What is the largest number you can write with the digits 4, 9, 0, 1?

20. What is the absolute value of –23?

    (A) 0   (B) 23   (C) –23   (D) 1

21. Which of the following is true?

    (A) The coefficient of y in the expression 2x + 7y is 7.
    (B) The expression 2x + 7y contains only 1 variable.
    (C) The expression 5x – 2 = 13 returns a non–real result.
    (D) The expression 4a – 8 = 29 has two terms.

22. Which list contains numbers ordered from least to greatest?

    (A) $\frac{4}{7}, \frac{5}{11}, \frac{1}{2}, \frac{5}{2}$ (B) $\frac{27}{3}, \frac{15}{3}, \frac{12}{3}, \frac{9}{3}$
    (C) $\frac{3}{9}, \frac{3}{12}, \frac{3}{15}, \frac{3}{27}$ (D) $\frac{3}{27}, \frac{4}{16}, \frac{3}{9}, \frac{5}{11}$

23. What is the absolute value of –5?

    (A) –5   (B) 0   (C) 1   (D) 5

24. Which of the following numbers could replace the variable h?

    $$\frac{3}{2} < h \leq \pi$$

    (A) 1.30   (B) 2.98   (C) 3.80   (D) 4.00

26

Number System

25. Audrey rode her horse 5.2 miles on Monday, $5\frac{1}{2}$ miles on Tuesday, and $5\frac{1}{3}$ miles on Thursday. Which of the following statements is true?

    (A) Audrey rode further on Monday than on Tuesday.
    (B) Audrey rode further on Tuesday than on Thursday.
    (C) Audrey rode further on Monday than on Thursday.
    (D) Audrey rode further on Thursday than on Tuesday.

26. Which numeral is in the ten–thousandths place in the number 34,156,954.35782468?

    (A) 5 (B) 6 (C) 7 (D) 8

27. The diameter of a hole is $2\frac{3}{10}$ inches.

    Which is the largest diameter below that can fit through the hole?

    (A) $2\frac{1}{2}$ inches (B) $2\frac{1}{3}$ inches
    (C) $2\frac{1}{4}$ inches (D) $2\frac{1}{5}$ inches

28. Which of the following is equal to a terminating decimal?

    (A) $\frac{1}{3}$ (B) π (C) $\frac{1}{4}$ (D) $\frac{1}{7}$

29. What is the absolute value of –3?

30. Solve: $2\sqrt{3} + 3\sqrt{3}$

    (A) $5\sqrt{3}$ (B) $6\sqrt{3}$ (C) $5\sqrt{6}$ (D) 18

31. Which of the following is rational?

    (A) $\sqrt{3}$ (B) $\sqrt{5}$ (C) $\sqrt{7}$ (D) $\sqrt{9}$

32. Which of the following sets of numbers does $4\frac{3}{4}$ belong to?

    (A) Whole numbers
    (B) Integers
    (C) Rational numbers
    (D) Irrational numbers

33. Order $\frac{1}{2}, \frac{1}{3}, \frac{1}{4}$, and $\frac{4}{5}$ from least value to greatest value.

    (A) $\frac{1}{2}, \frac{1}{3}, \frac{1}{4}, \frac{4}{5}$ (B) $\frac{1}{4}, \frac{1}{3}, \frac{1}{2}, \frac{4}{5}$
    (C) $\frac{4}{5}, \frac{1}{2}, \frac{1}{3}, \frac{1}{4}$ (D) $\frac{1}{4}, \frac{4}{5}, \frac{1}{2}, \frac{1}{3}$

34. Which of the following is an irrational number?

    (A) $\frac{2}{7}$ (B) $\sqrt{2}$ (C) 2 (D) 2^2

35. The number π belongs to which of the following number families?

    (A) Rational numbers
    (B) Irrational numbers
    (C) Integers
    (D) Imaginary numbers

36. Mary got between 5.15 and 5.33 on a national math test. What could her grade have been?

    (A) 5.149 (B) 5.169
    (C) 5.390 (D) 5.442

Number System

37. Which of the following is a rational number?
    (A) π (B) $\sqrt{2}$ (C) $\frac{22}{7}$ (D) $\sqrt[3]{3}$

38. Which list below has the numbers ordered from least to greatest?
    (A) 6, −5, −4, −3   (B) −3, −4, −5, 6
    (C) 6, −3, −5, −6   (D) −5, −4, −3, 6

39. The number $6i$ belongs to which of the following number families?
    (A) Imaginary numbers
    (B) Irrational numbers
    (C) Integers
    (D) Rational numbers

40. A measuring cup has lines marking the fractions $\frac{2}{3}, \frac{3}{4}, \frac{1}{2}$, and $\frac{2}{5}$ of a cup. In what order should the lines on the cup be labeled, starting with the bottom line of the measuring cup?
    (A) $\frac{2}{3}, \frac{3}{4}, \frac{1}{2}, \frac{2}{5}$ (B) $\frac{2}{5}, \frac{1}{2}, \frac{2}{3}, \frac{3}{4}$
    (C) $\frac{1}{2}, \frac{2}{3}, \frac{2}{5}, \frac{3}{4}$ (D) $\frac{1}{2}, \frac{2}{5}, \frac{2}{3}, \frac{3}{4}$

41. The absolute value of −118 is ___.

42. Which of the following is irrational?
    (A) $0.\overline{154797}$
    (B) 0.15479724032153947...
    (C) 0.2
    (D) $0.\overline{3}$

43. Joe works from 6 a.m. until 5 p.m. without a break, how long does he work?
    (A) 1 hour   (B) 11 hours
    (C) 12 hours   (D) 13 hours

44. Which number is not a multiple of 8?
    (A) 8   (B) 14   (C) 56   (D) 72

45. The wizard mixed a magical potion using salt. He tried $3\frac{1}{2}$ grams of salt, but it was not enough. He added $\frac{1}{4}$ gram more salt, but it was too much. Which of the following could be the right amount of salt?
    (A) $3\frac{1}{5}$ g (B) $3\frac{1}{4}$ g (C) $3\frac{2}{3}$ g (D) $3\frac{4}{5}$ g

46. The number $\sqrt{3}$ belongs to which of the following number families?
    (A) Imaginary numbers
    (B) Integers
    (C) Rational numbers
    (D) Irrational numbers

47. Which set of numbers below contains only irrational numbers?
    (A) $-\sqrt{15}, -4.\overline{96}, -\sqrt{49}, -3.9523...$
    (B) $-\sqrt{12}, -7.643..., \frac{1}{5}, \sqrt{12}$
    (C) $5.6, 6.\overline{329}, \sqrt{72}, \sqrt{100}$
    (D) $-\sqrt{15}, -3.467..., \sqrt{50}, 12.9762801...$

Number System

48. Circle all of the numbers below which would make the following inequality true.
$\frac{2}{5} < x < 0.73$

$\frac{3}{10}$ 0.42 $\frac{1}{3}$ $\frac{7}{10}$ $\frac{3}{4}$

Explain in words why each number you circled could replace the variable x.

---

49. Find the two integers one place value from the value of $\sqrt{144}$.
    (A) 11, 13 (B) 10, 11
    (C) 11, 12 (D) 13, 14

50. The absolute value of 7 is ___.

51. Three–fifths of the people in a small Canadian village speak more than one language. Which one of the following statements is definitely *not* true?
    (A) 60% speak more than one language.
    (B) More than $\frac{1}{2}$ speak more than one language.
    (C) 40 don't speak more than one language.
    (D) More than $\frac{3}{4}$ speak more than one language.

52. The distance from the Earth to the Sun is 93 million miles. What is this number expressed in scientific notation?
    (A) 9.3×10^7 (B) 93×10^6
    (C) $.93 \times 10^8$ (D) 9.3×10^5

53. Between what two numbers does $\sqrt[3]{40}$ lie?
    (A) 1 and 2 (B) 2 and 3
    (C) 3 and 4 (D) 4 and 5

54. The Great Wall of China is approximately 253,440,000 inches long. Which value is equivalent in inches?
    (A) 253.44×10^4 (B) $.25344 \times 10^9$
    (C) 2.5344×10^{10} (D) 25.344×10^{10}

55. Which percentage is equivalent to $\frac{3}{5}$?
    (A) 20% (B) 30% (C) 40% (D) 60%

56. The newsstand price of a newspaper is discounted 25% for subscribers. The newsstand price is $5.00. What is the subscription price?
    (A) $1.25 (B) $2.50
    (C) $3.75 (D) $4.75

57. Which of the following is not true?
    (A) $\frac{2}{5} = 0.4 = 40\%$ (B) $\frac{3}{9} = 0.3 = 33.3\%$
    (C) $\frac{6}{10} = 0.6 = 60\%$ (D) $\frac{5}{6} = .83 = 8.3\%$

Number System

58. In a survey, 85% of people said they preferred the color blue to the color green. What fraction is equivalent to this percentage?

    (A) $\frac{13}{20}$ (B) $\frac{3}{4}$ (C) $\frac{17}{20}$ (D) $\frac{9}{10}$

59. What is 0.035 expressed in scientific notation?

    (A) 3.5×10^{-3} (B) 3.5×10^{-2}
    (C) 3.5×10^{2} (D) 3.5×10^{3}

60. A carpenter tries a $\frac{5}{8}$ inch wrench to loosen a bolt. The wrench almost fits but it is slightly too small. Which of the following wrench sizes is the next largest wrench?

    (A) $\frac{3}{4}$ inches (B) $\frac{7}{8}$ inches
    (C) $\frac{11}{16}$ inches (D) $\frac{9}{16}$ inches

61. Express 3,210 in proper scientific notation.

    (A) 3.21×10^{4} (B) 3.21×10^{3}
    (C) 3.21×10^{-3} (D) 3.21×10^{-4}

62. Mary and John are eating pizza. Mary ate 25% and John ate $\frac{3}{8}$ of the pizza. What percent of the pizza is left?

    (A) 30% (B) 40%
    (C) 25% (D) 37.5%

63. The sun is 9.3×10^{7} miles from the Earth. Express this number in standard notation.

    (A) 930,000 (B) 9,300,000
    (C) 93,000,000 (D) 930,000,000

64. Express 0.000735 in proper scientific notation.

    (A) 7.35×10^{-3} (B) 7.35×10^{-4}
    (C) 735×10^{-4} (D) 735×10^{-7}

65. Base your answer to the following question on the following information.

    Jane selected some students in her school at random and asked what they ate for lunch each day. Her results are shown in the table below.

    ### Jane's Results

Type of Lunch	Number of Students
Hamburger	19
Chicken	24
Pizza	43

    What percent of the students in the table above eat chicken for lunch each day?

    Show your work. Round your answer to the nearest percent.

66. What is the standard notation for 4.22×10^{-3}?

    (A) 0.000422 (B) 0.00422
    (C) 42.2 (D) 422

67. Which of the following would give a repeating decimal as its quotient?

    (A) $\frac{9}{6}$ (B) $\frac{3}{16}$ (C) $\frac{8}{40}$ (D) $\frac{73}{9}$

Number System

68. Juan and his little brother had to share a candy cane that was 12 inches long. Juan took $\frac{2}{3}$ of the candy cane. How many inches of the candy cane did his little brother get?

    (A) $\frac{1}{3}$ inches (B) 3 inches
    (C) 4 inches (D) 6 inches

69. There are 57 million grains of sand on the beach. What is the number of grains of sand on the beach in scientific notation?

    (A) 5.7×10^6 (B) 57×10^6
    (C) 5.7×10^7 (D) 57×10^7

70. Mr. Franks is organizing his drill bits while cleaning up his tools. If the drill bits are to be arranged in size from smallest to largest, which list is in the correct order?

    (A) $\frac{1}{4}, \frac{2}{5}, \frac{1}{2}, \frac{2}{3}$ (B) $\frac{1}{4}, \frac{1}{2}, \frac{2}{3}, \frac{2}{5}$
    (C) $\frac{2}{3}, \frac{1}{4}, \frac{1}{2}, \frac{2}{5}$ (D) $\frac{2}{5}, \frac{1}{4}, \frac{1}{2}, \frac{2}{3}$

71. Town A and Town B are 156,000 meters away from each other. What is this number in scientific notation?

    (A) 15.6×10^3 (B) 156×10^{-3}
    (C) 1.56×10^5 (D) 1.56×10^{-5}

72. The sum of two numbers is 8. The sum of the squares of the same two numbers is 40. What are the numbers?

    (A) 0 and 8 (B) 1 and 7
    (C) 2 and 6 (D) 3 and 5

73. The expression $\left(\frac{1}{9} + \frac{2}{3}\right) \div \frac{2}{3}$ is equivalent to

    (A) $\frac{6}{7}$
    (B) $\frac{7}{6}$
    (C) $\frac{1}{9}$
    (D) 9

74. Which of the following would give a repeating decimal as its quotient?

    (A) $\frac{28}{7}$ (B) $\frac{38}{5}$ (C) $\frac{33}{9}$ (D) $\frac{42}{15}$

75. What is the prime factorization of 156?

    (A) $2 \cdot 3 \cdot 13$ (B) $2 \cdot 3 \cdot 26$
    (C) $2 \cdot 3^2 \cdot 13$ (D) $2^2 \cdot 3 \cdot 13$

76. Which is equivalent to 9.25×10^3?

    (A) 0.00925 (B) 0.0925
    (C) 925 (D) 9,250

77. Cindy uses $\frac{1}{8}$ L of lemonade in each cup she sells at her lemonade stand. If she has a pitcher which holds $\frac{12}{16}$ L. How many cups can she sell?

    (A) 3 (B) 4 (C) 5 (D) 6

78. 250 people attended the beach on July 4th last year. This year, 20% less people attended on that date. How many people went to the beach this year on July 4th?

    (A) 150 (B) 200 (C) 350 (D) 400

Number System

79. Which of the following represents this number?

    $2 \times 10^5 + 6 \times 10^3 + 1 \times 10^0$

    (A) 9 (B) 206,001
    (C) 26,100 (D) 900,000

80. Which of the following expressions represents the least value?

    (A) $245 \times \frac{1}{3}$ (B) $245 + \frac{1}{3}$
    (C) $245 - \frac{1}{3}$ (D) $245 \div \frac{1}{3}$

81. Shane is thinking of a number. The number:
    – is between 9 and 25
    – is not divisible by 5
    – is divisible by 7
    – is even

    What is Shane's number?

    (A) 14 (B) 21 (C) 23 (D) 28

82. Laura bought 7 pencils at the prices show below.

    | Plain Pencil | $0.55 |
    | Colored Pencil | $0.65 |

    Which could be the amount she spent for all the pencils?

    (A) $3.75   (B) $4.10
    (C) $4.15   (D) $4.65

83. What is the least common denominator of $\frac{1}{2}$, $\frac{1}{4}$ and $\frac{1}{5}$?

    (A) 20 (B) 10 (C) 40 (D) 80

84. What is the next greatest prime number after 23?

    (A) 25 (B) 27 (C) 28 (D) 29

85. Base your answer to the following question on the diagram below, which shows two sets of numbers, set A and set B.

    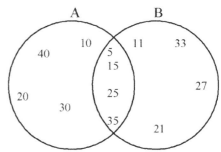

    What is the lowest 3–digit whole number that could be placed in the intersection of sets A and B?

86. What is the prime factorization of 156?

    (A) $2(3)^2(13)$ (B) $2^2(3)(13)$
    (C) $3(4)(13)$ (D) $2^2(3^2)(13)$

Number System

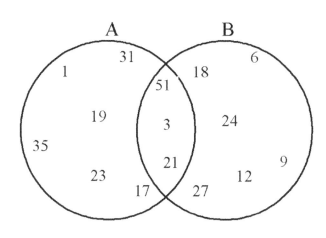

87. Set A is described as a set of odd whole numbers. Write a description for set B.

88. Which is true for any number n?

    (A) $n \times 0 = 0$ (B) $n \times 1 = 1$
    (C) $n + 0 = 0$ (D) $n \times \frac{1}{2} = 0$

89. Which of the following numbers is a composite number?

    (A) 1 (B) 2 (C) 39 (D) 89

90. Justin and Mark invented a new game called "Guess or Lose". The following are the clues to the game:

    A) The person's number is between 200 and 240.
    B) The person's number is evenly divisible by 2.
    C) The person's number is evenly divisible by 3.
    D) The person's number is evenly divisible by 5.
    E) The person's number is a prime number.

    1) If possible, write a number that meets criteria A and B. If it is not possible, tell why.

    2) If possible, write a number that meets criteria A, C, and D. If it is not possible, tell why.

    3) If possible, write a number that meets criteria A, B, C, and D. If it is not possible, tell why.

    4) If possible, write a number that meets criteria A, B, C, D, and E. If it is not possible, tell why.

91. Which expression is equal to –0.36?

    (A) $-0.4 - 0.04$ (B) $-2.4 + 2.76$
    (C) $-0.6 \times (-0.6)$ (D) $9 \times (-25)$

92. Write 432,000 in proper scientific notation.

    (A) 432×10^3 (B) 432×10^{-3}
    (C) 4.32×10^5 (D) 4.32×10^{-5}

93. What is the proper scientific notation for 299,800,000?

    (A) 2998×10^6 (B) 2.998×10^7
    (C) 2.998×10^8 (D) 2.998×10^9

Number System

94. Which of the following would give a terminating decimal as its quotient?

    (A) $\frac{31}{2}$ (B) $\frac{34}{9}$ (C) $\frac{13}{6}$ (D) $\frac{1}{3}$

95. The Earth's minimum distance to the sun is about 91 million miles. The maximum distance is about 3.5 million miles greater than the minimum distance. What is the scientific notation of the Earth's maximum distance from the sun in miles?

    (A) 9.45×10^5 (B) 9.45×10^6
    (C) 9.45×10^7 (D) 9.45×10^8

96. What is 6.3×10^{-3} in standard form?

    (A) 0.0063 (B) 0.063
    (C) 6,300 (D) 63,000

97. Harry deposited $5,000 into a bank account. At the end of 4 years, the account had earned $800 in simple interest. What rate of interest did the account earn per year?

    (A) 2.38% (B) 4%
    (C) 5% (D) 16%

98. What is the standard notation for 2.97×10^5?

    (A) 29,700 (B) 297,000
    (C) 2,970,000 (D) 2,970

99. Which of the following would result in the largest number?

    (A) 23×18
    (B) 10^3
    (C) $5^3 + 7^3$
    (D) $30 \times 20 + 10 \times 25$

100. The speed of an object going at Mach 1 is 343 meters per second. If Mach 10 is ten times the speed of Mach 1, what is the value of Mach 10 in meters per second?

    (A) 3.43×10^{-3} (B) 3.43×10^{-2}
    (C) 3.43×10^2 (D) 3.43×10^3

Conversion and Temperature

1. Lindsay parked her car 47 feet from her apartment. How far is this in yards?

    (A) 12 yards (B) $15\frac{2}{3}$ yards
    (C) $16\frac{1}{3}$ yards (D) 141 yards

2. Frank needs 8 pints of milk for milkshakes. How else can this amount be represented?

    (A) 1 cup (B) 1 quart
    (C) 1 gallon (D) 1 liter

3. In her science book, Melissa reads that escape velocity from Earth is 7 miles per second. What is that in miles per hour?

    (A) 420 (B) 1,640
    (C) 16,400 (D) 25,200

4. A box contains weights. Altogether, the box weighs 328 ounces. How many pounds does the box weigh?

    (A) 15.5 lb (B) 20 lbs.
    (C) 20.5 lb (D) 22 lb

5. Evaluate 194 cm + 100,000 mm

    (A) 101.94 centimeters
    (B) 100,194 meters
    (C) 101.94 meters
    (D) 100,194 millimeters

6. An airplane was traveling at 340 miles per hour. What is another way to express this amount? (1 mile = 5,280 feet)

    (A) 1.7952×10^1 ft/hr (B) 1.7952×10^3 ft/hr
    (C) 1.7952×10^4 ft/hr (D) 1.7952×10^6 ft/hr

7. Which of the following is the longest time?

    (A) 1,300 minutes (B) 1 day
    (C) 36,000 seconds (D) 12 hours

8. A drink contains 4 ounces of orange juice, 1 pint of cranberry juice, and 12 ounces of pineapple juice. How much liquid is contained in the drink?

    (A) 24 ounces (B) 1.5 pints
    (C) 1 quart (D) 1 quart and 1 pint

9. A kilometer is about $\frac{6}{10}$ of a mile. If a caution sign says the speed limit is 40 kilometers per hour, then what is the approximate speed limit in miles per hour?

    (A) 20 kilometers per hour
    (B) 24 kilometers per hour
    (C) 26 kilometers per hour
    (D) 32 kilometers per hour

10. Stan is driving his car through Europe. His speedometer reads 60 miles per hour. He wants to convert this into kilometers per hour. Which is the closest to his speed in kilometers per hour, if one kilometer is about 0.6 miles?

    (A) 36 (B) 64 (C) 100 (D) 120

Conversion and Temperature

11. There are 5,280 feet in a mile. There are 3 feet in a yard. How many yards are in $\frac{3}{4}$ of a mile?

    (A) 1,320 (B) 1,760
    (C) 3,960 (D) 5,280

12. Car 1 traveled 60 miles per hour. Car 2 traveled at 90 kilometers per hour. Which traveled faster?

    (A) Car 1
    (B) Car 2
    (C) The answer cannot be determined.

13. Put the following measurements in order from smallest to largest:
    1.5 feet, 1 yard, 15 inches, 1 foot

14. How can $7\frac{1}{2}$ feet also be written?

    (A) 15 inches   (B) $2\frac{1}{2}$ yards
    (C) 22.5 yards   (D) 22.5 inches

15. Aditiya is standing under a 9 foot doorway. He is 70 inches tall. How much space is between his head and the door?

    (A) 37 inches   (B) 3 feet 2 inches
    (C) 40 inches   (D) 4 feet

16. Steve's car weighs 4320 pounds. How many tons is that equivalent to?

    (A) 0.0216   (B) 0.216
    (C) 2.16   (D) 21.6

17. The graphite on Jason's pencil is 7 centimeters long. What is this length in millimeters?

    (A) .07 mm   (B) .7 mm
    (C) 70 mm   (D) 700 mm

18. Mr. Adams is buying water for his water cooler. His water cooler can fit a six gallon jug of water. How many quarts of water is equivalent to the six gallons?

    (A) 12 quarts   (B) 18 quarts
    (C) 24 quarts   (D) 36 quarts

19. Sam's kitchen has an area of 40 square yards. What is this area in square feet?

    (A) 40 (B) 80 (C) 120 (D) 360

20. Elliot is 6 feet and 1 inch tall while his friend Vaughn is 64.5 inches tall. How much taller is Elliot than Vaughn?

    (A) 0.5 feet   (B) 8.5 inches
    (C) $\frac{3}{4}$ feet (D) 10.5 inches

21. The distance between the John F. Kennedy International Airport in New York City and the Los Angeles International Airport in Los Angeles is approximately 2780 miles. If one mile is approximately 1.6 kilometers, which of the following is closest to the number of kilometers between these two airports?

    (A) 1738 kilometers (B) 2564 kilometers
    (C) 4448 kilometers (D) 5236 kilometers

Conversion and Temperature

22. Justin can type 4,920 words in an hour. On the average, how many words can he type in a minute?

23. Which is faster, 60 miles per hour or 60 feet per second?

    (A) 60 miles per hour
    (B) 60 feet per second
    (C) Both are the same

24. Evaluate: 189 g + 10,000 mg

    (A) 189.1 g   (B) 190 g
    (C) 199 g   (D) 289 g

25. The average weight of a cow is 6,600 pounds. How many tons does the average cow weigh?

    (A) 2.2 tons   (B) 2.6 tons
    (C) 3.3 tons   (D) 3.6 tons

26. A submarine travels 300 nautical miles in 8 hours and continues at this rate. Which is closest to the number of hours it will take the submarine to travel another 300 <u>miles</u>? (1 nautical mile ≈ 1.15 miles)

    (A) 5 hours   (B) 6 hours
    (C) 7 hours   (D) 8 hours

27. Farmer John milked 100 gallons of milk. He then sold his milk to the local grocery store at a rate of $0.50 per quart. How much money did Farmer John make from the 100 gallons of milk?

    (A) $100.00   (B) $200.00
    (C) $400.00   (D) $800.00

28. For his science project, Benjy measured that there are 2,640 feet in a half–mile. Based on his measurement, how many yards are there in a mile?

    (A) 880   (B) 1,280
    (C) 1,760   (D) 5,280

29. Three sticks, measuring 8 inches, 9 inches, and 10 inches, are connected end to end. How long are they when put all together?

    (A) 2 feet 3 inches   (B) 2 feet 4 inches
    (C) 2 feet 7 inches   (D) 2 feet 8 inches

30. Which is equivalent to 30 meters?

    (A) 0.3 centimeters
    (B) 300 centimeters
    (C) 3000 centimeters
    (D) 30000 centimeters

31. Evaluate: 371 mm + 27.8 cm

    (A) 0.649 m   (B) 3.988 m
    (C) 398.8 m   (D) 649 m

32. Karen the Kitten weighs 58 ounces. What is its weight in pounds and ounces?

    (A) 3 pounds 4 ounces
    (B) 3 pounds 10 ounces
    (C) 4 pounds 10 ounces
    (D) 5 pounds 8 ounces

Conversion and Temperature

33. How many liters is 180 milliliters (mL)?

    (A) .18 L (B) .36 L
    (C) 1.8 L (D) 3.6 L

34. An 18 foot round pool holds approximately 1102 ft³ of water. About how many cubic meters is this equivalent to if 35.3 ft³=1 m³?

    (A) 15.6 m³   (B) 31.2 m³
    (C) 20563 m³ (D) 38901 m³

35. Jonathan needs to purchase 3 pounds of butter for baking. The local grocery store sells sticks of butter that weigh 4 ounces. How many sticks of butter would Jonathan need to purchase?

    (A) 9 (B) 10 (C) 11 (D) 12

36. How many quarts are in $3\frac{1}{4}$ gallons?

    (A) 7 (B) 9 (C) 11 (D) 13

37. Which of the following metric units would be the best conversion choice for an area of land that is 3 miles long by 4 miles wide?

    (A) cm³ (B) cm² (C) km³ (D) km²

38. The Persian Gulf War lasted 213 days. Calculate the number of seconds that the war lasted.

    Show your work.

39. Susie can run 21 yards in 7 seconds. How fast can she run in feet per second?

    (A) 3 feet per second
    (B) 9 feet per second
    (C) 10 feet per second
    (D) 12 feet per second

40. In air, a sound wave travels at 343 meters per second. How many kilometers does a sound wave travel in an hour?

    (A) 20.580 km   (B) 1,234.800 km
    (C) 20,580 km   (D) 1,234,800 km

41. A recipe calls for 2 cups of sugar per quart of lemonade. How much sugar is needed for a gallon of lemonade?

    (A) 1 cup   (B) 4 cups
    (C) 8 cups (D) 16 cups

42. Jos\'{e} is 75 inches tall. Which of the following is the same height?

    (A) 6 feet 0 inches (B) 6 feet 1 inch
    (C) 6 feet 2 inches (D) 6 feet 3 inches

43. A recipe calls for 250,000 milligrams of flour. How many kilograms of flour does this equal?

    (A) 0.025 kg (B) 0.25 kg
    (C) 2.5 kg   (D) 250 kg

44. How many inches are in 3 yards?

    (A) 36 (B) 108 (C) 156 (D) 300

Conversion and Temperature

45. In order to finance his college education, Leon took out a loan to pay back in 58 monthly payments. About how long will it take him to pay for his college education?

    (A) 4 years (B) 5 years
    (C) 6 years (D) 58 years

46. Joan is watering her flower pot for a science experiment. The experiment calls for 2 liters of water. She only has a 50 mL measuring cup. How many times must she fill the measuring cup and pour it into the pot?

    (A) 50 times (B) 100 times
    (C) 20 times (D) 40 times

47. Which of the following lengths is shortest?

    (A) 40 millimeters
    (B) 0.4 centimeters
    (C) 0.04 meters
    (D) 0.0004 kilometers

48. A rock weighs 2,300 grams. How many kilograms is this?

    (A) 0.23 (B) 2.3 (C) 23 (D) 230

49. Which of the following is the greatest measurement?

    (A) 400 pounds (B) .3 tons
    (C) 8000 ounces (D) 650 pounds

50. A steel rod of 1.25 feet was cut into 5 equal pieces. How long was each piece in inches?

    (A) 0.25 in. (B) 2.40 in.
    (C) 3.00 in. (D) 15.00 in.

51. A rectangular block of cheese has a volume of 3 cubic feet. How many cubic inches is this?

    (A) 36 (B) 108
    (C) 432 (D) 5184

52. If a certain meteor passes by the earth every $5\frac{2}{3}$ years, how many **months** will it take for the meteor to pass the earth?

    (A) 5 months (B) 8 months
    (C) 60 months (D) 68 months

53. How many inches are in 5.5 yards?

    (A) 66 (B) 124 (C) 198 (D) 208

54. How can 3 yards also be written?

    (A) 1 foot (B) 3 feet
    (C) 6 feet (D) 9 feet

55. A model of the solar system uses a scale of $3 \text{ inches} = 2 \times 10^8$ kilometers. The distance between the Sun and the Earth is about 1.496×10^8 kilometers. In the model, how far apart are the Sun and the Earth?

    (A) 0.465 inches (B) 0.748 inches
    (C) 1.496 inches (D) 2.244 inches

Conversion and Temperature

56. Ms. Fanny requires 8 pints of milk to make her famous cake. How many gallons is this?

    (A) 8   (B) 4   (C) 2   (D) 1

57. Turkey at a delicatessen sells for $4.00 per pound. Based on this rate, how much does it cost per ounce of turkey?

    (A) $0.25 per ounce   (B) $0.33 per ounce
    (C) $48.00 per ounce   (D) $64.00 per ounce

58. A man who is 72 inches tall is

    (A) 5 feet 10 inches tall.
    (B) 6 feet 0 inches tall.
    (C) 6 feet 4 inches tall.
    (D) 7 feet 2 inches tall.

59. A square chocolate bar measures 4 inches by 4 inches. What is the least number of chocolate bars needed to cover a rectangular tray of 2 feet by 3 feet?

    (A) 3.75 chocolate bars
    (B) 4.5 chocolate bar
    (C) 45 chocolate bars
    (D) 54 chocolate bars

60. Four boys measured their height.

    Julio was 1.66 meters.
    Yang was 155 centimeters.
    Leonard was 1.7 meters.
    Sam was 160 centimeters.

    Which boy was the tallest?

    (A) Julio   (B) Yang
    (C) Leonard   (D) Sam

61. Put the following measurements in order from smallest to largest:
    0.5 yards, 14 inches, 2 feet, 1 foot

    (A) 0.5 yards, 14 inches, 2 feet, 1 foot
    (B) 1 foot, 14 inches, 2 feet, 0.5 yards
    (C) 1 foot, 14 inches, 0.5 yards, 2 feet
    (D) 14 inches, 1 foot, 2 feet, 0.5 yards

62. A path is 4 miles long. How many yards is this? (5280 ft = 1 mile)

    (A) 440 yards   (B) 7040 yards
    (C) 21120 yards   (D) 63360 yards

63. Convert: 48 ounces = ____ pounds

    (A) 3   (B) 4   (C) 6   (D) 8

64. Convert: 48 fluid ounces = ____ gallons

    (A) $\frac{3}{8}$ (B) $\frac{1}{2}$ (C) $\frac{5}{8}$ (D) 2

Conversion and Temperature

65. A grass field has dimensions 450 yards by 935 yards. Which of the following is closest to the dimensions in miles? (1 mile = 5,280 feet)

    (A) 0.028 mi × 0.059 mi
    (B) 0.085 mi × 0.177 mi
    (C) 0.232 mi × 0.482 mi
    (D) 0.256 mi × 0.531 mi

66. There are 5,280 feet in a mile. There are 3 feet in a yard. There are 91.5 centimeters in a yard. How many meters are in $\frac{3}{4}$ of a mile, to the nearest meter?

    (A) 1,208   (B) 1,610
    (C) 12,074   (D) 16,090

67. A race car travels at 180 miles per hour. If there are 5,280 feet in a mile, how many feet can the race car travel in an hour?

    (A) 528,000 feet   (B) 950,400 feet
    (C) 29.33 feet   (D) 15,840 feet

68. The length of a calculator is 10 cm. What is the length in mm?

    (A) 1 mm   (B) 100 mm
    (C) 1000 mm   (D) 10000 mm

69. Jose has a 1 quart pitcher.

    Approximately how many pitchers of water will Jose have to empty into his fish tank to have at least 10 gallons of water?

    (A) 5   (B) 20   (C) 40   (D) 60

70. Convert: 3 yards = ___ inches

    (A) 12   (B) 36   (C) 72   (D) 108

71. The temperature in Charlotte is measured each morning. On March 7th, it was 53°F. The temperature rose 8°F on March 8th and dropped 11°F on March 9th. What was the temperature on March 9th?

    Show your work.

72. The difference between two temperature readings is 13 degrees Fahrenheit. Which of the following could be the two temperature readings?

    (A) −5°F and 12°F   (B) −1°F and 14°F
    (C) −6°F and 7°F   (D) −3°F and 11°F

73. A certain beach will not open unless the water temperature is at least 65°F. Today, the water temperature was 53°F. How many more degrees must the temperature increase so that the beach can open?

    (A) 10°F   (B) 11°F
    (C) 12°F   (D) 13°F

74. The difference between two temperature readings is 9 degrees Fahrenheit. Which of the following could be the two temperature readings?

    (A) 2°F and −11°F   (B) 3°F and 11°F
    (C) −10°F and 1°F   (D) −4°F and 5°F

Conversion and Temperature

75. Pure water boils at 212°F. If a certain chemical is added to the water then the boiling point changes by −16°F. What is the new boiling point of the water?

    (A) 194°F (B) 196°F
    (C) 200°F (D) 228°F

76. Which temperature is coldest?

    (A) 37°F   (B) 37°C
    (C) 37 K   (D) 320 K

77. On January 21st the temperature at 4 P.M. was 9°F. By 2 A.M. the temperature had dropped to −3°F. Which of the following equations could you use to find x, the number of degrees the temperature dropped?

    (A) $9 - 3 = x$ (B) $9 - x = -3$
    (C) $9 - (-x) = 3$ (D) $x - (-3) = 9$

78. The temperature in Miami was 75°F, while the temperature in Alaska was −18°F. How much colder was it in Alaska?

    (A) 57°F (B) 93°F (C) 90°F (D) 18°F

79. Measured in Celsius, normal body temperature is 37°C. How much colder is room temperature, which is 23.5°C?

    (A) 13°C   (B) 13.3°C
    (C) 13.5°C (D) 56.3°C

80. Robyn heats a cup of tea to 90°F but she likes to drink it when it is 70°F. If the tea cools 4°F every 5 minutes, how long will Robyn have to wait to drink her tea?

    (A) 16 minutes (B) 20 minutes
    (C) 23 minutes (D) 25 minutes

81. Which temperature is cooler, 20 degrees Fahrenheit or 20 degrees Celsius?

    (A) 20 degrees Fahrenheit.
    (B) 20 degrees Celsius.
    (C) They both would feel the same.

82. A honeybee must have a body temperature of at least 86° Fahrenheit (°F) to be able to fly. What is this temperature in Celsius?

    (A) 30°C (B) 48°C
    (C) 66°C (D) 97°C

83. Coffee cools 2°F per minute and Martin likes to drink his coffee when it is 74°F. What was the original temperature of Martin's coffee if he waited 9 minutes for it to cool?

    (A) 56°F (B) 83°F
    (C) 92°F (D) 96°F

84. The temperature in New York is measured each morning. On January 10th, it was 10°C below zero (−10°C). The temperature rose 6°C on January 11th and dropped 2°C on January 12th. What was the temperature on January 12th?

    (A) −6°C (B) −2°C
    (C) 12°C (D) 14°C

Conversion and Temperature

85. Which temperature is warmer, 40 degrees Fahrenheit or 10 degrees Celsius?

    (A) 40 degrees Fahrenheit.
    (B) 10 degrees Celsius.
    (C) They both would feel the same.

86. What is 104°F equivalent to in Celsius? Show the work you used to reach this conclusion.

87. Measured in Fahrenheit, normal dog body temperature is 102°F. How much hotter is the boiling point of water, 212°F?

    (A) 110°F   (B) 314°F
    (C) 114°F   (D) 200°F

88. The melting point of nitrogen is –209°C and the boiling point is –195°C. How much greater is the boiling point than the melting point?

    (A) 14°C   (B) 24°C
    (C) 30°C   (D) 404°C

89. The record low temperature in New York City is –4°F and the record high temperature is 105°F. What is the difference between the record high and record low temperatures?

90. The temperature on Tuesday was 8°F. On Wednesday, the temperature was –7°F. How much colder was Wednesday?

    Show your work.

91. The high temperature yesterday was –8°F. Today the high temperature was six degrees higher. What was today's high temperature?

    (A) –14°F   (B) –2°F
    (C) 2°F   (D) 6°F

92. The temperature on Sunday was 12°F. On Monday, the temperature was –8°F. How much colder was Monday?

    (A) 4°F   (B) 6°F
    (C) 20°F   (D) 30°F

93. The melting point for bromine is –7°C and the boiling point is 58°C. How much greater is the boiling point than the melting point?

    (A) 65°F   (B) 51°C
    (C) 45°C   (D) 41°C

94. At sunrise (7 A.M.) the temperature is 59°F. If the temperature rises 3°F every hour until 2 P.M. and then decreases 1°F until 5 P.M., what is the temperature at 4 P.M.?

    (A) 77°F   (B) 78°F
    (C) 80°F   (D) 81°F

Conversion and Temperature

Base your answers to questions **95** through **97** on the following information. The daily high temperature in New York over a five day period in June is as follows: 83°F, 91°F, 76°F, 83°F, 72°F.

95. What is the range of the data above?

    (A) 9°F
    (B) 13°F
    (C) 17°F
    (D) 19°F

96. What is the mode of the data above?

    (A) 76°F
    (B) 80°F
    (C) 83°F
    (D) 91°F

97. What is the average high temperature over the five day period?

    (A) 72°F
    (B) 81°F
    (C) 83°F
    (D) 91°F

98. The record low temperature in Antarctica is –126°F and the record high temperature is 59°F. What is the difference between the record high and record low temperatures?

    (A) 126°F
    (B) 67°F
    (C) 59°F
    (D) 185°F

99. At sunset (6 P.M.) the temperature is 73°F. If the temperature drops one degree Fahrenheit every half an hour, what will the temperature be at 11 P.M.?

    (A) 61°F
    (B) 63°F
    (C) 68°F
    (D) 70°F

100. Which temperature is warmer, 25°C or 77°F?

    (A) 25°C.
    (B) 77°F.
    (C) They both would feel the same.

Square roots, Exp, OP

1. Which of the following represents the solution(s) to the following equation?

   $x = \sqrt[3]{8}$

   (A) $x = -2, 2$ (B) $x = -2$
   (C) $x = 2$ (D) $x = -4, 4$

2. Solve for v: $v^7 = 2{,}187$

   (A) 2   (B) 3   (C) 4   (D) 5

3. Roger used the equation below to solve a math problem.

   $5^A \times 5^B = 5^{A+B}$

   Using this equation, find the equivalent solution to $12^8 \times 12^{-2}$.

   (A) 12^{-6} (B) 12^6 (C) 12^{10} (D) 24^5

4. Perform the indicated operation: $5^{10} \times 5^{-6}$

   (A) 5^{-60} (B) 25^{-60}
   (C) 5^4 (D) 25^4

5. A minute is 0.0000019 of a year. What is this number expressed in scientific notation?

   (A) 1.9×10^{-5} (B) 1.9×10^{-6}
   (C) 1.9×10^6 (D) 1.9×10^5

6. Which value of x will make the equation below true?

   $2^x = 256$

   (A) 6   (B) 7   (C) 8   (D) 9

7. Which is equal to 12^1?

   (A) 0   (B) 1   (C) 12   (D) 144

8. Which of the following measurements would most likely be given with a negative exponent in scientific notation?

   (A) The mass of the sun in pounds
   (B) The distance to Mars in miles
   (C) The weight of a bowling ball in ounces
   (D) The length of a bacterium in inches

9. Find the square root of 9^2.

   (A) 3   (B) 9   (C) 18   (D) 27

10. Write 2^{-2} as a fraction.

11. Between which two whole numbers will you find $\sqrt{23}$?

    (A) 3 and 4   (B) 4 and 5
    (C) 5 and 6   (D) 7 and 8

12. Find $(\sqrt{9})^3$

    (A) 3   (B) 9   (C) 27   (D) 729

Square roots, Exp, OP

13. Which of the following represents the largest number?

    (A) $20^2 + 20^2$ (B) $21 \times 19 + 20^2$
    (C) $10^2 + 29 \times 31$ (D) 10^3

14. Which expression is equivalent to the one shown below?

    $(-5x^2)(3x^3)$

    (A) $-2x^6$ (B) $15x^5$
    (C) $-15x^5$ (D) $-15x^6$

15. Simplify: $3^{-2} \times 3^8 =$

    (A) 9^{-16} (B) 3^{-16} (C) 3^6 (D) 9^6

16. Simplify $3^4 \times 4^4$.

    (A) 12^4 (B) 7^4 (C) 7^8 (D) 12^8

17. Between what two numbers does the square root of 175 fall?

    (A) 11, 12   (B) 12, 13
    (C) 13, 14   (D) 14, 15

18. Solve for x: $3^4 = x$

    (A) 12   (B) 27   (C) 64   (D) 81

19. The difference between two numbers is 4. The sum of the squares of the same two numbers is 80. What are the two numbers?

    (A) 12 and 8   (B) 10 and 6
    (C) 8 and 4   (D) 9 and 5

20. What is the square root of 2^8?

    (A) 8   (B) 16   (C) 64   (D) 256

21. Write -2^{-2} as a fraction.

    (A) $-\frac{1}{4}$ (B) $\frac{1}{4}$ (C) -4 (D) 4

22. Perform the indicated operation: $5^3 \times 2^3$

    (A) 7^3 (B) $1{,}000$
    (C) 10^6 (D) 10^9

23. Perform the indicated operation: $4^{-2} \times 2^4$

    (A) 8^{-8} (B) 1   (C) 6^2 (D) 8^2

24. If $2^n = \frac{1}{128}$, what does n equal?

    (A) -8 (B) -7 (C) 7   (D) 8

25. Evaluate $\left(\frac{7}{10}\right)^3$.

    (A) 0.0343   (B) 0.343
    (C) 0.49   (D) 34.3

Square roots, Exp, OP

26. Between which two numbers does $\sqrt{24}$ lie on a number line?

    (A) 3 and 4 (B) 4 and 5
    (C) 5 and 6 (D) 6 and 7

27. Which of the following yields a positive result?

    (A) $-2^3(2^4)$ (B) -10^2
    (C) $(-6)^5(-4)^2$ (D) $(-3)^7(-1)^3$

28. Which is equal to 9^2?

    (A) 1 (B) 9 (C) 81 (D) 92

29. Simplify the expression: $4^5 \times 2^{-6}$

    (A) 4^{-1} (B) 8 (C) 16 (D) 4^8

30. To make the following true, what must be the value of v?

    $$2^v = 64$$

    (A) 3 (B) 4 (C) 5 (D) 6

31. Billy was told that 25 is a perfect square of a number. Which of these could Billy use to find out what number squared equals 25?

    (A) 25^2 (B) 25
    (C) $\sqrt{25}$ (D) $25 \cdot 2$

32. Which of the following represents the solution(s) to the following equation?

    $x^2 = 81$

    (A) $x = -9$ (B) $x = -9, 9$
    (C) $x = 9$ (D) $x = 10$

33. Find the value of $\left(\frac{2}{3}\right)^3 \times \left(\frac{1}{2}\right)^2$.

34. Between which two numbers does $\sqrt{42}$ lie?

    (A) 3 and 4 (B) 4 and 5
    (C) 5 and 6 (D) 6 and 7

35. Simplify: $A^n \times A^{-n} =$

    (A) A^{2n} (B) A^n (C) A (D) 1

36. What is the positive square root of 18?

    (A) $-2\sqrt{3}$ (B) $-3\sqrt{2}$
    (C) $2\sqrt{3}$ (D) $3\sqrt{2}$

37. Evaluate.

    $3^4 - 2^4$

    (A) 1 (B) 3 (C) 64 (D) 65

Square roots, Exp, OP

38. To make the following true, what must be the value of v?

$$4^v = 64$$

(A) 3 (B) 4 (C) 5 (D) 6

39. Simplify: $\left(\frac{3}{4}\right)^2$

(A) $\frac{3}{4}$ (B) $\frac{r}{4}$ (C) $\frac{9}{16}$ (D) $\frac{3}{2}$

40. What is 2^0 equal to?

(A) 0 (B) 1 (C) 2 (D) 4

41. What is 0^2 equal to?

(A) 0 (B) 1 (C) 2 (D) 4

42. $\sqrt{195}$ is closest to which whole number?

(A) 13 (B) 14 (C) 15 (D) 16

43. Find $(\sqrt{2})^4$.

(A) $\sqrt{2}$ (B) 2 (C) 4 (D) 16

44. What is the positive square root of 36?

(A) −18 (B) −6 (C) 6 (D) 18

45. Evaluate the following expression:

$$2^4 \cdot 2^5$$

(A) 128 (B) 256
(C) 512 (D) 1024

46. What expression is equivalent to
y • y • z • z • z • z?

(A) $y^2 + z^4$ (B) $(yz)^2 z^2$
(C) $y^4 z^2$ (D) $2(y + 2z)$

47. Evaluate the expression: 1^{12}

(A) −1 (B) 0 (C) 1 (D) 12

48. Find $(\sqrt{169})^2$

(A) 13 (B) 26 (C) 88 (D) 169

49. Find $(\sqrt{12})^2$.

50. Which is equal to 6^3?

(A) 6 (B) 36
(C) 216 (D) 1296

51. Simplify: $9 \div 3^2 + 5 \times 6$

(A) 31 (B) 36 (C) 48 (D) 33

Square roots, Exp, OP

52. What is the value of the expression below?

    $\frac{(7-3)}{4+8\times 4}$

    (A) $.\overline{1}$ (B) .25   (C) $.\overline{3}$ (D) .5

53. What is the value of the expression below?
    $1 + (3 - 2) \div 4 \times 9$

    (A) $\frac{37}{36}$ (B) $\frac{13}{9}$ (C) $\frac{13}{4}$ (D) $\frac{9}{2}$

54. Which of these operations should be performed first in order to evaluate the expression?
    $1 + 5 \times 3 \div 7 - 9$

    (A) addition   (B) subtraction
    (C) multiplication   (D) division

55. Which of the following operations should be performed last in order to solve the following problem?
    $6(10 - 4) \div 3 + 9$

    (A) +   (B) −   (C) ×   (D) ÷

56. Which of these operations should be performed first in order to solve the following equation?
    $[3 - 2(11 + 5)] \div 4$

    (A) addition   (B) subtraction
    (C) division   (D) multiplication

57. What is the sum of $(10 - 6)^2 + 21 - 2^2$ divisible by?

    (A) 2   (B) 5   (C) 9   (D) 11

58. $10 + (16 - 8) \div 2 \bullet 3$

    What is the value of the expression above?

    (A) 10   (B) 14   (C) 18   (D) 22

59. Which of the following operations should be performed first in order to solve the following problem?
    $6 + 2(3 \div 2) - 5$

    (A) +   (B) −   (C) ×   (D) ÷

60. Which of the following statements is false?

    (A) $-7 + 7 = 7 - 7$
    (B) $7(5 - 3) = 7(5) - 7(3)$
    (C) $(8 - 3) + 7 = 7 - 3 + 8$
    (D) $(-7)(-7)(-7) = 3(-7)$

61. Meghan is solving the following problem:

    $(5^3 \times 3)^2 = ?$

    Which step is correct in the process of solving this problem?

    (A) $(125 \times 3)^2$ (B) (125×3^2)
    (C) $(5 \times 3)^6$ (D) $(8^3)^2$

62. To solve the following expression, which operation must you perform first?

    $a + b(c - d) \div e$

    (A) +   (B) −   (C) ×   (D) ÷

Square roots, Exp, OP

63. Gary, Henry, and Iris are trying to find the value of the expression $4^2 + 2(2 + 6) \times 8$. All 3 students have different ideas on how to find the value.

    Gary plans to multiply 2 and 2 first.

    Henry plans to add 2 and 6 first.

    Iris plans to multiple 6 and 8 first.

    Which statement is true?

    (A) Only Gary has a correct strategy.
    (B) Only Henry has a correct strategy.
    (C) Only Iris has a correct strategy.
    (D) None of the three students has a correct strategy.

64. Find the value of the expression.
    $$(6 \times 4) + (1 \div 5^1) - (2 + 3) \times 3^2$$

    (A) $-20\frac{4}{5}$ (B) 0
    (C) 9 (D) $15\frac{1}{2}$

65. Evaluate using proper order of operations:

    $(31 - 19) \div 4$

    (A) $-11\frac{3}{4}$ (B) 3
    (C) 12 (D) $26\frac{1}{4}$

66. What is the value of the expression below?

    $|5 - 2 \times 9| - 4$

    (A) 9 (B) 13 (C) 17 (D) 23

67. Bob looks at the following equation and realizes he forgot to add parenthesis.

    $30 + 5 \times 2 - 17 - 2$

    How would the equation look if he wanted it to equal 55?

    (A) $30 + 5 \times 2 - (17 - 2)$
    (B) $(30 + 5) \times 2 - 17 - 2$
    (C) $(30 + 5) \times 2 - (17 - 2)$
    (D) $30 + 5 \times (2 - 17) - 2$

68. Which statement is correct?

    (A) $7 - (3 \times 6) \div 2 = 12$
    (B) $7 - 3 \times (6 \div 2) = 12$
    (C) $(7 - 3 \times 6) \div 2 = 12$
    (D) $(7 - 3) \times 6 \div 2 = 12$

Square roots, Exp, OP

69. (a) Evaluate the two expressions below.

   Show your work.

   (b) Explain why the results are not the same.

   $\frac{(8 \times 3 + 2)}{2}$ $\frac{8 \times (3 + 2)}{2}$

---

70. Evaluate using proper order of operations:
    $27 + (9 \div 3)$

    (A) 3   (B) 12   (C) 24   (D) 30

71. Solve the following expression if $x = 3$:
    $5(x + 1)^2$

    (A) 4   (B) 16   (C) 15   (D) 80

72. Which of the following operations should be performed first in order to solve the following problem?
    $6(10 - 4) \div 3 + 9$

    (A) +   (B) −   (C) ×   (D) ÷

73. To solve the following expression, which operation must you perform first?

    $8 - 3(4 + 3) \div 2$

    (A) +   (B) −   (C) ×   (D) ÷

74. Simplify the following expression:

    $3 - 4 \times 5 + 8$

    (A) −25   (B) −9   (C) 9   (D) 25

75. Solve the following expression.

    $18 - 4(8 - 4) \div 2$

    (A) 1   (B) 10   (C) 28   (D) 54

76. Jackie and Kirk are trying to find the value of the expression $8 \cdot 2^3$.

    Jackie plans to cube 2 first, then multiply the result by 8.

    Kirk plans to multiply 8 by 2 first, then cube the product.

    Which statement is true?

    (A) Only Jackie has a correct strategy.
    (B) Only Kirk has a correct strategy.
    (C) Both Jackie and Kirk have a correct strategy.
    (D) Neither Jackie nor Kirk has a correct strategy.

Square roots, Exp, OP

77. (a) Evaluate the two expressions below.

    Show your work.

    (b) Explain why the results are not the same.

    $(9+4)^2 \qquad 9^2 + 4^2$

---

78. Which of these operations should be performed last in order to solve the following expression?
    $65 - 7(43+2) \div 5$

    (A) addition (B) subtraction
    (C) multiplication (D) division

79. Which is equivalent to $3^3 - 2^3$?

    (A) 1 (B) 3 (C) 18 (D) 19

80. Which of these operations would be performed first in order to solve the following?
    $7(2^4 + 1) - 8$

    (A) addition (B) subtraction
    (C) multiplication (D) exponentiation

81. Jerry and Elaine are trying to find the value of the expression $(2+7)^2$.

    Jerry plans first to square 2, then square 7, and then add the results together.

    Elaine plans to first add 2 and 7, then square the sum.

    Which of the following statements are true?

    (A) Only Jerry has a correct strategy.
    (B) Only Elaine has a correct strategy.
    (C) Both Jerry and Elaine have correct strategies.
    (D) Neither Jerry nor Elaine has a correct strategy.

82. Isabella and Ethan are trying to figure out the value of the expression $(4-15)^2$.

    Isabella plans to first square 4, then square 15, and then subtract the results.

    Ethan plans to first square 15, then square 4, and then subtract the results.

    Which of the following is a correct statement?

    (A) Only Isabella has a correct strategy.
    (B) Only Ethan has a correct strategy.
    (C) Both Isabella and Ethan have correct strategies.
    (D) Neither Isabella nor Ethan has a correct strategy.

Square roots, Exp, OP

83. Simplify: $(6 \times 3 - 2) \div \frac{1}{4}$

    (A) 4   (B) 16   (C) 24   (D) 64

84. Evaluate using proper order of operation.
    $48 \div (3 - 1)$

    (A) 15   (B) 24   (C) 45   (D) 46

85. Which operation should be performed first in the expression $9 - 3(3 + 9 \div 3)^2$?

    (A) $3 + 9$ (B) $9 - 3$
    (C) $-3(3)$ (D) $9 \div 3$

86. The school choir needs to take the train to get to a performance. There are thirty–six students, two choir teachers, and five parents taking the train. Train tickets are $4.50 for each student and $7.50 for each adult. How much will it cost for all of the students and the adults to take the train?

    (A) $214.50   (B) $199.50
    (C) $177.00   (D) $162.00

87. Lucy is solving the following problem:

    $(5^2 - 2^2)^2 = ?$

    Which step is correct in solving this problem?

    (A) $(3^2)^2$ (B) $(5^2 - 2^4)$
    (C) $(25 - 4)^2$ (D) $(25^2 - 4^2)$

88. In simplifying the expression below, which operation should be performed first?
    $500 - 4 \times 5^3 + 35$

    (A) exponentiation   (B) subtraction
    (C) multiplication   (D) division

89. What is the first operation that should be performed to simplify the expression below?
    $2 \times 5 + 3 - 10$

    (A) addition   (B) subtraction
    (C) multiplication   (D) division

Square roots, Exp, OP

90. (a) Evaluate the two expressions below.

    Show your work.

    (b) Explain why the results are not the same.

    $9 \times (8 + 7) \times 6$ $9 \times 8 + 7 \times 6$

---

91. Simplify: $10(2 + (7 - 3)) - (5 \times 4)$

92. Justin placed parentheses in the expression $4 + 2 \times 9 + 3$ and got an answer of 28. Which of the following expressions correctly shows where Justin put parentheses?

    (A) $(4 + 2) \times (9 + 3)$ (B) $(4 + 2) \times 9 + 3$
    (C) $4 + 2 \times (9 + 3)$ (D) $(4 + 2 \times 9 + 3)$

93. Simplify: $3^3 + 9 \times 3 - (-12 \times 4)$

    (A) 6   (B) 15   (C) 33   (D) 42

94. What is the last operation to perform in the following expression given that $x = 3$?
    $3 + (2x - 3)^2$

    (A) addition   (B) subtraction
    (C) multiplication (D) division

95. Which of these operations should be performed first in order to simplify the following expression?
    $18 - 4(18 + 4) \div 2$

    (A) division   (B) multiplication
    (C) addition   (D) subtraction

96. Lana and Manny are trying to find the value of the expression $(11 - 5)^3$.

    Lana plans to first cube 11, then cube 5, and then subtract the results.

    Manny plans to subtract 11 and 5, then cube the result.

    Which statement is true?

    (A) Only Lana has a correct strategy.
    (B) Only Manny has a correct strategy.
    (C) Both Lana and Manny have a correct strategy.
    (D) Neither Lana nor Manny has a correct strategy.

97. $36 - (4 + 3) \cdot 4$ is equal to which of the following?

    (A) 6   (B) 8   (C) 16   (D) 37

98. Simplify: $5 + 3 \times 9 \div (2 + 1)$

    (A) 37   (B) 24   (C) 17   (D) 14

99. Which statement is correct?

    (A) $(5 \times 2) + 6 \div 2 = 20$
    (B) $(5 \times 2 + 6) \div 2 = 20$
    (C) $5 \times (2 + 6) \div 2 = 20$
    (D) $5 \times 2 + (6 \div 2) = 20$

100. Simplify: $5(2 + 7) \div (2 + 4)$

   (A) 6   (B) 6.5   (C) 7   (D) 7.5

Number Line and Algebra Part 1

1. What is the distance on a number line from –45 to 0?

2. Base your answer to the following question on the diagram below.

   Which of the following inequalities is graphed above?

   (A) $-3 > x \geq 2$ (B) $-3 \geq x > 2$
   (C) $-3 \leq x < 2$ (D) $-3 < x \leq 2$

3. How many units apart are –7 and 2 on the number line?

4. Which point on the number line below could represent $\frac{3}{5}$?

   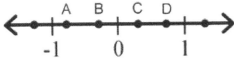

   (A) A (B) B (C) C (D) D

5. 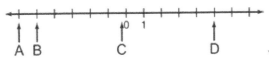 Which letter represents the location of the smallest absolute value of a number on the number line?

   (A) A (B) B (C) C (D) D

6. Which point on the number line below could represent –4?

   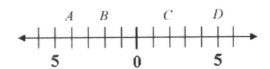

   (A) A (B) B (C) C (D) D

7. Which graph represents the solution to the equation $|x| \leq 1$?

   (A)

   (B)

   (C)

   (D)

8. Base your answer to the following question on the number line below.

   Which inequality is represented above?

   (A) $-6 < x < 4$ (B) $-6 \leq x < 4$
   (C) $4 < x \leq 6$ (D) $-6 < x \leq 4$

Number Line and Algebra Part 1

9. Point D will be placed to the right of point C and the distance between C and D will be equal to the distance between A and B.

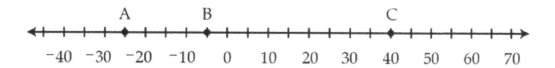

What will be the distance on the number line between points A and D?

(A) 70   (B) 75   (C) 80   (D) 85

Base your answers to questions **10** and **11** on the number line below.

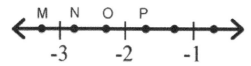

10. Which point best represents $-3\frac{1}{3}$?

    (A) M   (B) N   (C) O   (D) P

11. Which point best represents $-2\frac{2}{3}$?

    (A) M   (B) N   (C) O   (D) P

---

12. Base your answer to the following question on the timeline below.

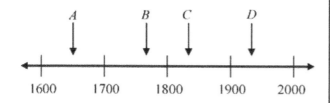

Which arrow most closely represents the year 1776?

(A) A   (B) B   (C) C   (D) D

13. Which number line represents the solution for the equation $2x - 2 > 12$?

(A)
(B)
(C)
(D)

14. How many units apart are –3 and 5 on the number line?

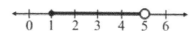

15. Which inequality represents the number line above?

(A) $1 \leq X \leq 5$
(B) X X < 1 and X > 5
(C) $1 \leq X < 5$
(D) $1 < X < 5$

57

Number Line and Algebra Part 1

16. Which number line shows r, s, t, and u from least to greatest?
    r = 2.4
    s = −3.03
    t = $2\frac{1}{2}$
    u = −3.11

    (A)
    (B)
    (C)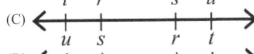
    (D)

17. Graph the inequality $4 < x \le 11$.

    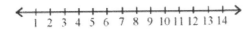

18. Which inequality is represented below?

    (A) $-1 < x < 3$ (B) $-1 \le x < 3$
    (C) $-1 < x \le 3$ (D) $-1 \le x \le 3$

19. Which inequality represents the graph below?

    (A) x < 10   (B) x ≤ 10
    (C) x > 10   (D) x ≥ 10

20. Which is the best estimate for the location of 3.25 on the following number line?

    (A) A   (B) B   (C) C   (D) D

21. Create a number line on your paper and plot the following points: 0.5, $\frac{3}{4}$

Number Line and Algebra Part 1

22. Solve the inequality below for *x* and graph the solution set on the number line provided.

    $4x + 19 > 27$

    Show your work.

23. How many units apart are –6 and 4 on the number line?

24. Which ordered pair is located in Quadrant IV?

    (A) (–2, –3)   (B) (1, 3)
    (C) (–3, 5)   (D) (3, –5)

25. Which number line shows *r*, *s*, *t*, and *u* from least to greatest?
    $r = -2.4$
    $s = 3.03$
    $t = -2\frac{1}{2}$
    $u = 3.11$

    (A)
    (B)
    (C)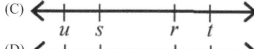
    (D)

26.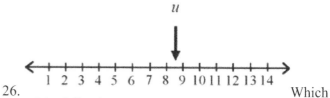
    Which of the following could be the value of *u*?

    (A) 6.9   (B) 7.6   (C) 8.7   (D) 9.3

27. What is the distance on a number line between –5 and 8?

    (A) 3   (B) 5   (C) 8   (D) 13

28. Which of the following numbers could be represented by the point in the figure below?

    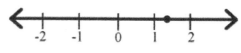

    (A) $\frac{1}{3}$ (B) $\sqrt{2}$ (C) 1.7   (D) $\frac{3}{2}$

29. Which quadrants does the line $y = 2$ run through?

    (A) I and II   (B) II and III
    (C) III and IV (D) I and III

Number Line and Algebra Part 1

30. What is the distance on a number line between 3 and 7?

    (A) 3   (B) 4   (C) 7   (D) 11

31. Create a number line on your paper and plot the following points: 0.3,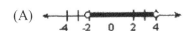

32. Which of the graphs below represents the inequality $-2 \leq x < 4$?

    (A)
    (B)
    (C)
    (D)

33. Which arrow most closely represents the year 2,082?

    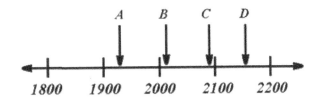

    (A) A   (B) B   (C) C   (D) D

34. Which point on the number line best represents the value $\sqrt{18}$?

    (A) A   (B) B   (C) C   (D) D

Number Line and Algebra Part 1

35. How many units apart are –9 and 8 on the number line?

36. Which number line shows the solution set to the inequality $-5 < x \leq 6$?

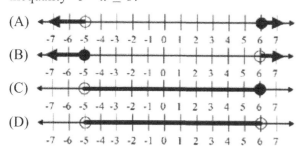

37. Which point on the number line below could represent $|-0.2|$?

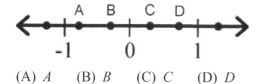

(A) A (B) B (C) C (D) D

Base your answers to questions **38** and **39** on the number line below.

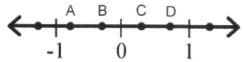

38. Which point best represents $\frac{1}{3}$?

(A) A (B) B (C) C (D) D

39. Which point best represents $-\frac{2}{3}$?

(A) A (B) B (C) C (D) D

40. Which number line shows r, s, t, and u from least to greatest?
  $r = -3.5$
  $s = 1.65$
  $t = -2\frac{1}{2}$
  $u = 1\frac{3}{5}$

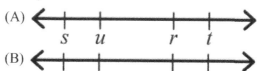

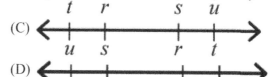

41. What is the value of the expression $11y - 9p$ if $y = 8$ and $p = 5$?

(A) 43 (B) 45 (C) 88 (D) 133

42. Which operation represents the distributive property?

(A) $a + b = b + a$
(B) $ab + 0 = ab$
(C) $a(b + c) = ab + ac$
(D) $(a + b) + c = a + (b + c)$

43. Which of the following is in the expression $3x + 4$?

(A) constant equation
(B) variable equation
(C) constant inequality
(D) coefficient variable

Number Line and Algebra Part 1

44. If *a* and *b* are integers, which statement is *always* true?

    (A) $a - b = b - a$ (B) $a + b = b + a$
    (C) $\frac{a}{b} = \frac{b}{a}$ (D) $a + 2b = b + 2a$

45. What is the identity for addition?

    (A) 0   (B) 1
    (C) $-x$ (D) $1 + x$

46. Select the property of addition that this equation demonstrates.
    $5(9 + 3) = 5(9) + 5(3)$

    (A) commutative   (B) associative
    (C) distributive   (D) closure

47. Select the property of addition that this equation demonstrates.
    $6 + 7 + 8 = 8 + 7 + 6$

    (A) commutative   (B) associative
    (C) distributive   (D) closure

48. Which of the following demonstrates the associative property of addition?

    (A) $a(b + c) = a(c + b)$
    (B) $a(b + c) = ab + ac$
    (C) $a + b = b + a$
    (D) $(a + b) + c = a + (b + c)$

49. What is the additive inverse of $\frac{3}{4}$?

    (A) $\frac{-3}{1}$ (B) $\frac{-1}{3}$ (C) $\frac{3}{4}$ (D) $\frac{4}{3}$

50. Which of the following is closed under addition?

    (A) numbers that are divisible by 3
    (B) odd integers
    (C) prime numbers
    (D) square numbers

51. What is the value of the expression $7m + 3d$ if $m = 6$ and $d = 7$?

    (A) 21   (B) 42   (C) 63   (D) 67

52. What is the identity for multiplication?

    (A) 0   (B) 1   (C) $\frac{1}{x}$ (D) $\frac{-1}{x}$

53. Select the property of addition that this equation demonstrates.
    $(2 + 3) + 4 = 2 + (3 + 4)$

    (A) commutative   (B) associative
    (C) distributive   (D) closure

54. Simplify: $(x + 5) - (2x + 1)$.

    (A) $-x + 4$ (B) $-x + 6$
    (C) $3x + 4$ (D) $3x + 6$

55. Base your answer to the following question on the equation below.

    $2 + 5 + 9 = 9 + 5 + 2$

    What property does this equation demonstrate?

    (A) associative   (B) commutative
    (C) distributive   (D) closure

Number Line and Algebra Part 1

56. James bought lollipops to give out to his class on Valentine's Day. He bought 3 large bags of 20 lollipops each. There are 20 students in his class. James wants to give each student a bag with the same amount of lollipops.

    (*a*) Write an equation to find the number of lollipops each student will receive.

    (*b*) Solve your equation to find the number of lollipops each student will receive.

    (*c*) This situation and your equation are examples of which mathematical property?

57. Which of the following is an example of the distributive property?

    (A) It doesn't matter the order one puts coins into a vending machine.
    (B) 5 packages each containing one red marble and one blue marble is the same as a package of five red marbles and a package of five blue marbles.
    (C) One set of N objects always contains N objects.
    (D) C sets of N objects is equal to N sets of C objects.

58. Which equation illustrates the commutative property?

    (A) $ab = ba$
    (B) $a(bc) = (ab)c$
    (C) $(ab) = ab$
    (D) $a(b + c) = ab + ac$

59. Which property does the equation below demonstrate?

    $(2 \times 3) \times 4 = 2 \times (3 \times 4)$

    (A) commutative (B) distributive
    (C) identity   (D) associative

60. Which of the following is an example of the multiplicative identity?

    (A) It doesn't matter the order one puts coins into a vending machine.
    (B) 5 packages each containing one red marble and one blue marble is the same as a package of five red marbles and a package of five blue marbles
    (C) One set of N objects always contains N objects.
    (D) C sets of N objects is equal to N sets of C objects.

61. George wants to simplify the expression $6(2 + 3)$. If he applies the distributive property, what will be his next step?

    (A) 6×5 (B) $(6 + 2) \times 3$
    (C) $12 + 18$ (D) $6(3 + 2)$

62. Which expression show the distributive property for the following equation?

    $5(9 + 14)$

    (A) $5(23)$ (B) $5(9) + 14$
    (C) $59 + 14$ (D) $5(9) + 5(14)$

Number Line and Algebra Part 1

63. Which of the following illustrates the identity property of multiplication?

    (A) $5 \times 0 = 0$
    (B) $5(3 + 2) = (5 \times 3) + (5 \times 2)$
    (C) $5 \times (9 \times 8) = (5 \times 9) \times 8$
    (D) $5 \times 1 = 5$

64. Mr. Johnson is playing a math game with his class. He takes a number, squares it, multiplies it by 2, then subtracts 1. Which of the following tables shows the relationship between the number Mr. Johnson starts with and the number he ends up with?

    (A)
In	1	2	3	4
Out	1	4	9	16

    (B)
In	1	2	3	4
Out	1	7	17	31

    (C)
In	1	2	3	4
Out	2	8	18	32

    (D)
In	1	2	3	4
Out	3	9	19	33

65. Which of the following illustrates the multiplicative inverse property?

    (A) $5 \times \frac{1}{5} = 1$ (B) $5 \times 0 = 0$
    (C) $5 \times 1 = 5$ (D) $5 \times 6 = 6 \times 5$

66. The distributive property is used to simplify the expression below.

    $-5a(7ab - 2c) + 2ac$

    Which of the following is the result?

    (A) $-35a^2b + 12ac$
    (B) $-35a^2b + 8ac$
    (C) $35a^2b - 10ac + 2ab$
    (D) $-35a^2b - 10ac + 2ab$

67. Which of the following is an example of the multiplicative commutative property?

    (A) It doesn't matter the order one puts coins into a vending machine.
    (B) 5 packages each containing one red marble and one blue marble is the same as a package of five red marbles and a package of five blue marbles
    (C) One set of N objects always contains N objects.
    (D) C sets of N objects is equal to N sets of C objects.

68. Rewrite the following expression: $(19 - 5) \times 4$

    (A) $(19 \times 4) - (5 \times 4)$
    (B) $(19 \times 4) \times (5 \times 4)$
    (C) $(19 - 5) - (19 - 4)$
    (D) $(19 \times 5) - (5 \times 4)$

69. Which of the following illustrates the associative property of multiplication?

    (A) $5 \times 8 = 8 \times 5$
    (B) $5 \times 0 = 0$
    (C) $5 \times 1 = 5$
    (D) $5 \times (9 \times 3) = (5 \times 9) \times 3$

70. Which of the following is a factor of the polynomial shown below?

    $12x^6 + 9x^3y + 15x^4y^2$

    (A) $9x^2$ (B) $3x^2y$ (C) $3x^3$ (D) $6x^2$

71. What is the value of x if $\frac{3}{5}(5 - x) = 9$?

    (A) -10 (B) 5 (C) 10 (D) 20

Number Line and Algebra Part 1

72. Simplify: $(9xy^3)(2x^2y)$

    (A) $18x^2y^3$ (B) $11x^2y^3$
    (C) $11x^3y^4$ (D) $18x^3y^4$

73. If x represents a negative integer, which of the following expressions would have the greatest value?

    (A) $\frac{x}{4}$ (B) $x - \frac{1}{4}$
    (C) $x + \frac{1}{4}$ (D) $x \div \frac{1}{4}$

74. Which is a solution for $4x + 2 = 8x - 8$?

    (A) $\frac{-5}{2}$ (B) $\frac{-3}{2}$ (C) $\frac{3}{2}$ (D) $\frac{5}{2}$

75. Use the expression below to answer the question.

    $$\frac{(x+4)(x-5)}{x}$$

    What is the value of this expression when $x = 8$?

    (A) $\frac{9}{4}$ (B) $\frac{9}{2}$ (C) 9   (D) $\frac{43}{2}$

76. What is the value of x in the following equation:

    $\frac{x}{7} + 15 = 85$

    (A) 440   (B) 490   (C) 500   (D) 510

77. If x represents a positive integer, which of the following expressions would have the greatest value?

    (A) $x - \frac{1}{2}$ (B) $x + \frac{1}{2}$
    (C) $\frac{x}{2}$ (D) $x \div \frac{1}{2}$

78. What value of p makes $10(p - 0.35) = 1.2$ true?

    (A) −0.23   (B) 0.47
    (C) 11.65   (D) 12.35

79. If $219 + 3(x - 1) = 6x - 22$, what is the value of x?

    (A) 52.5   (B) 58   (C) 59.5   (D) 63

80. What is the value of x in the equation $-3x + 6 = 27$?

    (A) −11   (B) −7   (C) 7   (D) 11

81. Find the solution to $\frac{x-7}{40} = 150$.

    (A) 407   (B) 507   (C) 607   (D) 707

82. Simplify: $(6x - 4y) - (-6x - 4y)$

    (A) $-8y$ (B) 0
    (C) $12x$ (D) $12x - 8y$

83. Evaluate $5(3 + 12x^2) - 2$ when $x = -2$.

    (A) 253   (B) 298
    (C) 2,893   (D) 4,498

84. Simplify as a binomial:

    $$2(4x - 5) + 5(-2x + 3)$$

Number Line and Algebra Part 1

85. Evaluate the following:

    $4(w + 5) = 30$

    (A) $w = 2.5$ (B) $w = 5.5$
    (C) $w = 7.5$ (D) $w = 12.5$

86. What is the value of x in the equation below?

    $3(x + 3) - 2(x - 1) = 24$

    (A) 4   (B) 12   (C) 17   (D) 21

87. Ms. Smith is a salesperson. She receives a weekly base salary of $350.00 and an extra 6% of her weekly sales as commission. At the end of one week, she received a paycheck in the amount of $710. Below is an equation representing this situation, where s is the dollar amount of Ms. Smith's sales for the week..

    $350 + 0.06s = 710$

    How much did Ms. Smith sell that week?

    (A) $400   (B) $600
    (C) $4000   (D) $6000

88. Simplify: $(t - 7) - (4 + t)$

    (A) -11 (B) -3
    (C) $2t - 11$ (D) $2t + 3$

89. Solve: $\frac{6x+3}{12} = \frac{x}{4}$

    (A) -1 (B) $\frac{-1}{4}$ (C) $\frac{1}{4}$ (D) 1

90. Solve for x:

    $\frac{x}{15} = \frac{45}{10}$

    (A) 25   (B) 35.5   (C) 67.5   (D) 90

91. What is the value of x in the following equation?

    $4x + 56 - x - 23 = 0$

    (A) -33 (B) -11 (C) 11   (D) 33

92. Which of the following is equal to the expression below?

    $(-8)(-x)(-x)$?

    (A) $-16x$ (B) $-8x^2$
    (C) $16x$ (D) $8x^2$

93. If $\Delta\Delta + \otimes = \otimes\otimes\otimes\otimes\otimes$, then

    (A) $\Delta = \otimes\otimes\otimes\otimes\otimes\otimes$ (B) $\Delta = \otimes\otimes\otimes\otimes$
    (C) $\Delta = \otimes\otimes\otimes$ (D) $\Delta = \otimes\otimes$

94. Simplify the expression below.

    $4p + 8pq - 6p$

    (A) $2pq + 4p$ (B) $12pq - 6p$
    (C) $6pq$ (D) $8pq - 2p$

95. Simplify: $3x(2x^2 - y^3)$

    (A) $5x^2 - 3x^3y^3$ (B) $5x^2 + 3x^3y^3$
    (C) $6x^3 - 3xy^3$ (D) $6x^3 + 3xy^3$

Number Line and Algebra Part 1

96. What is the value of n in the equation $2n^2 + 14 = 64$?

    (A) 3   (B) 5   (C) 9   (D) 25

97. Simplify as a binomial:

    $$4(3y - 3) - 2(4y - 5)$$

    (A) $20y - 22$ (B) $4y - 2$
    (C) $4y - 22$ (D) $20y - 2$

98. Justine is going to solve the following equation:

    $$3y - 5x = -3x + 4y$$

    (*a*) Simplify the equation.
    (*b*) Let $y = -14$. Simplify the equation further.

99. Which is a solution of $3(2x - 2) = 12$?

    (A) 1   (B) 2   (C) 3   (D) 4

100. Jaleel divided both sides of the equation below by 9.

    $$9x = 28$$

    Which other operation would have produced the same result?

    (A) Multiplying both sides by $\frac{1}{9}$
    (B) Subtracting 9 from both sides
    (C) Subtracting 28 from both sides
    (D) Multiplying both sides by $\frac{1}{28}$

Algebra part 2

1. Bonnie purchased an area rug for her dorm room at college. The dimensions of the area rug are 2 feet by 4 feet. If the store she purchased the rug from charges $2.00 per square foot of material, how much was Bonnie's area rug?

   (A) $8.00 (B) $10.00
   (C) $12.00 (D) $16.00

2. Bridgette has 6 cookies. Georgia has 4 times of 3 less cookies than Bridgette. How many cookies does Georgia have?

   (A) 3 (B) 12 (C) 21 (D) 24

3. Mr. Smith is purchasing a microwave from an appliance store. All microwaves at the store are on sale at $\frac{2}{3}$ of the original price, c. Mr. Smith also has a coupon for $20 off. Which equation models the total price, t, of a microwave after the sale and $20 discount?

   (A) $t = \frac{2}{3}(c - 20)$ (B) $t = \frac{1}{3}(c - 20)$
   (C) $t = \frac{1}{3}c - 20$ (D) $t = \frac{2}{3}c - 20$

4. Car rental company A charges $80 initially and $0.55 per mile. Car rental company B charges $25 initially but charges $0.75 per mile. If a person drives 1000 miles, how much money does one save by choosing car rental company A?

   (A) $40 (B) $65
   (C) $145 (D) $165

5. Elaine is selling knives for a company. Each month, she pays the company $30 plus 20% of her total monthly sales, s. Which of the following represents the total amount of money that Elaine must pay the company for one month?

   (A) $30(0.2s)$ (B) $30s + 0.2$
   (C) 30 (D) $30 + 0.2s$

6. The diameter of a circle is x. If the area of the circle is 30, which equation could be used to find the diameter of the circle?

   (A) $\pi \frac{x}{2} = 30$
   (B) $\pi x = 30$
   (C) $\pi x^2 = 30$
   (D) $\pi \left(\frac{x}{2}\right)^2 = 30$

7. Eileen's average on 10 quiz grades in math class is 90. If her teacher drops her lowest score, 75, which of the following equations can be used to find her new quiz average?

   (A) $\dfrac{(90 \times 10) - 75}{10}$
   (B) $\dfrac{90(75 - 10)}{10}$
   (C) $\dfrac{(90 \times 9) - 75}{10}$
   (D) $\dfrac{(90 \times 10) - 75}{10}$

Algebra part 2

8. Andrew and Allison were counting their marbles. Andrew said, "When I pick up three more marbles, I will have 4 times as many marbles as you." Allison said, "You have three times as many as I do right now." Which of the following systems of equations represents this situation, where x = Andrew's marbles and y = Allison's marbles?

   (A) $4x = y + 3$
       $3x = y$
   (B) $3x = y + 4$
       $4x = y$
   (C) $4y = x + 3$
       $3y = x$
   (D) $3y = x + 4$
       $4y = x$

9. Bill and Ingrid are sharpening #2 pencils. Bill says "I will have 9 pencils sharpened if I sharpen this one and 3 more." Ingrid says "I will have 8 pencils if I sharpen this one and one more." Which of the following is a true statement?

   (A) Bill has more pencils sharpened than Ingrid.
   (B) Bill has sharpened 9 pencils.
   (C) Ingrid has sharpened 6 pencils.
   (D) Bill has sharpened 6 pencils.

10. Kerri wants to buy a computer for college that costs $2,250. She will put $100 down on the computer and pay the rest in 5 equal payments. Which equation can be used to find the amount of each payment, where c is the amount of each payment?

    (A) $5c = \$2,250$
    (B) $5c = \$2,250 + \$100$
    (C) $5c = \$2,250 - \$100$
    (D) $5c + \$2,250 = \$100$

11. Sandra's bag of marbles weighed 2 pounds and 7 ounces. After she gave Dennis 6 marbles, the box weighed 1 pound and 11 ounces. How much did each marble weigh?

12. If x represents an even integer, then which of the following represents the next three consecutive even integers?

    (A) $x, x + 2, x + 4$
    (B) $x + 2, x + 4, x + 6$
    (C) $x + 1, x + 2, x + 3$
    (D) $x + 1, x + 3, x + 5$

13. The perimeter of a rectangular house is 40 feet. The length of the house is 2 feet more than twice the width. Which system of equations will determine the length, l, and the width, w, of the house?

    (A) $2l + 2w = 40$
        $l = 2w + 2$
    (B) $2l + 2w = 40$
        $l = 2w - 2$
    (C) $2l + 2w = 40$
        $l = 4w$
    (D) $2l + w = 40$
        $w = 2l + 2$

14. Alex's car gets 24 miles per gallon and can travel at most 428 miles without refueling. What is the maximum whole number of gallons that Alex's car tank can hold based on this information?

    (A) 16 gallons   (B) 17 gallons
    (C) 18 gallons   (D) 19 gallons

Algebra part 2

15. Maria's parents were married for 12 years before she was born. Which expression can be used to show how long Maria's parents have been married when Maria is m years old?

    (A) $\frac{12}{m}$ (B) $12 \times m$
    (C) $12 - m$ (D) $12 + m$

16. John bought M apples. He ate K of them. How many does he have left?

    (A) MK (B) $M + K$
    (C) $M - K$ (D) $M \div K$

17. A grocer noticed that a farmer delivered twice as many brown eggs as white eggs. There are 144 eggs in the delivery, and the grocer wants to determine how many of them are brown.

    Which equation will help you solve this problem?

    (A) $2x = 144$ (B) $2x = 144 + x$
    (C) $x + 2x = 144$ (D) $x = 144 + 2x$

18. A hexagon has 3 sides of length $9x + 1$ and 3 sides of $2x + 6$. What is the perimeter of the hexagon?

    (A) $33x + 21$ (B) $54x + 6$
    (C) $12x + 36$ (D) $66x + 42$

19. Jane went to the mall. In total, she spent $45. She spent $9 on food. She bought 3 shirts at the same price in a store. Which of the following equations could be used to solve for the cost, C, of each shirt?

    (A) $3C + 9 = 45$ (B) $45C + 9 = 3$
    (C) $9C + 3 = 45$ (D) $3C + 45 = 9$

20. The art teacher has three colors of construction paper: red, yellow, and blue. The paper is distributed in a ratio of 3:5:12, respectively. Determine the percent of each color of paper.

    Show your work.

21. If x represents an odd integer, then which of the following represents the next three consecutive odd integers?

    (A) $x + 1, x + 2, x + 3$
    (B) $x + 1, x + 3, x + 5$
    (C) $x + 2, x + 3, x + 4$
    (D) $x + 2, x + 4, x + 6$

22. The average of five numbers is 63. What number can be added to the five numbers so that the average of all six numbers is 67?

    (A) 90 (B) 67 (C) 87 (D) 70

23. Setauket Middle School Bookstore currently displays 23 pencils in the window. They plan to increase the number of pencils each day by 3 until they triple the amount of pencils in the window. Which of the following equations correctly solves for d, the number of days needed to triple the amount of pencils in the window?

    (A) $3(23 + d) = 69$ (B) $23 + 3d = 69$
    (C) $3d - 23 = 69$ (D) $23 - 3d = 69$

Algebra part 2

24. A bag contains 37 candies. Mike and Hallie want to share the candies such that Hallie has 5 more candies than Mike. Which of the following equations represents that situation?

    (A) $x + 5 = 37$ (B) $2x = 37$
    (C) $x = 37 - 5$ (D) $x + (x + 5) = 37$

25. Solve for x: $3x - 3.67 = 8.42$

    (A) $x = 1.58$ (B) $x = 3.37$
    (C) $x = 4.03$ (D) $x = 4.75$

26. Jake is a pizza delivery boy. He gets paid $2 for every day he works plus $0.50 for each delivery he makes. Which equation represents Jake's daily income (I) in terms of the number of deliveries he makes (D)?

    (A) $I = 2 + .5D$ (B) $I = 2 - .5D$
    (C) $I = .5(2 + D)$ (D) $I = D(2 + .5)$

27. Jeff will win a prize if he can figure out the number of beans in a jar. He knows that there are only red, white, and blue beans in the jar. There are twice as many red beans as white beans, and six more blue beans than white beans. How many beans are in the jar in total if he counts 8 red beans?

28. Dave had 90 unsharpened pencils. He told Mike that for every three pencils Mike sharpens, Mike can keep one. Mike sharpened $\frac{2}{3}$ of the pencils. What equation can be solved to find the number of pencils Mike could keep?

    (A) $\frac{2}{3}n = 90$ (B) $3n = 45$
    (C) $3n = 60$ (D) $3n = (\frac{1}{3})(\frac{2}{3})(90)$

29. A telephone company charges $30 a month and $0.10 per minute. If Bill spent $100 in the past 2 months, how many minutes did he use in these 2 months?

    (A) 40   (B) 70   (C) 400   (D) 700

30. A bag of gummy candies contains 13% blue, 26% yellow, 17% green, 31% red and 13% orange candies. Monica put 175 candies into her bag. Which of the following proportions can be used to find x, the number of red candies in the bag?

    (A) $\dfrac{100}{31} = \dfrac{x}{175}$
    (B) $\dfrac{31}{100} = \dfrac{175}{x}$
    (C) $\dfrac{31}{100} = \dfrac{x}{175}$
    (D) $\dfrac{175}{x} = \dfrac{69}{100}$

31. Rachel is reading a 435 page book. She reads 10 pages on the first day and each day reads 5 pages more than the previous day until the book is done. On what day will the book be finished?

    (A) Day 10   (B) Day 11
    (C) Day 12   (D) Day 13

32. Daniel's weight is equal to 4 less than 3 times the weight of his dog Mittens. Which expression shows this relationship?

    (A) $4x - 3$ (B) $3x - 4$
    (C) $3x + 4$ (D) $\frac{x}{3} - 4$

Algebra part 2

33. Billy and Susan are playing a math game. Billy says "twice my number minus 62 is 79". What is the corresponding expression to find her number?

    (A) $62 - 79 = 2n$ (B) $2n = 141$
    (C) $2n + 62 = 79$ (D) $2n = 17$

34. Lauren works in a factory. She can make 8 products in 56 minutes.

    (*a*) In the space below, write an equation that can be used to find how many products (*p*) Lauren can make in (*t*) minutes.

    (*b*) If Lauren makes products for 7 hours, how many products can she make?

35. Penelope is making Valentine's Day lollipops for her class. She needs one bag of sticks to make 3 dozen lollipops. A bag of sticks costs $1.09. Penelope is planning to make 9 dozen lollipops. Which expression tells Penelope how much it will cost for the sticks to make the lollipops?

    (A) $(36 \div 9) \times \$1.09$ (B) $(9 \div 3) \times \$1.09$
    (C) $(36 \times 9) \times \$1.09$ (D) $(9 \times 3) \times \$1.09$

36. The length and width of a rectangle are represented by $(x + 7)$ and $(x - 3)$. If the area of the rectangle is 24, which equation below can be used to find x?

    (A) $(x + 7) + (x - 3) = 24$
    (B) $2(x + 7) + 2(x - 3) = 24$
    (C) $(x + 7)^2 + (x - 3)^2 = 24$
    (D) $(x + 7)(x - 3) = 24$

37. Henry is 5 years younger than double Marc's age, *m*. Which expression represents Henry's age?

    (A) $2m - 5$ (B) $2m + 5$
    (C) $\frac{5m}{2}$ (D) $10m - 5$

38. Jack ran *M* miles up the hill. Jill ran *N* miles up the hill. Which represents the average (mean) distance of their trips?

    (A) $(M + N) \div 2$
    (B) $MN \div 2$
    (C) $\sqrt{MN}$
    (D) $\sqrt{M} + \sqrt{N}$

39. When 14 is divided by x, the result is greater than 14. Which of the following conclusions can be drawn from this?

    (A) $x < 1$ (B) $x = 1$
    (C) $0 < x < 1$ (D) $x = 14$

40. The total value of *d* dimes and *q* quarters is *C* dollars. Which of the following must be true?

    (A) $d + q = C$ (B) $0.1d + 0.25q = C$
    (C) $10d + 25q = C$ (D) $10dq = C$

41. The tree in Enrique's backyard was planted 5 years before he was born. Which expression could be used to show the tree's age when Enrique is *d* years old?

    (A) $5 + d$ (B) $5 \times d$
    (C) $\frac{d}{5}$ (D) $d - 5$

Algebra part 2

42. Richard took a taxi cab that is charging $1.25 for the first $\frac{1}{4}$ of a mile, then $1.10 for every $\frac{1}{2}$ of a mile. Richard paid $12.25 for his trip. How many miles did Richard travel in the taxi cab?

    (A) 5.25 mi (B) 5.5 mi
    (C) 11 mi   (D) 12 mi

43. Jerry is a dog. On a hot summer day, he drinks water at a constant rate from his bowl such that, after every hour the height of the water is one inch lower. Let t be the height of the water before he drinks, and let d be the height of the water two hours later.

    Which equation below would you use to find the height of the water after Jerry drinks some water?

    (A) $d = t - 2$ (B) $d - t = 2$
    (C) $d = 2 - t$ (D) $t = d - 2$

44. Chris is a plumber. He charges $12.00 per hour along with an initial fee of $7.95. If x represents the amount of time he worked on a customer's house, in hours, which expression represents how much he was paid?

    (A) $12x + 7.95$ (B) $12 + 7.95x$
    (C) $12x - 7.95$ (D) $7.95x - 12$

45. Mr. Dirp paid $11.99 per pound of bird feed and also bought a new bird house for $20.00. If x represents the pounds of bird seed, then which expression models how much he spent?

    (A) $11.99 + 20x$ (B) $20 - 11.99x$
    (C) $11.99x - 20$ (D) $11.99x + 20$

46. The total value of 6 nickels and q half dollars is equal to $1.80. Which of the following statements is true?

    (A) $6 + q = 1.80$
    (B) $(6 + 1)q = 1.80$
    (C) $0.30 + 0.5q = 1.80$
    (D) $(0.30 + 0.5)q = 1.80$

47. A water tank contains 2,000 gallons. A faucet attached to the tank releases water at a constant rate of 8 gallons per minute. If the faucet is left open for 1.5 hours and no other water is released, which equation can be used to find x, the number of gallons of water remaining in the tank?

    (A) $x = 2,000 - 60(8)$ (B) $x = 2,000$
    (C) $x = 2,000 - 90(8)$ (D) $x = 2.000$

48. Felipe has 6 fewer hats than Carly, and Gordon has 4 times as many hats as Felipe. If Carly has n hats, how many hats does Gordon have, in terms of n?

    (A) $4(n - 6)$ (B) $6 - 4n$
    (C) $n - 6$ (D) $4n - 6$

49. Susan is playing a game where she has to guess a number using clues. She is given the clue that 17 more than half of a number is 250. What is the number?

    (A) 167 (B) 205 (C) 233 (D) 466

Algebra part 2

50. In the formula below, C represents the total charge in dollars for babysitting and H represents the number of hours the child is watched. How much should Jamie be paid after she has babysat for 2 hours?

    $C = 2.50 + 4.50H$

    (A) $9.50 (B) $10.00
    (C) $11.50 (D) $12.50

51. The distance, d, in feet that a ball falls in t seconds is given by the equation, $d = 16t^2$. Based upon this equation, how many feet would a ball fall in 15 seconds?

    (A) 900 feet   (B) 1,800 feet
    (C) 3,600 feet (D) 6,400 feet

52. Jack always pays 1.5 times more for lunch than Jim. Jim paid $1.50 today. How much did they pay all together?

    (A) $1.50 (B) $2.25
    (C) $2.50 (D) $3.75

53. Dave is riding a cab. The ride costs $1.30 for the first one mile and $0.80 for each additional mile. The trip costs $12.50. How many miles was the cab ride?

    (A) 9.6 miles (B) 10 miles
    (C) 14 miles   (D) 15 miles

54. A software company uses the formula

    $$P = \$150N - \$200E$$

    to calculate its weekly profits, P, where N is the number of programs sold and E is the number of people employed by the company. If the company's profits for the last week were $850 and there are 16 employees, how many programs did the company sell?

    (A) 16 programs (B) 52 programs
    (C) 50 programs (D) 27 programs

55. In the equation below, what is the value of y?

    $6y + 5 + 2 = 31$

    (A) 4 (B) 5 (C) 7 (D) 8

56. For which of the following values of x and y is the following inequality true?

    $x < 2\sqrt{30} < y$

    (A) $x = 9, y = 11$ (B) $x = 7, y = 10$
    (C) $x = 11, y = 12$ (D) $x = 5, y = 9$

57. What is the value of n in the following equation?

    $535 + 0.6n = 1,069$

    (A) 320 (B) 890
    (C) 962 (D) 2,673

58. When $x = 5$, find the value of the expression.

    $$x^2 - 11x + 25$$

    (A) −55 (B) −5 (C) 55 (D) 105

Algebra part 2

59. A repair shop charged Jamie $150 for repairs, plus $40 for each hour he worked. The bill totaled $210. About how long did the repair shop work on this Jamie's car?

    (A) 1 hr (B) 1.5 hr
    (C) 2.5 hr (D) 5.25 hr

60. If $4(6x - 1) = 2$, then what is the value of $6x - 1$?

    (A) $\frac{1}{4}$ (B) $\frac{1}{2}$ (C) 4 (D) 8

61. The same number is to be placed on each of the boxes below. Which of these numbers would make a true statement?

    $\square \times \square = 2 \times \square$

    (A) 2 and 0 (B) 2 only
    (C) 2 and −2 (D) 0 only

62. What is the value of $6w + 2w + 2 \times 8$, when $w = 3$?

    (A) 36 (B) 37 (C) 40 (D) 208

63. Adam and Emma were gathering twigs together. Adam said to Emma, "If I gather this twig and two more, then I will have a total of 3 twigs." Emma said to Adam, "Well, if I gather this twig and four more, I will have a total of of 6 twigs."

    Which statement below is correct?

    (A) Adam has 1 twig.
    (B) Emma has 1 twig.
    (C) Adam had 3 twigs.
    (D) Emma has 4 twigs.

64. If $8r - 3t = 6$, what is the value of $15t - 40r$?

    (A) 30 (B) 6 (C) −24 (D) −30

65. Based on the formula below:

    $$\frac{1}{x} + \frac{1}{y} = \frac{1}{z}$$

    When $x = 15$ and $y = 5$, what would be the value of z?

    (A) $\frac{1}{20}$ (B) $\frac{4}{15}$ (C) $\frac{15}{4}$ (D) 20

66. Evaluate when $x = 2$ and $y = -2$:
    $5 - y(x + 3)$

    (A) 3 (B) 15 (C) 12 (D) 35

67. Solve for x: $7x + 1 > \frac{13}{2}x$

    (A) $x > 2$ (B) $x > -2$
    (C) $x < 2$ (D) $x < -2$

68. In order to solve the equation below, what should you do first?

    $\frac{1}{3}x + 2 = 9$

    (A) Multiply both sides of the equation by 3.
    (B) Add 2 to both sides of the equation.
    (C) Subtract 2 from both sides of the equation.
    (D) Subtract $\frac{1}{3}$ from both sides of the equation.

69. Use a calculator to determine the value of $3(a - b^3)^2$ when $a = 2$ and $b = -1$.

    (A) 7 (B) 9 (C) 12 (D) 27

Algebra part 2

70. Solve for x: $x - 6 = 10$

71. Solve for y when $x = 7$ and $b = 4$.
    $y = 4x - 2b$

    (A) 2 (B) 5 (C) 20 (D) 24

72. A mechanic charged Evan $60 for parts, plus $20 for each hour he worked. The bill totaled $180. About how long did the mechanic work on this Evan's car?

    (A) 2.25 hr (B) 3 hr
    (C) 6 hr   (D) 9 hr

73. In the equation below, which value for x will make this statement true?
    $$3(x - 7) = 69$$

    (A) 4 (B) 10 (C) 21 (D) 30

74. Find all the possible values of x:
    $\frac{x}{3} + 2 < x - \frac{1}{3}$

75. The conversion from Celsius to Fahrenheit can be computed using the expression
    $F = \frac{9}{5}C + 32$

    where F is the degree measure in Fahrenheit and C is the degree measure in Celsius. What is the temperature in Fahrenheit when it is 35° Celsius?

    (A) 32° (B) 63° (C) 90° (D) 95°

76. Let $\frac{50}{x} = 2y$. Which of the following (x, y) is correct?

    (A) (50, 1)   (B) (25, 2)
    (C) (5, 5)   (D) (10, 10)

77. Which of the following could replace x in the following inequality?
    $$\frac{x}{2} + \frac{1}{3} < x$$

    (A) $\frac{1}{3}$ (B) $\frac{2}{5}$ (C) $\frac{2}{3}$ (D) 1

78. A butcher sells ham for $4.25 per pound and turkey for $3.00 per pound. A customer buys twice as many pounds of ham as turkey and spends a total of $23.00. How many pounds of each did the customer buy from the butcher?

    (A) 2 lb. of ham and 1 lb of turkey
    (B) 3 lb. of ham and 1.5 lb of turkey
    (C) 4 lb. of ham and 2 lb of turkey
    (D) 5 lb. of ham and 2.5 lb of turkey

79. If $5 - 9n = 4m$, what is the value of $16m - 20$?

    (A) $18n$ (B) $-9n + 4$
    (C) $-36n$ (D) $-9n + 20$

80. What value for c makes the following statement true?
    $$243 = 3^c$$

    (A) 3 (B) 4 (C) 5 (D) 6

Algebra part 2

81. What are the solutions to the equation below?

    $|2x + 6| = 4$

    (A) $x = 1$ or 5 (B) $x = -1$ or 5
    (C) $x = -1$ or -5 (D) $x = -5$ or 1

82. What is the value of $6y \div y + 5 - 8y$, when $y = 3$?

    (A) -13 (B) -16 (C) -3 (D) -6

83. What does x equal in this equation?

    $x + 4 = 2$

84. Solve for x: $2x + 3 = 17$

85. If $3x - 4y = 7$, what is the value of $21 + 12y$?

    (A) $3x + 14$ (B) $9x$
    (C) $6x$ (D) $3x - 7$

86. An ice cream man says that his daily profit can be calculated by counting the number of children, n, that come to his truck in an hour and then using the following equation.
    $6(n - 2) + 4 =$ profit in dollars

    How much money did he make if he counted 18 children in an hour?

    (A) $96 (B) $100
    (C) $108 (D) $112

87. What is the value of the expression below when $x = 15$ and $y = -15$?

    $x^2 - y^2$

    (A) -15 (B) 0 (C) 225 (D) 900

88. What are all the whole numbers that make $9 + \_\_\_ < 13$ true?

    (A) 0, 1, 2, 3, 4 (B) 0, 1, 2, 3
    (C) 0, 1, 2 (D) 0, 1

89. Kate wants to buy a pony that costs $900. At her job, she makes $43.00 a week while spending $15.00 a week and saving the rest. How many weeks will it take her to have enough money to buy the pony if all of her savings are used for the pony?

    (A) 33 weeks (B) 21 weeks
    (C) 16 weeks (D) 11 weeks

Algebra part 2

90. Shantelle wants to rent a mid-size car for one day. Value Rent-a-Car charges $20 a day plus $0.20 per mile, and Best Rent-a-Car charges $30 a day plus $0.10 per mile for rental of the same mid-size car.

    (*a*) Determine the mileage where the rental charges are the same.

    (*b*) For what mileage is it more economical to rent from Value Rent–a–Car? Explain your answer.

---

91. If $\frac{3}{2}x + 1$ is an odd integer, then which of the following could be the value of *x*?

    (A) 2   (B) 4   (C) 6   (D) 10

92. + ⊕⊕⊕⊕⊕ =

    Therefore,

    (A) = 0   (B) = ⊕⊕⊕⊕⊕
    (C) ⊕ =   (D) ⊕ = 0

93. If a = –5 and b = 7, what is the value of the expression below?

    $\frac{3a-7}{2b-3}$

    (A) –2   (B) 0   (C) 5   (D) 7

94. What is the value of *X* when *V* = 2, *A* = 1, and *D* = 17?

    $X = \overline{InvalidEquationInvalidEquation \mp 2AD}$

95. Solve for *y* when *x* = 9 and $b = 1\frac{1}{2}$.
    $y = \frac{1}{2}x + b$

    (A) 5   (B) 6   (C) 7   (D) $19\frac{1}{2}$

96. When *x* = 4, find the value of the expression.

    $\frac{2x^3 - 4x}{2}$

    (A) 56   (B) 72   (C) 110   (D) 224

97. If *x* = 3 and *y* = 5, what is the value of the expression 2*x* – (–2*y*)?

    (A) –4   (B) 0   (C) 4   (D) 16

98. Wilma runs three times as far as Jane each day. They ran for a combined 12 miles. How far did Wilma run?

    (A) 4 miles   (B) 8 miles
    (C) 9 miles   (D) 12 miles

99. The following equation shows the relationship between a distance traveled (*d*), the time traveled (*t*), and the rate (*r*):

    $\frac{d}{t} = r$.

    As time *t* increases, the distance *d* remains the same. What happens to the rate *r*?

    (A) It increases.
    (B) It decreases.
    (C) It remains the same.
    (D) There is not enough information given to tell.

Algebra part 2

100. What is the value of x when $2x < -3x + 15$?

    (A) $x < 3$ (B) $x > 5$
    (C) $x > 3$ (D) $x < 5$

Angles, Triangle and, Circle

1. What is the measure of angle A in the following triangle?

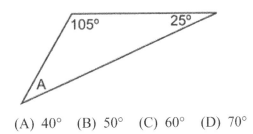

(A) 40° (B) 50° (C) 60° (D) 70°

2. The triangle below is an isosceles right triangle.

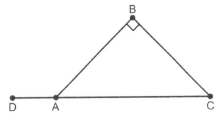

What is the difference between ∠ BAC and ∠ BAD?

(A) 90° (B) 100° (C) 120° (D) 180°

3. What is the measure of angle X?

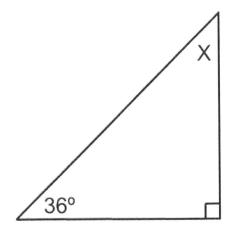

(A) 36° (B) 54° (C) 64° (D) 90°

4. Which two angles are complementary?

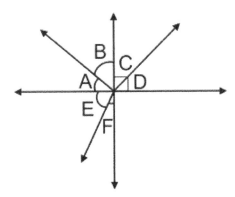

(A) ∠A and ∠F (B) ∠C and ∠D
(C) ∠B and ∠C (D) ∠A and ∠D

5. What is the value of x in the triangle shown?

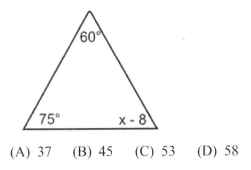

(A) 37 (B) 45 (C) 53 (D) 58

6. Look at the diagram:

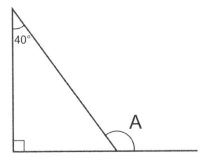

What is the measure of ∠A ?

(A) 50° (B) 90° (C) 130° (D) 150°

Angles, Triangle and, Circle

7. John is trying to make a bank shot in a game of pool. He wants to end the game by getting the eight ball into the corner pocket as shown below.

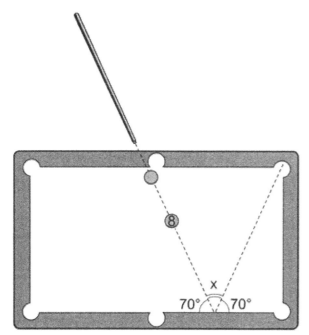

What angle x must the eight ball take so that it will go into the corner pocket as shown?

(A) 40° (B) 140° (C) 180° (D) 210°

8. The measures of the angles of a triangle are $2x + 15$, $4x - 10$, and $3x - 5$ degrees. What is the difference between the largest and smallest angles of the triangle?

(A) 15° (B) 35° (C) 40° (D) 45°

9. The measures of the angles of a triangle are $2x + 15$, $4x - 10$, and $3x - 5$ degrees. What type of triangle is this?

(A) scalene   (B) isosceles
(C) right   (D) equilateral

10. The measures of the angles of a triangle are $2x + 15$, $4x - 10$, and $3x - 5$ degrees. What is the measure of the largest angle of the triangle?

(A) 70° (B) 75° (C) 80° (D) 90°

11. The measures of the angles of triangle are $3x$, $3x + 30$, and $2x - 10$ degrees. What is the difference between the largest and smallest angles of this triangle?

(A) 30° (B) 45° (C) 60° (D) 90°

12. Ciara measured all but two angles of an octagon. The total degree measure for the angles she measured was 810°. What is the average degree measure for the angles she did not measure?

(A) 100°   (B) 120°
(C) 135°   (D) 270°

13. Marsha measured all but two angles of a hexagon. If the total degree measure for the angles she measured was 530°, then what is the total degree measure of the angles she did not measure?

(A) 170°   (B) 190°
(C) 200°   (D) 210°

14. Calen measured all but one angle of a pentagon. If the total degree measure for all of the angles he measured was 410°, then what is the measure of the remaining angle?

(A) 130°   (B) 150°
(C) 310°   (D) 360°

Angles, Triangle and, Circle

15. One angle in a right triangle is measured to be 56°. The measurements of the other angles are 90° and

    (A) 24°. (B) 34°. (C) 44°. (D) 54°.

16. An angle measures 39°. What would an angle complementary to it measure?

    (A) 39° (B) 41° (C) 51° (D) 141°

17. An angle measures 63°. What is the measure of an angle supplementary to that angle?

    (A) 27° (B) 113° (C) 117° (D) 127°

18. A round blueberry pie is cut into 8 pieces. What is the measure of the central angle of each piece?

    (A) 30° (B) 45° (C) 60° (D) 75°

19. A round apple pie is cut into 6 pieces. What is the measure of the central angle of each piece?

    (A) 30°   (B) 60°
    (C) 90°   (D) 120°

20. The second hand on a clock travels from the 12 to the 9. How many degrees has the second hand traveled?

    (A) 45°   (B) 90°
    (C) 135° (D) 270°

21. What is the measure of angle x?

    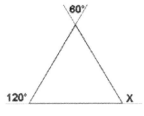

    (A) 60°   (B) 90°
    (C) 120°   (D) 180°

22. In the picture below, what is the measure of angle A?

    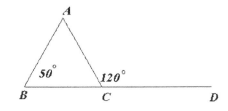

    (A) 50° (B) 60° (C) 70° (D) 80°

Angles, Triangle and, Circle

Base your answers to questions **23** and **24** on a pool game between Darren and Mark. Mark tried to make a shot as shown below.

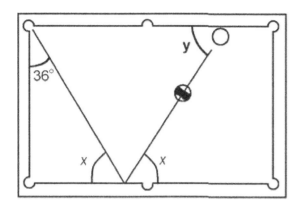

23. What angle must *y* be? Explain.

24. Knowing the angle measure shown in the diagram, what angle *x* must the path of the ball take so it will go in the corner pocket?

---

25. a pool game between Joe and Dave, Joe tried to make a shot as shown below.

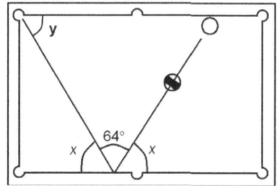

Joe estimated the angle measure shown in the diagram. What angle *x* must the path of the ball take so that it will go in the corner pocket?

26. The largest angle in △DEF measures 94°. What kind of triangle is △DEF?

   (A) acute (B) obtuse
   (C) equilateral (D) right

27. If the length of the altitude of a triangle is *a* and the length of the base is *b*, then which of the following represents the area of the triangle?

   (A) ab (B) $\frac{1}{4}ab$ (C) $\frac{1}{2}ab$ (D) $2ab$

28. In △MSU, $\overline{MS} = \overline{MU}$

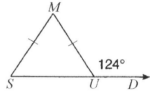

The measure of ∠M is

   (A) 124° (B) 56°
   (C) 68°   (D) 112°

29. What is the measure of ∠*x* ? (The figure is not drawn to scale.)

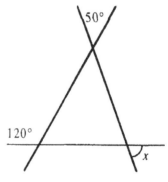

   (A) 40° (B) 50° (C) 60° (D) 70°

83

Angles, Triangle and, Circle

30. In △ABC, AC = BC.

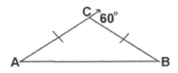

The measure of ∠B is

(A) 30°. (B) 50°.
(C) 60°. (D) 120°.

31. Dave and Bob both started in the same location. Bob walked due east for 40 feet. Dave walked 50 feet, and, when both had finished, Dave was x feet due north of Bob. What is distance x, separating Bob and Dave?

(A) 10 feet (B) 30 feet
(C) 64 feet (D) 90 feet

Angles, Triangle and, Circle

32. A guy wire is needed to hold a tent in place. The guy wire attaches to the ground 14 feet away from the base of the tent. The guy wire attaches to the tent at a point 23 feet high.

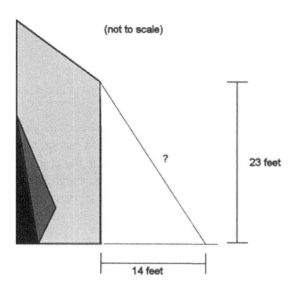

What is the length of the guy wire to the **nearest** tenth of a foot?

Show your work.

---

33. The diagonal of a square is 25 units long. What is the approximate length of a side of the square?

    (A) 20 units   (B) 18 units
    (C) 15 units   (D) 5 units

34. The lengths of the legs of a right triangle are 5 centimeters and 10 centimeters. Which of the following measures is closest to the length of the hypotenuse?

    (A) 3.9 centimeters   (B) 5.8 centimeters
    (C) 11 centimeters   (D) 11.2 centimeters

35. Base your answer to the following question on the diagram of rectangle *ABCD* below.

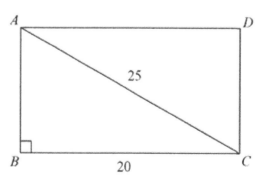

What is the area of rectangle *ABCD*?

(A) 400   (B) 300   (C) 625   (D) 500

85

Angles, Triangle and, Circle

36. Jenny and Abby were standing next to each other. Jenny walked due south for 24 feet. Abby walked due east for 18 feet. How many feet apart are they now?

    (A) 24 feet (B) 18 feet
    (C) 30 feet (D) 42 feet

37. What is the length of the hypotenuse of the triangle below?

    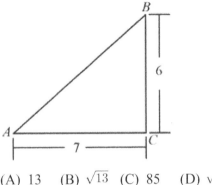

    (A) 13 (B) $\sqrt{13}$ (C) 85 (D) $\sqrt{85}$

38. The Pythagorean Theorem is used to relate the sides of what figure?

    (A) Right triangle (B) Circle
    (C) Square (D) Isosceles triangle

39. The fire department needs a ladder to get into a window that is 35 feet high. The bottom of the ladder must be 15 feet away from the base of the building. The length of the ladder will be closest to

    (A) 40 feet. (B) 32 feet.
    (C) 25 feet. (D) 20 feet.

40. Mr. Schwartz drove 16 miles south and then 12 miles east. How far away is he from his starting point?

    (A) 20 miles (B) 24 miles
    (C) 28 miles (D) 30 miles

41. Coach Toad wanted to decide how to make his track team run. He looked at the school's rectangular field. He can either make them run the entire perimeter, or run on the diagonal back and forth. The field is 300 yards by 400 yards. How many yards less is the diagonal run?

    (A) 200 yards (B) 400 yards
    (C) 500 yards (D) 700 yards

Angles, Triangle and, Circle

42. Base your answer to the following question on the map below that shows the distances between three towns.

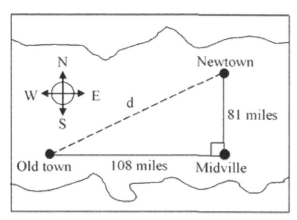

What is the distance, *d*, between Old town and Newtown?

Show your work.

43. The area of a rectangle is 200 square inches. The width is 20 inches. Find the length of its diagonal to the nearest thousandth.

   (A) 5.477 in (B) 10.000 in
   (C) 22.361 in (D) 30.000 in

44. A 25 foot pole leans against a tall building. The bottom of the pole is 7 feet away from the base of the building. How far up the side of the building does the pole reach?

   (A) 13 ft (B) 12 ft (C) 20 ft (D) 24 ft

45. Using the Pythagorean theorem, which of the following is a right triangle?

   (A) 3, 4, 6 (B) 4, 5, 6
   (C) 6, 8, 10 (D) 6, 8, 11

46. A flagpole is 10 feet high and casts a shadow 12 feet long. Calvin, standing nearby, is 5 feet tall. How long is the length of his shadow?

   (A) 6 feet (B) 6.5 feet
   (C) 7 feet (D) 7.2 feet

47. In the figure below, $\triangle ABC$ is similar to $\triangle DEF$.

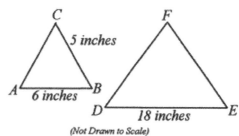

(Not Drawn to Scale)

What is the length of side $\overline{EF}$?

   (A) 5 in (B) 15 in
   (C) 18 in (D) 135 in

Angles, Triangle and, Circle

48. 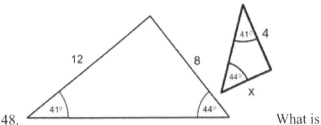 What is the length of side x?

(A) 2.7 (B) 6 (C) 8 (D) 24

49. △ABC ~ △CDE.

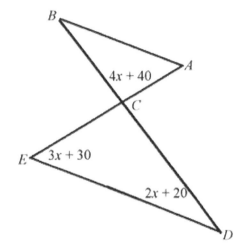

Find the measure of ∠DCE.

(A) 10° (B) 30° (C) 50° (D) 80°

50. Steve had to enlarge a picture. The picture was originally 6 inches by 9 inches. After the enlargement, the longer side was 15 inches. Find the length of the shorter side.

(A) 9 inches (B) 10 inches
(C) 12 inches (D) 15 inches

51. Base your answer to the following question on the diagram below.

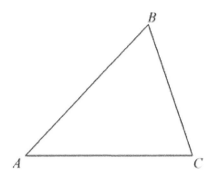

Which of the following triangles is similar to △ABC?

(A)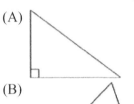

(B)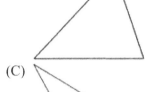

(C)

(D)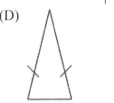

Angles, Triangle and, Circle

52. The lengths of the sides of equilateral △S are three times the lengths of the sides of equilateral △T. How many of △T can fit in △S?

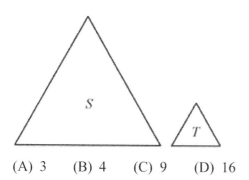

(A) 3   (B) 4   (C) 9   (D) 16

53. John is enlarging a picture that was originally 4 inches wide and 6 inches long. If he keeps the picture in proportion and the new length is 9 inches, what is the new width?

(A) 9 inches   (B) 6 inches
(C) 4 inches   (D) 7 inches

 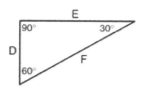

54. Which of the following proportions is true for these similar triangles?

(A) $\frac{A}{C} = \frac{D}{F}$ (B) $\frac{A}{B} = \frac{D}{F}$
(C) $\frac{A}{C} = \frac{D}{E}$ (D) $\frac{A}{D} = \frac{D}{B}$

55. Base your answer to the following question on the diagram of two similar triangles below.

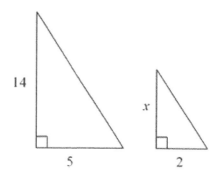

Find the value of x.

(A) 5.6   (B) 11.2   (C) 3.5   (D) 6.5

56. In the figure below, △ABC ~ △DEF.

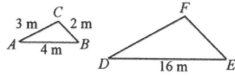

What is the length of side $\overline{EF}$?

(A) 2 m   (B) 4 m
(C) 8 m   (D) 16 m

57. Mrs. Williams drew an isosceles triangle on the chalkboard. She then drew its dilation with a scale factor of 4.2 cm. If the length of the legs in the original triangle was 5 cm, what is the length of each of the legs in the dilated image?

(A) .8   (B) 2.1   (C) 9.2   (D) 21

Angles, Triangle and, Circle

58. Triangles *ABC* and *DEF* are similar. The lengths of the sides of △*DEF* are one–fourth the lengths of the corresponding sides of △*ABC*. How do the areas of the triangles compare?

   (A) The area of △*DEF* is $\frac{1}{12}$ times the area of △*ABC*.
   (B) The area of △*DEF* is $\frac{1}{16}$ times the area of △*ABC*.
   (C) The area of △*DEF* is 4 times the area of △*ABC*.
   (D) The area of △*DEF* is 12 times the area of △*ABC*.

59. △$\overline{ABC}$ is similar to △$\overline{DBE}$.

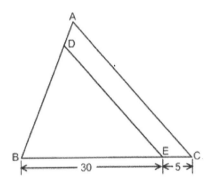

   What is the ratio of the length of the sides of △$\overline{ABC}$ to △$\overline{DBE}$?

   (A) 1:3 (B) 30:35
   (C) 7:6 (D) 7:1

60. The lengths of the sides of equilateral triangle *A* are twice the lengths of the sides of equilateral triangle *B*. How many of triangle *A* can fit in triangle *B*?

   (A) 2 (B) 4 (C) 6 (D) 8

61. Which of the following is similar, but not congruent, to a triangle with sides 3, 4 and 5?

   (A) A triangle with sides 3, 4 and 5
   (B) A triangle with sides 6, 8, and 9
   (C) A triangle with sides 6, 8 and 10
   (D) A triangle with sides 3, 4, and 6

62. Triangle *ABC* is similar to triangle *DEF*.

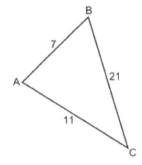 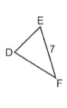

   What is the length of $\overline{DE}$?

   (A) $\frac{7}{21}$ (B) $\frac{7}{7}$ (C) $\frac{11}{7}$ (D) $\frac{7}{3}$

Angles, Triangle and, Circle

63. △ABC is similar to △XYZ

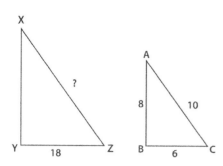

What is the length of $\overline{XZ}$?

(A) 10 (B) 20 (C) 30 (D) 40

64. Refer to the figures below. △NOP ~ △NLM.

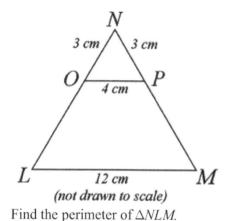

Find the perimeter of △NLM.

(A) 24 (B) 28 (C) 30 (D) 40

65. The triangles below are similar.

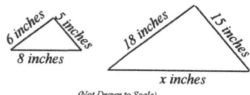

What is the value of x?

(A) 6 (B) 16 (C) 21 (D) 24

66. The ratio between sides of two similar triangles ABC and DEF is 3:2, respectively. What is the ratio between the areas of triangles DEF and ABC, respectively?

(A) 3:2 (B) 2:3 (C) 9:4 (D) 4:9

67. The two triangles below are similar. Find x.

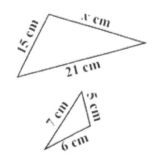

(A) 12 (B) 18 (C) 24 (D) 36

Angles, Triangle and, Circle

68. The two triangles below are similar. Find *x*.

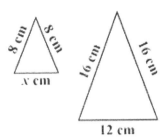

(A) 4 cm (B) 6 cm
(C) 8 cm (D) 10 cm

Base your answers to questions **69** and **70** on the diagram below.

Jane is 5 feet tall. At a certain time during the day, Jane casts a shadow of 7 feet.

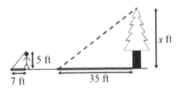

69. The tree casts a shadow of 35 feet at the same time of the day. How tall is the tree?

(A) 25 ft (B) 33 ft (C) 37 ft (D) 49 ft

70. Find the length of the shadow of a tree that is 30 feet tall at the same time of day.

(A) 22 feet (B) 28 feet
(C) 32 feet (D) 42 feet

71. The figure below shows two similar triangles.

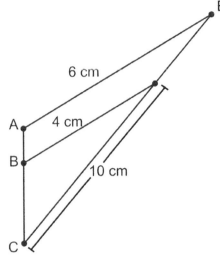

Based on this diagram, what is the distance between Point E and Point D?

(A) 5 cm (B) 10 cm
(C) 15 cm (D) 25 cm

Base your answers to questions **72** and **73** on the diagram below. $\triangle ABC \sim \triangle DEF$.

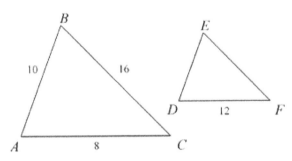

72. What is the length of side $\overline{EF}$?

(A) 20 (B) 18 (C) 16 (D) 24

73. What is the length of side $\overline{ED}$?

(A) 10 (B) 15 (C) 16 (D) 14

Angles, Triangle and, Circle

74. Terri is building a replica of a triangle from an original that looks like the following:

Which triangle could be a replica of the original triangle?

(A)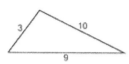

(B)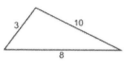

(C)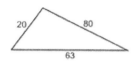

(D)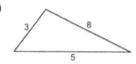

75. Henry cut three pairs of triangles in Industrial Technology class. Which of the following pairs of triangles are not congruent?

(A)

(B)

(C)

(D) They are all congruent.

76. How many times larger is the area of circle B than the area of circle A?

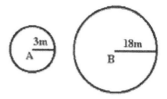

(A) 1   (B) 6   (C) 36   (D) 216

77. Which is the closest to the area of a circle whose diameter is 6 cm?

(A) 18.84 cm^2 (B) 28.26 cm^2
(C) 62.82 cm^2 (D) 113.04 cm^2

78. A pie has a radius of 6 cm. If 6 people share the pie equally, what is the circumference of each individual sector in centimeters?

(A) π (B) 2π (C) 4π (D) 6π

79. What is the approximate area of a circle with a radius of 6 meters?

(A) 6 m^2 (B) 36 m^2
(C) 72 m^2 (D) 113 m^2

Angles, Triangle and, Circle

80. A dog is on a leash with a length of 5 meters, as shown in the picture below.

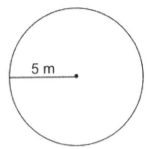

What is the circumference of the dog's path around the circle?

(A) 12.6 m (B) 15.7 m
(C) 20.5 m (D) 31.4 m

81. Joe put a circular garden in his backyard. The garden has a diameter of 16 feet. He needed to cover the garden with dirt, which is sold in bags. Each bag can cover 75 square feet. How many bags did he need?

(A) 1 bags (B) 2 bags
(C) 3 bags (D) 4 bags

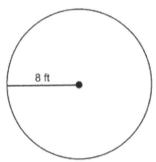

82. What is the approximate area of this circle?

(A) 50 square ft (B) 64 square ft
(C) 195 square ft (D) 200 square ft

83. A wheel has a radius of 16 inches. Approximately how many square inches is the area of the wheel?

(A) 50 square inches
(B) 201 square inches
(C) 804 square inches
(D) 3215 square inches

84. What is the approximate area of the circle?

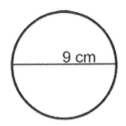

(A) 20 cm^2 (B) 64 cm^2
(C) 81 cm^2 (D) 254 cm^2

85. What is the radius of a circle with a circumference of 20π?

(A) 2π (B) 10π (C) 2 (D) 10

86. Will had a circular window with a radius of 9 feet. In the middle of this piece of wood he cut out a 4×4 foot square piece.

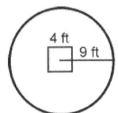

Will now plans to cover the edges of the circular area and square area with copper to protect the edges. How much copper edging will Will need? Show all work.

Angles, Triangle and, Circle

87. A circular window has a diameter of 4 feet. Approximately how many feet is the circumference of the window?

    (A) 6 feet (B) 8 feet
    (C) 13 feet (D) 50 feet

88. What is the approximate area of the circle?

    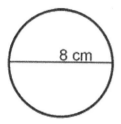

    (A) 16 cm²   (B) 50 cm²
    (C) 64 cm²   (D) 201 cm²

89. Base your answer to the following question on a circle.

    Find the area of the circle if the circumference of the circle is 40π inches.

90. A bicycle wheel travels 240 inches in 3 full rotations. What is the diameter of the wheel to the nearest inch?

    (A) 23 inches (B) 25 inches
    (C) 50 inches (D) 76 inches

91. A circular place mat has a diameter of 11 inches. Approximately how many inches is the circumference of the place mat?

    (A) 22 (B) 35 (C) 69 (D) 380

92. Ann needed to enlarge a circular hole in her fence. Currently, the hole has a radius of 1 foot. She wants to increase the radius of the hole to 2 feet. How much greater is the area of the new hole than the old hole?

    (A) half   (B) double
    (C) triple   (D) quadruple

93. How many times larger is the area of circle B than the area of circle A?

    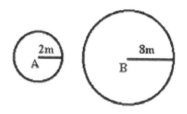

    (A) 2   (B) 4   (C) 8   (D) 16

94. Steve had a circular piece of wood with a radius of 12 feet. In the middle of this piece of wood he cut out a 2 × 2 foot square piece of wood.

    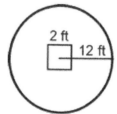

    Steve now plans to cover the edges of the circular area and square area with copper to protect the edges. How much copper edging will Steve need? Show all work.

Angles, Triangle and, Circle

95. The radius of a circle is 3 inches. Between what two whole numbers does the circumference fall in?

   (A) 9 ft and 10 ft (B) 10 ft and 11 ft
   (C) 18 ft and 19 ft (D) 19 ft and 20 ft

96. Michael's patio is in the shape of a square with a semicircle on each side as shown below.

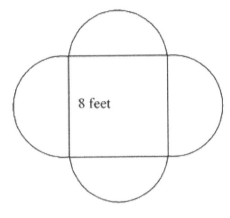

   What is the perimeter of the patio to the nearest foot? (Use $\pi = 3.14$)

97. A ferris wheel car travels 202 feet in two complete rotations. What is the radius of the ferris wheel to the nearest foot?

   (A) 16 feet (B) 25 feet
   (C) 32 feet (D) 33 feet

98. Observe:

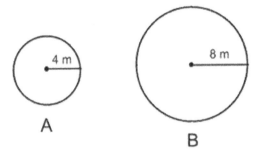

   Which is a correct relationship between circles A and B?

   (A) The area of A is half that of B
   (B) The area of A is a quarter that of B
   (C) The circumference of A is equal to that of B
   (D) The circumference of A is a quarter that of B

Angles, Triangle and, Circle

99. A cylindrical column 13 inches in diameter is strengthened by wrapping one steel band around the base, with no overlap.

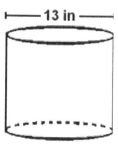

What should be the length of the steel band?

---

100. What is the circumference of this circle?

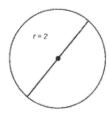

(A) 2π (B) 4π (C) 8π (D) 16π

Area, Volume

1. Betty had 40,000 cubic centimeters of water. How many tanks like this can she fill?

   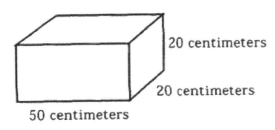

   (A) $\frac{1}{2}$ (B) 1   (C) $1\frac{1}{2}$ (D) 2

2. Base your answer to the following question on the diagram below. (Note: Figure is not drawn to scale.)

   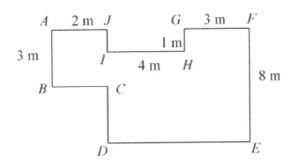

   What is the total area of the figure?

   (A) 39 m²   (B) 60 m²
   (C) 72 m²   (D) 58 m²

3. Gillian's Candy Factory makes candy in cylinders with a radius of 4 cm and a height of 2 cm. Which is closest to the total surface area of the candy.

   (A) 50 cm²   (B) 100 cm²
   (C) 125 cm²   (D) 150 cm²

4. A model of a floor plan has a scale of 1 in = 5 ft.

   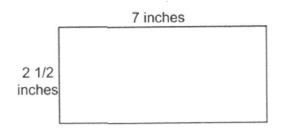

   What is the area of the room below?

   (A) 9.5 ft²   (B) 17.5 ft²
   (C) 437.5 ft²   (D) 967.5 ft²

5. A cylindrical soup can has a diameter of 2 inches and a height of 5 inches. Which is the closest to the volume of the soup can?

   (A) 10 in³   (B) 15.7 in³
   (C) 31.4 in³   (D) 62.8 in³

6. If the length of each side of a rectangle is cut to $\frac{1}{4}$ of its original size, what happens to the area?

   (A) It is $\frac{1}{64}$ the original area.
   (B) It is $\frac{1}{16}$ the original area.
   (C) It is $\frac{1}{8}$ the original area.
   (D) It is $\frac{1}{4}$ the original area.

7. A box has a width of 1, a height of 4, and a length of 2. What is the surface area of the box?

   (A) 7 sq cm   (B) 8 sq cm
   (C) 14 sq cm   (D) 28 sq cm

Area, Volume

8. The volume of a sphere is:

   Judith has two spheres, one with a diameter of 4 and one with a diameter of 2. What conclusion can be drawn from the preceding information?

   (A) One sphere is twice the volume of the other sphere
   (B) One sphere is triple the volume of the other sphere
   (C) One sphere is four times the volume of the other sphere
   (D) One sphere is eight times the volume of the other sphere

9. The parallelogram below is divided into a rectangle and two right triangles. What is the area of this quadrilateral?

   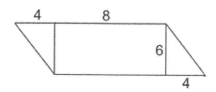

   (A) 60 square units   (B) 72 square units
   (C) 78 square units   (D) 96 square units

10. Farmer Bob is going to store grain in a silo. If his silo is a cylinder with a height of 20 meters and diameter of 10 meters, approximately what is the maximum volume of grain can Farmer Bob fit in the silo?

    (A) 524 m³   (B) 1571 m³
    (C) 2094 m³   (D) 6283 m³

11. A company needs to figure out what the surface area of their soup cans are going to be. If the cans are cylindrical, as in the diagram below, what will the approximate surface area be?

    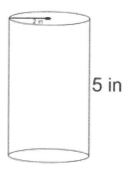

    (A) 76.3 in²   (B) 87.9 in²
    (C) 200 in²   (D) 254.3 in²

12. Base your answer to the following question on the figure below.

    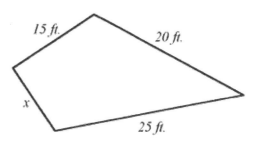

    Find the perimeter of this figure in terms of x.

    (A) $70 + x$
    (B) $60 + x$
    (C) $60x$
    (D) $(15 + 20 + 25) \div 3 + x$

13. A sphere has a diameter of 8 inches. What is its approximate volume in cubic feet?

    (A) $0.05\,\pi$ (B) $0.4\,\pi$
    (C) $85\frac{1}{3}\pi$ (D) $682\frac{2}{3}\pi$

Area, Volume

14. If the area of this triangle is 168, what is the height h of the triangle?

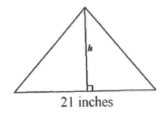

(A) 8   (B) 9   (C) 16   (D) 21

15. Base your answer on the circle below.

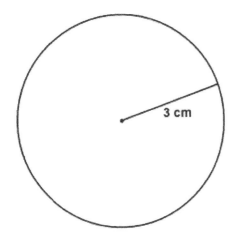

(a) What is the diameter of this circle?

(b) What is the circumference of this circle?

(c) What is the area of this circle?

(d) Draw a chord on the above diagram.

Area, Volume

16. The shape below is a triangular prism.

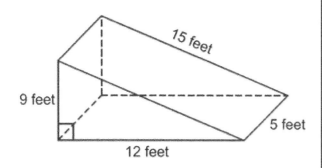

What is the volume of this triangular prism in square feet?

(A) 270 sq feet (B) 450 sq feet
(C) 540 sq feet (D) 900 sq feet

17. The height of a cylinder is twice the length of its radius. If the length of its diameter is 10 inches, what is the surface area of the cylinder?

(A) 120π in^2 (B) 136π in^2
(C) 144π in^2 (D) 150π in^2

18. Which of the following has the same area as a square with side 6?

(A) a rectangle with length 4 and width 8
(B) a rhombus with side 6 and height 5
(C) a trapezoid with bases 4 and 8, and height 6
(D) a triangle with base 6 and height 6

19. What is the length of one side of a square with an area of 169 in^2?

(A) 5.5 in (B) 13 in
(C) 16.9 in (D) 23 in

20. ABCD is a rectangle. Diagonals $\overline{AC}$ and $\overline{BD}$ intersect at E, m∠ABD = 35°.

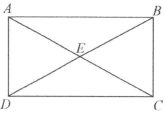

What is m∠AED?

(A) 35° (B) 55° (C) 70° (D) 110°

21. Base your answer to the following question on the following information.

Mr. Simon is remodeling his backyard. He has a square pool that is 12 feet by 12 feet. He wants to make a brick walkway around the pool that is 2 feet wide as shown in the diagram below.

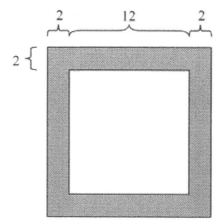

The bricks are sold in packages made to cover 8 square feet. How many packages of bricks will Mr. Simon have to buy to make his brick walkway?

Show your work.

101

Area, Volume

22. A triangle has a perimeter of 40 centimeters. If each of the sides are increased by 25%, what will the perimeter of the new triangle be?

    (A) 10 cm (B) 42 cm
    (C) 50 cm (D) 60 cm

Base your answers to questions **23** and **24** on the following information.

The local hockey rink needs some maintenance. The hockey rink is made of two semicircles on the sides of a rectangle. The diagram below shows a birds-eye view of the rink.

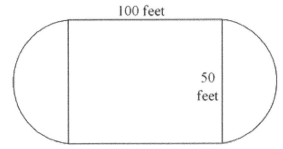

23. The insulation underneath the ice also needs to be replaced. The insulation is sold in packages that cover 50 square feet. How many packages of insulation must be bought to cover the entire rink?

    Show your work. Use $\pi = 3.14$.

24. The wall surrounding the rink needs to be replaced. How long is the wall surrounding the rink?

    Show your work. Use $\pi = 3.14$.

    _____

25. Luc is a tycoon who recently purchased an estate 4 miles wide and 8 miles long. What is the area of his new estate?

    (A) 12 square miles (B) 24 square miles
    (C) 32 square miles (D) 36 square miles

26. The Parkview Community Center is going to paint a 20–yard by 66–yard wall. Each person has enough paint to paint a section with an area of 15 square yards. If each person's paint costs $5.75, what would be the total cost of the paint to complete the wall?

27. A company is manufacturing a weighted cube for Enrichment Center research activities.

    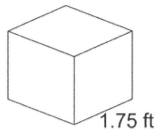

    What is the volume of the cube?

    (A) 5.36 ft³ (B) 6.48 ft³
    (C) 7.49 ft³ (D) 9.28 ft³

Area, Volume

Base your answers to questions **28** and **29** on on the following information.

A swimming pool has a length of 40 feet and a width of 20 feet. The pool is partially filled to a depth of 5.5 feet.

28. Which of the following is the volume of the water in the pool?

    (A) 330 ft³   (B) 4,400 ft³
    (C) 4,800 ft³   (D) 5,000 ft³

29. During a rainstorm, the water level in the pool rises from 5.5 feet to 5.8 feet. By how much has the volume in the pool changed?

    (A) 120 ft³   (B) 200 ft³
    (C) 240 ft³   (D) 4,640 ft³

30. The perimeter of the figure below is

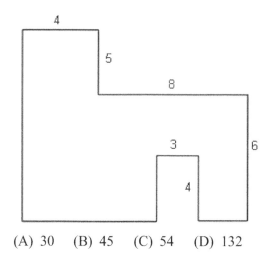

    (A) 30   (B) 45   (C) 54   (D) 132

31. What is the area of a square whose side measures $2 + \sqrt{3}$ units?

    (A) 7 units   (B) $4 + 4\sqrt{3}$ units
    (C) $7 + 4\sqrt{3}$ units   (D) 14 units

32. Base your answers on the parallelogram below.

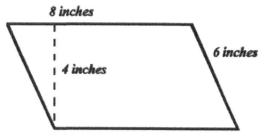

    (*a*) What is the area of this parallelogram?

    (*b*) What is the perimeter of this parallelogram?

    (*c*) What would be the area of a rectangle with the same side lengths?

33. The dimensions of a family portrait are 3 inches by 5 inches. If the dimensions are both increased by a factor of 3, then how many times greater will the area of the new photo be?

    (A) 3   (B) 6   (C) 8   (D) 9

34. Joan is setting up a circular table in her kitchen with an opening in the middle.

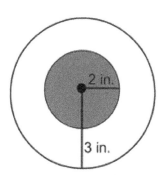

What is the approximate surface area of the top face of the table?

    (A) 13 ft²   (B) 28 ft²
    (C) 66 ft²   (D) 78 ft²

Area, Volume

35. A square has an area of 36 square meters. What is the perimeter?

    (A) 6 meters (B) 12 meters
    (C) 24 meters (D) 36 meters

36. A cube has an edge that measures 4 inches. If each side is increased by 4 inches, how much greater will the volume of the cube be?

    (A) two times greater
    (B) three times greater
    (C) four times greater
    (D) eight times greater

37. The figure below is 4 squares connected in a line.

    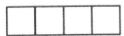

    The side of each square measures 5 feet. What is the perimeter of the figure?

    (A) 20 ft (B) 25 ft
    (C) 50 ft (D) 100 ft

38. The length of a rectangle is half its width. The perimeter is 36 centimeters. What is the width in centimeters?

    (A) 3 cm (B) 6 cm
    (C) 9 cm (D) 12 cm

39. A rectangular poster has an area of 360 square inches. The ratio of the width to the length of the poster is 2:5. What are the dimensions of the poster?

    (A) 8 in. × 20 in. (B) 10 in. × 25 in.
    (C) 12 in. × 30 in. (D) 14 in. × 35 in.

40. Refer to the trapezoid drawn below. The trapezoid has a perimeter of 66 feet.

    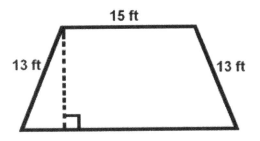

    (a) Find the altitude.
    (b) Find the area of the trapezoid.

41. Refer to the square in the diagram below.

    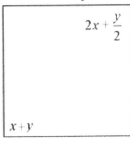

    Find x.

    (A) 30° (B) 45° (C) 60° (D) 90°

42. The total surface area of a cube is 37.5 square inches. Which of the following represents the length of its edge?

    (A) 1 inch (B) 1.25 inches
    (C) 2.5 inches (D) 6.25 inches

43. Find the surface area of a cube with side of length 2 cm.

    (A) 2 cm² (B) 4 cm²
    (C) 8 cm² (D) 24 cm²

Area, Volume

44. Two rooms have the same volume but different dimensions.

    Room 1: 12 ft × 8 ft × _____ ft
    Room 2: 18 ft × 8 ft × 9 ft

    What is the missing dimension in room 1?

    (A) 10 ft
    (B) 13.5 ft
    (C) 14.3 ft
    (D) 15 ft

45. Cylinder *A* and cylinder *B* have the same volume. Their dimensions are below, except for the height of cylinder *B*, which is unknown.

    Cylinder *A*: radius 1 in., height 36 in.
    Cylinder *B*: radius 3 in., height ??

    What is the height of cylinder *B*?

    (A) 4 in.
    (B) 12 in.
    (C) 18 in.
    (D) 36 in.

46. Manny wants to put wallpaper up in his bathroom. What measure of the room should he take?

    (A) Perimeter of the room
    (B) Volume of the room
    (C) Surface area of the walls
    (D) Length of the room

47. A box that measures 36 inches long, 26 inches wide, and 20 inches tall is one third full. How much space is left in the box?

    (A) 6,240 cubic inches
    (B) 12,480 cubic inches
    (C) 14,040 cubic inches
    (D) 18,720 cubic inches

48. Mark is using fence to build an enclosure for his backyard. If he uses 120 feet for the length, and the perimeter is 360 feet, what is the area of the enclosure.

    (A) 2160 ft^2
    (B) 7200 ft^2
    (C) 9600 ft^2
    (D) 12000 ft^2

Area, Volume

49. What is the area of the circle below if the square's area is 36 square inches? Leave your answer in terms of π.

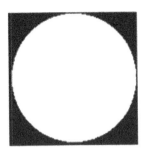

50. What shape does the formula $A = \frac{1}{2}h(b_1 + b_2)$ refer to?

    (A) parallelogram (B) trapezoid
    (C) circle (D) rhombus

51. Which of the following is the perimeter of a square whose sides measure $3a - 4$?

    (A) $7a - 8$ (B) $6a - 8$
    (C) $12a - 4$ (D) $12a - 16$

52. Determine the volume of a cylinder when the radius is 3 and the height is 20. Use $\pi = 3.14$.

    (A) 565.2 (B) 188.4
    (C) 3,768 (D) 11,304

53. A large freshly baked apple pie is sliced into 12 equal pieces. What is the measure of the central angle of each piece?

    (A) 12° (B) 25° (C) 30° (D) 36°

54. A rectangular farm has an area of 1,000 square yards. The length of the farm is 20 yards. Determine the farm's perimeter.

    (A) 25 yards (B) 50 yards
    (C) 70 yards (D) 140 yards

55. Base your answer to the following question on the drawing of the isosceles trapezoid shown below.

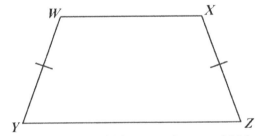

Suppose the trapezoid has a perimeter of 250. $\overline{WX}$ measures 57. $\overline{WY}$ measures 50. What does $\overline{YZ}$ measure?

(A) 50 (B) 57 (C) 93 (D) 97

Area, Volume

56. A company wants to build a smaller version of a rectangular prism

    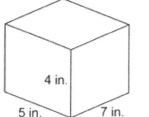

    If the smaller version is to have a height of 2 in, what will the new volume be?

    (A) 17.5 in³   (B) 23.75 in³
    (C) 64 in³   (D) 70 in³

57. Ms. Mackey told her students to draw rectangles with the following properties:

    The length is 3 inches longer than the width.

    The area is 40 square inches.

    What is the width of the rectangle?

    (A) 4 inches   (B) 5 inches
    (C) 7 inches   (D) 8 inches

58. Farmer Bill is putting up a fence in the corner of his yard as shown in the picture.

    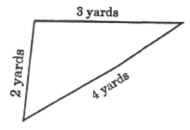

    How much fencing will he need?

    (A) 9 yards   (B) 10 yards
    (C) 12 yards   (D) 24 yards

59. A square-based pyramid has a height of 15 inches and one side of the base is 9 inches. What is the volume of the square-based pyramid?

    (A) 45 in³   (B) 135 in³
    (C) 405 in³   (D) 1215 in³

60. Base your answer to the following question on the diagram of a square inscribed in a circle shown below. The diagonal of the square is shown, running through the center of the circle (not shown).

    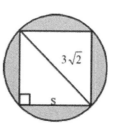

    Find the area of the shaded area.

    Show your work.

107

Area, Volume

61. Base your answer to the following question on the parallelogram below. (All units measured in inches)

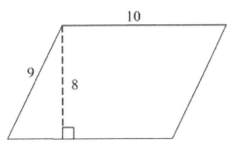

What is the perimeter of the parallelogram?

(A) 19 inches (B) 20 inches
(C) 38 inches (D) 40 inches

62. What is the volume of a cube with a side length of 5 inches?

(A) 5 in^3 (B) 25 in^3
(C) 50 in^3 (D) 125 in^3

63. Spooner township is 6 miles long and 6 miles wide. What is the area of the township?

(A) 6 square miles (B) 12 square miles
(C) 24 square miles (D) 36 square miles

64. The perimeter of a rectangle is 48 cm. The length is 3 more than double the width. What is the area of the rectangle?

(A) 17 cm^2 (B) 49 cm^2
(C) 119 cm^2 (D) 289 cm^2

65. The figure below is a right triangle.

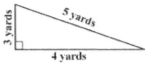

What is the area of this triangle?

(A) 6 yd^2 (B) 12 yd^2
(C) 24 yd^2 (D) 60 yd^2

66. The volume of a cube with an edge of 6 centimeters is

(A) 6 cm^3. (B) 36 cm^3.
(C) 216 cm^3. (D) 1246 cm^3.

67. Find the volume of the following cone.

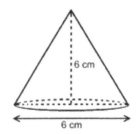

(A) 6π cm^3 (B) 18π cm^3
(C) 54π cm^3 (D) 64π cm^3

Area, Volume

68. The total perimeter of the figure below is 140 meters.

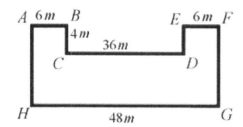

What is the measure of $\overline{AH}$?

(A) 9 m (B) 18 m
(C) 27 m (D) 36 m

69. Cube A has twice the length of Cube B. The volume of Cube B is ___ times smaller than the volume of Cube A.

(A) $\frac{1}{8}$ (B) $\frac{1}{4}$ (C) 4 (D) 8

70. The stage at the local playhouse needs to be coated with wood finish. The stage is a rectangle with a trapezoid that extends out into the audience, as shown in the diagram below.

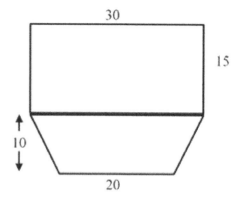

If a can of wood finish will coat 70 square feet, how many cans of wood finish will be needed to coat the stage?

(A) 5 cans (B) 7 cans
(C) 10 cans (D) 12 cans

71. Base your answer to the following question on the following information.

A storage company wants to optimize the storage bins that it uses. The current bins are right circular cylinders that have a radius of 2 feet and are 5 feet tall.

Find the volume of the current cylindrical bins to the nearest cubic foot. Use $\pi = 3.14$.

Show your work.

72. Samara wants to make a table cloth by cutting a circular piece of fabric out of a square piece. She needs the circle to have a radius of 3 feet. The square has sides 11 feet. How much material will be left after the circular piece is cut out?

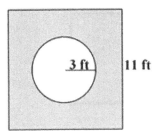

(A) $11^2 - 3^2\pi$ (B) $3^2 - 11^2\pi$
(C) $(11 - 3\pi)^2$ (D) $(3\pi - 11)^2$

74. Mr. Kim and his son own a farm. They built a fence to enclose their farm as shown in the diagram below.

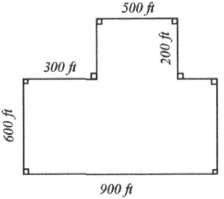

How many feet of fencing was used?

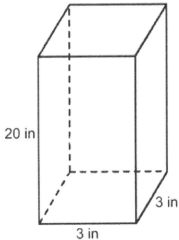

73. Find the surface area of the rectangular prism.

(A) 180 square inches (B) 220 square inches
(C) 258 square inches (D) 264 square inches

Area, Volume

75. Base your answer to the following question on the diagram below of a trapezoid.

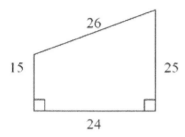

Find the area of this trapezoid in square inches.

Show your work.

---

76. Mr. Joe is building a house. It is going to be 30 feet long and 60 feet wide. What is the perimeter of the house?

    (A) 30 feet   (B) 90 feet
    (C) 180 feet (D) 1,800 feet

77. Hector's landscaping company is building a garden. The dimensions are 1.5 ft by 3 ft by 8 ft. How many cubic feet of soil will he need to fill the garden?

    (A) 12.5 (B) 20   (C) 24   (D) 36

78. What is the perimeter of a rectangle with sides 9 feet and 5 feet?

    (A) 14 ft   (B) $22\frac{1}{2}$ ft
    (C) 28 ft   (D) 45 ft

79. Mr. Johnson wants to build a large rectangular sandbox for his kids to play in. He has 82 feet of lining material for the perimeter of the sandbox.

    If the length and width can only be whole numbers, and Mr. Johnson can only use 82 feet of lining:

    (1) What dimensions for the sandbox will provide the maximum area in the sandbox?
    (2) What is the area of this sandbox?

    Show your work.

80. The length of a rectangle is doubled and its width is halved. What happens to its area?

    (A) It's quartered   (B) It's halved
    (C) It's doubled   (D) No change

Area, Volume

81. Base your answer to the following question on the diagram below.

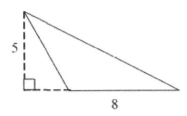

What is the area of the triangle above?

(A) 20   (B) 30   (C) 40   (D) 50

82. Base your answer to the following question on the following diagram of a cube with measurements in centimeters.

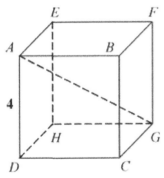

Find the volume of this cube.

Show your work.

83. A cube has a volume of 8 square inches. What is the length of one edge of this cube?

(A) 2 inches   (B) 4 inches
(C) 6 inches   (D) 8 inches

84. FGHI is a rhombus whose diagonals intersect at J. m∠IFG = 40°

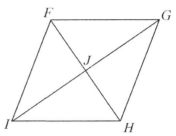

Find m∠FJG.

(A) 20°   (B) 50°   (C) 70°   (D) 90°

85. Martin measured his bedroom and found that it was 9 feet by 12 feet. The ceiling was 8 feet high. What is the volume of Martin's room in cubic feet?

(A) 32 ft^3 (B) 96 ft^3
(C) 864 ft^3 (D) 2,592 ft^3

86. A square has an area of 36 square inches. If the length of each side is increased by 4 inches, what will be the area of the new square?

(A) 4 square inches   (B) 16 square inches
(C) 40 square inches   (D) 100 square inches

87. Mr. Bill wants to build a fence around his garden. The garden is 50 feet long and 20 feet wide. How many feet of fencing will he need?

(A) 30 feet   (B) 70 feet
(C) 140 feet   (D) 280 feet

Area, Volume

88. The length of rectangle E is four times the base of right triangle F. The width of rectangle E is the same as the height of right triangle F. How many of triangle F can fit in rectangle E?

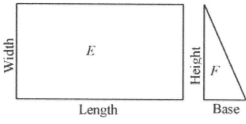

(A) 4 (B) 6 (C) 8 (D) 12

89. The figure below is 3 equilateral triangles connected together.

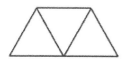

The length of a side of the triangles is 4 feet. What is the perimeter of the figure?

(A) 12 ft (B) 20 ft (C) 28 ft (D) 36 ft

90. Robert is wrapping a present for his friend's birthday party. The present is in the box below:

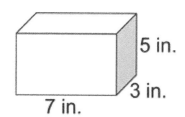

How much wrapping paper will Robert need?

(A) 105 in² (B) 142 in²
(C) 255 in² (D) 360 in²

91. If the volume of cube A is 64 times larger than the volume of cube B, what could be the length of the sides of cube A and cube B?

(A) cube A: 8, cube B: 2
(B) cube A: 2, cube B: 8
(C) cube A: 4, cube B: 6
(D) cube A: 6, cube B: 4

92. If the side of cube A is 3 times larger than that of cube B, the volume of cube A is ___ times larger than cube B

(A) $\frac{1}{9}$ (B) 3 (C) 9 (D) 27

Area, Volume

93. A soup company needs to know how much soup it can fit in one of their new cans. One such can is showed below.

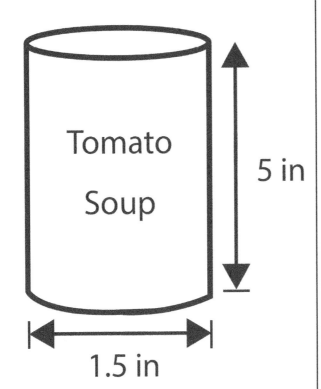

What is the volume of the can?

(A) 1.25π in³   (B) 1.75π in³
(C) 3.5π in³   (D) 7.5π in³

94. What is the length of a side of a square if its perimeter is 16 centimeters?

(A) 2 cm   (B) 4 cm
(C) 6 cm   (D) 8 cm

95. What is the area of $\triangle ABC$?

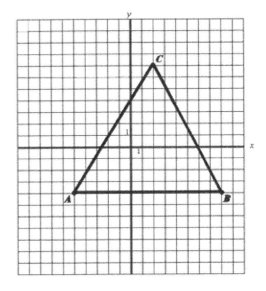

96. What is the area of the triangle below?

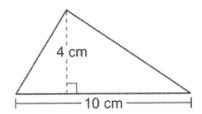

Note: The figure is not drawn to scale.

(A) 10 cm²   (B) 20 cm²
(C) 30 cm²   (D) 40 cm²

Area, Volume

97. Two rectangular prisms are shown below.

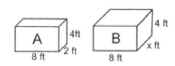

If B has double the width of A, how many times greater is the volume of B compared to A?

(A) 2 times (B) 4 times
(C) 6 times (D) 8 times

98. If the dimensions of the figure below were increased by 100%, what would be the change in the perimeter of the figure?

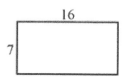

(A) $\frac{1}{4}$ as long (B) $\frac{1}{2}$ as long
(C) 2 times longer (D) 4 times longer

99. Base your answer to the following question on a rectangle whose length is twice the width. The width is $3x$ cm.

Find the perimeter in terms of x.

100. What is the approximate volume of a sphere (in cubic inches) with an 8 inch diameter if the volume of a sphere is given by the formula $V=\frac{4}{3}\pi r^3$? (Use $\pi = 3.14$)

(A) 66.99 (B) 136.78
(C) 267.95 (D) 2143.57

115

Area, Volume Part 2

1. Carpenter Cliff is constructing the door below which measures 1.2 meters by 2.3 meters. There will be 4 special square panels measuring 0.3 meters on each side placed on the door. Cliff needs to know the surface area of the door that will still be showing after the panels are added.

   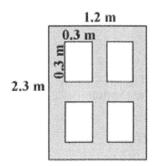

   Which expression below represents this area?

   (A) $1.2(2.3) - 4(0.3)^2$ (B) $4(0.3)^2$
   (C) $1.2(2.3) - (0.3)^2$ (D) $1.2(2.3)$

---

2. The total surface area of a cube is 67 inches. Which of the following measures is closest to the length of its edge?

   (A) 6.9 inches   (B) 6.6 inches
   (C) 3.3 inches   (D) 3.1 inches

3. Box *A* and box *B* have the same volume. Their dimensions are below, except for the width of box *B*, which is unknown.

   Box A: height 6 in., width 4 in., length 2 in.
   Box B: height 8 in., width ??, length 2 in.

   What is the width of box *B*?

   (A) 2 in.   (B) 3 in.   (C) 4 in.   (D) 6 in.

4. Which of the following is the ratio between the volume of a cone and the volume of a cylinder of same base and height?

   (A) 1:2   (B) 1:3   (C) 1:4   (D) 1:5

5. Lori has a page of stamps measuring 3 inches by 6 inches. If each stamp is half an inch by half an inch, what is the maximum number of stamps that the page can hold?

   (A) 3   (B) 6   (C) 18   (D) 72

Area, Volume Part 2

6. Base your answer on the model below which is made up of cubes. Each cube has a side of 4 centimeters.

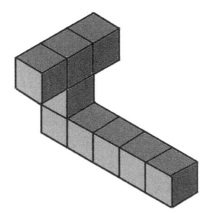

   What is the volume of this figure?

   (A) 144 cm³   (B) 304 cm³
   (C) 576 cm³   (D) 864 cm³

7. The width of a rectangle is 4 inches shorter than the length of a rectangle and the area of the rectangle is 46 square inches. Which of the following equations could be used to solve for the width of the rectangle?

   (A) $x(x + 4) = 46$ (B) $4x + x = 46$
   (C) $x(x - 4) = 46$ (D) $x + x + 4 = 46$

Base your answers to questions **8** and **9** on the following information.

    Jiadi's father has hired her to paint a silo that he uses to store grain on his farm. The silo is in the shape of a right circular cylinder with a diameter of 20 feet and a height of 38 feet.

8. What is the lateral surface area of the silo?

   (A) 58π ft²   (B) 380π ft²
   (C) 550π ft²   (D) 760π ft²

9. If Jiadi knows that one can of paint will cover 500 square feet, then what is the least number of cans she will need to paint the entire lateral surface area of the silo?

   (A) 5   (B) 6   (C) 8   (D) 10

---

10. Box *A* and box *B* have the same volume. Their dimensions are below, except for the length of box *B*, which is unknown.

    Box *A*: height 3 in., width 4 in., length 2 in.
    Box *B*: height: 6 in., width 1 in., length ??

    What is the length of box *B*?

    (A) 2 in.   (B) 3 in.   (C) 4 in.   (D) 5 in.

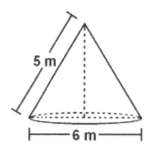

11. Find the volume of the cone.

Area, Volume Part 2

12. A middle school has an indoor running track with **semicircular** ends shown below. Each straightaway of the track is 100 feet long. The field surrounded by the track is 40 feet across.

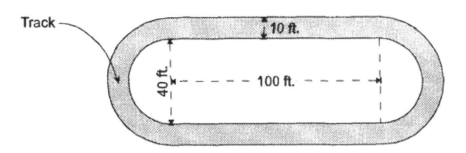

(*a*) One mile is 5,280 feet. In order to jog one mile, how many laps, rounded to the nearest lap, would a person jogging along the inside edge of the track have to jog? Show your work.

(*b*) Another person jogs the outside edge of the track. In each lap, how much further (to the nearest foot) does that person have to jog than the person who jogs the inside edge of the track? Show your work.

---

13. A cylinder has a volume of 512 in³ and a diameter of 11.5 in. What is the approximate height of the cylinder?

    (A) 2.75 in (B) 3 in
    (C) 4.5 in   (D) 5 in

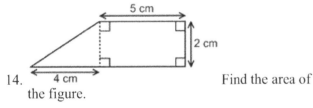

14. Find the area of the figure.

    (A) 10 cm   (B) 14 cm
    (C) 18 cm   (D) 20 cm

15. Base your answer to the following question on the diagram below. (Note: Diagram is not drawn to scale.)

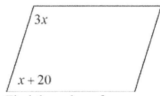

Find the value of x.

(A) 20   (B) 30   (C) 40   (D) 50

118

Area, Volume Part 2

16. Observe the figure below:

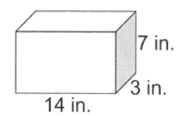

    What is the surface area of the figure?

    (A) 294 in² (B) 332 in²
    (C) 447 in² (D) 508 in²

17. A circle and a triangle have the same area. The radius of the circle is 5 millimeters. The base of the triangle is 2 millimeters long. What is the height of triangle? Use $\pi = 3.14$.

    (A) 157.2 mm (B) 78.5 mm
    (C) 10.9 mm   (D) 2.3 mm

18. Walter is painting a rectangular wall measuring 10 feet by 16 feet. A door in the wall measures 7 feet by 3 feet. What is the area of the wall that needs to be painted, excluding the door?

    (A) 139 square feet (B) 145 square feet
    (C) 160 square feet (D) 181 square feet

19. The lawn in Veronica's backyard is a 30 foot by 60 foot rectangle. Veronica converts part of the lawn in a circular garden 10 feet in diameter. What fractional part of her backyard is garden space?

    (A) $\frac{100\pi}{1,800}$ (B) $\frac{10\pi}{1,800}$ (C) $\frac{25\pi}{1,800}$ (D) $\frac{100\pi}{1,800-100\pi}$

20. How many square centimeters of construction paper does Eli need if she wants to exactly cover four sides of a cube with sides that measure 8 inches long?

    (A) 64 in²   (B) 256 in²
    (C) 328 in² (D) 512 in²

21. The width of a rectangle is 2 inches shorter than the length of a rectangle and the area of the rectangle is 30 square inches. Which of the following equations could be used to solve for length of the rectangle?

    (A) $x(x + 2) = 30$ (B) $x + (x - 2) = 30$
    (C) $x - (x - 2) = 30$ (D) $x(x - 2) = 30$

Area, Volume Part 2

22. What is the volume of the below trapezoidal prism?

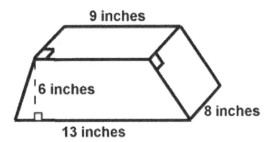

23. What will the area of a square whose area is 25 square inches be if its sides are then extended by 2 inches?

24. The length of a side of a cube is 3.5 inches. What is its volume in cubic inches?

   (A) 12.25 inches cubed
   (B) 42.875 inches cubed
   (C) 45.875 inches cubed
   (D) 105 inches cubed

Base your answers to questions **25** and **26** on the following information.

Mr. Simon is remodeling his backyard. He has a square pool that is 12 feet by 12 feet. He wants to make a brick walkway around the pool that is 2 feet wide as shown in the diagram below.

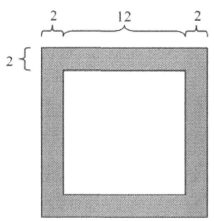

25. The bricks are sold in packages made to cover 8 square feet. How many packages of bricks will Mr. Simon have to buy to make his brick walkway?

    Show your work.

26. What is the area of the surface of the pool floor?

27. The volume of a cylinder is equal to the volume of the cone shown below.

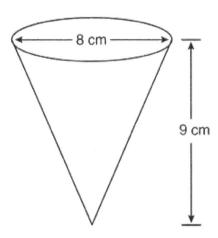

What is the radius of the cylinder if the cylinder and cone have the same height, to the nearest hundredth of a cm?

(A) 2.15 cm (B) 2.31 cm
(C) 2.57 cm (D) 5.33 cm

28. Evan needs to calculate how much grass seed is needed to cover his entire lawn. If his lawn is 60 feet wide and 20 feet long, how many bags of grass seed will he need if one bag covers 80 square feet?

(A) 1 (B) 15 (C) 18 (D) 20

29. The diameter of a cone is 8 inches and the height of the cone is 9 inches. Which of the following is closes to the volume of the circular cone?

(A) 75.4 in^3 (B) 113.1 in^3
(C) 150.8 in^3 (D) 452.4 in^3

30. Mr. Wie has 36 feet of fencing to make a caged area for his dog. What should the dimensions of the rectangular region be to have the largest possible area for the dog?

(A) 6 feet by 12 feet (B) 10 feet by 8 feet
(C) 9 feet by 9 feet (D) 11 feet by 7 feet

31. A triangle has an area of 10 square inches. Which of the following pairs could be the height and length of the triangle?

(A) 2 inches by 5 inches
(B) 3 inches by 4 inches
(C) 10 inches by 4 inches
(D) 5 inches by 4 inches

32. Base your answer to the following question on the following figure is a rectangle

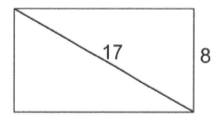

What is the area of this rectangle?

(A) 95 (B) 105 (C) 120 (D) 136

Area, Volume Part 2

33. Base your answer to the following question on the diagram below of a square and a circle with measurements in inches.

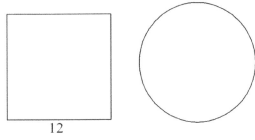

12

If the square and the circle have the same area, what is the radius of the circle? Use $\pi = 3.14$

Show your work. Round your answer to the nearest tenth of an inch.

34. The area of square A is 9 square units. The sides of square B are twice as long as the sides of square A. What is the area of Square B?

(A) 18 square units (B) 27 square units
(C) 36 square units (D) 81 square units

35. Base your answer to the following question on the figure below.

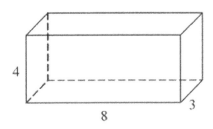

What is the volume of the figure?

(A) 12 cubic units   (B) 32 cubic units
(C) 96 cubic units   (D) 15 cubic units

36. What is the volume of the box below to the nearest tenth?

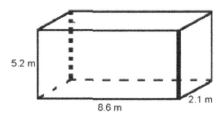

(A) 87.4 m³   (B) 93.9 m³
(C) 99.7 m³   (D) 100.4 m³

37. Lisa wants to create a cylinder for her water with a radius of 7 inches and a height of 12 inches. What is the volume of water that the cylinder can hold? (Use $\pi = 3.14$)

(A) 263 in³   (B) 1846 in³
(C) 3165 in³   (D) 4005 in³

38. Find the perimeter and the area of a rhombus whose diagonals are 6 meters and 8 meters.

39. The figure below is 3 squares connected in a line.

The side of each square measures 8 feet. What is the perimeter of the figure?

(A) 32 ft (B) 64 ft (C) 80 ft (D) 96 ft

Area, Volume Part 2

40. Base your answer to the following question on the diagram below, showing a circle with radius 3 inscribed in a square.

    Find the area of the shaded region.

    Show your work. Use π = 3.14.

41. To the nearest hundredth, what is the volume of this box?

    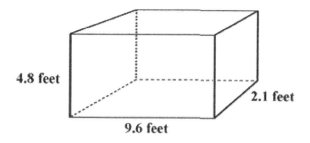

    (A) 96. ft³ (B) 96.8 ft³
    (C) 96.77 ft³ (D) 96.768 ft³

42. $\overline{AB} \cong \overline{EF}$. What is the length of $\overline{AB}$ in the figure below?

    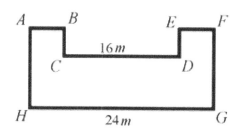

    (A) 4 m (B) 5 m
    (C) 8 m (D) 24 m

43. The drawing below shows an equilateral triangle placed on a square.

    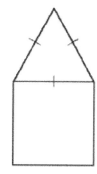

    If one side of the triangle is 10, then
    (a) what is the area of the square?
    (b) what is the perimeter of the figure?

44. If the length of the sides of a cube are doubled, then how many times greater will the surface area of the cube be?

    (A) 4 times (B) 5 times
    (C) 8 times (D) 10 times

Area, Volume Part 2

45. The height of the right triangle below is represented by a certain positive number x. The triangle's base is represented by $x + 8$..

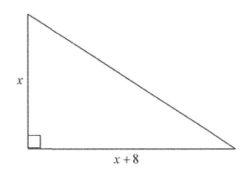

Which expression represents the area of the triangle?

(A) $\frac{x+x+8}{2}$ (B) $\frac{x(x+8)}{2}$
(C) $x(x + 8)$ (D) $2x + 2(x + 8)$

46. Which of the following is the area of a square whose sides measure $2a - 1$?

(A) $4a^2 - 4a + 1$ (B) $4a^2 - 4a - 1$
(C) $8a^2 - 4a + 1$ (D) $8a - 4$

47. The formula $A = bh$, where A is the area, b is the base, and h is the height, applies to which of the figures below?

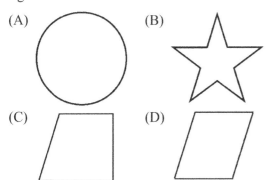

Base your answers to questions **48** and **49** on the following information.

A storage company wants to optimize the storage bins that it uses. The current bins are right circular cylinders that have a radius of 2 feet and are 5 feet tall.

48. Find the volume of the current cylindrical bins to the nearest cubic foot. Use $\pi = 3.14$.

Show your work.

49. The material to make the bins is costly. Which storage bin needs more material for its outer covering?

Show your work.

---

50. How does doubling the height of a cylinder affect its volume?

(A) Halves the volume
(B) Doubles the volume
(C) Quadruples the volume
(D) No effect

51. Mrs. Lasner needed to paint a rectangular wall that was 75 feet long and 8 feet high. When she stopped to take a break she still had 175 square feet unpainted. How many square feet of wall did she paint before taking a break?

(A) 425 ft²   (B) 300 ft²
(C) 150 ft²   (D) 92 ft²

Area, Volume Part 2

52. The area of square A is 16 square units. The area of square B is 36 square units. What is the difference between the length of the sides in square A and the sides in square B?

    (A) $\frac{2}{3}$ units (B) $\frac{3}{2}$ units
    (C) 2 units (D) 20 units

53. The volume of a cylinder is 21π cubic feet. If the height of the cylinder is 3 times its radius, how tall is the cylinder?

    (A) 1 foot (B) 3 feet
    (C) 9 feet (D) 27 feet

54. If the dimensions of a rectangle are halved, the area of the rectangle is

    (A) quartered. (B) halved.
    (C) doubled. (D) quadrupled.

55. Which of the following has the same area as a triangle with base 4 and height 6?

    (A) a rectangle with length 4 and length 6
    (B) a rhombus with side 4 and height 3
    (C) a square with side 6
    (D) a trapezoid with bases 4 and 8, and height 3

56. Look at the triangle below.

    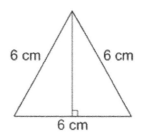

    Which of the following is the area of the triangle in square centimeters?

    (A) $3\sqrt{3}$ (B) $6\sqrt{3}$
    (C) $9\sqrt{3}$ (D) $18\sqrt{3}$

57. Find the volume of the box below.

    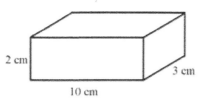

    (A) 30 cm³ (B) 60 cm³
    (C) 112 cm³ (D) 120 cm³

58. The diameter of a cylinder is 18 and the height is 12. What is the volume of the cylinder? Use $\pi = 3.14$. Round your answer to he nearest tenth.

    (A) 216.0 (B) 678.3
    (C) 3,052.0 (D) 3,052.1

59. The inside of a plastic box has a volume of 2,400 cubic inches and measures 5 inches long and 24 inches high. How deep is the inside of the plastic box?

    (A) 10 inches (B) 15 inches
    (C) 20 inches (D) 40 inches

Area, Volume Part 2

60. Square *A* has 4 times the perimeter of Square *B*. Square *A* has an area of 48 units squared. What is the area of Square *B* in units squared?

    (A) 3 (B) 6 (C) 12 (D) 24

Base your answers to questions **61** through **65** on the diagram below. (Note: Figure is not drawn to scale.)

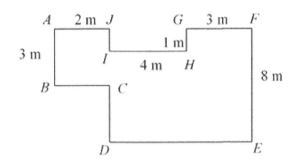

61. What is the total area of the figure?

    (A) 39 m^2 (B) 60 m^2
    (C) 72 m^2 (D) 58 m^2

62. What is the length of $\overline{DE}$?

    (A) 3 m (B) 7 m (C) 4 m (D) 5 m

63. What is the perimeter of the figure?

    (A) 36 m (B) 40 m
    (C) 22 m (D) 30 m

64. What is the length of $\overline{CD}$?

    (A) 3 m (B) 4 m (C) 5 m (D) 6 m

65. What is the length of $\overline{BC}$?

    (A) 3 m (B) 1 m (C) 2 m (D) 4 m

---

66. Mr. Diaz wants to build a fence around his yard. The yard is 140 feet long and 30 feet wide. How many feet of fencing will he need?

    (A) 170 ft (B) 200 ft
    (C) 340 ft (D) 420 ft

67. The area of square *A* is 4 square units. The sides of square *B* are twice as long as the sides of square *A*. What is the area of square *B*?

    (A) 8 square units   (B) 16 square units
    (C) 32 square units (D) 64 square units

68. If a model is made of 3 cubes, each with a side length of 5 inches, what is the total volume of the model?

    (A) 125 cubic inches
    (B) 250 cubic inches
    (C) 375 cubic inches
    (D) 3375 cubic inches

69. Which is the closest to the area of a circle with diameter of 8 inches?

    (A) 45 in^2 (B) 50 in^2
    (C) 192 in^2 (D) 201 in^2

Area, Volume Part 2

70. The total perimeter of the figure below is 36 meters.

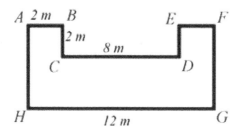

What is the measure of $\overline{FG}$?

(A) 4 m (B) 5 m
(C) 8 m (D) 10 m

71. Below is a diagram of a restaurant. Which expression represents the area of the dining room?

(A) $(xy)(ab)$
(B) $(x+y)(a+b)$
(C) $(x+y)(a+b) - ay$
(D) $(x+y)(a+b) + ay$

72. What is the volume V of a right circular cylinder in terms of π with radius $r = 4$ and height $h = 10$?

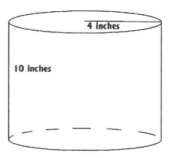

(A) 26π inches^3 (B) 80π inches^3
(C) 160π inches^3 (D) 504π inches^3

Base your answers to questions **73** and **74** on the parallelogram below. (All units measured in inches)

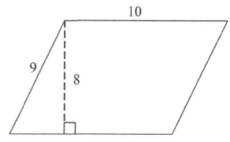

73. What is the perimeter of the parallelogram?

(A) 19 inches (B) 20 inches
(C) 38 inches (D) 40 inches

74. What is the area of the parallelogram?

(A) 45 square inches (B) 90 square inches
(C) 40 square inches (D) 80 square inches

Area, Volume Part 2

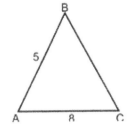

75. Find the area of isosceles triangle $\triangle \overline{ABC}$.

    (A) 6 sq. units (B) 12 sq. units
    (C) 16 sq. units (D) 24 sq. units

76. The figure below is 3 connected squares.

    The side of each square measures 3 feet. What is the area of the figure?

    (A) 9 ft (B) 24 ft (C) 27 ft (D) 48 ft

77. Barbara bought a cage for her dog that measured 24 in. by 36 in. by 48 in. What is the volume of the cage in cubic inches?

    (A) 24 in³   (B) 52 in³
    (C) 288 in³   (D) 41,472 in³

78. In the Johnson's home, the living room is 156 inches long and 132 inches wide and the dining room is 10 feet long and 8 feet wide. What is the difference, in square feet, between the areas of these rooms?

    (A) 46 square feet   (B) 63 square feet
    (C) 6624 square feet (D) 9072 square feet

79. Base your answer to the following question on the following rhombus.

    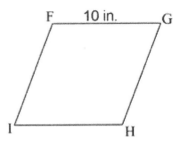

    What is the area of this figure?

    (A) 10 square inches
    (B) 40 square inches
    (C) 100 square inches
    (D) 10,000 square inches

80. Stacy needs a sphere that fits in a hole. A sphere with a radius of $\frac{4}{5}$ inches was too small so it fell through, but a sphere with a radius of $\frac{3}{2}$ inches was too big. What radius sphere could possibly fit in the hole?

    (A) $\frac{13}{20}$ in (B) 1 in (C) $\frac{5}{3}$ in (D) $\frac{8}{3}$ in

81. Rectangle A has an area of 10 square inches and rectangle B has an area of 20 square inches. If the length of rectangle B is half that of rectangle A, how many times larger is the width of rectangle B compared to rectangle A?

    (A) Same width
    (B) Twice the width
    (C) Four times the width
    (D) Eight times the width

Base your answers to questions **82** and **83** on the figure below.

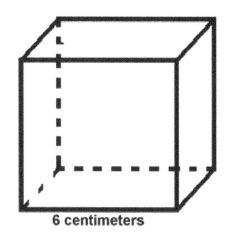

6 centimeters

82. What is the volume of this cube?

   (A) 18 cm³ (B) 108 cm³
   (C) 216 cm³ (D) 288 cm³

83. What is the surface area of this cube?

   (A) 18 cm² (B) 108 cm²
   (C) 216 cm² (D) 288 cm²

84. A circular pool has a diameter of 10 ft. What is the area of the pool?

   (A) 25 ft²   (B) 31 ft²
   (C) 78.54 ft² (D) 100 ft²

85. The base perimeter of a square pyramid is tripled. What is the ratio of the volume of the original pyramid to the volume of the new pyramid?

   (A) 1:3 (B) 1:6 (C) 1:9 (D) 1:12

86. Base your answer to the following question on the figure below.

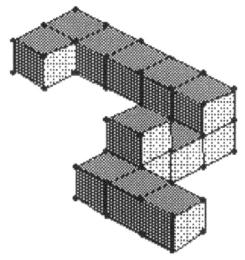

The total volume of the figure is 104 cubic inches. What is the height of each cube?

   (A) 1 inch   (B) 2 inches
   (C) 3 inches (D) 4 inches

87. Determine the volume of a cylinder when the diameter is 16 and the height is 12. Round your answer to the nearest whole number. Use $\pi = 3.14$.

   (A) 28   (B) 88
   (C) 2,411 (D) 2,412

Area, Volume Part 2

Base your answers to questions **88** and **89** on the following diagram of a cube with measurements in centimeters.

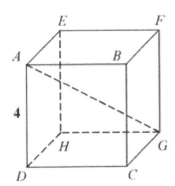

88. Find the volume of this cube.

    Show your work.

89. Find the surface area of this cube.

    Show your work.

90. If a rectangle's length was tripled and width was halved, the area increased by a factor of

    (A) $\frac{2}{3}$.   (B) 1.5.   (C) 3.   (D) 6.

91. Below is a rectangle prism with dimensions 8 in. by 7 in. by 4 in.

    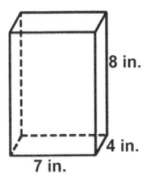

    What is the surface area of this rectangular prism?

    (A) 116 in^2 (B) 224 in^2
    (C) 232 in^2 (D) 256 in^2

92. A table measures 7 feet by 14 feet. What is the area of the tabletop?

    (A) 2 ft^2 (B) 54 ft^2
    (C) 98 ft^2 (D) 112 ft^2

93. Find the area of the parallelogram below.

    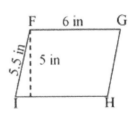

    (A) 11.5 in^2 (B) 16.5 in^2
    (C) 30 in^2 (D) 33 in^2

Area, Volume Part 2

94. What is the area of the triangle below?

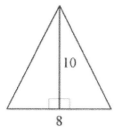

(A) 40   (B) 80   (C) 110   (D) 121

95. A cone has a height of 6 inches and a base circumference of 10π inches. What is the volume of the cone?

(A) 50 cubic inches   (B) 150 cubic inches
(C) 200 cubic inches   (D) 600 cubic inches

96. The circle below has a radius of 5 inches. What is the area of the shaded region? Use $\pi = 3.14$.

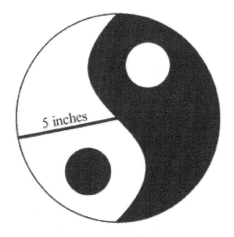

131

Area, Volume Part 2

97. The volume of the rectangular solid below is 396 cubic inches.

    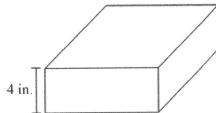

    4 in.

    What could be the length and width of this rectangular solid?

    (A) 4 inches by 9 inches
    (B) 10 inches by 11 inches
    (C) 7 inches by 13 inches
    (D) 9 inches by 11 inches

98. Jane is filling her new pool with water. It is a rectangular pool that measures 30 feet long, 12 feet wide, and 8 feet deep. The pool is half filled. How many more cubic feet of the pool does she have to fill?

    (A) 25 cubic feet   (B) 50 cubic feet
    (C) 1,440 cubic feet (D) 2,880 cubic feet

99. Jarred builds an aquarium with a length of 3.5 feet, a width of 0.75 feet, and a height of 1.5 feet. If he fills up half the tank with water, how much water is in the tank?

    (A) 1.54 ft^3 (B) 1.97 ft^3
    (C) 2.51 ft^3 (D) 3.94 ft^3

100. What is the volume of a box that has width of 5 cm, height of 10 cm, and length of 6 cm?

    (A) 60 cm^3 (B) 300 cm^3
    (C) 400 cm^3 (D) 600 cm^3

Data Analysis

1. Barney recorded the points that his favorite basketball team scored in each game for 16 games. These were his results:

   77 66 86 94
   92 97 70 91
   60 85 93 96
   64 66 75 91

   What is a correct stem–and–leaf plot for these scores?

   (A) 6 | 60 64 66 66
       7 | 70 75 77
       8 | 85 86
       9 | 91 91 92 93 94 96 97

   (B) 6 | 0 4 6 6
       7 | 0 5 7
       8 | 5 6
       9 | 1 1 2 3 4 6 7

   (C) 6 | 60 64 66
       7 | 70 75 77
       8 | 85 86
       9 | 91 92 93 94 96 97

   (D) 6 | 0 4 6
       7 | 0 5 7
       8 | 5 6
       9 | 1 2 3 4 6 7

2. Aaron kept a record of his test scores on the 12 math tests he took this year. These were his results:

   85 79 91
   68 75 89
   85 80 79
   92 83 88

   What is a correct stem–and–leaf plot for these scores?

   (A) 6 | 8
       7 | 5 9
       8 | 0 3 5 8 9
       9 | 1 2

   (B) 6 | 8
       7 | 5 9 9
       8 | 0 3 5 5 8 9
       9 | 1 2

   (C) 6 | 68
       7 | 75 79 79
       8 | 80 83 85 85 88 89
       9 | 91 92

   (D) 6 | 68
       7 | 75 79
       8 | 80 83 85 88 89
       9 | 91 92

Data Analysis

3. Wayne measured the temperature outside his house every day at noon for 16 days. These were his results:

   33 49 53 23
   30 11 49 56
   25 41 39 49
   54 23 43 18

   What is a correct stem–and–leaf plot for these scores?

   (A) 1 | 1 8
        2 | 3 5
        3 | 0 3 9
        4 | 1 3 9 2
        5 | 4 6

   (B) 1 | 11 18
        2 | 23 25
        3 | 30 33 39
        4 | 41 43 49
        5 | 52 54 56

   (C) 1 | 11 18
        2 | 23 23 25
        3 | 30 33 39
        4 | 41 43 49 49 49
        5 | 52 54 56

   (D) 1 | 1 8
        2 | 3 3 5
        3 | 0 3 9
        4 | 1 3 9 9 9
        5 | 2 4 6

Base your answers to questions **4** and **5** on the stem-and-leaf plot below of the scores on Mrs. Jackson's last science test.

Stem	Leaves
6	8
7	2 2 7 9
8	0 1 1 6 6 6 8 9
9	0 0 2 5 9

4. How much higher was the highest score than the lowest score?

   (A) 29   (B) 31   (C) 35   (D) 26

5. What was the highest score on the test?

   (A) 9   (B) 89   (C) 90   (D) 99

Base your answers to questions **6** and **7** on the following histogram of the scores on Mr. Steven's last math test.

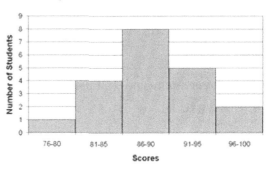

6. How many more students scored in the 86–90 range than in the 76–80 range?

   (A) 7 students   (B) 6 students
   (C) 5 students   (D) 4 students

7. How many students scored between 91 and 100 on the test?

   (A) 5 students   (B) 2 students
   (C) 7 students   (D) 8 students

Base your answers to questions **8** and **9** on the following box and whisker plot that shows the median points scored per game by the players on the Scott Middle School Basketball team.

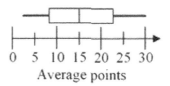
Average points

8. What was the highest score on the team?

   (A) 7 points   (B) 15 points
   (C) 23 points   (D) 30 points

9. What was the average score on the team?

   (A) 7 points   (B) 15 points
   (C) 23 points   (D) 30 points

Data Analysis

Base your answers to questions **10** through **12** on the following box and whisker plot of the family members at the Claire Family Reunion.

Age of Attendees to Family Reunion

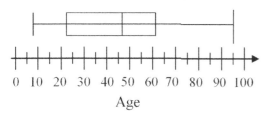

Age

10. The youngest 25% of the Claire family is under how many years of age?

    (A) 8 years old (B) 23 years old
    (C) 47 years old (D) 61 years old

11. What is the mean age of the family members attending the family reunion?

    (A) 8 years old (B) 23 years old
    (C) 47 years old (D) 61 years old

12. According to the box and whisker plot, what is the age of the oldest person at the family reunion?

    (A) 23 years old (B) 47 years old
    (C) 61 years old (D) 95 years old

13. The two box-and-whisker plots below show the number of magazine subscriptions sold by the members of the senior and junior classes for a fundraiser.

Number of Magazine Subscriptions Sold

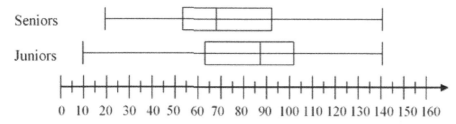

What statement about the two data plots must be true?

(A) The seniors and juniors sold the same number of subscriptions.
(B) The same median number was sold by both classes.
(C) The same upper quartile number was sold by both classes.
(D) The same upper extreme number was sold by both classes.

Data Analysis

14. The students in Mrs. Smith's class made a chart to show how they come to school. Each student made a mark beside one of the pictures to show how he or she comes to school.

    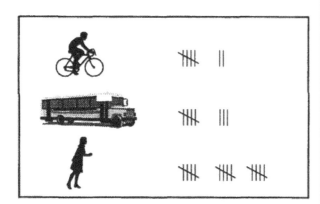

    Sally is a student in Mrs. Smith's class. Which one of the following statements is correct?

    (A) It is more likely that Sally rides a bike than that she walks to school.
    (B) It is more likely that Sally walks than that she takes the bus to school.
    (C) It is more likely that Sally takes the bus than that she walks to school.
    (D) It is more likely that Sally rides her bike than that she takes the bus to school.

15. Base your answer to the following question on The speed for a sample of twenty-five cars is shown in miles per hour (mph) in the box-and-whiskers graph below.

    Speed (mph)

    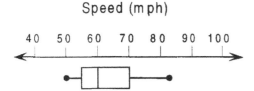

    If an officer is writing speeding tickets to each driver in the sample whose speed is more than 70 mph, about what percentage of the drivers will be ticketed?

    (A) 25%
    (B) 40%
    (C) 75%
    (D) cannot be determined

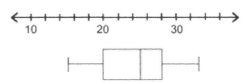

16. In which of the following intervals does 50% of the data exist?

    (A) 15–20 (B) 20–28
    (C) 25–28 (D) 15–28

17. What information can you not determine from a box and whisker plot?

    (A) Median (B) Highest value
    (C) 3rd quartile (D) Mode

18. The miles walked each day by someone were recorded in a stem and leaf plot.

Stem	Leaf
1	0
2	1,3
3	2,7
4	5,6
5	0,1

    Which number set represents this data?

    (A) {10, 213, 233, 327, 372, 456, 501}
    (B) {10, 21, 37, 46, 51}
    (C) {10, 13, 21, 23, 32, 27, 50, 51}
    (D) {10, 21, 23, 32, 37, 45, 46, 50, 51}

Data Analysis

19. The chart below shows the score distribution of Mrs. Fleisher's 8th grade class' previous math test.

Score Range	Number of Students
≤ 65	1
65-70	2
70-75	4
75-80	3
80-85	2
≥ 85	5

Which histogram best represents this data?

(A)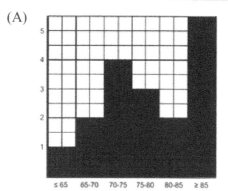

(B)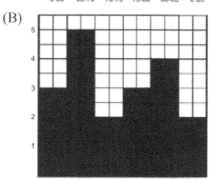

(C)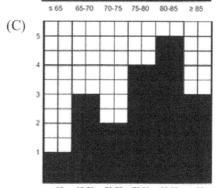

(D)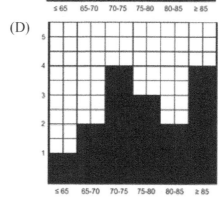

Data Analysis

Marbles Won

```
1 | 0
2 | 5, 9
3 | 1, 4, 7
4 | 3, 8, 9
5 | 2
```

20. George recorded the marbles he won each day in a week using a stem and leaf plot:

    What is the total number of marbles George won during the week?

    (A) 329   (B) 358   (C) 408   (D) 422

21. What is the mode of the test scores?

Final Exam Scores

```
4 | 5 7
5 | 3 8 9
6 | 5 6 7 9
7 | 0 5 6 8 8
8 | 2 4 4 4 7
9 | 0 1 2 3 5 6 8 9
```

(A) 45   (B) 78   (C) 84   (D) 99

22. Review the following values of stocks on a certain day:
    41, 59, 67, 52, 79, 85, 55, 68

    Which stem and leaf plot correctly displays this data?

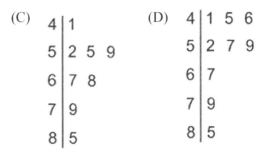

(A)
```
4 | 1
5 | 3
6 | 2
7 | 1
8 | 1
```

(B)
```
4 | 1 3
5 | 0 2 4
6 | 8
7 | 9
8 | 5
```

(C)
```
4 | 1
5 | 2 5 9
6 | 7 8
7 | 9
8 | 5
```

(D)
```
4 | 1 5 6
5 | 2 7 9
6 | 7
7 | 9
8 | 5
```

23. Consider the following scores that Scott got on his last 8 science tests:

    90, 92, 88, 91, 89, 97, 85, 87

    Which box and whisker plot correctly shows these data points?

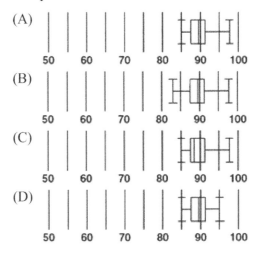

Data Analysis

Base your answers to questions **24** through **29** on the map below that James made of his hometown. The roads are shown by the lines drawn.

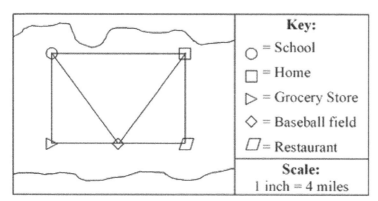

24. On Saturday, James leaves his home to go to a baseball game. After the game, the coach takes the team to the restaurant for a victory celebration. Then James goes back home. Approximately how long is his trip?

    (A) 3 miles   (B) 6 miles   (C) 9 miles   (D) 12 miles

25. James is finished working at the grocery store and is going home. Which of the following routes home is the shortest?

    (A) grocery store → school → home
    (B) grocery store → baseball field → restaurant → home
    (C) grocery store → baseball field → home
    (D) grocery store → school → baseball field → home

26. James has to travel from his home to school, and then to the grocery store where he works. Approximately how long is this trip?

    (A) 10 miles   (B) 7 miles   (C) 6 miles   (D) 2 miles

27. Approximately how far is it from James' home to the baseball field?

    (A) 3 miles   (B) 5 miles   (C) 7 miles   (D) 9 miles

28. Approximately how far is it from James' home to the restaurant?

    (A) 2 miles   (B) 3 miles   (C) 4 miles   (D) 5 miles

29. Approximately how far is it from James' home to school?

    (A) 1 mile   (B) 2 miles   (C) 4 miles   (D) 6 miles

---

30. The scale on a map is 1 inch: 3 miles. Using a proportion, how can you find the actual distance between two cities if the distance on the map is 2 feet?

    (A) $\dfrac{24}{3} = \dfrac{1}{x}$ (B) $\dfrac{1}{3} = \dfrac{2}{x}$ (C) $\dfrac{1}{3} = \dfrac{24}{x}$ (D) $\dfrac{1}{3} = \dfrac{24}{x}$

Data Analysis

31. The floor of Justin's bedroom is shaped like a rectangle with dimensions of 8 feet by 12 feet. His bed is positioned in one corner of the room. His bed measures 6 feet by 3 feet.

    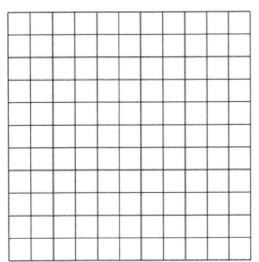

    On the grid above, draw a scale diagram of Justin's bedroom floorplan. Make sure to include and label his bed in the drawing in a correct place. Be sure to provide the scale that you used to draw your diagram.

32. Jacob made a drawing of his front yard using the scale of 1 centimeter = 5 feet. His driveway is drawn 7 centimeters long. How many feet is the actual length of his driveway?

    (A) 7 feet   (B) 35 feet
    (C) 25 feet   (D) 40 feet

33. Joe is standing at the corner of Green Street, Deli Street, and Main Street.

    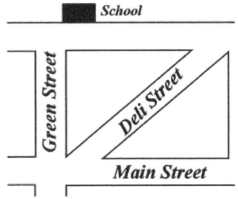

    The shortest distance for Joe to take to school would be

    (A) along Green Street.
    (B) along Main Street.
    (C) along Deli Street.
    (D) along Main and Deli Streets.

34. This speedometer shows the speed at which Helen's car is traveling.

    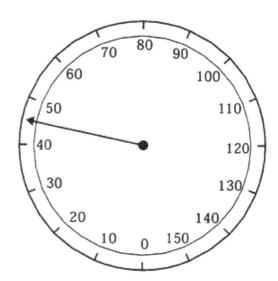

    How many miles per hour faster must she go to be travelling at 65 miles per hour?

    (A) 20 miles per hour   (B) 45 miles per hour
    (C) 65 miles per hour   (D) 25 miles per hour

Data Analysis

35. It takes Jimmy 16 minutes to walk around his block.

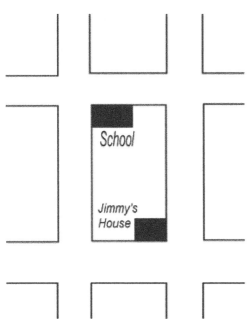

What is the best approximation of the amount of time it takes him to walk to school?

(A) 4 minutes (B) 8 minutes
(C) 12 minutes (D) 16 minutes

36. An architect is drawing blueprints using a scale where $3\frac{3}{4}$ inches = 15 feet. If the length of a section is 7 inches, how long is the actual section going to be?

(A) 28 feet (B) 30 feet
(C) 43 feet (D) 51 feet

37. Bill built a scale model of a car using $\frac{1}{2}$ inch = 1 foot. If the chassis of the car ended up being 12.5 inches, what was the actual length of the car?

(A) 20 ft (B) 25 ft (C) 30 ft (D) 35 ft

38. A car is traveling at a constant velocity. Which of the following velocity (v) vs. time (t) graphs best illustrates this situation?

(A)
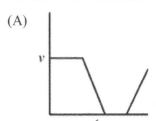

(B)
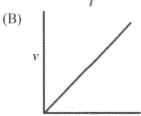

(C)
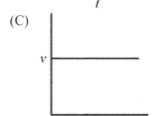

(D)
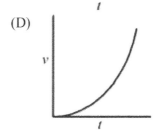

39. What type of graph best shows a continuation over time?

(A) bar graph (B) line graph
(C) pictograph (D) circle graph

141

40. Base your answer to the following question on the Venn diagram below. C is the set of all of Ham's Burgers' customers yesterday. H is the set of customers who bought hamburgers. F is the set of customers who bought French fries.

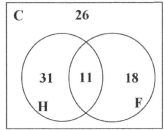

How many customers bought both hamburgers and French fries?

(A) 11   (B) 26   (C) 31   (D) 49

41. Base your answer to the following question on the following information and table.

A group of high school students were asked what they prefer for lunch. The table below shows the number of students who prefer each food.

Food	Number of Students
Pizza	37
Hamburger	26
Sandwich	51
Hot Dog	12
Others	23

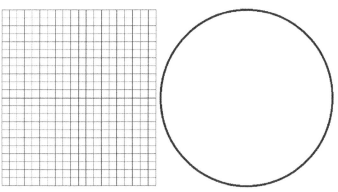

On the grid, create a bar graph.

42. Johnny is making a graph for his Social Studies class. He wants to show the population of several nations in terms of millions of people. What kind of graph should he use?

(A) circle graph   (B) line graph
(C) histogram   (D) pictograph

Data Analysis

43. Ms. Grace drove her car to the store. She started off by increasing her speed, then drove at a constant speed for a while. Then, she slowed down to a complete stop.

    Which graph best illustrates Ms. Grace's trip?

    (A) 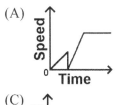   (B)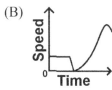

    (C) 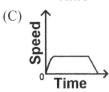   (D)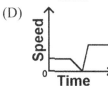

44. Sean surveyed 100 classmates about their favorite foods. The results of the survey are shown in the table below.

Food	Number of People
Pizza	50
Bagel	10
Hamburger	20
Salad	5
Pasta	15

    Which pie chart best represents this data?

    (A)    (B)

    (C)    (D)

Data Analysis

45. A car accelerates to a constant speed. Then, after some time passes, it accelerates again. Which of the following velocity vs. time graphs best illustrates this situation?

    (A) 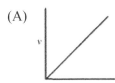   (B)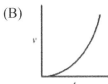

    (C) 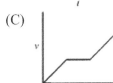   (D)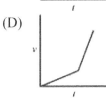

46. The graph below shows the amount of Betamax and VCR players in the U.S.

    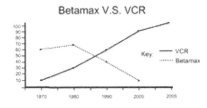

    In which year did VCRs overtake Betamax players?

    (A) 1975 (B) 1980
    (C) 1990 (D) 2000

47. Base your answer to the following question on the following circle graph which shows the portion of the time Billy spends at home, work, school, and in his car.

    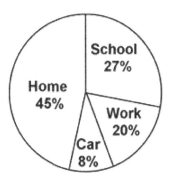

    About how many hours in a day does he work?

    (A) 3   (B) 5   (C) 8   (D) 20

48. Steve is designing a graph to show the populations of several towns. Which graph would be the best type for Steve to use?

    (A) 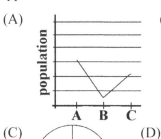   (B)

    (C) 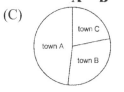   (D)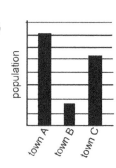

Data Analysis

49. In data analysis, correlation is often used to see if there is a relationship between data. The greater the correlation number, the more the data follows a trend. Correlation spans between −1 and 1. A correlation of 1 is the largest positive correlation, a correlation of −1 is the largest negative correlation, and 0 is no correlation at all. Which is the closest to the correlation of the scatterplot below?

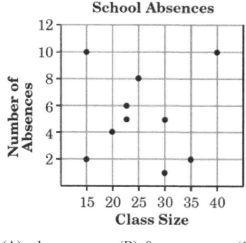

(A) −1 (B) 0 (C) .7 (D) 1

50. What type of graph best uses pictures to illustrate data?

    (A) bar graph   (B) line graph
    (C) pictograph (D) circle graph

51. The graph below shows the number of televisions bought from a store each year.

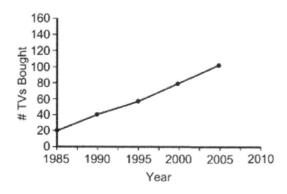

What is a reasonable prediction for the number of TV's bought in 2010?

(A) 80 (B) 100 (C) 120 (D) 140

52. Joe measured temperatures at various times of the day. A graph of his temperature information is given below.

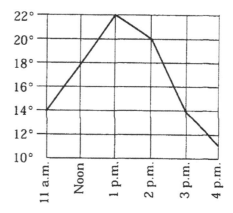

Using the graph of Joe's information, how much did the temperature fall between 1 p.m. and 3 p.m.?

(A) 6° (B) 2° (C) 8° (D) 9°

145

Data Analysis

53. Base your answer to the following question on the following pictogram of the number of salt cubes sold over a six-month period by a salt-making company.

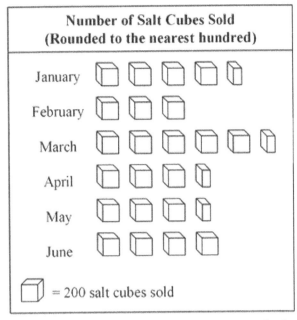

During which month was the least amount of salt cubes sold?

(A) February (B) April
(C) May (D) June

54. Helen measured temperatures at various times of the day and night. A graph of her temperature information is given below.

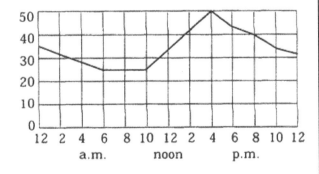

Helen's graph shows that the hottest time of the day was at?

(A) 4 a.m. (B) 10 a.m.
(C) 4 p.m. (D) 6 p.m.

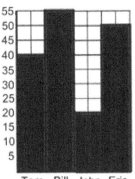

55. Which statement can be drawn from this graph?

(A) Bill and Tom have an equal number of apples.
(B) Tom has twice the number of apples that John has.
(C) Tom has half the apples that Bill has.
(D) Eric has a third of the apples that John has.

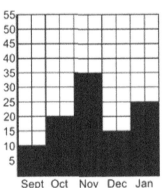

56. Which month had twice the books taken out compared to September?

(A) October (B) November
(C) December (D) January

146

Data Analysis

57. The circle graph below shows ice cream flavors that students of Morton Middle school prefer.

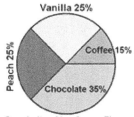

Popularity of Ice Cream Flavors

Which ice cream flavor is most preferred?

(A) chocolate (B) coffee
(C) peach   (D) vanilla

58. Ralph is designing a graph to show the percent of the total money earned that will be used to buy new computers. Which graph would be the best type for Ralph to use?

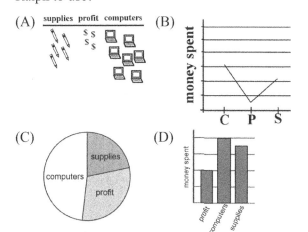

59. The following Venn diagram represents the students in the 10th grade of Phiment High School, and the languages they speak.

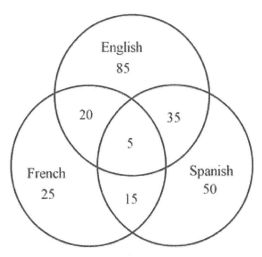

How many students speak both English and Spanish?

(A) 5   (B) 15   (C) 40   (D) 75

60. The graph represents the percentage of students passing in each subject.

Class	% of Students Passing
Math	82%
Social Studies	88%
English	78%
Science	75%
Language	70%

There are 2,000 students taking science. How many students are passing?

(A) 1,000   (B) 1,250
(C) 1,500   (D) 2,000

61. Mrs. Smith is making a graph to show the scores of her students on her last test. She wants to show the number of students within specific ranges of scores. What type of graph should she use?

(A) circle graph   (B) line graph
(C) histogram   (D) pictograph

Data Analysis

62. The graph shows computer purchases from last year.

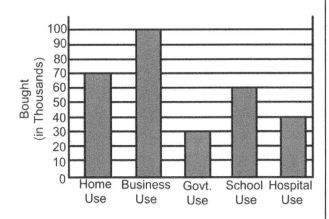

Which use of purchase is closest to the mean of the data?

(A) Home Use   (B) Business Use
(C) Government Use   (D) School Use

63. The graph below shows the decline of video rentals during a week at the end of a month.

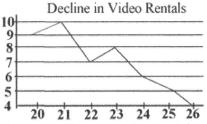

How many fewer rentals were taken during the 25th then the 22nd?

(A) 1   (B) 2   (C) 3   (D) 4

64. The circle graph below shows the eye color of 200 students at Mountain Middle School.

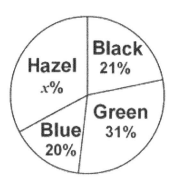

How many of the 200 students have hazel eyes?

(A) 18 students   (B) 28 students
(C) 36 students   (D) 56 students

65. Base your answer on the following question on the graph below.

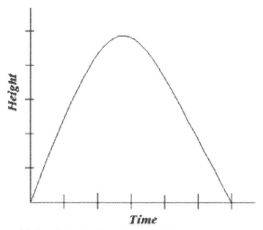

Which of the following could be represented by this graph?

(A) The height of a candle as it burns
(B) The height of a ball thrown upward
(C) The height of an elevator applying a constant upward acceleration
(D) the height of water filling a spherical tank at a consistent pace

Data Analysis

66. The graph below shows the popularity of certain foods in a school cafeteria.

    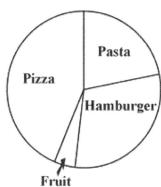

    Which group represents over 50 percent of the population?

    (A) pizza
    (B) pizza and fruit
    (C) hamburger and fruit
    (D) pasta and hamburger

67. A car accelerates from rest to a constant speed and then comes to a complete stop. Which of the following graphs illustrates this situation on a velocity vs. time graph?

    (A) 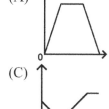 (B)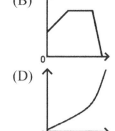

    (C) (D)

Data Analysis

68. Which graph shows the line of best fit for the data points shown?

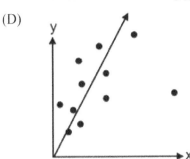

69. Base your answer to the following question on the following line graph of the daily temperature variation in Hotville, FL.

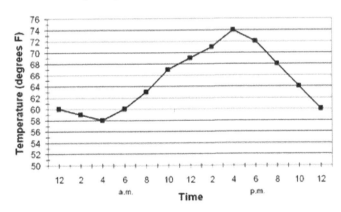

When was the coldest time of the day?

(A) 2 a.m.   (B) 3 a.m.   (C) 4 a.m.   (D) 5 a.m.

Data Analysis

Base your answers to questions **70** and **71** on the following Venn diagram.

A restaurant serves hamburgers, french fries, and soda pop.

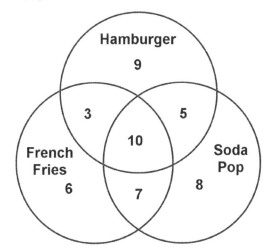

70. How many customers ordered exactly two of them?

    (A) 10   (B) 15   (C) 23   (D) 48

71. How many customers did the restaurant have?

    (A) 10   (B) 15   (C) 23   (D) 48

72. Which type of graph would be least effective in displaying population data over several years?

    (A) circle graph
    (B) line graph
    (C) vertical bar graph
    (D) horizontal bar graph

73. Base your answer to the following question on the following graph of the number of students in each grade at Pi Delta Middle School.

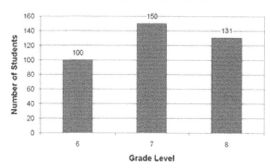

How many total students are in Pi Delta Middle School?

(A) 250   (B) 381   (C) 365   (D) 291

Base your answers to questions **74** through **76** on the following bar graph of the number of visitors to the Beetown Visitor Center over 9 years.

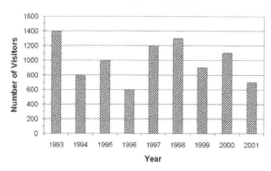

74. Over these 9 years, approximately what was the mean number of visitors to Beetown?

    (A) 800 visitors   (B) 1000 visitors
    (C) 700 visitors   (D) 1200 visitors

75. How many years did the number of visitors exceed 850?

    (A) 5 years   (B) 6 years
    (C) 7 years   (D) 8 years

76. How many more visitors came in 1993 than in 1996?

    (A) 500   (B) 600   (C) 700   (D) 800

Data Analysis

77. Base your answer to the following question on the table and information below about the test scores from Mr. Jackson's last math test.

    92, 84, 96, 82, 74, 99, 88, 89, 81, 71, 79, 80, 81, 90, 91

Grade	71-80	81-90	91-100
# of students			

    (a) Organize the test scores into the table above.

    (b) Which group in the table has the most students?

    (c) How many students scored 81 or higher on this test?

    (d) What is the mean score in Mr. Jackson's class (round to the nearest tenth)?

78. The chart below represents the approximate population of various U.S. cities.

    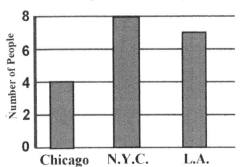

    Approximate City Population (in millions)

    To the nearest million, how many more people does New York City have than Chicago?

    (A) 1   (B) 2   (C) 3   (D) 4

79. The table below shows the results of a survey on favorite fruit juices. From a sample of 500 people, how many would you expect to choose orange juice?

Favorite Fruit Juices	Frequency
Orange	21
Grapefruit	6
Pineapple	10
Apple	15
Tomato	8

    (A) 150   (B) 175   (C) 210   (D) 225

Data Analysis

80. Sam surveyed kids as they got off their school buses in the morning to determine how many hours a night they sleep. Below is a chart displaying this data.

Hours Slept	Frequency
Less Than 7	85
Between 7 and 8	93
More Than 8	22

Sam now wants to extend this survey to the entire school of 1700 students. Based on the data in the table, how many students in the entire school can he expect to get more than 8 hours of sleep?

(A) 149   (B) 187   (C) 205   (D) 374

81. The chart below shows the results of an eating contest.

Contestant	Number of pies	Time (min)
Joey	12	24
Julia	4	48
Lee	7	10
Kim	6	8

Who ate at the fastest rate?

(A) Joey   (B) Julia   (C) Lee   (D) Kim

82. Base your answer to the following question on the chart below that shows the distance traveled by four different airplanes and how long it took each airplane.

Airplane	Distance (miles)	Time (min)
A	350	45
B	450	60
C	200	20
D	250	30

Which airplane flew at the fastest average speed?

(A) A   (B) B   (C) C   (D) D

83. To make one cake, a baker needs:
$\frac{2}{3}$ cups of shortening
$\frac{3}{4}$ cups of white sugar
$2\frac{1}{3}$ cups of brown sugar
$4\frac{1}{2}$ cups of flour
3 cups of water

You can use $\frac{1}{4}$, $\frac{1}{3}$, and $\frac{1}{2}$ cup measuring cups, but not 1 cup measuring cups.

(a) How many $\frac{1}{2}$ cup measurements of flour must the baker use? Explain how you reached your answer.

(b) Explain how the baker should use the measuring cups to successfully measure the brown sugar.

(c) How much shortening will you use to make 6 cakes for a birthday party next weekend?

84. According to the table below, what is the total amount of protein contained in two eggs and one-half cup of whole milk?

Amount of Protein

	Protein
Egg	4
1 Cup of Milk	1

(A) 14   (B) 17.5   (C) 30.5   (D) 35

Data Analysis

85. The table below shows the population of Los Angeles between the years 1940 and 1960.

Population of Los Angeles

Year	Population
1940	24,200,000
1950	24,800,000
1960	25,200,000

How many more people were living in Los Angeles in 1960 than in 1940?

(A) 100,000 (B) 500,000
(C) 800,000 (D) 1,000,000

86. How many passengers used the Grange airport for the six months shown in the table below? (Please note that numbers in the chart show hundreds of passengers.)

AIRPORTS	JAN	FEB	MAR	APR	MAY	JUN	TOTAL
BAY CITY	9	3	5	7	2	4	30
CAMDEN	6	8	1	5	8	2	30
DOOVER	8	5	9	6	6	3	37
FISKE	5	6	6	1	3	7	28
GRANGE	1	2	3	6	7	10	29
TOTAL	29	24	24	25	26	26	154

*Numbers show passenger use in hundreds.

(A) 29 (B) 290 (C) 2,900 (D) 29,000

87. The table below shows the height of a plant every 3 months for a year.

PLANT HEIGHT

Months (x)	Height (in inches) (y)
3	2
6	3
9	4
12	5

What is the slope of the equation that best represents the data?

(A) 3 (B) $\frac{1}{3}$ (C) $\frac{1}{2}$ (D) 1

Data Analysis

Base your answers to questions **88** through **90** on the following table showing the number of food cans and the pounds of clothes collected by Spring Middle School for a collection drive for the needy.

Week	Number of Food Cans	Pounds of Clothes
1	29	14
2	43	25
3	52	34
4	19	29
5	39	41

88. What was the mean amount of clothes collected each week?

    (A) 36.4 pounds (B) 28.6 pounds
    (C) 30.2 pounds (D) 25.5 pounds

89. Did Spring Middle School collect more food cans or more pounds of clothes over the five-week period?

    (A) More food cans.
    (B) More pounds of clothes.
    (C) They collected equal amounts of both.
    (D) Not enough information is given.

90. What was the total number of food cans collected?

    (A) 133 cans (B) 143 cans
    (C) 182 cans (D) 153 cans

91. The chart below shows the population of Nowheresville, NY over the past 30 years.

Year	Population (in thousands)
1970	1
1975	2
1980	4
1985	8
1990	16
1995	32
2000	64

If the rate of growth remains constant in the future, what will be the population of Nowheresville in 2010?

(A) 96,000   (B) 128,000
(C) 256,000 (D) 512,000

92. Galileo discovered that there is a relationship between the time it takes for a clock pendulum to swing back and forth and the length of the pendulum.

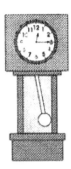

Time of Swing	Length of Pendulum
1 second	1 unit
2 seconds	4 units
3 seconds	9 units
4 seconds	16 units

(a) According to the pattern shown in the table, what would be the length of the pendulum if the swing took 6 seconds?

(b) On the grid in your Student Answer Booklet, draw a graph from this data to show the relationship between the time of the swing and the length of the pendulum.

(c) Describe how the length of the pendulum can be calculated for swings of up to 12 seconds.

(d) Write an equation that shows the relationship between the pendulum length, l, and the number of seconds, t, of the swing.

93. The chart below shows the hair color of students at Smallville Middle School.

Hair Color	Number
Black	75
Blond	60
Brown	210
Red	15

In a circle graph, how many degrees should be used for red hair?

(A) $15°$ (B) $45°$ (C) $54°$ (D) $162°$

Data Analysis

94. The diagram below represents the number of people in Acresville owning either a dog, cat, or bird.

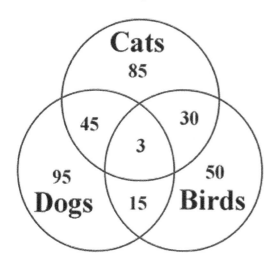

How many people have both a dog and a cat?

(A) 3   (B) 5   (C) 45   (D) 48

---

95. 3 friends each played a spinner game at a carnival. Each spinner had 3 sections of equal area with different colors. The results were as follows:

Name	Results
Mike	Red, Red, Green
Mark	Blue, Red, Green
Tom	Green, Green, Green

If the red section is worth 1 point, the blue section is worth 2 points, and the green section is worth 3 points, which matrix displays this situation correctly?

(A) $\begin{array}{c} \\ \text{Mike} \\ \text{Mark} \\ \text{Tom} \end{array} \begin{array}{ccc} 1 & 2 & 3 \\ \left[\begin{array}{ccc} 2 & 0 & 1 \\ 1 & 1 & 1 \\ 0 & 0 & 3 \end{array}\right] \end{array}$

(B) $\begin{array}{c} \\ \text{Mike} \\ \text{Mark} \\ \text{Tom} \end{array} \begin{array}{ccc} 1 & 2 & 3 \\ \left[\begin{array}{ccc} 2 & 0 & 3 \\ 1 & 2 & 3 \\ 0 & 0 & 9 \end{array}\right] \end{array}$

(C) $\begin{array}{c} \\ \text{Mike} \\ \text{Mark} \\ \text{Tom} \end{array} \begin{array}{ccc} 1 & 2 & 3 \\ \left[\begin{array}{ccc} 2 & 1 & 0 \\ 1 & 2 & 0 \\ 3 & 3 & 3 \end{array}\right] \end{array}$

(D) $\begin{array}{c} \\ \text{Mike} \\ \text{Mark} \\ \text{Tom} \end{array} \begin{array}{ccc} 1 & 2 & 3 \\ \left[\begin{array}{ccc} 0 & 0 & 0 \\ 1 & 1 & 1 \\ 2 & 2 & 2 \end{array}\right] \end{array}$

96. Samuel and Jackson want to survey the students at Adams Middle School to determine the students' favorite sports. What is the best way of surveying to get the best sample of 200 students?

(A) Ask 200 students as they get on the school bus after school

(B) Ask 200 students in the cafeteria

(C) Ask 200 boys only

(D) Ask 200 students randomly by choosing names from the enrollment list

Data Analysis

97. Base your answer to the following question on the information below.

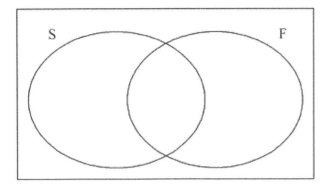

There are 97 students in the ninth grade at Klein Junior High. 23 do not participate in an intramural sport. Of the remaining students, 50 play soccer (S) and 46 play football (F). How many students play both soccer and football? Fill in the correct numbers in the Venn diagram above and explain your answer in the space below.

98. Midland Records opened a store, spending $6000 in start-up expenses. The store's total income and expenses for the first four months are plotted on the graph below.

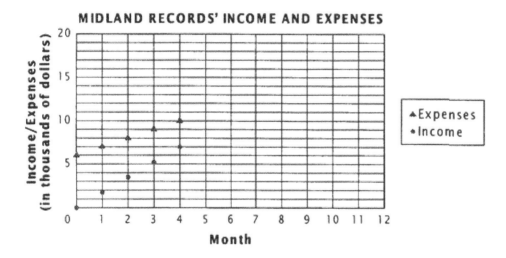

If the store's income and expenses continue to follow the pattern in the graph, during which month will Midland Records begin to make a profit (income will exceed expenses)?

(A) 4   (B) 6   (C) 8   (D) 10

Data Analysis

99. Base your answer to the following question on the following information and table.

For an assignment, Becki read 3 books. Each of the books were 300 pages long. The table below shows how many pages she read per day.

Day	Pages Read
1	51
2	48
3	53
4	47

Assuming Becki read at approximately a constant rate, estimate the time it took Becki to finish her reading assignment.

(A) 3 days (B) 6 days
(C) 12 days (D) 18 days

100. Base your answer to the following question on the following information.

Lincoln Middle School had a fundraiser in which students collected as many pennies as possible.

Grade 6

Week	Number of Pennies
1	1083
2	1180
3	1240

Grade 7

Week	Number of Pennies
1	1572
2	1303
3	1421

Grade 8

Week	Number of Pennies
1	1521
2	1102
3	1201

Without using a calculator, rank the grades from *lowest* to *highest* collection of pennies.

Probability

1. At a pet store, there are 7 breeds of dogs. There are also 4 types of collars for dogs. How many unique dog and collar combinations are possible?

   (A) 4 combinations (B) 7 combinations
   (C) 11 combinations (D) 28 combinations

2. Rob's father is driving Rob, Marc, and Lisa to the movies. Rob's father can go 2 different ways to Marc's house, 5 different ways from Marc's house to Lisa's house, and 2 different ways from Lisa's house to River Cinemas. How many different routes can Rob's father take in all?

   (A) 5   (B) 10   (C) 20   (D) 40

3. The student council at your school wants to sponsor a family skating night at a local roller rink. The skating night is going to be a fundraiser to help purchase new sports equipment for the school. The students have discussed how to encourage ticket sales so that there will be a good turnout for the event.

   They decide that each of the 5 student officers will call 5 eighth graders to tell them about the skating night. Each of those eighth graders will call 3 seventh graders. Assuming that no person is called more than once, how many seventh graders would be called?

   (A) 5   (B) 25   (C) 75   (D) 125

4. How many ways can a committee consisting of three different leveled positions be made from a group of 5 people?

   (A) 8   (B) 10   (C) 15   (D) 60

5. Jon is getting dressed. He is choosing between 4 shirts and 3 pants. How many different clothing combinations are possible with these clothes?

   (A) 3   (B) 4   (C) 7   (D) 12

6. Chef Roberto has prepared five main courses, six vegetables, and three desserts. A meal includes one main course, one vegetable, and one dessert. How many different dinners can he serve?

   (A) 14   (B) 30   (C) 90   (D) 120

7. Neil has a box of tea that contains 5 types of tea. Sometimes he puts sugar in his tea, and sometimes he doesn't. Sometimes he adds milk, and sometimes he doesn't. How many different combinations of tea, milk, and sugar are there?

   (A) 5   (B) 9   (C) 10   (D) 20

8. Fun Land has two very popular games on the midway. One of the games has 3 different prizes you can win and the other game has 5 different prizes. How many different combinations of one prize from each game could a player win?

   (A) 3   (B) 5   (C) 8   (D) 15

9. Since all of her students just passed the Math 8 exam, Mrs. Francis made gifts for her class. Each gift had a white **or** black box wrapped in red, blue **or** green wrapping paper, with a yellow, purple, orange, **or** lime colored card. No two gifts were the same. How many combinations could Mrs. Francis have made?

   Show your work.

Probability

10. What is the exact number of coins that can be tossed to obtain a total of 128 different possible outcomes?

    (A) 5   (B) 6   (C) 7   (D) 8

11. If the circle must be placed first, how many ways can the shapes be arranged in the rectangle?

    (A) 3   (B) 6   (C) 12   (D) 24

12. The local delicatessen in Mathland lets the customer order custom sandwiches. The customer can choose from turkey, ham, roast beef, or salami as meats. For breads, the customer can choose between white bread, wheat bread, or Italian bread. The different cheeses available are Swiss cheese, provolone cheese, or American cheese. How many different sandwich combinations are there to choose from if a customer must choose one of each meat, bread, and cheese?

    (A) 4   (B) 10   (C) 27   (D) 36

13. In Dave's Ice Cream Palace, you have 3 choices of ice cream: chocolate, vanilla, and strawberry. You have 4 choices of toppings: sprinkles, fudge, nuts, and caramel. You can also choose whether you want a cup or a cone. How many desserts can you make with 1 kind of ice cream, 1 kind of topping, and the way you want it served?

    (A) 9   (B) 12   (C) 24   (D) 48

14. Ashley, Kyle, Mark, and Josh are running a race. How many different ways could they finish the race?

    (A) 4   (B) 16   (C) 24   (D) 64

15. Mr. Anderson has 1 son and 3 daughters, and all of Mr. Anderson's children had 4 children. Mr. Anderson bought each of his grandchildren 4 dolls. How many dolls did he buy?

    (A) $4+4+4+4$ (B) $4+4+4+4+4$
    (C) 4^3 (D) 4^4

16. Jamal has 3 pairs of pants, 5 shirts, and 3 pairs of socks. How many different ways could he get dressed in the morning?

17. Whitney needs to buy 2 flavors of ice cream for her class party. If she has 8 different flavors to choose from, how many ways can she choose the 2 flavors of ice cream?

    (A) 16   (B) 28   (C) 56   (D) 60

161

Probability

18. The five finalists in the school talent show will present their acts during a school assembly. Ms. Kung will decide the order in which the five contestants will participate. How many ways can Ms. Kung arrange the five acts?

    (A) 5 ways (B) 25 ways
    (C) 60 ways (D) 120 ways

19. Ming has ten cards labeled 1 through 10. What are all of the combinations of two cards such that the sum of the numbers on the two cards is even?

20. Joey has a choice of 4 main courses, 6 side dishes, and 5 beverages. How many different meals can he make?

    (A) 120 (B) 240 (C) 360 (D) 720

21. There are 4 different icons on a computer desktop. How many different combinations can they be ordered in, assuming that they are in a straight line?

    (A) 8 (B) 12 (C) 16 (D) 24

22. In every painting in Joanne's house, there are five old women, each with three girls, each with two cats and two dogs. There are five paintings in Joanne's house. What is the total number of cats and dogs in all of Joanne's paintings?

    (A) (5)(3)(2) (B) 5(3)(2) + 2
    (C) $(5^2)(4)(3)$ (D) $(5^2)3(2)$

23. Base your answer to the following question on the following hamburger menu posted by a restaurant.

    Types of Hamburgers

Weight	Bun	Toppings
1/4	Plain	Pickles
1/3	Sesame	Onions
1/2		Cheese

    How many different hamburgers with one meat weight, one type of bun, and one topping can be made?

    Show your work.

Probability

24. The following is a sign hanging at a local delicatessen advertising a lunch special.

Sandwiches	Soups	Beverages
Ham	Chicken Noodle	Soda
Turkey	Split Pea	Juice
Cheese		Milk

How many different combinations of 1 sandwich, 1 soup, and 1 beverage are possible?

(A) 8 (B) 10 (C) 16 (D) 18

---

25. The owner of Main St. Delicatessen is planning to advertise the variety of sandwiches he sells. If there are 8 choices of meats, 5 choices of vegetables, and 6 choices of dressings, which of the following most accurately states how many sandwiches are possible containing one each of meats, vegetables and dressings?

(A) 19 combinations   (B) 45 combinations
(C) 120 combinations (D) 240 combinations

26. A restaurant offers 4 different main courses, 2 different salads, 6 different appetizers, 3 different desserts, and 5 different drinks. How many different meals consisting of 1 main course, 1 salad, 1 appetizer, 1 dessert, and 1 drink are offered?

(A) 20 (B) 84 (C) 144 (D) 720

27. Megan's parents are getting her a dog for her birthday. There are 3 types of dogs that they can get. There are 4 types of flea collars that they can buy. There are also 4 types of leashes that they can buy. How many unique ways can Megan's parents get one type of dog, one flea collar, and two leashes?

(A) 48 (B) 72 (C) 144 (D) 192

28. You go to a coffee shop where you are presented with many options. You can have Regular, Decaffeinated, or French Vanilla coffee. You can have it with or without sugar. Also, you can have it with whole milk, half and half, one percent milk, or no milk. How many different ways are possible to have your coffee?

(A) 9 (B) 18 (C) 20 (D) 24

29. There is a sale at the local sports store for the simultaneous purchase of a bat, a glove, and a hat. There are 4 types of bats, 5 types of gloves, and 3 types of hats. How many unique purchase combinations qualify for the sale?

(A) 12 (B) 15 (C) 20 (D) 60

30. Jamie has 4 shirts, 5 pairs of pants, and 5 pairs of shoes that she can make outfits out of. How many outfits consisting of 1 of each article of clothing can Jamie create?

(A) 14 (B) 15 (C) 75 (D) 100

Probability

31. John is eating at a restaurant that offers 4 different meals, 3 different drinks, and 5 types of dessert. How many ways can John eat one meal, one drink, and one dessert?

    (A) 12   (B) 15   (C) 20   (D) 60

32. On a family trip to London, the Smiths want to visit Buckingham Palace, Westminster Abbey, the Tower of London, and the British Museum. If they want to go visit these sites in any order, how many different combinations are possible?

    (A) 4   (B) 12   (C) 16   (D) 24

33. This menu is posted in the restaurant at the ski lodge.

    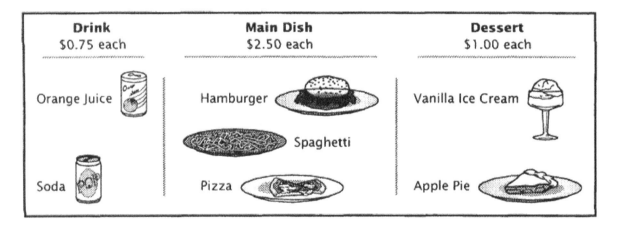

    How many lunch combinations are possible if Carl chooses one drink, one main dish, and one dessert?

    (A) 2   (B) 4   (C) 6   (D) 12

164

Probability

34. Michelle buys water in bulk. One bottle of water contains half a liter of water. One carton contains a dozen bottles of water. One box contains 5 cartons of water. If Michelle bought 7 boxes of water bottles, how many liters of water did she buy?

    (A) 35 liters   (B) 210 liters
    (C) 420 liters   (D) 168 liters

35. Manny has 4 different marbles. How many different combinations can they be arranged in, assuming they are lined up in a straight line.

    (A) 4   (B) 8   (C) 16   (D) 24

36. For a game, Justin must pick a colored card out of each of 2 bags without looking. There is one of each of red, orange, yellow, green, and blue cards in the first bag. There is one each of purple, turquoise, and gray cards in the second bag. How many different combinations of one card from each bag are possible?

    Show your work.

37. Calvin and Lorraine belong to a soccer league. There are eight teams and each team plays the other teams twice. How many total games are played?

    (A) 36   (B) 56   (C) 64   (D) 112

38. Martina is in an afterschool basketball league. There are 5 teams and each team plays the other teams twice. How many total games are played?

    (A) 10   (B) 15   (C) 20   (D) 40

39. Glenn wanted to order a hamburger. It can have ketchup, mustard, or nothing. It can also have cheese, bacon, both, or neither. How many different hamburgers can Glenn order? Show how you got your answer.

40. Nick is choosing a sandwich, a soft drink, and a dessert from a menu. The sandwich can have chicken, ham, or bacon. The soft drink is a choice between cola, orange soda pop, or root beer. For the dessert, Nick has a choice of ice cream or frozen yogurt.

    How many different meals can Nick have using one type of sandwich, one type of drink, and one type of dessert?

    (A) 8   (B) 12   (C) 18   (D) 27

41. Becky rolls a fair die. What is the probability that the number on top is even?

    (A) $\frac{1}{6}$ (B) $\frac{1}{3}$ (C) $\frac{1}{2}$ (D) $\frac{3}{4}$

42. Philip has a green marble, a red marble, a blue marble, and a yellow marble in a bag. Philip will select a single marble randomly and then put it back. If he does this three times, what is the probability that he will pick a blue marble all three times?

    (A) $\frac{1}{64}$ (B) $\frac{1}{24}$ (C) $\frac{1}{16}$ (D) $\frac{1}{4}$

Probability

43. Base your answer to the following question on the figure below.

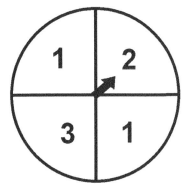

What is the probability of spinning a number spelled with three letters?

(A) $\frac{1}{4}$ (B) $\frac{1}{2}$ (C) $\frac{3}{4}$ (D) 1

44. There are yellow, blue, and red marbles in a box. If Greg takes a single marble out without looking, the probability that it will be yellow is $\frac{1}{2}$, the probability that it will be blue is $\frac{1}{4}$, and the probability that it will be red is $\frac{1}{4}$. What is the least number of marbles that can be in the box?

(A) 2 (B) 4 (C) 8 (D) 16

45. Matt surveyed his classmates about their favorite sports. He found that 3 out of every 5 of his classmates picked football as their favorite sport. Furthermore, 5 out of 6 of those classmates who picked football were boys. What is the probability that a classmate chosen at random is a girl whose favorite sport is football?

(A) 10% (B) 30% (C) 40% (D) 90%

46. Of the 14 songs on Chantal's new CD, 4 are her favorites. What is the probability that a randomly selected song will be one of her favorites?

(A) $\frac{3}{14}$ (B) $\frac{11}{14}$ (C) $\frac{2}{7}$ (D) $\frac{1}{7}$

47. There are 7 green peppers, 9 red peppers, and 14 orange peppers in a bag. What is the probability that a red pepper will be picked at random?

(A) $\frac{9}{29}$ (B) $\frac{21}{30}$ (C) $\frac{3}{10}$ (D) $\frac{9}{10}$

48. Phil has a bag of gum balls containing 8 blue gum balls and 2 yellow gum balls. What is the probability of him choosing a blue gum ball at random, keeping it, and then choosing a yellow gum ball?

(A) $\frac{4}{25}$ (B) $\frac{8}{45}$ (C) $\frac{1}{2}$ (D) $\frac{48}{90}$

49. 70% of the cars owned by John's Car Rentals have a standard transmission and 30% of the cars are blue. What is the probability that a randomly selected car will not have a standard transmission and not be blue?

(A) $\frac{21}{100}$ (B) $\frac{40}{100}$ (C) $\frac{79}{100}$ (D) $\frac{80}{100}$

50. Clarisse is playing a game that utilizes a coin and a deck of cards. Each move in the game is determined by the result of the coin toss and the suit the player pulls from the deck at random. What is the probability that Clarisse flips "heads" and pulls a spade?

(A) $\frac{1}{8}$ (B) $\frac{1}{4}$ (C) $\frac{1}{2}$ (D) $\frac{3}{4}$

51. The probability of an event happening is 39 out of 65. What is the probability of the event not happening?

(A) $\frac{26}{65}$ (B) $\frac{39}{65}$ (C) 1 (D) $\frac{65}{39}$

Probability

52. If Matt, Phil, Annie and Zoe are sitting at a circular table, then what is the probability that Phil and Zoe are not sitting next to each other?

    (A) $\frac{2}{3}$ (B) $\frac{1}{4}$ (C) $\frac{1}{3}$ (D) $\frac{1}{2}$

53. Ben's 8th grade math teacher gave him a probability assignment to do. The assignment asked what the probability is for rolling a 7 or a double with a pair of dice. If she gave him a hint that there are 36 total possible rolls for a pair of dice, what should Ben's answer be?

    (A) $\frac{1}{6}$ (B) $\frac{1}{3}$ (C) $\frac{1}{2}$ (D) $\frac{2}{3}$

54. Josie has a bag with 18 marbles. The bag contains red, blue, and green marbles. If the probability of picking a red marble is $\frac{1}{2}$, and the probability of picking a blue marble is $\frac{1}{3}$, how many green marbles are in the bag?

    (A) 2   (B) 3   (C) 5   (D) 6

55. Mike plays each week at a tennis club. Data from his first 200 serves were recorded.

Serve	Number of times
Ace	14
Double Fault	32
IN	154

    What is the probability, based on this data, that Mike's serve will be an ace?

    (A) 3%   (B) 7%   (C) 14%   (D) 61%

56. The table below shows the number, color, and gender of puppies at Selma's pet shop.

Color	Male	Female
Black	4	6
Brown	6	2
Gray	3	1
White	2	1
Blond	3	2

    What is the probability of selecting a gray male at random?

    (A) 0.1   (B) 0.25   (C) 0.33   (D) 0.4

57. John rolls a fair die and flips a coin. What is the probability of rolling a prime number and flipping heads?

    (A) $\frac{1}{4}$ (B) $\frac{1}{3}$ (C) $\frac{1}{2}$ (D) $\frac{2}{3}$

58. Vincent has a bag containing 8 green, 2 blue, 6 red, 4 yellow, and 8 white marbles. What is the probability of randomly choosing a green marble on the first pick, replacing it, and then randomly choosing a blue marble on the second pick?

    (A) $\frac{1}{49}$ (B) $\frac{4}{189}$ (C) $\frac{1}{14}$ (D) $\frac{68}{189}$

59. Once a month, Ms. Stevens selects one name out of a hat to win a free video tape. There are 15 girls' and 20 boys' names in the box. What is the probably that a girl will be selected?

    (A) $\frac{3}{7}$ (B) $\frac{4}{7}$ (C) $\frac{3}{4}$ (D) $\frac{4}{3}$

Probability

60. Which of the following numbers *cannot* be used to express a probability?

    (A) 0   (B) $\frac{1}{10}$

    (C) 70%   (D) 110%

61. A cooler has 5 diet soda and 10 regular soda. One soda is chosen at random from the cooler and removed. Then, another soda is chosen at random from the cooler.

    What is the probability that a diet soda will be pulled out first, followed by a regular soda?

    (A) $\frac{3}{24}$ (B) $\frac{5}{21}$ (C) $\frac{2}{9}$ (D) $\frac{14}{27}$

62. Bob has 16 equally sized marbles in a bag. The table below shows the number of each marble color in the bag.

    Bob's Marbles

Color	Number
Red	6
Blue	8
Green	2

    What is the probability that if Bob randomly selects one marble from the bag it will be red?

    (A) $\frac{3}{8}$ (B) $\frac{5}{2}$ (C) $\frac{5}{8}$ (D) $\frac{7}{8}$

63. In Kelly's refrigerator, there are several small cartons of juice: 4 apple, 3 orange, 2 cranberry, and 2 grapefruit. Kelly selects a carton of juice without looking. What is the probability that she will select an orange juice?

    (A) $\frac{1}{11}$ (B) $\frac{1}{8}$ (C) $\frac{3}{11}$ (D) $\frac{3}{8}$

64. What is the probability of rolling an odd prime with a single die?

    (A) $\frac{1}{6}$ (B) $\frac{1}{3}$ (C) $\frac{1}{2}$ (D) $\frac{2}{3}$

65. Stewart has 50 marbles in a bag. There are 20 red, 14 blue, and 16 black marbles. What is the approximate probability that he will pick out 2 red marbles in a row, assuming he picks out one at a time and with no replacement?

    (A) 10%   (B) 16%   (C) 23%   (D) 32%

66. Tyler is doing a probability experiment. He has a standard 52 card deck. Tyler first shuffles the cards, draws a card, records the suit, and then replaces the card and shuffles the deck. He does this 40 times. Below is a table with his results.

    Cards Drawn At Random

Suit	Number of Times Drawn
Diamonds	8
Clubs	14
Hearts	6
Spades	12

    What are the theoretical and experimental probabilities that, on the next draw, Tyler will draw a club?

    (A) Theoretical probability = 35%
        Experimental probability = 8.75%
    (B) Theoretical probability = 35%
        Experimental probability = 25%
    (C) Theoretical probability = 25%
        Experimental probability = 35%
    (D) Theoretical probability = 35%
        Experimental probability = 8.75%

Probability

67. Marcus is taking a 5 question long true/false exam. If Marcus did not understand the material and guessed each answer randomly, what is the probability that he would get 100% on the test?

    (A) $\frac{1}{8}$ (B) $\frac{1}{10}$ (C) $\frac{1}{16}$ (D) $\frac{1}{32}$

68. There are 19 sixth graders, 31 seventh graders, and 30 eight graders that work on the school newspaper. What is the probability that a randomly chosen newspaper worker is a sixth grader? Show all work needed to reach the answer.

69. Neil flipped a coin 8 times. What is the probability that he got 8 heads?

    (A) $\frac{1}{256}$ (B) $\frac{1}{128}$ (C) $\frac{1}{64}$ (D) 1

70. Jim is building a game for his school carnival where students can spin a wheel and win a prize. The spinner has 8 sections.

    If he wants there to be a 50% chance of winning a small prize, a 37.5% chance of winning a medium prize, and a 12.5% chance of winning a big prize, how many sections should be colored for winning a big prize?

    (A) 1 (B) 2 (C) 3 (D) 4

71. The probability that it will snow this week is 75%. Which of the following could simulate the days it will snow?

    (A) Spin a spinner that has 4 equal pieces. Let pieces 1, 2, and 3 represent snow.
    (B) Roll a number cube numbered 1 through 6. Let all even numbers represent snow.
    (C) Roll a number cube number 1 through 6. Let numbers 3 and 6 represent snow.
    (D) Flip a coin 20 times. Let tails represent snow.

72. Two fair dice are rolled. Which is most likely to happen?

    (A) The sum is 1. (B) The sum is 7.
    (C) The sum is 9. (D) The sum is 12.

73. What is the probability that a spin will result in a vowel?

    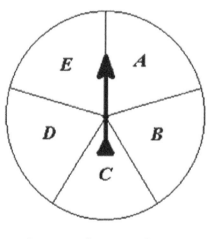

    (A) $\frac{1}{5}$ (B) $\frac{2}{5}$ (C) $\frac{1}{4}$ (D) $\frac{1}{2}$

Probability

74. Each spinner below is divided into three equal parts. The numbers obtained from spinning the two arrows once are multiplied. For example, the spin shown on the spinners below would result in 2 × 6 = 12, or an even answer. If you spin both arrows once and then multiply the numbers that each of the pointers land on, what is the probability that the product will be an odd number?

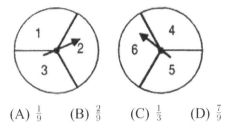

(A) $\frac{1}{9}$ (B) $\frac{2}{9}$ (C) $\frac{1}{3}$ (D) $\frac{7}{9}$

75. The football team needs to choose a captain. The team consists of 16 defensive players, 18 offensive players, and 6 special team players. If the captain is chosen at random, what is the probability the captain is a special team player?

(A) $\frac{3}{20}$ (B) $\frac{3}{8}$ (C) $\frac{3}{17}$ (D) $\frac{1}{3}$

76. Use the tree diagram below to answer the question.

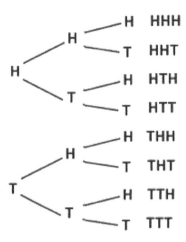

Determine the probability of flipping three coins and getting two tails and 1 heads.

77. According to the diagram, what is the probability of spinning, and getting an even number?

(A) $\frac{1}{4}$ (B) $\frac{1}{2}$ (C) $\frac{3}{4}$ (D) 1

78. Robert has a bag filled with 5 vanilla candies and 7 chocolate candies. He reaches in and eats one candy at random, and then reaches in again and eats that candy. What is the probability that he will eat two chocolate candies?

(A) $\frac{14}{24}$ (B) $\frac{42}{132}$ (C) $\frac{7}{22}$ (D) $\frac{7}{12}$

Probability

79. Sarah played a game by rolling a fair die and flipping a coin. She decided that if she got heads, she would subtract 1 from the number she rolled, and if she got tails, she would add 1 to the number.

    What are the odds of Sarah getting a 3 after the computation?

    (A) $\frac{1}{2}$ (B) $\frac{1}{4}$ (C) $\frac{1}{6}$ (D) $\frac{1}{12}$

80. Randy is playing a spinner game at a carnival.

    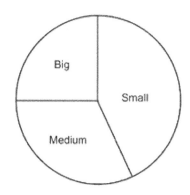

    What is the probability of winning the big prize?

    (A) 25%   (B) 33%   (C) 50%   (D) 67%

81. What is the probability of rolling an even number or the number 1 in one roll of a fair die?

    (A) $\frac{1}{12}$ (B) $\frac{1}{6}$ (C) $\frac{1}{3}$ (D) $\frac{2}{3}$

82. Jill usually makes 3 free throws out of every 5 attempts. To simulate her free throws, Jack puts 25 marbles in a bag. He uses red marbles to simulate "making a free throw" and blue marbles for a miss. How many blue marbles will Jack use?

    (A) 2   (B) 3   (C) 5   (D) 10

83. Two fair dice are rolled. Which is least likely to happen?

    (A) The sum is 1.   (B) The sum is 7.
    (C) The sum is 9.   (D) The sum is 12.

84. Use the chart below to answer the following question.

    Number of Band Members

	Grade 6	Grade 7	Grade 8
Number	18	26	42

    A band member is chosen at random to represent the band at a parent–teacher meeting. Which is the best estimate of the probability that an eighth grader will be chosen?

    (A) 33%   (B) 50%   (C) 67%   (D) 85%

85. The following table shows the results of an experiment involving colored marbles, taken with replacement.

Color	Number of Times Picked
Purple	6
Blue	5
Green	4
Yellow	6
Orange	2

    Which of the following is a valid conclusion?

    (A) There must be at least 2 orange marbles.
    (B) There are probably more green marbles than any other color.
    (C) There is a greater probability of pulling a blue marble than a green one.
    (D) There are the same number of purple and yellow marbles.

Probability

86. Edward has a bag full of 6 red, 3 green, and 17 black marbles. If he reaches in and pulls out one at random, what is the probability that it will be green?

    (A) $\frac{1}{2}$ (B) $\frac{3}{26}$ (C) $\frac{17}{9}$ (D) $\frac{17}{26}$

87. In a room with 400 people, can at least 2 of the people have the same birthday?

    (A) definitely
    (B) probably
    (C) probably not
    (D) There is no way to tell.

88. Aliza tossed three coins. What is the probability that she will toss one head and two tails?

    (A) 0   (B) $\frac{1}{4}$ (C) $\frac{3}{8}$ (D) $\frac{2}{3}$

89. What is the probability of winning a strictly chance game with three other people if everyone has an equal chance of winning?

    (A) $\frac{1}{4}$ (B) $\frac{1}{3}$ (C) $\frac{1}{2}$ (D) $\frac{3}{4}$

90. During a game, Steven was asked to pick a colored 6–sided die out of a hat without looking and then roll it. The dice were blue, purple, or black and each has 6 sides, each with a different number between 1 and 6. There was an equal number of each color die. What is the probability that Steven randomly picked a black die and then rolled a 5?

    (A) $\frac{1}{3}$ (B) $\frac{1}{6}$ (C) $\frac{1}{9}$ (D) $\frac{1}{18}$

91. Joe has a bag of marbles that contains 4 green marbles, 3 black marbles, 16 blue marbles, 2 yellow marbles, and 4 white marbles. What is the probability that Joe takes a white marble out of the bag?

    (A) $\frac{2}{29}$ (B) $\frac{3}{29}$ (C) $\frac{4}{29}$ (D) $\frac{5}{29}$

92. Bethany has a large box containing 250 animal crackers. She randomly chooses 15 animal crackers and 3 of them are lions. Based on this ratio, of the original 250 animal crackers, how many lions should she expect to find?

    (A) 36   (B) 40   (C) 45   (D) 50

93. A cube whose sides were numbered 1 to 6 was rolled once. What was the probability that the number rolled was a factor of 49?

    (A) $\frac{1}{6}$ (B) $\frac{1}{3}$ (C) $\frac{1}{2}$ (D) $\frac{5}{6}$

94. Once a week, Mr. Stevens picks a name out of a hat to win a free pencil. If there are 20 girls and 10 boys, what is the probability that a girl will win?

    (A) $\frac{1}{3}$ (B) $\frac{1}{2}$ (C) $\frac{2}{3}$ (D) 2

Probability

95. The game Jim is playing has him spin the spinner shown below. He spins once.

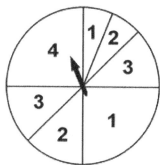

What is the probability he spins a 4?

(A) $\frac{1}{5}$ (B) $\frac{1}{4}$ (C) $\frac{2}{5}$ (D) $\frac{2}{3}$

96. Base your answer to the following question on the following information.

Igor asks his friend Matilda to choose a card from a deck of cards and place it on the table. He then asks her to choose a second card.

What is the probability that the second card has the same face value as the first card?

(A) $\frac{1}{51}$ (B) $\frac{1}{12}$ (C) $\frac{3}{51}$ (D) $\frac{3}{12}$

97. Base your answer to the following question on the following information

Forty people went to the movies. 30 had blonde hair and the other 10 had red hair.

One person is selected at random from the group, what is the probability he/she will have blonde hair?

(A) $\frac{1}{4}$ (B) $\frac{1}{3}$ (C) $\frac{1}{2}$ (D) $\frac{3}{4}$

98. Rose has a bag with 25 blue jelly beans, 75 white jelly beans, and 65 red jelly beans. What is the probability she will pick a blue and then a white jelly bean?

(A) $\frac{1875}{27060}$ (B) $\frac{1975}{27060}$ (C) $\frac{104}{169}$ (D) $\frac{79}{169}$

99. Base your answer to the following question on the following information.

Donald is playing a game where he rolls two fair, six-sided dice.

What is the probability that he rolls a sum of 7?

(A) $\frac{12}{36}$ (B) $\frac{7}{36}$ (C) $\frac{6}{36}$ (D) $\frac{18}{36}$

100. There are 8 red marbles and 6 blue marbles in a bag. What is the probability of picking one red marble and then, without replacing it in the bag, picking a blue marble?

(A) $\frac{14}{182}$ (B) $\frac{48}{182}$ (C) $\frac{14}{48}$ (D) $\frac{2}{48}$

Statistics, Functions and Patterns

1. Four samples of a product are taken from the production line every two hours and weighed to ensure conformance with the product's specifications. The table below shows the results of the samples taken on a particular day.

   SAMPLE RESULTS (in ounces)

9:00 A.M.	11:00 A.M.	1:00 P.M.	3:00 P.M.
15.93	15.89	15.94	15.91
15.97	15.93	15.93	15.94
15.85	15.96	15.92	15.92
15.91	15.89	15.94	15.92

   Which time had samples with a mean closest to the specification weight of 15.93 ounces?

   (A) 9:00 A.M. (B) 11:00 A.M. (C) 1:00 P.M. (D) 3:00 P.M.

2. The table below shows the number of miles Gary walked in a week.

Day	# of Miles
Monday	11
Tuesday	9
Wednesday	4
Thursday	15
Friday	0

   What is the mean distance that Gary walked?

   (A) 7.8 (B) 7.6 (C) 8 (D) 7.4

3. Base your answer to the following question on the chart below, which displays the measurements Sumayah made of each day's temperature.

   TEMPERATURE MEASUREMENTS

Day	Temperature °F
Monday	70.58
Tuesday	68.93
Wednesday	71.44
Thursday	74.05

   What is the median temperature, in degrees Fahrenheit, for the 4 days shown?

   Show your work.

Statistics, Functions and Patterns

4. Base your answer to the following question on the following information.

   Mrs. Fox gave a math test to her eighth grade class. The grades are shown below.

   92, 83, 90, 96, 81, 84, 90, 80, 87

   What is the mean (average) of the grades on the math test?

   (A) 83   (B) 84   (C) 90   (D) 87

5. The list below shows the grades students received in English class last semester.

   69, 79, 81, 83, 84, 87, 87, 87, 90, 92, 96, 97, 99

   Based on the information provided above, which of the following is *not* a true statement?

   (A) The median grade was 87.
   (B) The mean grade is 87.
   (C) The mode grade is 87.
   (D) The range of the scores is 87.

Statistics, Functions and Patterns

6. Base your answer to the following question on the graph below, which displays the number of cousins that each of the eighth-grade students surveyed has.

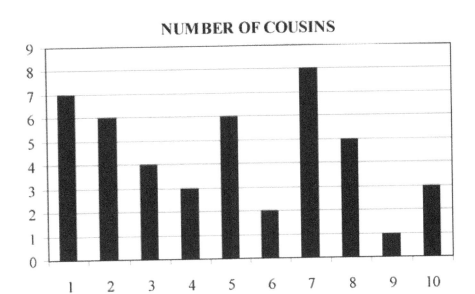

What is the median number of cousins?

Show your work.

---

7. A survey is conducted to find the most popular sport among students in the eighth grade at a school. Which of the following sampling methods would give the most accurate results?

   (A) Choose every eighth–grade teacher and parent.
   (B) Choose every third student in an alphabetical list of eighth–grade boys.
   (C) Choose every third student in an alphabetical list of eighth–grade students.
   (D) Choose every eighth–grade student athlete.

8. Eric earned $17, $18, and $23 for 3 weeks of chores. How much must he earn in the fourth week to average (mean) $20 for the 4-week period?

   (A) $4   (B) $20   (C) $22   (D) $23

9. Misty drove 38, 42, 51, and 49 miles on each of four days. She traveled 9 miles for every gallon of gasoline that she used. On average, how much gas did she use each day?

   (A) 3 gallons   (B) 5 gallons
   (C) 15 gallons (D) 25 gallons

10. In this set of data,

    4, 7, 1, 4, 9, 7, 3, 7,

    7 represents which of the following measures of data?

    (A) mean   (B) median
    (C) mode   (D) range

Statistics, Functions and Patterns

11. Halvey calculated the mean of four numbers to be 33. Then, he found that he had made an error by writing 40 for one of the numbers when it should have been 32. What is the mean of the correct four numbers?

    (A) 30   (B) 31   (C) 32   (D) 32.5

12. Currently, your grades this term are as follows:

    85, 89, 96, 86.

    What is the lowest grade you can get on the final quiz in order to have a final average (mean) of at least 90?

    (A) 93   (B) 94   (C) 95   (D) 96

13. Base your answer to the following question on the following information.

    The Eighth Grade Student Government is planning a spring dance. They are trying to estimate how many students will come to the dance based on the attendance at past dances. The table below shows the number of students who attended dances the previous 5 years.

Year	# of Students
1998	41
1999	136
2000	140
2001	126
2002	137

    Should the Student Government base their plans on the median or the mean? Justify your answer in the space below.

14. Scott earned $15.50, $21.50, and $24 for 3 weeks of labor. How much must he earn in the next week to average (mean) $24 for the 4 week period?

    (A) $22   (B) $24   (C) $26   (D) $35

15. Base your answer to the following question on the table below showing the distances that Joe ran over 5 days.

Day	Distance
Monday	20 miles
Tuesday	23 miles
Wednesday	16 miles
Thursday	21 miles
Friday	15 miles

    Find the median distance that Joe ran over the 5 days shown.

    (A) 17 miles   (B) 18 miles
    (C) 19 miles   (D) 20 miles

16. Marco hit 56, 61, 65, and 66 home runs in each of the past four years, respectively. What was the average (mean) of his home runs?

    (A) 61   (B) 62   (C) 248   (D) 63.5

Statistics, Functions and Patterns

Base your answers to questions **17** through **19** on the following table that shows the heights of several kids in a class.

Kid	Height
Dave	6'4"
Keith	6'
Mike	5'10"
Brandon	5'9"
Jon	5'9"
Josh	4'11"
Jeff	4'6"

17. What is the median?

    (A) 4'6" (B) 5'7" (C) 5'9" (D) 6'4"

18. What is the mode?

    (A) 4'6" (B) 5'7" (C) 5'9" (D) 6'4"

19. What is the mean height?

    (A) 5'3" (B) 5'5" (C) 5'7" (D) 5'9"

---

20. A certain cargo airplane can carry up to 1,200 pounds of cargo. If it is filled to its maximum weight capacity with 48 boxes, what is the mean (average) weight of each box?

    (A) 120 pounds (B) 60 pounds
    (C) 25 pounds   (D) 48 pounds

21. Billy has taken 4 out of 6 tests for this semester, and desires at least a 90 on his report card. His test scores so far are 91, 83, 85, and 93. What must his average (mean) score be on the next two tests in order to have an average of at least 90?

    (A) 93 (B) 94 (C) 95 (D) 96

22. Jane applied for a secretary job, and she wanted to know how fast she can type. She calculated her mean words per minute every day for a week as shown in the table below.

    Day Words per Minute
    Wednesday 60.44
    Thursday 54.86
    Friday 58.97
    Saturday 60.04
    Sunday 63.90
    Monday 59.87
    Tuesday 61.23

    What is Jane's median typing speed for the week?

    (A) 58.97   (B) 59.90
    (C) 60.04   (D) 60.44

23. Billy's grades so far this term are as follows:

    96, 90, 94, 88.

    What is the lowest grade he can get on his final quiz to keep his final average (mean) of at least 90?

    (A) 78 (B) 80 (C) 82 (D) 84

24. A group of three students has an average age of 14. When their teacher joins the group, the average age is 25. What is the age of the teacher?

    (A) 45 (B) 50 (C) 58 (D) 60

25. Carmen got 87, 95, 95, and 91 on her four math tests. What is her average?

    (A) 90 (B) 92 (C) 93.5 (D) 95

Statistics, Functions and Patterns

26. What is the average (mean) of 3, 9, 13, and 43?

    (A) 11.5 (B) 17   (C) 21   (D) 25

27. Six samples have been taken from the production line every hour and weighed to ensure conformance with the product's specifications. The table below shows the result of the samples taken on a particular day.

    Sample Results (in ounces)

8:00 A.M.	9:00 A.M.	10:00 P.M.
11.92	12.5	11.5
11.96	11.5	11.7
11.93	12.0	11.6
11.95	12.2	11.5
11.96	11.9	11.4
11.2	11.7	11.8

    Which time had samples with a mean closest to the specification weight of 11.82 ounces?

    (A) 8 A.M.
    (B) 9 A.M.
    (C) 10 A.M.
    (D) None of the above

28. The ages of puppies in a pet store front window are as following: 8 weeks, 12 weeks, 4 weeks, 15 weeks, 18 weeks, and 10 weeks. The mean (average) age is closest to

    (A) 10 weeks.   (B) 11 weeks.
    (C) 12 weeks.   (D) 13 weeks.

29. The past four years, Jake hit 210, 205, 265, and 294 hits, respectively. What was the average (mean) of Jake's hits?

    (A) 243   (B) 243.5
    (C) 244   (D) 245

30. A survey is conducted to find the least popular food among eighth–grade students at Harborview Middle School. Which of the following sampling methods would be the most accurate?

    (A) Choose every fourth student who enters the cafeteria one day.
    (B) Choose every eighth–grade teacher and parent.
    (C) Choose every fourth student in an alphabetical list of every eighth–grade girl.
    (D) Choose every fourth student in an alphabetical list of every eighth–grade student.

Statistics, Functions and Patterns

Base your answers to questions **31** and **32** on the graph below, which displays the scores of all eighth-grade students on a recent math exam.

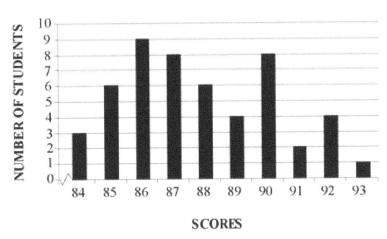

31. What is the median score?

    Show your work.

32. What is the mean score? Round to the *nearest whole number*.

    Show your work.

Base your answers to questions **33** and **34** on the grades on a test, which were 99, 96, 94, 89, 85, 82, 82, 81, 75, 73, 69, 54, 33, 21, and 2.

33. What is the median of the grades?

    (A) 2   (B) 69   (C) 75   (D) 81

34. What is the average (mean) of the grades?

    (A) 2   (B) 69   (C) 81   (D) 82

Statistics, Functions and Patterns

35. Base your answer to the following question on the chart below, which displays the number of calories in 6 cereals contains.

CALORIES IN CEREAL

Cereal	Calories
A	92.54
B	332.93
C	112.66
D	118.51
E	180.71
F	117.2

What is the median amount of calories for the 6 cereals shown?

Show your work.

36. Mike has an average (mean) of 84 on his first four tests of this semester. What grade must he get on his fifth test in order to bring his average up two points?

    (A) 69 (B) 84 (C) 86 (D) 94

37. The chart below shows the lengths of Mary's fingers.

Right	Left
3.0"	3.1"
3.2"	3.2"
3.0"	2.9"
2.5"	2.7"

What is the mean of the length of Mary's fingers?

(A) 2.91" (B) 2.93"
(C) 2.95" (D) 2.98"

38. 4, 9, 16, 9, 10, 3, 7

Which is the largest of the following for this data?

(A) Mean   (B) Median
(C) Mode   (D) Range

39. Noel bought 2.4 pounds of apples, 6.8 pounds of potatoes, and 3.6 pounds of chicken. Which is the closest to the mean weight of the items purchased?

(A) 13 pounds   (B) 10 pounds
(C) 5 pounds   (D) 4 pounds

40. Dan has test scores of 85, 89, 72, 80, and 85 in his math class. If he wants to bring his average up to an 85, what is the minimum test score that he needs on his next test?

(A) 95 (B) 97 (C) 99 (D) 100

Statistics, Functions and Patterns

41. Base your answer to the following question on the table below.

    A real estate agent surveyed the market values on 5 houses in a city block as listed below:

House A:	$ 73,000
House B:	$100,000
House C:	$ 50,000
House D:	$ 62,000
House E:	$ 65,000

    Find the mean (average) market value of the houses listed.

    (A) $50,000 (B) $65,000 (C) $70,000 (D) $80.000

42. Base your answer to the following question on the table below that shows the number of hours worked by the employees of a small company.

Employee	Hours
Jane	15
John	13
Alex	17
Chris	18
David	24
Julia	14
Lisa	18

    What was the mode of the number of hours worked?

    (A) 15 hours (B) 17 hours
    (C) 18 hours (D) 24 hours

43. Stacie drove at the speed of 30 miles per hour for 30 minutes, 50 miles per hour for 20 minutes, and 40 miles per hour for 10 minutes. What was her mean (average) speed?

    (A) 12.3 mph (B) 20.0 mph
    (C) 38.3 mph (D) 40 mph

44. Base your answer to the following question on the following table that shows the amount of time Allison has practiced her flute this week.

Day	Practice
Monday	2 hours
Tuesday	4 hours
Wednesday	1.5 hours
Thursday	3 hours
Friday	1 hour
Saturday	2 hours
Sunday	?

    What is the mean (average) amount of time that she practiced over the six days shown?

    (A) 1.25 hours (B) 2.20 hours
    (C) 2.25 hours (D) 1.65 hours

45. Mark hit 19, 28, and 25 home runs during the past 3 years, respectively. What was his average (mean) number of home runs for the 3 years?

    (A) 22 (B) 23 (C) 24 (D) 25

Statistics, Functions and Patterns

46. A student has an average (mean) score of 85 on three tests. On his fourth and final test, he received a grade of 92. What is his new average, rounded to the nearest whole number?

    (A) 85   (B) 86   (C) 87   (D) 88

47. The mean (average) of 4 numbers is 30. Maxim added the number 20 to the list of numbers and then recalculated the mean. What is the new mean?

    (A) 20   (B) 22   (C) 28   (D) 30

48. Base your answer to the following question on the grades of 10 students on a science test are listed below.

    Grades
    100 85
    95   85
    90   85
    90   80
    87   65

    What is the median of these grades?

    (A) 85   (B) 86   (C) 87   (D) 90

49. 4 students told each other what their scores were on a math test. 3 of the scores are shown below:

    74, 89, 85

    If the median score was 87, what could the fourth student's score be?

    (A) 90   (B) 87   (C) 83   (D) 70

50. John had 106, 203, and 171 hits the past three years, respectively. What was his average (mean) number of hits for the 3 years?

    (A) 160   (B) 170   (C) 477   (D) 480

51. What is the range of the following data?

    60, 93, 38, 26, 30, 123
    19, 39, 39, 72, 84, 73

    (A) 39   (B) 105   (C) 104   (D) 123

52. Fern forest is pictured below.

    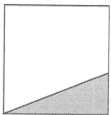

    The area that is shaded has 24 fern trees on it. If fern trees are evenly distributed throughout Fern Forest, what is the most reasonable estimate for the number of fern trees in the whole forest?

    (A) 30 – 90   (B) 90 – 150
    (C) 150 – 210   (D) 210 – 270

53. Diane wrote a set of a three numbers. The mean of the set is 10 and the range of the set is 15.

    Which of the following could be Diane's set of numbers?

    (A) {4, 10, 16}   (B) {5, 8, 20}
    (C) {3, 6, 21}   (D) {3, 9, 18}

Statistics, Functions and Patterns

54. The highest point in the United States is the peak of Mount McKinley, Alaska at 20,320 feet (above sea level). The lowest point is the bottom of Death Valley, California at –282 feet (below sea level). What is the range between the highest and lowest points in the U.S.?

    Show your work.

55. Jenna's test grades in math were 75, 91, 98, 84, and 92. What is the range of her scores?

    (A) 14   (B) 23   (C) 75   (D) 98

56. Two numbers are missing in the number pattern below.

    $\frac{-1}{27}, \frac{1}{9}, \frac{-1}{3}, \_\_\_, -3, \_\_\_, -27$

    Which two numbers are missing?

    (A) 1 and 9   (B) 1 and –9
    (C) –1 and 9   (D) –1 and –9

57. What is the sum of the first 10 terms of the following sequence?

    2, 0, 1, –2, 0, –1, 2, 0, 1, –2, 0, –1...

    (A) –2   (B) –1   (C) 0   (D) 1

58. Mark had 16 baseball cards in his collection. He traded half of them to his friend and received 2 cards back for every 1 he traded. How many cards does Mark have now?

    (A) 8   (B) 16   (C) 24   (D) 32

59. Which number x fits the following pattern?

    10, 11, x, 16, 20

    (A) 12   (B) 13   (C) 14   (D) 15

60. Use the number pattern below.

    $\frac{-1}{3}, \frac{1}{9}, \frac{-1}{27}, \frac{1}{81}, \frac{-1}{243}, \_\_\_, \_\_\_$

    What two numbers are missing?

    (A) $\frac{1}{2187}, \frac{1}{729}$ (B) $\frac{1}{729}, \frac{-1}{2187}$
    (C) $\frac{1}{91}, \frac{-1}{247}$ (D) $\frac{-1}{69}, \frac{-1}{2197}$

61. What number will complete this number sequence?

    2, 5, 12, 27, __

    (A) 46   (B) 47   (C) 57   (D) 58

62. A runner ran a marathon to earn money for a charity event. She earned donations based on the chart below.

Miles	0.1	0.2	0.3	0.4
Donation	$10	$20	$30	$40

    If the runner ran 22.6 miles, how much would she earn in donations?

    (A) $52.70   (B) $226.00
    (C) $1260.00   (D) $2260.00

Statistics, Functions and Patterns

63. Arthur performed an experiment to see how a ball bounces. After a few trials, he saw that every time the ball bounces, it bounces back up to $\frac{1}{5}$ its original height. If Arthur dropped the ball from an initial height of 100 feet, about how high will the ball be after 2 bounces?

    (A) .8 feet (B) 4 feet
    (C) 20 feet (D) 100 feet

64. The first five numbers in a series are listed below.

    3, 9, 7, 21, 19

    Based on the pattern indicated, what is the next number in this series?

    (A) 17   (B) 25   (C) 35   (D) 57

65. Summer is practicing the mile run for a track meet. The table below shows her mile times over 4 days.

Day	Time
Monday	6:54
Tuesday	6:38
Wednesday	6:22
Thursday	6:06
Friday	?

    If this pattern continues, what will be her mile time on Friday?

    (A) 6:00   (B) 5:50   (C) 5:30   (D) 5:40

66. The arrows below form a pattern.

    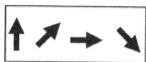

    Which of the arrows below comes next in the pattern?

    (A) ↓   (B) ↙
    (C) ←   (D) ↖

67. Abigail is making triangles out of craft sticks. She needs three sticks to make one triangle, 5 sticks to make a row of two triangles, and 7 sticks to make a row of three triangles.

    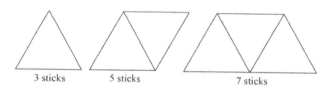

    3 sticks   5 sticks   7 sticks

    How many sticks will Abigail need to make a row of seven triangles?

    (A) 15   (B) 13   (C) 11   (D) 9

68. How many stars and moons altogether will be in the repeating pattern shown below if there are 45 shapes in the pattern? Show all work.

    SMPMP
    S = Star, M = Moon, P = Planet

Statistics, Functions and Patterns

69. Base your answer to the following question on the geometric pattern below.

    ⬠ ○ ○ ⬡ △ △ ⬠ ○ ○ ⬡ △ △ ...

    If the pattern continues, what will be the 16th shape in the pattern?

    (A) ⬠ (B) ⬡ (C) ○ (D) △

70. A segment having its endpoints on a circle is called a chord. If there are 2 points on a circle, 1 chord can be drawn. If there are 3 points on a circle, 3 chords can be drawn. If there are 4 points on a circle, 6 chords can be drawn. How many chords can be drawn from 6 points?

    (A) 5 (B) 10 (C) 15 (D) 20

71. What is next in this pattern? Why?

    Base your answers to questions **72** through **74** on the pattern below that Sean is working with:

    3, 9, 27, 81, ___

72. Does the following number pattern obey the same rule as the one above? Explain why or why not.

    2, 4, 8, 16, 32

73. On the space below, describe the pattern rule you used to find the correct answer to the previous question.

74. According to the pattern, which number would come next?

    _____

75. A segment having its endpoints on a circle is called a chord. If there are 2 points on a circle, 1 chord can be drawn. If there are 3 points on a circle, 3 chords can be drawn. If there are 4 points on a circle, 6 chords can be drawn. How many chords can be drawn from 5 points?

    (A) 5 (B) 10 (C) 15 (D) 20

76. What comes next in the following pattern?

    $a, b, ab, ab^2, a^2b^3, a^3b^5$

    (A) a^4b^6 (B) a^5b^6 (C) a^5b^8 (D) a^7b^6

77. What is the next term in this sequence?

    $x, x+y, x+2y, x+3y, x+4y$

    (A) $x + 5y$ (B) $x + 6y$
    (C) $2x + 6y$ (D) $2x + 3y$

Statistics, Functions and Patterns

78. The first ten positions in a pattern are shown below.

    U, D, L, R, U, D, L, R, U, D

    If this pattern continues, which letter would be found at the 86th position?

    (A) U (B) L (C) D (D) R

79. The following numeric sequence below could represent which of the following algebraic expressions?

    −8, −2, 2, 7

    (A) $x - 5, x + 1, x + 5, x + 10$
    (B) $x - 1, x + 4, x + 7, x + 10$
    (C) $x - 7, x - 2, x + 2, x + 8$
    (D) $x, x + 2, x + 4, x + 7$

80. Which comes next in this pattern?

    $\frac{x}{y}, \frac{x+2}{y+1}, \frac{x+4}{y+2}, \frac{x+6}{y+3}$

    (A) $\frac{x+8}{y+4}$ (B) $\frac{x+7}{y+4}$ (C) $\frac{x+8}{y+5}$ (D) $\frac{x+7}{y+5}$

81. The following algebraic expressions could represent which numeric sequence?

    $x - 4, x + 2, x + 5, x + 10$

    (A) −4, 1, 5, 10
    (B) −2, 4, 7, 12
    (C) 1, 7, 9, 14
    (D) 0, 6, 9, 13

82. What is the next term in the following pattern?

    $x + y, 2x + 3y, 3x + 5y$

    Justify your answer.

83. What is the next term in the following pattern?

    $a(x + 1), b(x + 2), c(x + 3), d(x + 4)$

    (A) $e(x + 6)$ (B) $e(x + 5)$
    (C) $d(x + 5)$ (D) $f(x + 5)$

84. What is the next term in the following pattern?

    $\frac{x}{y}, \frac{x+3}{y+2}, \frac{x+6}{y+4}, \frac{x+9}{y+6}$

    (A) $\frac{x+11}{y+8}$ (B) $\frac{x+10}{y+9}$ (C) $\frac{x+9}{y+9}$ (D) $\frac{x+12}{y+8}$

85. The following numeric sequence below could represent which of the following algebraic expressions?

    −3, 1, 5, 9

    (A) $x + 1, x + 4, x + 7, x + 11$
    (B) $x + 2, x + 6, x + 9, x + 11$
    (C) $x, x + 5, x + 9, x + 13$
    (D) $x, x + 4, x + 8, x + 12$

86. Which of the following pairs are based on the rule given below?

    First, square the number.
    Second, subtract the original number from the square.
    Third, double the result.

    (A) (1, 1) (B) (3, 12)
    (C) (2, 20) (D) (2, 10)

Statistics, Functions and Patterns

87. Ms. Saunders and her family members went to an amusement park. It cost C dollars for n people, where $C = 4 + 7.50n$. Which table below correctly shows the cost in dollars of tickets for 5, 10, and 15 people?

(A)
n	5	10	15
C	37.5	75	112.5

(B)
n	5	10	15
C	41.5	79	116.5

(C)
n	5	10	15
C	39.0	74	109.0

(D)
n	5	10	15
C	35.0	70	105.0

88. Which of the following pairs follows the rules to get the second number?

Rules:

1) Multiply the first number by 2.
2) then, square the answer.
3) then subtract 5 from the answer.

(A) (2, 16) (B) (4, 11)
(C) (5, 105) (D) (3, 31)

89. Jamie is having a party at the local bowling alley. The special group rate is described by the equation:

$C = 20 + 3n$,

where C is the total cost of the party and n is the number of people at the party. Which table below correctly shows the cost in dollars of a party for 10, 20, or 30 people?

(A)
C	10	20	30
n	30	60	90.0

(B)
C	10	20	30
n	20	40	60.0

(C)
C	10	20	30
n	50	80	110.

(D)
C	10	20	30
n	23	26	29.0

90. Mr. Al Gebra and his class went to a museum. It cost T dollars for n students, where $T = 7 + 1.50n$. Which table below correctly shows the cost in dollars of tickets for 20, 30, and 40 students?

(A)
n	T
20	27
30	37
40	47

(B)
n	T
20	30
30	45
40	60

(C)
n	T
20	44
30	64
40	84

(D)
n	T
20	37
30	52
40	67

Statistics, Functions and Patterns

91. At a restaurant, the tip is calculated by the equation:

    $T = 2 + 1.50n$,

    where T is the tip and n is the number of people served. Which table below correctly shows the tip in dollars for a group of 2, 4, or 6 people?

    (A)
T	2	4	6
n	2	5.00	8

    (B)
T	2	4	6
n	5	6.50	8

    (C)
T	2	4	6
n	6	12.	18

    (D)
T	2	4	6
n	5	8.0	11

92. Which graph represents an exponential relationship?

    (A)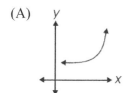

    (B)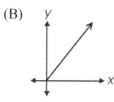

    (C)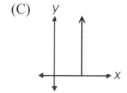

    (D)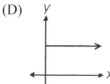

93. When a ball is dropped from a tall building, the relationship between the time (t) that the ball is in the air and the speed (s) of the ball is described in the equation:

    $s = 9.8t$.

    Which table fits this equation?

    (A)
t	1	2	3	4
s	9.8	19.6	29.4	39.2

    (B)
t	1	2	3	4
s	9.8	9.90	10.0	10.1

    (C)
t	1	2	3	4
s	9.8	4.90	2.50	1.30

    (D)
t	1	2	3	4
s	9.8	19.6	39.2	78.4

94. Greg's art class needs to make stickers to label classrooms 1 through 40. How many of each digit will they need to make? How did you reach this answer?

Statistics, Functions and Patterns

95. Which represents the graph of x = 3?

(A)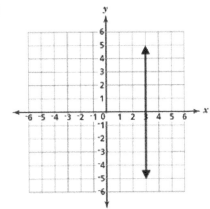

(B)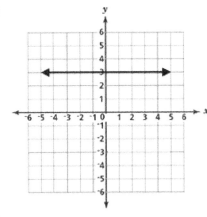

(C)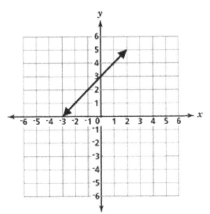

(D)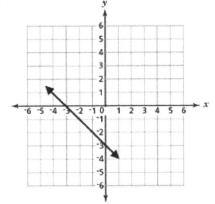

96. Emily has recorded the number of people (P) who attend the football game and the number of drinks (D) that are sold at the concession stand in the table below.

P	D
40	70
80	110
120	150
160	190

Which equation below describes the pattern in the table above?

(A) $D = 2P - 10$
(B) $D = P + 30$
(C) $D = 3P - 50$
(D) $D = 2P - 50$

97. Base your answer to the following question on the table below.

x	y
2	11
4	17
6	23

Which equation below would produce the pattern in the table above?

(A) $y = 3x + 5$
(B) $y = 2x + 7$
(C) $y = 4x + 3$
(D) $y = 6x - 1$

Statistics, Functions and Patterns

98. The table below compares the points on a graph.

x	y
2	3
4	15
5	24

Which of the following equations describes this relationship?

(A) $y = x + 1$ (B) $y = 4x - 1$
(C) $y = x^2$ (D) $y = x^2 - 1$

99. The table below compares the speed at which a ball hits a wall and the speed at which it bounces back.

x	y
10	6
15	9
25	15

Which equation describes this relationship?

(A) $y = x - 4$ (B) $y = x^2$
(C) $y = (x)\frac{3}{5}$ (D) $y = \frac{3}{5}x$

100. Steven's Video Store accepts used video cassette tapes in exchange for new tapes. The following table has been created for the exchange:

New Tapes Used Tapes
1 3
2 6
3 11
4 14
5 19
6 22

Assuming that the pattern will continue and that Jen has 30 used tapes to exchange, what is the greatest number of new tapes that she can get?

(A) 7   (B) 8   (C) 9   (D) 10

REVIEW TOPICS

Test 1: Numbers & Operations

GRID-IN QUESTIONS				
Questions 58 – 62				
58.	If $x + a = a + x = x$ for all values of x, what is the value of a?	61.	If 11 less than m is a negative number and 9 less than m is a positive number, what could be the integer value of m?
59.	George is 31 years older than Leo, who is 15 years younger than Carol. In how many years will Carol be the same age as George is now?	62.	Jim, Garry and Frank were eating pizza. Jim ate thrice as fast as Garry ate. Frank ate twice as slowly as Garry ate. If Frank ate 3 slices, how many slices did Jim eat?
60.	When Mr. Franklin came to the supermarket, there were 6 packages of hamburger buns. In two packages, there were 4 buns, and each of the others contained 6 buns. If Mr. Franklin bought all the buns and made 2 burgers a day, how many days could he eat hamburgers?		

MULTIPLE CHOICE QUESTIONS

Questions 63 – 68

63. Which of the following numbers is between $\frac{5}{3}$ and $\frac{7}{4}$?

   A. 1.31
   B. 1.66
   C. 1.71
   D. 1.77

64. The value of which expression is between 3 and 4?

   E. $(\sqrt{3+4})^2$
   F. $\sqrt{3} + \sqrt{4}$
   G. $(\sqrt{3} + \sqrt{4})^2$
   H. $\sqrt{3^2 + 4^2}$

65.

x	-1	1	3	5
y	-2	0	26	124

   Which of the following rules describes the table above?

   A. $y = 1 - x^2$
   B. $y = 1 - x^3$
   C. $y = x^2 - 1$
   D. $y = x^3 - 1$

66. Set A contains all integers from 10 to 37 inclusive. Set B contains all integers from 22 to 50 exclusive. How many integers are common in both sets?

   E. 15
   F. 16
   G. 40
   H. 41

67. How many integers are between $-\frac{11}{5}$ and $\frac{11}{5}$?

   A. 7
   B. 5
   C. 4
   D. 3

68. HIGH SCHOOL STUDENTS

	Algebra	Geometry	Total
Physics		1,150	
Chemistry			1,280
Total	1,430		3,200

   The table above is partially filled. Based on the information from the table, how many students who take Geometry are also taking Chemistry?

   E. 620
   F. 660
   G. 740
   H. 770

Questions 69 – 74

69. $828 \div 0.184 =$

A. 450,000
B. 45,000
C. 4,500
D. 450

70. A computer program randomly selects a positive two-digit number. If selected number is greater than 50, the number written in reverse order is printed on the piece of paper. If selected number is less than 50, the sum of the digits is printed on the piece of paper. Which of the following numbers couldn't be printed on the piece of paper?

E. 6
F. 16
G. 27
H. 61

71. When the positive integer b is divided by 7, the remainder is 3. Which of the following statements is true?

A. When $b + 3$ is divided by 7, the remainder is 0
B. When $b - 7$ is divided by 7, the remainder is 0
C. When $b - 3$ is divided by 7, the remainder is 0
D. When $b + 7$ is divided by 7, the remainder is 0

72. Emily has only nickels and dimes in her pocket. If there are 3 nickels for every dime, which of the following couldn't be the number of coins in Emily's pocket?

E. 16
F. 28
G. 32
H. 42

73. Everett noticed that in the queue he is 11th from the beginning and 11th from the end. In the same queue, what is the position from the beginning of a man who is 7th from the end?

A. 15
B. 14
C. 13
D. 12

74. Each term in the sequence is determined by multiplying the previous term by 3 and subtracting 5. If the second term is 4, what is the sum of the first and third terms?

E. 3
F. 7
G. 10
H. 12

	Questions 75 – 80		
75.	Two consecutive odd integers m and n are prime numbers. Which of the following is equal to mn? A. 110 B. 143 C. 156 D. 195	78.	If $q = -2$, which of the following numbers has the smallest value? E. $q - 4$ F. $q^2 - 3$ G. $q^3 - 2$ H. $q^4 - 1$
76.	The basket contained the same number of apples and pears. When Gwen took five apples and two pears from the basket, there were twice as many apples left in the basket as pears. How much apples and pears altogether were in the basket initially? E. 8 F. 10 G. 14 H. 16	79.	Which of the following numbers is divisible by 6? A. 1,197 B. 1,588 C. 2,394 D. 2,846
77.	If x, x^2 and $\frac{1}{x}$ lie on the number line as shown above, which of the following could be the value of x? A. $-\frac{3}{4}$ B. $-\frac{4}{3}$ C. $\frac{3}{4}$ D. $\frac{4}{3}$	80.	If n is an integer, what is the possible value of n for which $1,116n$ is the square of an integer? E. 24 F. 28 G. 31 H. 33

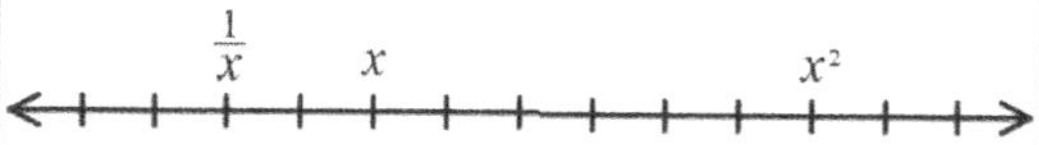

Questions 81 – 86

81. If $(x-y)(x+y) > 0$ and $x+y < 0$, which of the following statements must be true?

    A. $x < y$
    B. $x > y$
    C. $x < -y$
    D. $x > -y$

82. The cost of the purchased car decreases at a constant rate of $450 every six months. If the cost of the car is $13,200 now, for how many years has the price of the car been $18,150?

    E. 4.5 years
    F. 5 years
    G. 5.5 years
    H. 6 years

83. A particular number N is divisible by two different prime numbers p and q. Which of the following statements must be true?

    I. Number N is divisible by $p + q$
    II. When number N is divided by p, the quotient is q
    III. When number N is divided by pq, the remainder is 0

    A. II
    B. I and III
    C. II and III
    D. III

84. If x is a positive integer, what is the least value of x for which $\sqrt{\frac{27x}{8}}$ is an integer?

    E. 4
    F. 6
    G. 8
    H. 24

85. On the table lie nickels, dimes and quarters. Brad uses 6 of these coins to make the maximum possible amount of cents, and uses at least one coin of each value. What is the maximum amount of cents Brad can make?

    A. 150 cents
    B. 115 cents
    C. 100 cents
    D. 80 cents

86. $100 \div ((-2)^3 + (-2)^2) =$

    E. -50
    F. 50
    G. 25
    H. -25

Questions 87 – 92

87. **STUDENTS FAVORITE COLORS**

	Blue	Green	Red	Total
Boys	x	y	v	a
Girls	z	u	w	b
Total	c	d	e	s

The table above shows the students' distribution by their favorite colors. Each variable represents the number of students in each category. Which of the following is not equal to s?

A. $x + y + z + u + v + w$
B. $c + d + e + a + b$
C. $a + b$
D. $c + d + e$

88. A is the set of four consecutive integers. When the least two integers are added, the sum is a. When the greatest two integers are added, the sum is b. Which of the following statements is true about a and b?

E. $a = b$
F. $a = b + 4$
G. $b = a + 2$
H. $b = a + 4$

89. $8 \times (-3)^2 - (-3) \times 8^2 =$

A. 264
B. 120
C. -264
D. -120

90. **DISTRIBUTION OF CAR DRIVERS**

	Drive car	Do not drive car	Total
Men	225	120	345
Women	185	170	355
Total	410	290	700

The table above shows the distribution of car drivers. How many more women drive car than men do not drive car?

E. 65
F. 55
G. 50
H. 15

91. Which of the following is not equivalent to $\sqrt{225}$?

A. $\left(\sqrt{15^2}\right)^2$
B. $\sqrt{15^2}$
C. $\left(\sqrt{15}\right)^2$
D. 15

92. In different stores, the price of the Math book is in the range of $12 to $15. Mr. Terry can spend between $240 and $360 on books. What is the maximum number of books Mr. Terry can buy?

E. 16
F. 20
G. 24
H. 30

Questions 93 – 98			
93.	On the number line above, with endpoints −14 and 13, what is the value at point A? A. −1 B. 0 C. 1 D. 3	96.	The product of three consecutive integers is 24. What is their sum? E. 9 F. 11 G. 12 H. 15
94.	If n is an even number and m is an odd number, which of the following statements must be true? E. $n + m$ is an even number F. nm is an odd number G. $n + m - 2$ is an even number H. $nm + 1$ is an odd number	97.	If n is evenly divisible by 4, which of the following numbers must be evenly divisible by 6? A. $\frac{n}{2}$ B. $\frac{3n}{2}$ C. $\frac{n}{4}$ D. $\frac{3n}{4}$
95.	Which of the following expressions represents a non-repeating decimal? A. $\frac{3}{2} + \frac{2}{3}$ B. $\frac{3}{2} - \frac{2}{3}$ C. $\frac{2}{3} - \frac{1}{6}$ D. $\frac{2}{3} + \frac{1}{6}$	98.	If a and b are two consecutive integers and $b^2 = a^2 + 13$, what is the value of a? E. 6 F. 7 G. 8 H. 9

Questions 99 – 104			
99.	How many positive two-digit numbers are evenly divisible by 6? A. 10 B. 11 C. 14 D. 15	102.	How many positive three-digit numbers have the sum of the digits equal to 4? E. 5 F. 6 G. 8 H. 10
100.	Which of the following expressions is equivalent to -5? E. $(-1,000) \div (-200)$ F. $(-960) \div 160$ G. $800 \div (-200)$ H. $600 \div (-120)$	103.	How many integers in the set of all integers from 6 to 60, inclusive, are neither the square nor cube of an integer? A. 55 B. 53 C. 50 D. 48
101.	How many positive integers from 10 to 40 inclusive are multiples of neither 2 nor 3? A. 9 B. 10 C. 11 D. 12	104.	Jordan has two pennies, two nickels and one dime in his wallet. He randomly selects three coins from the wallet and finds the amount of cents he gets. Which of the following amounts of cents he cannot obtain? E. 11 cents F. 16 cents G. 17 cents H. 20 cents

Questions 105 – 110

105.

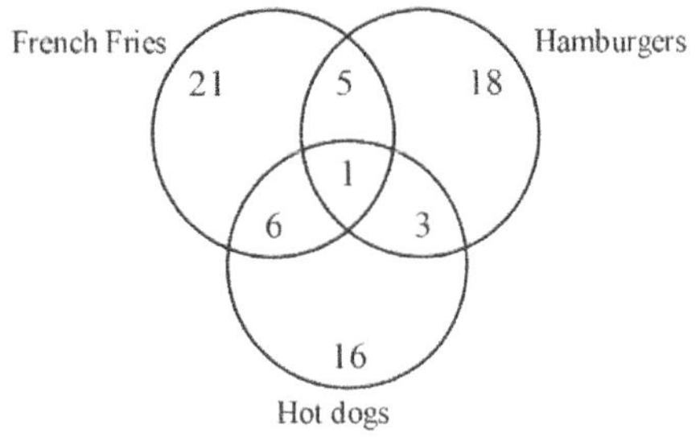

French Fries / Hamburgers / Hot dogs Venn diagram: French Fries only 21, Hamburgers only 18, Hot dogs only 16, French Fries ∩ Hamburgers only 5, French Fries ∩ Hot dogs only 6, Hamburgers ∩ Hot dogs only 3, all three 1.

A group of students was surveyed to determine which of three types of foods they liked. The diagram above shows the results of this survey. Which of the following statements is false?

A. Both French fries and hamburgers like 5 students
B. French fries, hamburgers and hot dogs like 15 students
C. Only hot dogs like 16 students
D. Hamburgers like 27 students

106. If x and y are positive integers less than 30, and $\frac{x}{2y} = 3$, what is the greatest possible value of y?

E. 6
F. 5
G. 4
H. 3

107. If $a \odot b = \frac{b^2}{2} - 2a$, what is the value of $2 \odot 4$?

A. 8
B. 4
C. −6
D. −2

108. The table below shows two rows of positive integers, Row X and Row Y, and the relationship between them.

X	1	3	5	7	9
Y	100	98	96	94	92

Assume each row continues in the pattern shown. Which of the following statements is true?

E. When X = 11, Y = 88
F. The difference between Y and X is always positive
G. When Y = 2, X = 101
H. The sum of X and Y in each column is 101

109. In how many ways can you make $0.40 using any combinations of dimes and pennies?

A. 5
B. 6
C. 7
D. 8

110. Judy's password contains two three-digit numbers.
- First number id divisible by 9;
- Second number is an even number divisible by 5.

Which of the following combinations could be Judy's password?

E. 546 – 215
F. 783 – 520
G. 807 – 630
H. 990 – 819

Questions 111 – 114

111.	$\dfrac{4.05}{0.003} \div 50 =$ A. 2.7 B. 27 C. 270 D. 2,700	113.	Number n is divisible by 4, 5, 6 and 9. If $n < 500$, what is the greatest possible value of n? A. 315 B. 360 C. 450 D. 480
112.	What is the sum of all odd integers from 3 to 22 inclusive? E. 100 F. 110 G. 120 H. 130	114.	How many positive integers x satisfy the inequality $5 \leq \sqrt{x} < 6$? E. 10 F. 11 G. 12 H. 13

Test 2: Percent

GRID-IN QUESTIONS			
Questions 58 – 62			
58.	There are 250 animals on Mr. Quint's farm. 30% of them are cows, 40% of the remaining animals are sheep, and the rest are chickens. How many chickens are on Mr. Quint's farm?	61.	An electronics store announced a sale of goods. A laptop went on sale from $800 to $720. A smartphone was discounted by the same percent. If the new price of the smartphone was $540, what was the old price of the smartphone?
59.	35% of the class are vegetarians. What is the minimum possible number of students in the class?	62.	15% of a equals to b. 75% of b equals to 18. What is the value of a?
60.	Ms. Timothy's dress costs 80% of Mrs. Roger's dress. If Mrs. Roger's dress costs $120, what is the cost of Ms. Timothy's dress?		

	MULTIPLE CHOICE QUESTIONS		
	Questions 63 – 68		
63.	Which of the following is equivalent to $\frac{1}{3}$ of 60% of number x? A. $0.02x$ B. $0.18x$ C. $0.2x$ D. $1.8x$	66.	In a set of 40 numbers, 35% are odd numbers. How many even numbers are in the set? E. 14 F. 16 G. 24 H. 26
64.	Which of the following is equivalent to 20% of $\frac{1}{5}$ of 432? E. 4% of 5 × 432 F. 20% of 5 × 432 G. 4% of 432 H. 20% of 432	67.	What percent of 96 is 75% of 72? A. 56.25% B. 55.75% C. 55.5% D. 54%
65.	5,000 people were surveyed about their favorite pets. The pie diagram below shows the results of the survey. Dogs, 36%; Guinea pigs, 13%; Hamsters, 18%; Rabbits; Cats, 23% How many people said that rabbit was their favorite pet? A. 750 B. 700 C. 550 D. 500	68.	BOOKS READ BY STUDENTS IN THE SUMMER | Number of books	Number of students
---	---
0	p
1	$0.3p$
2	$0.1p$
3	$0.05p$
4	$0.25p$
≥ 5	$0.3p$	 The table above shows the number of books read by students in the summer. What percent of students read at least 5 books in the summer? E. 1.5% F. 3% G. 15% H. 30%

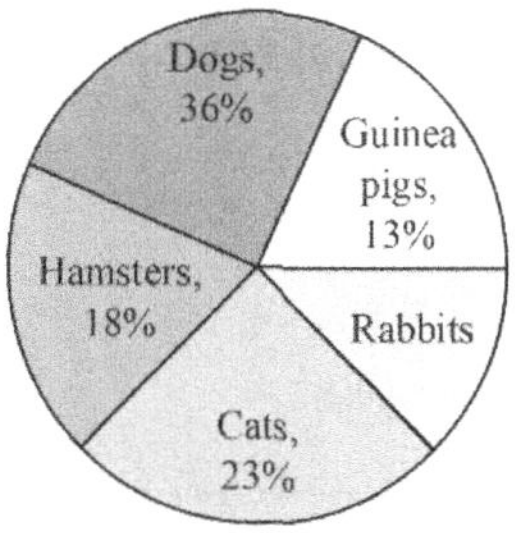

203

Questions 69 – 74

69.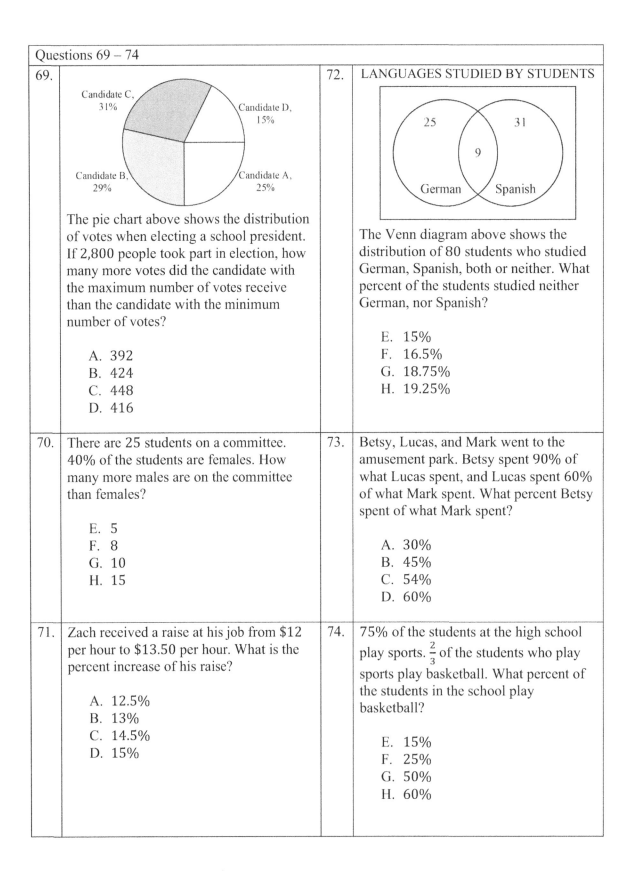

The pie chart above shows the distribution of votes when electing a school president. If 2,800 people took part in election, how many more votes did the candidate with the maximum number of votes receive than the candidate with the minimum number of votes?

A. 392
B. 424
C. 448
D. 416

70. There are 25 students on a committee. 40% of the students are females. How many more males are on the committee than females?

E. 5
F. 8
G. 10
H. 15

71. Zach received a raise at his job from $12 per hour to $13.50 per hour. What is the percent increase of his raise?

A. 12.5%
B. 13%
C. 14.5%
D. 15%

72. LANGUAGES STUDIED BY STUDENTS

The Venn diagram above shows the distribution of 80 students who studied German, Spanish, both or neither. What percent of the students studied neither German, nor Spanish?

E. 15%
F. 16.5%
G. 18.75%
H. 19.25%

73. Betsy, Lucas, and Mark went to the amusement park. Betsy spent 90% of what Lucas spent, and Lucas spent 60% of what Mark spent. What percent Betsy spent of what Mark spent?

A. 30%
B. 45%
C. 54%
D. 60%

74. 75% of the students at the high school play sports. $\frac{2}{3}$ of the students who play sports play basketball. What percent of the students in the school play basketball?

E. 15%
F. 25%
G. 50%
H. 60%

Questions 75 – 80

75. A school took a survey to see how many siblings each student had.

Number of siblings	Number of students
0	22%
1	36%
2	17%
3	14%
> 3	11%

The table above shows the percent distribution for 1,500 students. How many students had no more than 2 siblings?

A. 330
B. 540
C. 870
D. 1,125

76. A survey shows that between 70% and 80% of people buy promotional goods. If a supermarket is visited by about 5,000 people a day, what is the maximum number of people buying promotional goods?

E. 3,500
F. 3,750
G. 4,000
H. 4,250

77. The football team held a vote to determine the team captain. Among the 32 team members, 4 fewer people voted for the first candidate than for the second candidate. What percentage of votes did the winner receive?

A. 43.75%
B. 56.25%
C. 58.5%
D. 62.5%

78.

Algebra	Geometry	Statistics	Probability
33	28	35	29

The table above shows the classes that Mr. Morgan taught and the number of students in each class. If no student was enrolled in more than one class, what percent of the students in Mr. Morgan's classes did not take Statistics?

E. 28%
F. 32%
G. 68%
H. 72%

79. If the area of the square is increased by 44%, by what percent is increased each side?

A. 12%
B. 20%
C. 24%
D. 44%

80. A rectangle is 60 cm wide and 80 cm long. If the width of the rectangle is decreased by 10% and the length of the rectangle is increased by 10%, what is the new area of the rectangle?

E. $4,884\ cm^2$
F. $4,782\ cm^2$
G. $4,752\ cm^2$
H. $4,698\ cm^2$

Questions 81 – 86

81. The cost of the item was first increased by 15%, then a sale was announced and the price was reduced by 15%. How has the price of the item changed compared to the original price?

   A. Reduced by 2.25%
   B. Increased by 2.25%
   C. Reduced by 1.5%
   D. Didn't change

82. Jill has a parental restriction on the use of the phone: 2 hours on weekdays and 100% more on weekends. How many hours can Jill use the phone on the weekend?

   E. 2.5 hours
   F. 3 hours
   G. 3.5 hours
   H. 4 hours

83. Last night, George had 3 hours of homework. This night, George had 4.5 hours of homework. What percentage more hours did George have this night than last?

   A. 150%
   B. 100%
   C. 75%
   D. 50%

84. If x percent of 120 is 18, then x percent of what number is 24?

   E. 160
   F. 180
   G. 200
   H. 240

85. The percent decrease from 40 to 24 is equal to the percent increase from 50 to x. What is the value of x?

   A. 66
   B. 68
   C. 70
   D. 72

86. Which of the following expressions must $a + b$ equal if 15% of x equals a and $\frac{3}{4}$ of x equals b?

   E. $0.9x$
   F. $0.8x$
   G. $8x$
   H. $9x$

	Questions 87 – 92		
87.	If 75% of the number a is 24, then how much is 200% of the number a? A. 36 B. 48 C. 60 D. 64	90.	In the morning, Matt spent 20 minutes on breakfast. Lunch took him 150% more time than breakfast. How much time did Matt spend on lunch? E. 30 minutes F. 40 minutes G. 50 minutes H. 60 minutes
88.	SMARTPHONE FEATURES Quality, 29% Color, 15% Camera, 16% Brand, 40% The pie diagram below shows the main features that students pay attention to when choosing a phone. If 288 students pay attention to camera, how many students pay attention to brand? E. 720 F. 684 G. 640 H. 576	91.	In the school, there are two eight-grade classes: class A has 30 students and class B has 35 students. If $\frac{1}{6}$ of the students in class A and 60% of the students in class B get to school by school bus, what percent of all the students get to school by school bus? A. 35% B. 40% C. 45% D. 50%
89.	What is the difference of 30% of 60 and 60% of 30? A. 0 B. 18 C. 24 D. 36	92.	In a dance class, 30 students are male and 50 students are female. 40% of the male students and 20% of the female students are math students. What percentage of dance students are math students? E. 27.5% F. 30% G. 32.5% H. 35%

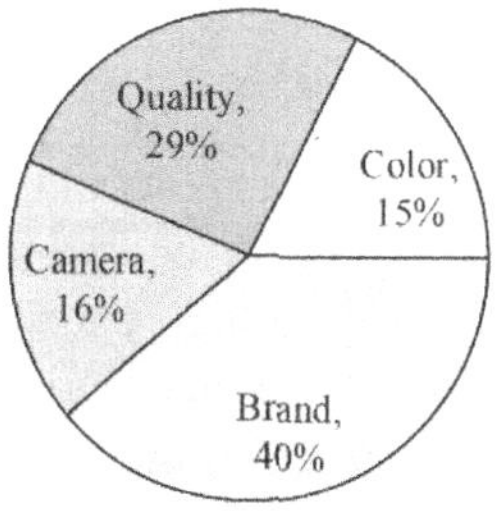

Questions 93 – 98

93. Number *a* is 20% of number *b*. Number *b* is 60% of number *c*. What percentage of number *c* is number *a*?

    A. 12%
    B. 24%
    C. 40%
    D. 80%

94. In the store, for a product that costs more than $100, there is a 15% discount. For a product that costs no more than $100, there is a 10% discount. How much less will one buyer pay for a product worth $102 than another buyer for a product worth $98?

    E. $2
    F. $1.75
    G. $1.50
    H. $1.25

95. When buying a house, the Adams paid a down payment of 40%. They paid 80% of the remaining balance in the first half-year and the rest $10,800 in the second half-year. How much did the Adams house cost?

    A. $108,000
    B. $100,000
    C. $98,000
    D. $90,000

96. There are 100 black and red balls in the bag. The clown randomly pulled out 20 balls, and it turned out that 30% of them were red and the rest were black. What is the smallest number of red balls that a clown must pull out so that the number of black and red balls pulled out is equal?

    E. 6
    F. 8
    G. 12
    H. 14

97. In Octavian Corporation, 55% of the total revenue $R is devoted to the advertising budget. Five-elevenths of this advertising budget was spent on Internet advertising. Which of the following represents the amount spent on Internet advertising?

    A. $\$\frac{R}{4}$
    B. $\$\frac{R}{11}$
    C. $\$\frac{R}{5}$
    D. $\$\frac{30R}{121}$

98. On Monday, the milkman brought 50 liters of milk to the market. On Tuesday, he brought 20% more milk than on Monday, and on Wednesday, 15% more than on Tuesday. How many more liters of milk did the milkman bring on Wednesday than on Monday?

    E. 19
    F. 17.5
    G. 16
    H. 15.5

	Questions 99 – 104		
99.	The bookstore had 7,000 books. 20% of them were detectives. After a purchase of detectives, the number of detectives at the bookstore was 30% of all books. How many detectives were at the bookstore after purchase? A. 2,100 B. 2,200 C. 2,300 D. 2,400	102.	Each month, Mrs. McMillan spent 65% of her salary on bills and 20% of the remaining on food. If she had $560 left, what is Mrs. McMillan's monthly salary? E. $1,800 F. $1,900 G. $2,000 H. $2,100
100.	A suit originally priced at $S was on sale for 10% off. Melanie has an additional discount coupon with 20% off the sale price. If Melanie used the coupon and paid $P for the suit, which of the following expressions represents this situation? E. $P = 0.72S$ F. $S = 0.72P$ G. $P = 0.7S$ H. $S = 0.7P$	103.	The retail price of a porcelain set was $70. It was marked down 25% on sale day and then marked back up 40%. What was the percent increase on the original price? A. 3.5% B. 0.5% C. 7% D. 5%
101.	Lori and her friend had 600 stamps together. If Lori had 8% more stamps than her friend did, how many stamps did Lori have? A. 348 B. 324 C. 312 D. 306	104.	A rope was cut it into two pieces. The first piece was 61% of the length of the original rope. If 44 cm was transferred from the first piece to the second piece, the two pieces would have the same length. How long was the second piece? E. 121 cm F. 156 cm G. 182 cm H. 244 cm

	Questions 105 – 110		
105.	A carpenter sold five chairs, which had the same cost. He sold three of them with a profit of 24% and the rest at the cost price. If he received $200.20, what was the cost of each chair? A. $30 B. $32 C. $35 D. $36	108.	Cindy had $\frac{1}{4}$ more money than Leo. After Cindy spent 50% of her money, she had $9 less than Leo. How much money did Cindy initially have? E. $18 F. $20 G. $30 H. $36
106.	Class A has 10% fewer boys than class B. If 1 boy transferred from class B to class A, there will be the same amount of boys in the two classes. How many boys are there in class A? E. 18 F. 20 G. 22 H. 24	109.	Alex invests $1,300 in an account that pays r% interest. After the first year, he receives $84.50 interest. What is the value of r? A. 5 B. 5.5 C. 6 D. 6.5
107.	Two farmers have 1,530 sheep. If the number of first farmer's sheep is equal to 80% of the number of second farmer's sheep, how many sheep does second farmer have? A. 810 B. 830 C. 850 D. 870	110.	A bank is offering 7.5% simple interest on a savings account. If you deposit $4,200, how much interest will you earn in four years? E. $1,230 F. $1,240 G. $1,250 H. $1,260

Questions 111 – 114

111. Mathew has lunch at a local restaurant and the cost of his meal is $36. Mathew pays $41.40 including a tip. What percentage of lunch is a tip?

   A. 12%
   B. 15%
   C. 16%
   D. 18%

112. How many gallons of a 15% acid solution must be mixed with 4 gallons of 30% acid solution to make a 25% acid solution?

   E. 1 gallon
   F. 1.5 gallons
   G. 2 gallons
   H. 2.5 gallons

113. Laura has a bag containing 60 coins.
   - 50% of coins are dimes.
   - There are twice as many nickels as quarters.

   How much, in dollars, does Laura have?

   A. $6
   B. $6.25
   C. $6.50
   D. $6.75

114. A bag contains 38 white balls and 2 black ball. How many white balls should be removed for the bag to contain 90% white balls?

   E. 30
   F. 25
   G. 20
   H. 15

Test 3: Fractions

GRID-IN QUESTIONS			
Questions 58 – 62			
58.	What is $\frac{1}{4}$ of S if $\frac{3}{4}$ of S is 81?	61.	What is $1 \div \frac{20}{16}$ in decimal form?
59.	A student has a bag containing 24 blue marbles and 9 green marbles. He puts more green marbles until the number of green marbles represented $\frac{1}{2}$ of the total number of marbles in the bag. How many green marbles has the student put in the bag?	62.	The train left the starting point half-full. At the next stop, 200 people boarded the train and 40 people got off, after which the train became three-fourths full. How many people can the train accommodate?
60.	$3\frac{1}{5} \div 5\frac{1}{3} =$		

MULTIPLE CHOICE QUESTIONS

Questions 63 – 68

63.

FRUIT PRICES

Fruit	Price per pound
Apples	$0.84
Pears	$0.88
Apricots	$1.48
Peaches	$0.96
Grapes	$1.28

The table below shows fruit prices at the certain supermarket. A customer plans to buy $\frac{3}{2}$ pounds of apples, $\frac{2}{3}$ pound of peaches, $\frac{5}{4}$ pounds of grapes and 2 pounds of apricots. How much will it cost the customer?

A. $6.12
B. $6.24
C. $6.38
D. $6.46

64. $\left(3\frac{1}{3} - \frac{10}{7}\right) \div \frac{100}{42} =$

E. 0.8
F. 0.6
G. 0.4
H. 0.2

65. In Mathwill, 12,600 people wear glasses. If $\frac{5}{8}$ of Mathwill population do not wear glasses, how many people live in the Mathwill?

A. 20,160
B. 33,600
C. 31,625
D. 20,475

66. Among 2,000 teachers and students, the school conducted a survey on the transition to distance studying. The table below shows the results of this survey.

	Yes	No	Neutral
Teachers	58	80	42
Students	696	608	516

What fraction of people preferring distance studying are students?

E. $\frac{87}{250}$
F. $\frac{174}{281}$
G. $\frac{38}{125}$
H. $\frac{12}{13}$

67. Fractions $\frac{2}{3}$ and $\frac{2+n}{12}$ are equivalent. What is the value of n?

A. 2
B. 4
C. 6
D. 8

68. Bryan gave Nancy $\frac{1}{5}$ of chocolate bar and gave Benjamin $\frac{1}{2}$ of the remaining chocolate bar. What fraction of chocolate bar did Bryan leave?

E. $\frac{2}{5}$
F. $\frac{3}{5}$
G. $\frac{1}{2}$
H. $\frac{3}{10}$

Questions 69 – 74

69. Let n be a positive integer. If $A_n = \frac{4}{n}$, what is the value of $A_1 A_3 - A_2 A_4$?

A. $\frac{32}{3}$

B. $\frac{28}{3}$

C. $\frac{22}{3}$

D. $\frac{10}{3}$

70. Sofia cut a 640-centimeter piece of fabric into four equal pieces. Then she cut one of the pieces into five identical ones and cut one of these pieces into 2 identical ones. What is the length of the smallest piece of fabric?

E. 32 cm
F. 16 cm
G. 8 cm
H. 4 cm

71. When buying a new car, the full insurance is one-fifth of the cost of the car. The buyer paid a 10% down payment and paid the full insurance, which was $3,600 in total. What was the cost of the car?

A. $36,000
B. $24,000
C. $18,000
D. $12,000

72. Every day, Emily's parents give her $10 pocket money. Every morning at school, Emily buys a hamburger for $2.50 and fresh juice for $1.50. What fraction of money does Emily have left for other expenses?

E. $\frac{3}{10}$

F. $\frac{2}{5}$

G. $\frac{3}{5}$

H. $\frac{7}{10}$

73. The numerator of the fraction is 5 less than the denominator of the fraction. If this fraction is equivalent to $\frac{3}{4}$, what is the numerator of the fraction?

A. 10
B. 15
C. 20
D. 25

74. In the fall, the clothing store announced the sale of the summer collection at a discount for $\frac{1}{3}$ off the retail prices. Max bought two identical shirts and paid $36. How much would Max pay for one such shirt in the summer?

E. $24
F. $27
G. $48
H. $54

	Questions 75 – 80		
75.	$\frac{4}{11}$ of the people in a pizzeria are children. If there are 27 more adults than children, how many adults are there in the pizzeria? A. 27 B. 36 C. 63 D. 99	78.	$2\frac{1}{2} + 3\frac{1}{4} - 1\frac{1}{8} =$ E. 4.25 F. 4.375 G. 4.5 H. 4.625
76.	Mila and Samuel had an equal amount of money for shopping. Mila spent $42 and Samuel spent $36. After that, Mila had $\frac{1}{2}$ of what Samuel had left. How much money Mila had initially? E. $54 F. $52 G. $50 H. $48	79.	At the festive concert dedicated to the school day, $\frac{1}{3}$ of speakers were sixth-graders, $\frac{1}{2}$ – seventh-graders and $\frac{2}{3}$ of the remaining – eighth-graders. What fraction of speakers were neither sixth-graders, seven-graders, nor eighth-graders? A. $\frac{1}{18}$ B. $\frac{1}{12}$ C. $\frac{1}{9}$ D. $\frac{1}{6}$
77.	$\frac{1}{8}$ of all animals at the farm are horses. $\frac{2}{7}$ of the remaining animals are cows. The rest are sheep. If there are 126 cows on the farm, how many more sheep than horses are there? A. 63 B. 126 C. 189 D. 252	80.	Today, Lucas's age is $\frac{2}{3}$ of Mark's age. In 12 years, Lucas's age will be $\frac{4}{5}$ of Mark's age. How old is Lucas today? E. 6 years old F. 9 years old G. 12 years old H. 18 years old

	Questions 81 – 86		
81.	If $m = ab$ and $n = \frac{a}{b}$, what is $\frac{n}{m}$ in terms of a and b? A. $\frac{1}{b^2}$ B. b^2 C. $\frac{1}{a^2}$ D. a^2	84.	Numbers a and b belong to the set $\{1, 2, 3, 4, 5, 6\}$. For which values of a and b the fraction $\frac{a+1}{b-1}$ has the maximum value? E. $a = 6, b = 1$ F. $a = 6, b = 2$ G. $a = 1, b = 6$ H. $a = 2, b = 6$
82.	⟵———A———B———⟶ $1\frac{1}{4}$ On the number line above, $AB = \frac{2}{3}$. Point C is the midpoint of AB. Where is point C located? E. $\frac{1}{12}$ to the left of 1 F. $\frac{1}{12}$ to the right of 1 G. $\frac{1}{6}$ to the left of 1 H. $\frac{1}{6}$ to the right of 1	85.	⟵——P——Q————R—S——⟶ On the number line above, $PR = 3\frac{1}{2}$, $QS = 2\frac{3}{4}$, and $RS = \frac{5}{6}$. What is the length of PQ? A. $1\frac{11}{12}$ B. $1\frac{7}{12}$ C. $1\frac{5}{12}$ D. $1\frac{1}{12}$
83.	Suppose $A, B, C,$ and D are fractions. If $B = \frac{1}{2}A, C = A \div \frac{1}{2}, D = A - \frac{1}{2}$, which variable has the least value? A. A B. B C. C D. D	86.	$$2\left(x - \frac{1}{x}\right) + 3\left(x + \frac{1}{x}\right)$$ If $x = \frac{5}{2}$, what is the value of the expression above? E. 11.8 F. 12.1 G. 12.9 H. 13.2

	Questions 87 – 92		
87.	The decimal 0.15 can be written as the fraction $\frac{x}{80}$. What is the value of x? A. 3 B. 6 C. 9 D. 12	90.	If x and y are positive integers and $\frac{x}{y} = 0.16$, what is the least possible value of $x + y$? E. 4 F. 25 G. 29 H. 58
88.	In Mr. Trade class of 28 students, $\frac{4}{7}$ of the students are taking Japanese, $\frac{1}{4}$ of the students are taking Chinese, and 8 students are taking neither Japanese, nor Chinese. How many students are taking both languages? E. 2 F. 3 G. 4 H. 5	91.	In the school, there are two eight-grade classes: class A has 30 students and class B has 35 students. If $\frac{1}{3}$ of the students in class A and $\frac{2}{7}$ of the students in class B get to school by school bus, what fraction of all the students get to school by school bus? A. $\frac{3}{13}$ B. $\frac{4}{13}$ C. $\frac{13}{21}$ D. $\frac{4}{21}$
89.	What is the fraction of prime numbers in the set of whole integers greater than 5 but less than 26? A. $\frac{3}{10}$ B. $\frac{2}{7}$ C. $\frac{1}{3}$ D. $\frac{7}{10}$	92.	In a dance class, 30 students are male and 50 students are female. $\frac{1}{3}$ of the male students and $\frac{3}{10}$ of the female students are math students. What fraction of dance students are not math students? E. $\frac{11}{16}$ F. $\frac{5}{16}$ G. $\frac{19}{30}$ H. $\frac{11}{30}$

Questions 93 – 98

93. If $a = 4b + 1$ and $b = \frac{1}{2^n}$ for $n = 1, 2,$ or 3, what is the least possible value of a?

    A. $\frac{1}{2}$

    B. 3

    C. 2

    D. $1\frac{1}{2}$

94. Melissa has x dollars in her savings account, and Rosie has y dollars in her savings account. Rosie gives Melissa $\frac{1}{4}$ of her money, which Melissa deposits into her savings account. Then Melissa spends $\frac{1}{3}$ of the total in her savings account. Express the amount of money Melissa spent in terms of x and y.

    E. $\frac{x}{3} + \frac{y}{4}$

    F. $\frac{x}{4} + \frac{y}{3}$

    G. $\frac{x}{3} + \frac{y}{12}$

    H. $\frac{x}{12} + \frac{y}{3}$

95. If $0.00036 = \frac{36}{10^k}$, what is the value of k?

    A. 4
    B. 5
    C. 6
    D. 7

96. How many integers are between $\frac{7}{3}$ and $\frac{47}{4}$?

    E. 8
    F. 9
    G. 10
    H. 11

97. There are 100 black, red and yellow balls in the bag. An illusionist randomly pulled out 30 balls, and it turned out that $\frac{1}{2}$ of them were red, $\frac{1}{3}$ of them were yellow and the rest were black. What is the number of yellow balls that the illusionist must pull out so that the number of yellow balls pulled out is equal to the total number of black and red balls?

    A. 5
    B. 10
    C. 15
    D. 20

98. Which of the following shows the fractions $\frac{16}{3}, \frac{21}{4}$ and $\frac{27}{5}$ in order from least to greatest?

    E. $\frac{16}{3}, \frac{21}{4}, \frac{27}{5}$

    F. $\frac{21}{4}, \frac{16}{3}, \frac{27}{5}$

    G. $\frac{21}{4}, \frac{27}{5}, \frac{16}{3}$

    H. $\frac{16}{3}, \frac{27}{5}, \frac{21}{4}$

Questions 99 – 104

99. A juice container is $\frac{1}{5}$ full; then, 2 liters of juice are added to the container, making it $\frac{1}{3}$ full. How many additional liters of juice could be added to the container to fill it completely?

A. 7
B. 8
C. 10
D. 15

100.

If all possible values of x are indicated by the shaded part of the number line above (from 6 to 15), what is the least possible value of $\frac{3}{x}$?

E. $\frac{1}{5}$
F. $\frac{1}{4}$
G. $\frac{1}{3}$
H. $\frac{1}{2}$

101. $$\frac{x}{2} - \frac{x}{3} + \frac{x}{4} - \frac{x}{5} = 13$$

In the equation above, what is the value of x?

A. 30
B. 60
C. 90
D. 120

102. Yesterday, Pamela read $\frac{5}{12}$ of her entire book. Today she read $\frac{3}{10}$ of the entire book. In lowest terms, what fraction of the book is left for her to read?

E. $\frac{17}{60}$
F. $\frac{17}{120}$
G. $\frac{43}{60}$
H. $\frac{43}{120}$

103. A chemist mixed three liquids, A, B, and C in a container. The amount of A is 4 times the amount of C, and the amount of B is $\frac{1}{2}$ the amount of C. What fraction of the amount of A is amount of B?

A. $\frac{1}{2}$
B. $\frac{1}{4}$
C. $\frac{1}{8}$
D. $\frac{1}{10}$

104. If $a = 3$ and $b = 4$, what is the value of $\frac{b-(3a-2b)}{7a-1}$?

E. 0.3
F. 0.2
G. 0.15
H. 0.05

Questions 105 – 110

105. Lenny rode $12\frac{2}{3}$ miles on Monday, $10\frac{5}{6}$ miles on Tuesday, and $11\frac{1}{2}$ miles on Wednesday. How many more miles did he ride on Tuesday and Wednesday together than on Monday?

   A. $10\frac{1}{3}$ miles
   B. $9\frac{2}{3}$ miles
   C. $9\frac{1}{3}$ miles
   D. 9 miles

106. Which statement must be true if $x \geq 10$?

   E. $\frac{1}{x} < \frac{1}{x+1}$
   F. $\frac{1}{x-1} > \frac{1}{x-2}$
   G. $\frac{1}{x+1} < \frac{1}{x+2}$
   H. $\frac{1}{x} > \frac{1}{x+2}$

107. Between which two consecutive integers is the fraction $\frac{48}{9}$ located?

   A. 2 and 3
   B. 3 and 4
   C. 4 and 5
   D. 5 and 6

108. Owen had $\frac{1}{5}$ more money than Oliver. After Owen spent $12, she had $\frac{2}{5}$ less money than Oliver. How much money did Owen initially have?

   E. $20
   F. $22
   G. $24
   H. $26

109.

   If AC = 21 cm, what is the length of BC?

   A. 15 cm
   B. 12 cm
   C. 10 cm
   D. 9 cm

110. What is $900 \times \left(\frac{2}{3}\right)\left(\frac{3}{4}\right)\left(\frac{4}{5}\right)\left(\frac{5}{6}\right)$?

   E. 900
   F. 600
   G. 450
   H. 300

Questions 111 – 114

111. What is the decimal value of $\frac{3\times 4\times 5}{6\times 8\times 10}$?

A. 0.5
B. 0.25
C. 0.125
D. 0.0625

112. The length of the rectangle is $\frac{4}{9}$ of its perimeter. Which fraction of the rectangle's perimeter is its width?

E. $\frac{1}{9}$
F. $\frac{2}{9}$
G. $\frac{5}{18}$
H. $\frac{1}{18}$

113. Gina has a bag containing 80 coins.
- $\frac{1}{4}$ of coins are dimes.
- There are twice as many nickels as quarters.

What fraction of all coins are nickels?

A. $\frac{2}{3}$
B. $\frac{1}{4}$
C. $\frac{1}{3}$
D. $\frac{1}{2}$

114. 6, 7, 8, 9, 10, 11, 12, 13, 14

If $\frac{x+8}{x-8}$ is a whole number, how many of the numbers listed above can be a value of x?

E. 8
F. 7
G. 6
H. 5

TEST 4: Ratio & Proportions

GRID-IN QUESTIONS

Questions 58 – 62

58.
1 colon = 5 soms
1 colon = 0.4 won

Ethan has 200 soms and 100 wons. If he exchanges the soms and woms for colons according to the rates above, how many colons will he receive?

59. Today in the amusement park, the ratio of girls to boys is 2 : 5. If there are 364 children in the park today, how many more boys than girls are there?

60. Ryan is reading a 300-page book. He read 50 pages in the first 75 minutes. At this rate, how many more hours does it take Ryan to finish reading the book?

61.

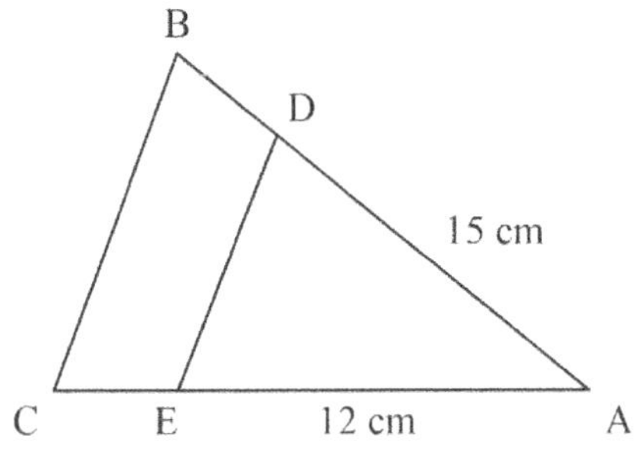

In the figure above, DE is parallel to BC, AD = 15 cm, and AE = 12 cm. If AB = 18 cm, what is the length of CE, in centimeters?

62. Imelda bought a package of dog food for her dog. If the package weighs 50,000,000 milligrams, how much does this package weigh in kilograms?

MULTIPLE CHOICE QUESTIONS

Questions 63 – 68

63.
$$\frac{4+n}{12+n} = \frac{3}{5}$$

What value of n makes the above equation true?

A. 16
B. 12
C. 10
D. 8

64. Nate's class has between 26 and 36 students. The ratio of girls to boys in the class is 5 : 9. How many boys are in Nate's class?

E. 9
F. 10
G. 18
H. 28

65. In a bouquet, the ratio of daises to roses is 7 : 3. What percent of the flowers in the bouquet are daises?

A. 30%
B. 50%
C. 70%
D. 90%

66. At an exchange office, Nicole exchanged 450 dollars and received 25 rinks. Based on that information, how many rinks are equal to 1 dollar? (Assume that there are no exchange fees.)

E. 18
F. $\frac{1}{9}$
G. $\frac{1}{18}$
H. 9

67. The scale on a map is 2 inches to 9 miles. What is the distance, in miles, between two towns that are d inches apart on the map?

A. $\frac{2d}{9}$
B. $\frac{9d}{2}$
C. $\frac{9}{2d}$
D. $\frac{2}{9d}$

68. A cake recipe calls for 280 g of flour for every 160 grams of sugar. If in total a cooker used 550 grams of flour and sugar, how much sugar did he use?

E. 350 grams
F. 300 grams
G. 250 grams
H. 200 grams

Questions 69 – 74

69.

BISCUIT RECIPE

Flour	150 grams (6 oz)
Butter	100 grams (4 oz)
Sugar	62.5 grams (2.5 oz)

How many ounces of sugar do you need to prepare biscuits using 240 grams of flour?

A. 3 oz
B. 3.5 oz
C. 4 oz
D. 4.5 oz

70. Mr. Baltimore has three types of pens in his store: with thick, medium and thin rods. The ratio of pens with thick rods to the pens with medium rods is 2 : 3. The ratio of pens with medium rods to the pens with thin rods is 4 : 5. If Mr. Baltimore has 165 pens with thin rods, how many pens with thick rods does he have?

E. 44
F. 88
G. 66
H. 132

71. The ratio of Oscar's weight to his sister's weight is 7 : 5. If Oscar got 1 kg and his sister lost 1 kg, the ratio of Oscar's weight to his sister's weight became 16 : 11. How much did Oscar weigh initially?

A. 56 kg
B. 63 kg
C. 64 kg
D. 70 kg

72. Otto has 40 coins, consisting of a mix of quarters and dimes. The total value of these coins is $6.40. What is the ratio of quarters to dimes in Otto's collection?

E. 2 : 3
F. 3 : 5
G. 3 : 2
H. 5 : 3

73. The students in Mrs. Grey's class played games.
- 10 boys played basketball
- 8 girls played basketball
- 6 boys played volleyball
- 9 girls played volleyball

What is the ratio of children playing volleyball to children playing basketball?

A. 5 : 6
B. 6 : 5
C. 4 : 5
D. 5 : 4

74. The ratio of Gordon's money to Arthur's money was 8 : 7 at first. After Arthur spent half of his money and Gordon spent $50, Arthur had twice as much money as Gordon had. How much money did Gordon have at first?

E. $96
F. $80
G. $64
H. $56

Questions 75 – 80

75. A store was selling 9 avocados for $15 at the farmers market. Which of the following statements is false?

   A. 6 avocados cost $10
   B. 12 avocados cost $20
   C. 15 avocados cost $25
   D. 18 avocados cost $35

78. In a class of 30 students, 12 students study only French, 9 students study only Spanish, and 6 students study both French and Spanish. What is the ratio of students who study French or Spanish to those who study neither?

   E. 6 : 1
   F. 7 : 1
   G. 8 : 1
   H. 9 : 1

76. If the ratio of the circumference of the circle to the area of the circle is 4 : 9, which of the following statements is true?

   E. The circumference of the circle is 18π units
   F. The diameter of the circle is 9 units
   G. The area of the circle is 9π square units
   H. The radius of the circle is $\frac{2}{9}$ units

79. Hermione travelled at a constant rate for 50 km and it took her 4 hours to complete the journey. Which of the following expression can be used to find Hermione's rate, in meters per second?

   A. $\frac{4 \times 3,600}{50 \times 1,000}$

   B. $\frac{50 \times 3,600}{4 \times 1,000}$

   C. $\frac{50 \times 1,000}{4 \times 3,600}$

   D. $\frac{4 \times 1,000}{50 \times 3,600}$

77. At a zoo, the ratio of spider monkeys to gibbons to mandrills is 9 : 2 : 4. If there are 8 more mandrills than gibbons, how many spider monkeys are at the zoo?

   A. 9
   B. 18
   C. 27
   D. 36

80. In a bag, the ratio of red balls to green balls is 5 : 2, the ratio of green balls to blue balls is 4 : 3. What is the ratio of blue balls to red balls in the bag?

   E. 5 : 6
   F. 6 : 5
   G. 10 : 3
   H. 3 : 10

Questions 81 – 86

81. On the number line above, the ratio of PQ to RS is 3 : 2, the ratio of QS to PR is 5 : 6. If QR = 12 cm, what is the length of PS?

   A. 20 cm
   B. 24 cm
   C. 28 cm
   D. 32 cm

82. In the online game, every 15 points won can be exchanged for 3 small prizes and every 36 points won can be exchanged for 2 large prizes. How many large prizes are worth 72 small prizes?

   E. 5
   F. 10
   G. 15
   H. 20

83. The company offers its customers two types of transactions: online and offline. The ratio of time spent on online transaction to the time spent on offline transaction is 3 : 5. If it takes 1 hour and 15 minutes to deal with offline transaction, how long will the same online transaction last?

   A. 40 minutes
   B. 45 minutes
   C. 50 minutes
   D. 55 minutes

84. $$\frac{4m - 3n}{m} = \frac{5n}{3m}$$
In the proportion above, $m \neq 0$. What is the value of m in terms of n?

   E. $\frac{6}{7}n$
   F. $\frac{7}{6}n$
   G. $\frac{5}{6}n$
   H. $\frac{6}{5}n$

85. Pink paint is made by mixing white paint with red paint in the ratio 4 : 3. Emilia wants to paint her room in pink and needs 9.1 L of pink paint. How much red paint does she need?

   A. 3.9 L
   B. 4.2 L
   C. 4.9 L
   D. 5.2 L

86. In the basket, the ratio of fruit to vegetables is 3 : 2. What percent of fruit is in the basket?

   E. 20%
   F. 30%
   G. 40%
   H. 60%

Questions 87 – 92

87.

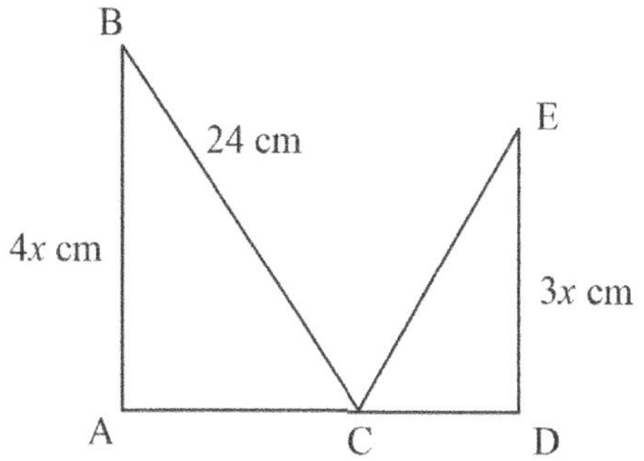

The figure above shows two similar triangles ABC and DEC. What is the length of the side CE?

A. 12 cm
B. 14 cm
C. 16 cm
D. 18 cm

88. A student draws a scale diagram of the art class, using a scale of 2 : 25. The actual width of the art class is 12 m. What is the width of the art class on the diagram?

E. 96 cm
F. 48 cm
G. 24 cm
H. 12 cm

89. A hen can lay an average of 5 eggs per week. At this rate, how many eggs can two hens lay in 14 days?

A. 10
B. 20
C. 40
D. 80

90.

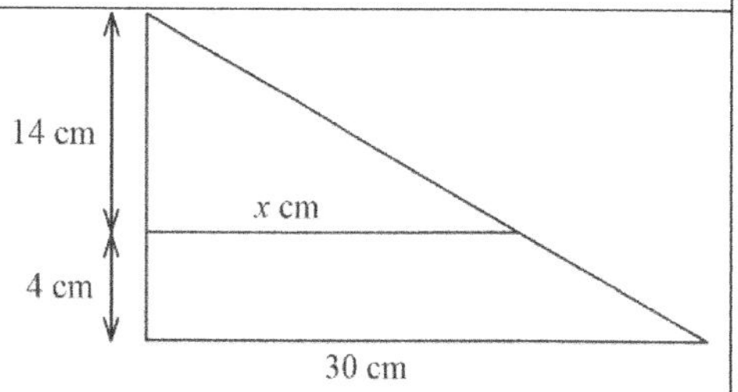

In the figure above, what is the value of x?

E. $8\frac{2}{3}$
F. 8.2
G. $23\frac{1}{3}$
H. 28.4

91. If $\frac{8a}{3x} = \frac{a}{9}$, and $x \neq 0, a \neq 0$, what is the value of x?

A. 72
B. 48
C. 36
D. 24

92. Every morning, Ian runs 10 kilometers in 40 minutes. Today, Ian plans to increase his running time by 10 minutes. If he runs at the same rate as before, how many kilometers will Ian run today?

E. 12.5 km
F. 12 km
G. 15 km
H. 14.5 km

227

Questions 93 – 98

93. On a sunny day, an 8-meter tree casts a maximum shade of 2.4 meters in length. At the same time, of what length will be the shadow of a 180-cm man?

   A. 5.4 cm
   B. 9.375 cm
   C. 93.75 cm
   D. 54 cm

94. Triangle CAT is similar to triangle DOG. Corresponding sides AC and OD have lengths 48 inches and 36 inches respectively. If the perimeter of the triangle DOG is 117 inches, what is the perimeter of the triangle CAT?

   E. 87.75 inches
   F. 156 inches
   G. 78 inches
   H. 175.5 inches

95. A plane can fly an average of 800 km in 50 minutes. If the distance between two cities is 2,000 km, how long will the flight last?

   A. 2 hours
   B. 2 hours 5 minutes
   C. 2 hours 10 minutes
   D. 2 hours 15 minutes

96. A farmer has 6 horses that can eat all the grass in a field in 12 days. If the farmer sold 2 of his horses, how many days would it take the remaining horses to eat all the grass on the field?

   E. 24 days
   F. 20 days
   G. 18 days
   H. 15 days

97. In a class of a students, there are b boys. What is the ratio of the number of boys to the number of girls in the class?

   A. $\frac{b}{a}$
   B. $\frac{b}{a-b}$
   C. $\frac{b}{a+b}$
   D. $\frac{a-b}{a+b}$

98. The measures of two complementary angles are in the ratio 7 : 8. What is the measure of the smaller angle?

   E. 35°
   F. 42°
   G. 48°
   H. 49°

	Questions 99 – 104		
99.	$56 \div x = 63 \div 72$ What is the value of the x in the proportion shown above? A. 1 B. 8 C. 24 D. 64	102.	In a bag, there are 3 different color beads. There are red, white, and black beads. The ratio of red beads to white beads is 3 : 4. The ratio of white beads to black beads is 6 : 11. If there are 387 beads in total, how many red beads are in the bag? E. 108 F. 81 G. 54 H. 27
| 100. | ```
<—+—+—+♦—+—+—+—+—+—+—+♦—+—+—+—>
    6                        15
```<br>If point A divides above segment in the ratio 5 : 1, where is point A located?<br><br>E. 7.5<br>F. 8.5<br>G. 13.5<br>H. 14.5 | 103. | In a museum, the ratio of boys to girls is 3 : 5. Some girls leave the museum such that the number of boys and the number of girls become the same. What percent of the total number of children is the number of girls who leave the museum?<br><br>A. 20%<br>B. 25%<br>C. 40%<br>D. 45% |
| 101. | If a car travels 150 km in 2 hours and a bus travels 100 km in 2.5 hours at constant rates, what is the ratio of the car's rate to the bus's rate?

A. 16 : 7
B. 15 : 8
C. 14 : 9
D. 13 : 10 | 104. | In a school, the ratio of boys to girls in year 8 is 3 : 2. In year 8, the ratio of boys preferring basketball to the boys preferring tennis is 5 : 4. If there are 24 girls in year 8, how many boys in year 8 preferred tennis to basketball?

E. 20
F. 18
G. 16
H. 15 |
```

Questions 105 – 110			
105.	In a school, the number of utility rooms is $\frac{1}{6}$ of the number of all rooms. The ratio of the number of large classrooms to small classrooms is 1 : 3. If the number of small classrooms rooms is 45, what is the number of utility rooms in the school? A. 12 B. 15 C. 30 D. 60	108.	A juice mixture contains water and juice concentrate in the ratio of 7 : 2. If the mixture contains 300 ml more water than juice concentrate, how many milliliters of the mixture are there? E. 420 ml F. 450 ml G. 480 ml H. 540 ml
106.	Karen is cooking a birthday cake. The ratio of flour to sugar to nuts to butter is 5 : 2 : 1 : 3. If Karen uses 180 g of butter, what will be the weight of the cake? E. 660 g F. 600 g G. 540 g H. 480 g	109.	In a farm, the ratio of the number of geese to ducks to hens is 4 : 3 : 8. There are 20 more hens than ducks. If each goose eats 0.65 pound of grass per day, what is the total daily consumption of grass by all geese, in pounds? A. 7.8 B. 9.2 C. 10.4 D. 11.6
107.	The diagram above shows a triangle with a square inside. The ratio of the triangle's area to the square's area is 5 : 2. If the area of the shaded region is 54 cm^2, what is the length of the square's side? A. 9 cm B. 8 cm C. 7 cm D. 6 cm	110.	In triangle ABC, lines AC and DE are parallel. The ratio of BD to BA is 3 : 5. What percent of the triangle is shaded? E. 36% F. 40% G. 64% H. 60%

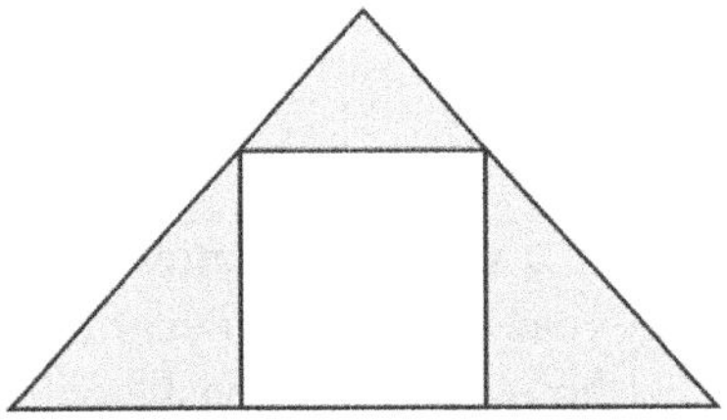

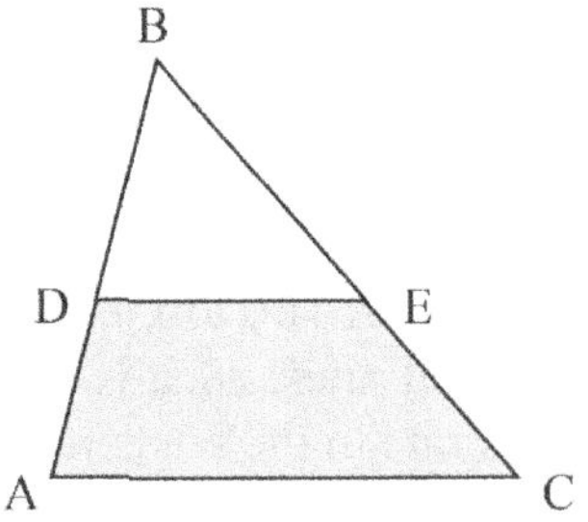

Questions 111 – 114

111. Water is poured into a glass for 5 seconds. The graph above shows the depth of the water in the glass. What is the meaning of point P?

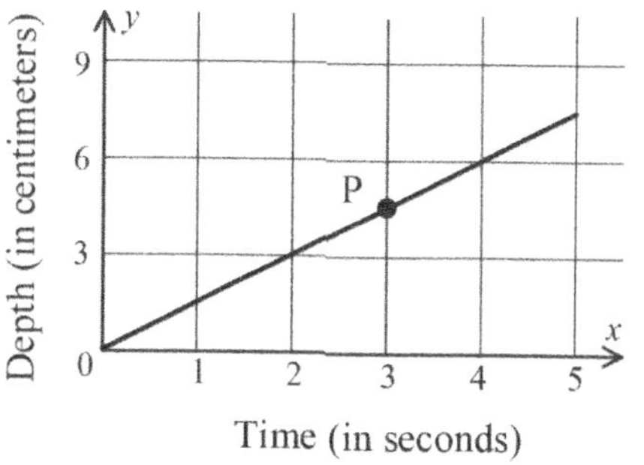

A. In 4.5 seconds the depth of the water is 3 cm
B. In 5 seconds the depth of the water is 3 cm
C. In 3 seconds the depth of the water is 4.5 cm
D. In 5 seconds the depth of the water is 4.5 cm

112. The diagram below shows a square attached to the base of a regular hexagon. The side lengths of the square and the hexagon are equal.

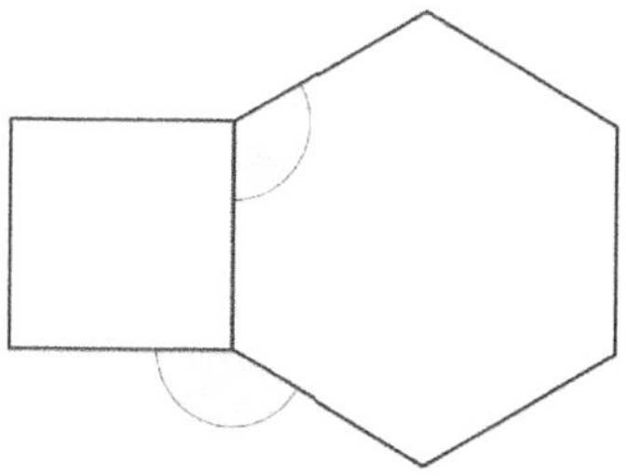

What is the ratio of the measure of the greater angle to the measure of the smaller angle?

E. 7 : 6
F. 6 : 5
G. 5 : 4
H. 4 : 3

113. Wendy needs a apples for b cupcakes. The table below shows proportional relationship between the number of apples and the number of cupcakes Wendy used for the same recipe.

Number of apples	Number of cupcakes
5	20
6	24
7	28

Which of the following statements is true?

A. $a = 2b$
B. $b = 4a$
C. $a = 4b$
D. $b = 2a$

114. Harvey has two mathematically similar wooden bears. He wants to paint them. Harvey spent $2.80 to paint the smaller bear. How much will it cost him to paint the larger one?

E. $1.75
F. $2.24
G. $3.50
H. $4.48

Test 5: Factors, Multiples, Exponents & radicals, absolute value, Scientific Notation

GRID-IN QUESTIONS			
Questions 58 – 62			
58.	If $\approx a \approx = 2 - 3a + a^2$, what is the value of $\approx (-4) \approx$?	61.	If $2^x \times 3^y \times 5^z = 1{,}200$, what is the value of $x \times y \times z$?
59.	A code contains three digits. How many different codes can be made with the digits 0 – 9 if no digit is used more than once and the first digit is neither 0, nor 1?	62.	The surveillance camera on the first house updates the video surveillance recording every half an hour. The surveillance camera on the second house updates the video surveillance recording every 40 minutes. If they both started recording at 9 a.m., in how many hours will they start recording again at the same time?
60.	$\lvert a - 2 \rvert = 4$ $\lvert 3 - b \rvert = 7$ If a and b are two positive solutions of the equations above, what is the value of $b - a$?		

MULTIPLE CHOICE QUESTIONS

Questions 63 – 68

63. What is the value of $\sqrt{\frac{81}{64}}$?

   A. $1\frac{1}{2}$

   B. $1\frac{1}{4}$

   C. $1\frac{3}{4}$

   D. $1\frac{1}{8}$

64. $|-6| + |6| - |-6| \div |6| + 6 =$

   E. 5
   F. 17
   G. 18
   H. 19

65. What is the value of 0.0000001012 in scientific notation?

   A. 1.12×10^{-7}
   B. 1.12×10^{7}
   C. 1.012×10^{7}
   D. 1.012×10^{-7}

66. The cleaning company has 12 workers. How many ways can you choose a cleaning group of 3 workers to service the order?

   E. 220
   F. 660
   G. 1,320
   H. 1,728

67. If $a \therefore b = ab + |b - a|$, what is the value of $6 \therefore (-3)$?

   A. -27
   B. -18
   C. -9
   D. 9

68. What is the greatest common factor of 350 and 420?

   E. 7
   F. 14
   G. 35
   H. 70

Questions 69 – 74

69. $|-100 + 60| - b - |-100 + 80| = 40$
In the equation above, what is the value of b?

A. 20
B. -20
C. 60
D. -60

70. What is the greatest prime factor of 260?

E. 2
F. 5
G. 13
H. 26

71. Damek has five number cards lying on the table. There are two number cards with digit 1, two number cards with digit 2 and one number card with 0. How many different three-digit numbers can Damek form? (Number cannot begin with 0)

A. 6
B. 12
C. 14
D. 60

72. Express 107,000 in scientific notation.

E. 1.07×10^5
F. 1.7×10^3
G. 1.07×10^3
H. 1.7×10^5

73. If $2^{3x} = 64$, what is the value of 3^x?

A. 729
B. 81
C. 27
D. 9

74. $a \boxtimes b = 2(b + a) - 3(a - b)$
What is the value of $a \boxtimes 2$ in terms of a?

E. $10 - a$
F. $7a - 2$
G. $10 + a$
H. $7a + 2$

Questions 75 – 80

75. Payton has 12 photos of her family. She wants to choose four photos to make a collage. How many different collages can Payton form? (If the same photos are placed in a different order, the collage is considered to be different)

   A. 11,880
   B. 20,736
   C. 990
   D. 495

76. What is the value of the numerical expression $(1.2 \times 10^2) \times (0.5 \times 10^3)$ in scientific notation?

   E. 0.6×10^5
   F. 6.0×10^4
   G. 0.6×10^4
   H. 6.0×10^5

77. If $*x* = |4x - 5|$, what is the value of $*(-3)*$?

   A. −17
   B. −7
   C. 17
   D. 7

78. What is the value of $-|-M| - |M|$ if $M = -|-12|$?

   E. 0
   F. −24
   G. 24
   H. −12

79. If $\sqrt{9-x} = 2$, what is the value of $\sqrt{125x}$?

   A. 5
   B. −5
   C. 25
   D. −25

80. Boxes that are 10 inches tall are being stacked next to boxes that are 12 inches tall. What is the smallest number of shorter boxes for which the two stacks will be of the same height?

   E. 5
   F. 6
   G. 10
   H. 12

Questions 81 – 86

81. What is the value of the expression
$$\frac{(4)^2(3)^3}{(2)^5(9)^2}?$$

   A. $\frac{1}{6}$

   B. $\frac{3}{2}$

   C. $\frac{2}{3}$

   D. 6

82. On Monday, two school teams are sharing the field for their practices. The first team meets for practice every 3 days, and the second team meets every 2 days. When will they have to share the field again?

   E. On Monday
   F. On Wednesday
   G. On Friday
   H. On Sunday

83. $$|x - 1| - |2 - x|$$
   If $x < 0$, and $|x + 3| = 5$, what is the value of the expression above?

   A. −1
   B. 1
   C. −19
   D. 19

84. An airplane sensor shows that the plane flew 5.02×10^3 kilometers this week. What expression shows this number in meters?

   E. 502,000,000
   F. 50,200,000
   G. 5,020,000
   H. 502,000

85. In a cafe, a boy met a girl. She wrote down him her phone number on a napkin. When the boy came home, he saw that the first two digits were erased. How many phone number combinations does he have to go through to call the girl in the worst-case scenario?

   A. 90
   B. 100
   C. 45
   D. 50

86. For some operation $\oplus$, $a \oplus b = b \oplus a$. Which of the following options gives possible expression for $\oplus$?

   E. $x \oplus y = \frac{x^2}{y^2}$

   F. $x \oplus y = \sqrt{x^2 - y^2}$

   G. $x \oplus y = \frac{1}{2}x^2 + \frac{1}{3}y^2$

   H. $x \oplus y = \frac{1}{4}x^2 + \frac{1}{4}y^2$

Questions 87 – 92

87. $$\propto x = \frac{4}{x} + x^2$$
If $\propto x = 15$, what is the value of x?

A. -1
B. -2
C. -4
D. -8

88. Alexa puts the books in the bookcase. She has 9 books with green covers and 15 books with red covers. How many ways can Alexa order books on the bookshelf if she wants to put all books with red covers first?

E. $15! \times 9!$

F. $\frac{15!}{9!}$

G. $15! + 9!$

H. $\frac{15!}{(15-9)!}$

89. What is the value of 2.7×10^{-4} in standard form?

A. 0.27
B. 0.027
C. 0.0027
D. 0.00027

90. $$|x - 12| = 5 - y,$$
$$|3 - y| = 18$$
In the equations above, $x > 0, y < 0$. What is the value of x?

E. 38
F. 36
G. 34
H. 32

91. $$\frac{17^2 \times 9^2}{(-51)^2}$$
What is the value of the expression above?

A. -9
B. 9
C. -27
D. 27

92. The table below shows the number of students in the school choir.

Boys	32
Girls	48

The choir teacher plans to arrange the students in equal rows. Only girls or boys will be in each row. What is the greatest possible number of rows?

E. 4
F. 5
G. 7
H. 16

Questions 93 – 98

93. $A = 2^6 \times 3^4 \times 5^2$,
$B = 2^2 \times 3^4 \times 5^6$
What is the least common multiple of numbers A and B?

A. $2^8 \times 3^8 \times 5^8$
B. $2^6 \times 3^4 \times 5^6$
C. $2^4 \times 3^6 \times 5^4$
D. $2^4 \times 3^4 \times 5^4$

94. For any number x, the symbol $< x >$ means the greatest integer that is smaller than or equal to x. What is the value of $< \sqrt{190} >$?

E. 12
F. 13
G. 14
H. 15

95. If $15 - 2x > 29$, what is the smallest possible integer value of $|x|$?

A. 6
B. 7
C. 8
D. Cannot be defined

96. How many composite numbers are between 6 and 26 inclusive?

E. 6
F. 7
G. 15
H. 14

97. If $X = 27^2$ and $Y = 81^2$, which of the following statements is false?

A. $\frac{X}{Y} = \frac{1}{3^2}$

B. $XY = 3^{48}$

C. $X + Y = 3^6 \times 10$

D. $\frac{Y}{X} = 9$

98. The distance from Seren's home to the school is 2.8×10^3 meters. The distance from Seren's school to the amusement park is 3.6×10^3 meters. In standard form, what is the distance from Seren's home to the amusement park walking through the school?

E. 0.8 km
F. 4.6 km
G. 5.2 km
H. 6.4 km

Questions 99 – 104

99. If $f(x) = x^4$, then how many times greater is $f(8)$ then $f(4)$?

    A. 2
    B. 4
    C. 8
    D. 16

100. Which of the following is equivalent to $5^4 + 5^4 + 5^4 + 5^4 + 5^4$?

    E. 5^5
    F. 5^{10}
    G. 5^{15}
    H. 5^{20}

101. The menu at a restaurant offers 4 different soups, 5 salads and 7 desserts. How many different combinations of a soup, a salad and a dessert are possible from the menu?

    A. 16
    B. 140
    C. 63
    D. 70

102. When expressed in scientific notation, the number 62,500,000,000 is written as 6.25×10^M. What is the value of M?

    E. 8
    F. 9
    G. 10
    H. 11

103. Willy, Billy, Molly, Dolly and Olli run a race. In how many different ways can the first and the second places be shared?

    A. 5×5
    B. 5×4
    C. $5!$
    D. $2!$

104. The designer of the fantasy book painted the starry sky on the cover, using a scale $1 : 3 \times 10^7$. If the distance between two stars on the cover is 3 cm, what is the actual distance between these two stars?

    E. 900 km
    F. 90,000 km
    G. 10,000,000,000 km
    H. 90,000,000,000 km

Questions 105 – 110

105. If $a \square b = a^2b - 2ab + 3b^3$, what is the expression for $a \square (-a)$?

   A. $2a^2(a-1)$
   B. $-2a^2(a-1)$
   C. $2a^2(2a-1)$
   D. $-2a^2(2a-1)$

106. The set of possible values of k is $\{-6, -4, 2, 3, 5\}$. If $m = 2k - 3$, what is the greatest possible absolute value of m?

   E. 15
   F. 11
   G. 7
   H. 3

107. In a sample of 20 cards, 8 are red and 7 are blue, and the rest are green. How many different ways can two cards of different colors be selected?

   A. 380
   B. 131
   C. 171
   D. 280

108. Which of the following numbers has factors that include the smallest factor (greater than 1) of 299?

   E. 63
   F. 65
   G. 69
   H. 72

109. There are 9 color pencils in the box. Kate will choose 2 of these pencils to draw a two-color striped flag. How many different pairs of two-color striped flags can she draw? (Note that the red-black and black-red flags are different)

   A. 72
   B. 17
   C. 81
   D. 36

110. How many multiples of 6 are greater than 6 but less than 10 times the 6?

   E. 6
   F. 8
   G. 10
   H. 12

Questions 111 – 114			
111.	How many even 6-digit numbers can be created using the digits 2, 3, 5, 6, 7, and 8 without repeating any digits within that 6-digit number? A. 20 B. 120 C. 360 D. 720	113.	Holly thinks about two whole numbers a and b. She calculates that the greatest common factor between numbers a and b is 12 and the least common multiple between these numbers is 420. Which of the following pairs of numbers can represent a and b? A. 12, 84 B. 60, 84 C. 12, 210 D. 60, 210
112.	If $a^x \times a^5 = a^{12}$ and $(b^3)^y = b^{21}$, which of the following statements is true? E. $y = 18$ F. $x = 2.4$ G. $x = y + 1$ H. $x = y$	114.	The age difference between Emma and Sophia is 3 years. If Emma is 12 years old and it is unknown who of them is older, how to write an equation to determine the age of Sophia? E. $\|x - 12\| = 3$ F. $\|x + 12\| = 3$ G. $\|x - 3\| = 12$ H. $\|x + 3\| = 12$

Test 6: Algebra (Part 1)

GRID-IN QUESTIONS			
Questions 58 – 62			
58.	Storm's age is 6 years more than twice Ellie's age. If the sum of their ages is 57 years, what is Storm's age?	61.	Linette and Celeste have a total of 56 marbles. If Celeste has 16 fewer marbles than Linette has, how many marbles does Celeste have?
59.	Zooey has 12 fewer quarters than nickels. If the total value of her coins is $3.30, how many quarters does Zooey have?	62.	If $\frac{x^2}{2y} = 8$, $y = 9$, and $x > 0$, what is the value of $\frac{2x-y}{2y-x}$?
60.	$\frac{5}{11} = \frac{x-15}{x+15}$ What is the value of x in the equation above?		

MULTIPLE CHOICE QUESTIONS

Questions 63 – 68

63. The difference of two positive integers is 24. If the greater integer is thrice the smaller integer, what is the greater integer?

    A. 12
    B. 24
    C. 36
    D. 48

64. If $\frac{a}{b} = 7$ and $5 - b = 1$, what is the value of a?

    E. 1.75
    F. 4
    G. 28
    H. 42

65. If $m = -3$, which of the following is equivalent to $5 - mx + m^2x$?

    A. $5 + 6x$
    B. $5 + 12x$
    C. $5 - 6x$
    D. $5 - 12x$

66. The second angle of a triangle is 3 times the first angle. The third angle is 20° less than the first. What is the measure of the smallest angle of the triangle?

    E. 40°
    F. 30°
    G. 20°
    H. 10°

67. $12 - 2(x - 3) = x$

    In the equation above, what is the value of x?

    A. -6
    B. -3
    C. 3
    D. 6

68. If $x = -5$, which of the following expressions has the greatest value?

    E. $(x - 1)(x - 4)$
    F. $(x - 1)(x + 4)$
    G. $(x + 1)(x - 4)$
    H. $(x + 1)(x + 4)$

	Questions 69 – 74		
69.	A sofa and a table together costs $504. The sofa costs 200% more than the table costs. How much does the sofa cost? A. $126 B. $254 C. $378 D. $402	72.	Abigail is 8 years older than Daisy is. 4 years ago, Daisy's age was half of Abigail's age. How old is Abigail now? E. 16 F. 18 G. 20 H. 22
70.	The perimeter of a rectangle is 76 cm. The length of the rectangle is 5 cm more than twice its width. What is the area of the rectangle? E. $242\ cm^2$ F. $255\ cm^2$ G. $276\ cm^2$ H. $297\ cm^2$	73.	A freight train starts from city A for city B at a rate of 50 mph. One hour later, a passenger train leaves from city A for city B at a rate of 80 mph. How long in total will the freight train be on the way when a passenger train overtakes it? A. 1 hour 40 minutes B. 2 hour 10 minutes C. 2 hour 20 minutes D. 2 hour 40 minutes
71.	If $(x-4)^2 = 49$ and $x < 0$, what is the value of $(2-x)^2$? A. 81 B. -3 C. 9 D. 25	74.	If $ab = -6$, what is the value of $$\frac{1}{3} \times \frac{a^2}{b} \times b^3?$$ E. 12 F. -12 G. 36 H. -36

Questions 75 – 80

75.

Input	Output
1	1
2	3
5	9
14	27
63	x

Which of the following is represented by x in the table above?

A. 125
B. 126
C. 127
D. 128

76. Tickets for the basketball game were $4.50 for adults and $2.50 for children. If adult tickets were sold for 40 more than children's, and total receipts were $740, how many adult tickets were sold?

E. 80
F. 120
G. 160
H. 200

77. If $2x - y = 12$, and $25x - 11x = 49$, what is the value of y?

A. 5
B. -5
C. 2
D. -2

78. It takes Jacob and Hannah a hours to do a certain job, it takes Jacob and Ethan b hours to do the same job and it takes Hannah and Ethan c hours to do the same job. How long would it take Jacob, Hannah and Ethan to do the same job if all of them worked together?

E. $2a + 2b + 2c$ hours
F. abc hours
G. $2abc$ hours
H. $a + b + c$ hours

79. If $1.8a + 0.6b = 2.4b - 3.6a$, what is the value of b in terms of a?

A. $b = a$
B. $b = -a$
C. $b = 3a$
D. $b = \frac{1}{3}a$

80. The Girl Club made some cakes to sell during school festival to raise money for a trip. The local bakery helped them by donating two cakes to the club. Each cake was then cut into twelve pieces and sold. There were a total of 156 pieces sold. How many cakes did the club make?

E. 9
F. 10
G. 11
H. 12

Questions 81 – 86

81. $$\frac{2x-1}{x+1} = 1.8$$
What is the value of x in the equation above?

   A. 14
   B. 15
   C. 16
   D. 17

82. Mr. Roderick used 10 more gallons of fuel oil in June than in May, and 3 times as much fuel oil in July as in May. Which of the following expressions can be used to find the total number of gallons of fuel oil used in the three months, if x represents the number of gallons of fuel oil used in June?

   E. $5x + 10$
   F. $5x - 40$
   G. $5x - 10$
   H. $5x + 40$

83. 115, 109, 103, 97, 91, 85, ...
The first six terms of a sequence are shown. Each term after the first is found by subtracting 6 from the immediately preceding term. Which term in the sequence is preceding $3(x-2)$?

   A. $3x - 12$
   B. $3x - 6$
   C. $3x$
   D. $3x + 6$

84. If $280{,}000 = 2{,}000(m - 2)$, then $m =$

   E. 138
   F. 16
   G. 142
   H. 12

85. On his business trip in Chicago, Xavier's expenses for food and lodging combined were $450 less than twice the flight cost. Which of the following expressions can be used to find Xavier's expenses for food and lodging in terms of flight cost?

   A. $x - 450$
   B. $x + 450$
   C. $2x - 450$
   D. $2x + 450$

86. If $2a = 3b, 2b = 3c, 2c = 3d$, and $a, b, c,$ and d are all positive integers, which of the following is true?

   E. $a < c < b < d$
   F. $d < c < b < a$
   G. $d < b < c < a$
   H. $a < b < c < d$

246

Questions 87 – 92

87. Austin is half as old as his professor, Dr. Martins. Sebastian is three years older than Austin. If Sebastian is 21 years old, how ald is Dr. Martins?

A. 36 years old
B. 39 years old
C. 45 years old
D. 48 years old

88. If $a(x + y) = 156$, and $ay = 14$, what is the value of $150 - ax$?

E. -20
F. 136
G. -6
H. 8

89. "The square root of the difference of a and b is the difference of b and the square root of a".
Which of the following expressions represents the statement above?

A. $\sqrt{a-b} = \sqrt{a} - b$
B. $\sqrt{a-b} = a - \sqrt{b}$
C. $\sqrt{a-b} = b - \sqrt{a}$
D. $\sqrt{a-b} = \sqrt{b} - a$

90. $$\frac{0.12}{0.09} = \frac{3.2}{2x}$$
What is the value of x in the equation above?

E. 0.12
F. 1.2
G. 12
H. 120

91. $5x^2y^2 - 12xy^2z + 4xyz^2 - 8y^2z^2$
The coefficient of xz^2 in the expression above is ...

A. $-12y^2$
B. $4y$
C. $-\frac{12y^2}{z}$
D. 4

92. Expression $2a - (b - 3c)$ is the same as expression $a - c + (*)$. What should stand in the place of $*$ in the last expression?

E. $a - b + 4c$
F. $a - b + 2c$
G. $a - b - 2c$
H. $a - b - 4c$

Questions 93 – 98

93. A taxi service charges $2.25 per km and a fixed charge of $5.50. If the taxi is hired for x km, which of the following expressions represents the total expenses?

A. $\$(2.25 + 5.50)x$
B. $\$(2.25x + 5.50)$
C. $\$(2.25 + 5.50x)$
D. $\$(2.25x + 5.50x)$

94. If $a + b = 15$, and $\frac{a}{b} = 2$, what is the value of $a - b$?

E. 5
F. 10
G. -5
H. -10

95. If $2y = 9x$, what value of x does $x = -y$?

A. 0
B. $-\frac{2}{9}$
C. $-\frac{9}{2}$
D. Does not exist

96. Steve works in a mall and is paid $6.50 per hour. Last week he worked for 36 hours and this week he worked for x hours. If Steve was paid $507 in total, what is the value of x?

E. 38
F. 40
G. 42
H. 44

97. "The product of $2x$ and $\frac{3}{8}$ is equal to the quotient of 0.24 and $3x$".

Which of the following expressions represents the statement above?

A. $2x \times \frac{3}{8} = \frac{0.24}{3x}$

B. $2x \times \frac{3}{8} = \frac{3x}{0.24}$

C. $2x \times \frac{3}{8} = 0.24 \times 3x$

D. $2x \times \frac{3}{8} = 0.24 \div \frac{1}{3x}$

98. When 10 more than $3x$ is doubled, the result is the same as when $2x$ is subtracted from 100. What is the value of x?

E. 10
F. 20
G. 30
H. 40

	Questions 99 – 104		
99.	Finn and Hugo have to collect different kinds of leaves for biology project. They go to a park where Finn collects 35 leaves and Hugo collects x leaves. After some time Finn loses 2 leaves and Hugo collects 13 more leaves. If they ended up with the same number of leaves, what is the value of x? A. 12 B. 16 C. 20 D. 24	102.	If $454{,}545 = 45(x + 101)$, what is the value of x? E. 10,000 F. 1,000 G. 100 H. 10
100.	The sum of four consecutive integers is 134. If g represents the greatest of these integers, which of the following statements is true? E. $4g = 128$ F. $4g = 132$ G. $4g = 136$ H. $4g = 140$	103.	If $x - y = 2$, $y = 4z$, and $z = \frac{3}{8}$, what is the value of $x + y + z$? A. $5\frac{1}{4}$ B. $5\frac{3}{4}$ C. $5\frac{3}{8}$ D. $5\frac{7}{8}$
101.	The rate of planting the grass is \$$x$ per square meter. What is the cost of planting the grass on a triangular lawn with the base of a meters and height of h meters? A. $\$\frac{\frac{1}{2}ah}{x}$ B. $\$\frac{1}{2}xah$ C. $\$\frac{ah}{x}$ D. $\$xah$	104.	$$\frac{1}{3}n^2 + \frac{1}{6}n$$ The sum of the first n numbers in the sequence is given by formula above. What is the second term in the sequence? E. $\frac{1}{2}$ F. $\frac{5}{3}$ G. $\frac{7}{6}$ H. $\frac{13}{6}$

Questions 105 – 110

105.	Nathan buys 30 avocados at x cents each and 72 oranges at $x - 24$ cents each. He packs them into 6 bags containing the same number of avocados and the same number of oranges and sells the bags for $11.57 each. If Nathan's total profit on selling fruit is $10.20, what is the value of x? A. 75 B. 61 C. 51 D. 85	108.	Working together, it takes Tyler and Gabriel six hours to paint one room. When Tyler works alone, he can paint one room in 8 hours. How long will it take Gabriel to paint the room alone? E. 4 hours F. 12 hours G. 16 hours H. 24 hours
106.	If $2 + 8x = 13$, what is the value of $11 - 8x$? E. 2 F. 1 G. 0 H. −1	109.	Luke walked 5 kilometers to his friend's house and returned home. His speed to home was 1 kilometer per hour faster than speed to his friend's house, and it took him 25 fewer minutes to get to home. The total time for both trips was 2 hours 55 minutes. What was Luke's initial walking speed? A. 4.5 km/h B. 4 km/h C. 3.5 km/h D. 3 km/h
107.	If $\frac{3}{8}$ of b is 60, what is $\frac{5}{8}$ of b? A. 4 B. 20 C. 40 D. 100	110.	If $\frac{4}{9}$ of a number is 32, what is $\frac{2}{3}$ of this number? E. 16 F. 24 G. 36 H. 48

Questions 111 – 114

111. If $5a^1 - 25a^0 = 0$, what is the value of $a^2 + a + 1$?

A. 29
B. 31
C. 26
D. 24

112. In a moneybox, there are nickels and dimes. The total value of all 56 coins is $4.40. Which of the following equations can be used to find the number of dimes in moneybox?

E. $5x + 10(56 - x) = 440$
F. $5(56 - x) + 10x = 440$
G. $5x + 10(56 - x) = 4.40$
H. $5(56 - x) + 10x = 4.40$

113. If $k = -4$, which of the following expressions is equivalent to $(1 - k)x^2 + 2kx - (3 + k)$?

A. $5x^2 - 8x - 1$
B. $-3x^2 - 8x - 1$
C. $-3x^2 - 8x + 1$
D. $5x^2 - 8x + 1$

114. If $x - 5y = 45$ and $xy = -20$, which of the following statements is true?

E. $y^2 + 9y + 4 = 0$
F. $y^2 + 9y - 4 = 0$
G. $y^2 - 9y - 4 = 0$
H. $y^2 - 9y + 4 = 0$

TEST 7: Algebra (part 2)

GRID-IN QUESTIONS			
Questions 58 – 62			
58.	The range of the heights in Ms. Nancy's class could be described as $\|x - 165\| \leq 7$. How many integer values are included in the range?	61.	$39 < x^2 < 60$ $53 < y^2 < 100$ If x and y are positive integers, what is the smallest possible value of xy?
59.	$3x - 7 < 56$ What is the greatest integer solution to the inequality above?	62.	$\|x - 9\| < 3$ $\|x + 5\| < 13$ What integer value of x satisfies both inequalities above?
60.	The cost, in dollars, of producing y chairs is $1{,}320 + 24y$. The chairs are sold for \$35 each. What number of chairs would need to be sold so that the revenue received is greater than the cost of producing chairs?		

MULTIPLE CHOICE QUESTIONS

Questions 63 – 68

63. If $2a - 13 \geq -7a + 23$, what is the smallest possible value of $4a + 1$?

   A. 15
   B. 16
   C. 17
   D. 18

64. To edit a text, Otto charges $60 for the first two hours and $22 per hour after the first two hours. Which of the following inequalities could be used to find the minimum number of hours, x, Otto should edit the text in order to earn at least $478?

   E. $60 + 22x \leq 478$
   F. $60 + 22x \geq 478$
   G. $60 + 22(x - 2) \leq 478$
   H. $60 + 22(x - 2) \geq 478$

65. $$4 - 9x \leq -14$$
   What is the solution to the inequality above?

   A. $x \geq 2$
   B. $x \leq 2$
   C. $x \geq -2$
   D. $x \leq -2$

66. If x is greater than $-\frac{1}{2}$ but less than $\frac{1}{4}$, which of the following expressions has the largest value?

   E. $x + 1$
   F. x^2
   G. $2x$
   H. $-x^2$

67. Each morning, Don jogs at 8 kilometers per hour and rides a bike at 15 kilometers per hour. His goal is to cover a total of at least 10 kilometers in one hour. If Don rides his bike for b hours, which of the following inequalities represents Don's goal?

   A. $8(1 - b) + 15b \geq 10$
   B. $8(1 - b) + 15b \leq 10$
   C. $8b + 15(1 - b) \geq 10$
   D. $8b + 15(1 - b) \leq 10$

68. If $8 - 3a < -4$, which of the following is not a possible value of a?

   E. $5\frac{1}{2}$
   F. 5
   G. $4\frac{1}{2}$
   H. 4

	Questions 69 – 74		
69.	$-x, -4x, -16x, -64x$ If $x < 0$, which of the four values has the smallest value? A. $-x$ B. $-4x$ C. $-16x$ D. $-64x$	72.	If $\frac{m}{b} = -2$, and $b \neq 0$, what does $10b$ equal in terms of m? E. $\frac{m}{5}$ F. $-\frac{m}{5}$ G. $5m$ H. $-5m$
70.	If n represents an odd integer, which of the following expressions represents an even integer? E. $2n - 5$ F. $3n + 4$ G. $4n - 3$ H. $5n - 1$	73.	If $2a - 4b < 4a - 2b$, which of the following statements must be true? A. $-a < b$ B. $-a < b$ C. $-a > -b$ D. $-a < -b$
71.	If $a < 0$ and $b > 0$, which of the following expressions must be negative? A. $(-a)^2 \times b$ B. $(-a) \times b^2$ C. $(-a^2) \times b$ D. $a^2 \times (-b)^2$	74.	If Bonnie is now x years old and Danielle is 5 years older than Bonnie is, which of the following expressions shows Danielle's age a years ago? E. $x - 5 + a$ F. $x - 5 - a$ G. $x + 5 - a$ H. $x + 5 + a$

Questions 75 – 80

75. If $1 - a$ represents an even number, which of the following expressions represents an even number greater than $1 - a$?

    A. $5 - a$
    B. $a - 5$
    C. $3 + a$
    D. $a - 3$

76. Mr. Douglas sold x hamburgers. Mr. and Mrs. Douglas together sold $4x - 7$ hamburgers. In terms of x, how many more hamburgers did Mrs. Douglass sell?

    E. $3x - 7$
    F. $2x - 7$
    G. $x - 7$
    H. x

77. $$3 - 5x \leq 4x + 30$$
    Which of the following inequalities is equivalent to the inequality above?

    A. $-x \geq -3$
    B. $-x \leq -3$
    C. $3x \leq -9$
    D. $2x \geq -6$

78.

	Distance
Isaac	2.1t meters
Joyce	2.4t meters

Isaac and Joyce are running on a 400-meter track. The expressions in the table above show the distances both of them run t seconds after they started the race. How many meters will Isaac have left to finish the race when Joyce is on the finish line?

    E. 50 meters
    F. 45 meters
    G. 40 meters
    H. 35 meters

79. Julian wants to rent a car for three days and pay no more than $220. How far can he drive the car if the car rental cost $20 per day plus $0.50 per mile?

    A. At most 320 miles
    B. At most 310 miles
    C. At most 300 miles
    D. At most 290 miles

80. If $x > 2y$ and $-y < 3z$, which of the following statements must be true?

    E. $x > -6z$
    F. $x < -6z$
    G. $-x > -6z$
    H. $-x < -6z$

Questions 81 – 86

81. The composite figure above is made up of two congruent rectangles. What is the perimeter of the figure in terms of x and y?

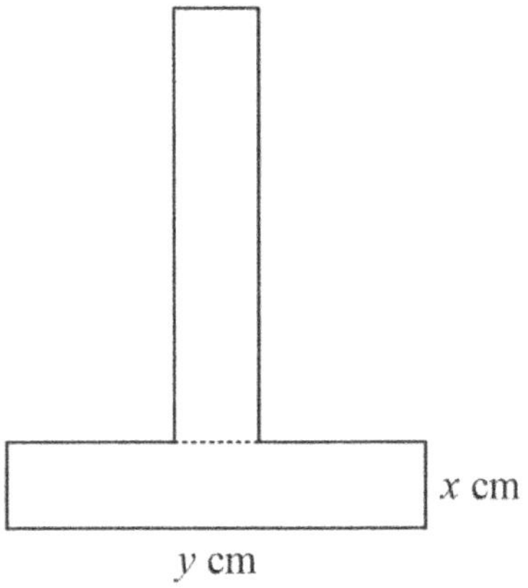

A. $4y + 3x$ cm
B. $4y + 2x$ cm
C. $3y + 4x$ cm
D. $3y + 3x$ cm

82. If $4x = 5y$ and $2x = 3z$, what is z in terms of y?

E. $\frac{5}{6}y$

F. $\frac{10}{3}y$

G. $\frac{6}{5}y$

H. $\frac{3}{10}y$

83. If x and y are two positive consecutive even integers, and $x > y$, what is the value of $(y - x)^2$?

A. 2
B. −2
C. 4
D. −4

84. $5 + x - 1 > 4x + 4$

Which of the following number lines shows the solution to the inequality above?

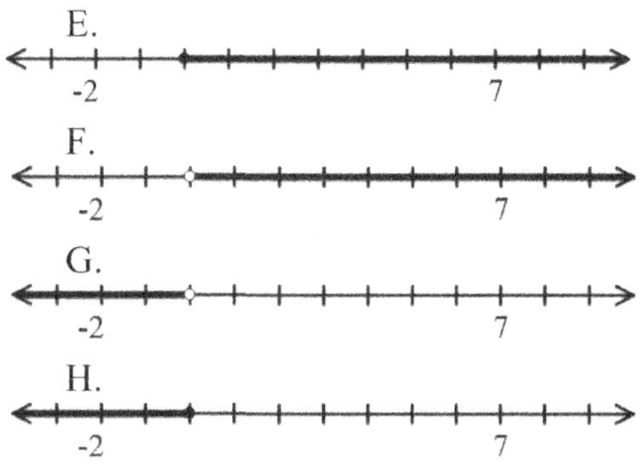

E. (number line from −2 to 7, shaded right of a closed point)
F. (number line from −2 to 7, shaded right of an open point)
G. (number line from −2 to 7, shaded left of an open point)
H. (number line from −2 to 7, shaded left of a closed point)

85. If $ab = c$, $ac = mb$, and $ab \neq 0$, which of the following is equal to m?

A. 1

B. $\frac{1}{a^2}$

C. $(ab)^2$

D. a^2

86. If x and y are two even integers, which of the following is an odd number?

E. $3x(2y - 1)$
F. $(3x - 1)(2y)$
G. $(3x + 1)(2y - 1)$
H. $3x(2y + 1)$

Questions 87 – 92

87.

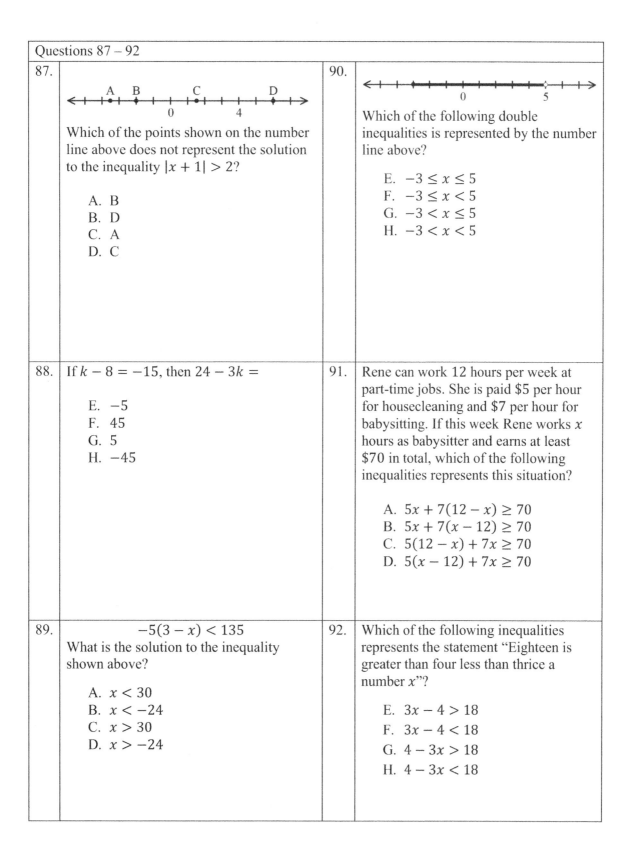

Which of the points shown on the number line above does not represent the solution to the inequality $|x + 1| > 2$?

A. B
B. D
C. A
D. C

88. If $k - 8 = -15$, then $24 - 3k =$

E. -5
F. 45
G. 5
H. -45

89.
$$-5(3 - x) < 135$$
What is the solution to the inequality shown above?

A. $x < 30$
B. $x < -24$
C. $x > 30$
D. $x > -24$

90.

Which of the following double inequalities is represented by the number line above?

E. $-3 \leq x \leq 5$
F. $-3 \leq x < 5$
G. $-3 < x \leq 5$
H. $-3 < x < 5$

91. Rene can work 12 hours per week at part-time jobs. She is paid $5 per hour for housecleaning and $7 per hour for babysitting. If this week Rene works x hours as babysitter and earns at least $70 in total, which of the following inequalities represents this situation?

A. $5x + 7(12 - x) \geq 70$
B. $5x + 7(x - 12) \geq 70$
C. $5(12 - x) + 7x \geq 70$
D. $5(x - 12) + 7x \geq 70$

92. Which of the following inequalities represents the statement "Eighteen is greater than four less than thrice a number x"?

E. $3x - 4 > 18$
F. $3x - 4 < 18$
G. $4 - 3x > 18$
H. $4 - 3x < 18$

Questions 93 – 98

93. A zoo worker weighed all 30 monkeys in the enclosure. The lightest monkey weighed 2 kg 400 g, the heaviest weighed 36 kg 800 g. Which of the following inequalities represents the range, in grams, of monkeys' weights?

    A. $2.4 \leq x \leq 36.8$
    B. $2.4 < x < 36.8$
    C. $2,400 < x < 36,800$
    D. $2,400 \leq x \leq 36,800$

94. Which of the following inequalities indicates that a positive number x is less than or equal to half the value of y?

    E. $0 \leq x \leq \frac{1}{2}y$
    F. $0 < x \leq \frac{1}{2}y$
    G. $0 \leq x < \frac{1}{2}y$
    H. $0 < x < \frac{1}{2}y$

95. Nicole worked 6 more hours than Phil did. If together they worked no more than 90 hours, what was the maximum possible number of hours Nicole worked?

    A. 42
    B. 44
    C. 48
    D. 50

96. A salad contains a total of at most 1.8 kg of tomatoes and chicken. If the amount of chicken in the salad is twice the amount of tomatoes, which of the following inequalities represents this situation?

    E. $x + 2x \geq 1.8$
    F. $x + 2x \leq 1.8$
    G. $x + 1.8 \leq 2x$
    H. $x + 1.8 \geq 2x$

97. The Students Committee must consist of 6 to 9 representatives from the junior and senior classes. Which of the following inequalities represents the range of representatives?

    A. $6 \leq x \leq 9$
    B. $6 \geq x \geq 9$
    C. $6 < x < 9$
    D. $6 > x > 9$

98. A delivery company is hired to deliver 150 antique vases for $28 each. The company agrees to pay $56 for each vase that is broken during transportation. If the delivery company needs to receive at least a payment of $3,640, what is the maximum number of vases that can be broken during transportation?

    E. 10
    F. 9
    G. 8
    H. 7

Questions 99 – 104

99.	Each term of the sequence is three more than half the previous term. If the value of the second term is at most 18, what could be the maximum value of the first term? A. 42 B. 6 C. 12 D. 30	102.	Barry has x muffins. He gives y muffins to his friend and then bakes z more muffins. He divides all muffins he has now into w gift boxes with equal numbers of muffins in each box. Which of the following expressions represents the number of muffins in each gift box? E. $\frac{x-y+z}{w}$ F. $\frac{x+y-z}{w}$ G. $w(x-y+z)$ H. $w(x+y-z)$
100.	If the average of three numbers a, b and c is k, what is the average of four numbers $a, b, c,$ and d? E. $\frac{k+d}{4}$ F. $\frac{3k+d}{4}$ G. $\frac{k+d}{2}$ H. $\frac{3k+d}{2}$	103.	If $8x + 9 = 6y - 11$, what is the value of $3y - 4x$? A. -10 B. -20 C. 10 D. 20
101.	An electronic store has a sale for 12% off the price of laptops. Which expression shows how much a company would save if it buys a laptops for $\$p$ each? A. $\$ap - \$0.12ap$ B. $\$0.12ap$ C. $\$\frac{0.12p}{a}$ D. $\$\frac{p}{a} - \$\frac{0.12p}{a}$	104.	A florist can make x bouquets of y roses in each. He decided to increase the number of roses in each bouquet by 2, which leaves him 5 extra roses. How many such bouquets can the florist make? E. $\frac{xy-5}{y+2}$ F. $\frac{xy+5}{y+2}$ G. $\frac{xy-5}{x+2}$ H. $\frac{xy+5}{x+2}$

Questions 105 – 110

105. A movie ticket costs $s. The cinema announced a promotion: every third ticket is for half price. How much will the customer save by buying 9 promotional tickets?

A. $0.5s
B. $s
C. $1.5s
D. $3s

106. If $x = 8$, what is the least integer value of y that satisfies the inequality $x - 3y < -3$?

E. 2
F. 3
G. 4
H. 5

107. $$-\frac{1}{2} \leq x - 3 < 2$$
How many integers satisfies the inequality above?

A. 2
B. 3
C. 4
D. 5

108. Florence earns $9 per hour delivering pizzas and is charged $4 for each late delivery. She worked for a hours this week and had b late deliveries. Which of the following expressions shows how much Florence earned?

E. $(4a + 9b)$
F. $(4a - 9b)$
G. $(9a + 4b)$
H. $(9a - 4b)$

109. If $\frac{1}{n} = \frac{5}{m}$ and $\frac{m-1}{5} = 1$, what is the value of $m + n$?

A. $7\frac{1}{5}$

B. $6\frac{4}{5}$

C. $7\frac{5}{6}$

D. $6\frac{5}{6}$

110. There are a players on the school basketball team. In the game, the team scored a total of 85 points. Kirk scored 3 more points than the average number of points per player. How many points did Kirk score?

E. $\frac{85}{a} - 3$

F. $\frac{85}{a+3}$

G. $\frac{85}{a} + 3$

H. $\frac{85}{a-3}$

260

Questions 111 – 114

111. Rafael has x in his savings account, and Whitney has y in her savings account. Rafael has $15 more than the average amount of money they have in total. Which of the following equations represents this situation?

A. $x - 15 = \frac{x+y}{2}$

B. $x + 15 = \frac{x+y}{2}$

C. $y - 15 = \frac{x+y}{2}$

D. $x + y = \frac{x+y}{2} + 15$

112. If $x + y = a$, $x + z = a^2$, and $y + z = 1$, what is the value of $x + y + z$ in terms of a?

E. $a^2 + a + 1$
F. $\frac{1}{2}(a^2 + a + 1)$
G. $2(a^2 + a + 1)$
H. $0.2(a^2 + a + 1)$

113. Paula has 156 stamps in her collection. Her school is hosting a stamp donation. There are f students planning to donate the same amount of stamps and reach a total donation of s stamps. How many stamps will Paula have in her collection after her donation?

A. $\frac{s-156}{f}$

B. $156 - \frac{s}{f}$

C. $\frac{156-s}{f}$

D. $\frac{s}{f} - 156$

114. If $x - 5y = 2y - 27x$ and $xy = 1$, which of the following statements cannot be true?

E. $x = \frac{1}{2}$

F. $y = 2$

G. $y = -1$

H. $x = -\frac{1}{2}$

Test 8: Probability & Statistics

GRID-IN QUESTIONS

Questions 58 – 62

58.	If the mean of the numbers a, $4a$, $12a$ and 5 is 65, what is the value of a?	61.	For a math test, Ms. Rudolf divided the class into two parts. The first 12 students wrote one version and received an average of 81 points. The other 13 students wrote the second version and received an average of 86 points. What is the average score in the whole class?
59.	Erin's playlist includes rock songs and lyric songs. There are 18% more rock songs than lyric songs. What is the probability that a randomly chosen song to listen to will be lyric?	62.	Tobias's box of 80 candies contains mint caramels, chocolate circles and vanilla lozenges. The probability of randomly picking out a mint caramel is $\frac{1}{5}$, the probability of randomly picking a chocolate circle is $\frac{3}{8}$. If Tobias ate all the chocolate circles, what is his probability of picking out a vanilla lozenge after that?
60.	The set A contains all multiples of 3, which are not multiples of 4 greater than 11 but less than 37. What is the median number in the set A?		

MULTIPLE CHOICE QUESTIONS

Questions 63 – 68

63. A bowl contains 12 red marbles, 13 blue marbles and 15 green marbles. If one marble is selected at random, what is the probability that it will be green?

A. 0.3
B. 0.325
C. 0.35
D. 0.375

64.
$$2, 3, 5, 6, 9, 11, 13, 17$$
Which number should be added to the list of numbers above for the median to become 9?

E. 4
F. 6
G. 8
H. 10

65. There is a rule on the TV channel: each 50-minute episode of the series can be interrupted at any time by 4.5-minute advertising. Usually, a housekeeper watches three episodes of her favorite series every day. What is the probability that if she randomly turns on the TV, she will get on advertising?

A. 0.09
B. 0.075
C. 0.05
D. 0.045

66. A bean's container contains 90 beans. 27 of them are red, 18 of them are black and the rest are white. If one bean is selected at random, what is the probability that it will not be a red one?

E. 0.2
F. 0.3
G. 0.7
H. 0.8

67. Passing three math tests, Katya scored an average of 78 points. Which of the following could be the results of these three tests?

A. 72, 76, 80
B. 73, 77, 81
C. 74, 79, 81
D. 75, 77, 80

68. Waiting for an unexpected shot, the photographer sat in the jungle for 6 hours. To have fun, he counted the birds he noticed at that time. The results of his observations are shown in the table below.

Time	13.00-14.00	14.00-15.00	15.00-16.00	16.00-17.00	17.00-18.00	18.00-19.00
Number of birds	26	17	24	32	21	23

What is the range of the numbers of birds the photographer noticed?

E. 9
F. 12
G. 15
H. 17

Questions 69 – 74

69.

Number of pens

(line plot from 1 to 9)

The line plot above represents the number of pens in students' pencil cases. What is the median number of pens in student's pencil cases?

A. 4
B. 4.5
C. 5
D. 5.5

70.

Number of pens

(line plot from 1 to 9)

The line plot above represents the number of pens in students' pencil cases. What is the mean number of pens in student's pencil cases?

E. 4.4
F. 4.5
G. 4.6
H. 4.8

71. Beryl's pencil case contains 8 grey pencils, 5 red pencils and 4 green pencils. He loses 2 pencils, one of which is green. If Beryl then picks one pencil at random from the pencil case, what is the probability that this pencil will be green?

A. 0.5
B. 0.4
C. 0.3
D. 0.2

72. The game is that the participant opens one of 20 cells. 15 of these cells contain balloons, and the remaining cells contain prizes of $5, $10, $15, $20, and $25. What is the probability that a participant will win more than $10?

E. 0.25
F. 0.2
G. 0.15
H. 0.1

73. A sport bag contains w white and r red tennis balls. If one ball is picked at random, from the bag, the probability that this ball is red is $\frac{4}{9}$. What is the value of $\frac{w}{r}$?

A. $\frac{4}{9}$

B. $\frac{5}{4}$

C. $\frac{9}{13}$

D. $\frac{5}{9}$

74. If the mean of x and $3x$ is 96, what is the mean of $2x$ and 100?

E. 94
F. 96
G. 98
H. 100

Questions 75 – 80			
75.	A basket of fruit contains 12 apricots, 10 peaches, 14 plums, and 16 figs. Alberto randomly grabs one apricot and one plum from the basket. What is the probability that the next fruit taken will be a fig or a peach? A. 0.13 B. 0.26 C. 0.44 D. 0.52	78.	8, 3, 13, 10, 5, 9, 8 For the list of numbers above, which of the following statements is false? E. The median number is 8 F. The mean number is 8 G. The range is 8 H. The mode number is 8
76.	Geert tossed a fair coin in the air 20 times and found that it lands on its head 11 times. If he tosses the coin in the air 180 times, what is the total number of times Geert can expect the coin to land on its head? E. 77 F. 88 G. 99 H. 110	79.	If x is the mean of a and 5, y is the mean of $3a$ and 25, what is the mean of x and y in terms of a? A. $8a + 60$ B. $4a + 30$ C. $2a + 15$ D. $a + 7.5$
77.	In a sample of 15 cards, 9 are red and 6 are black. If two cards are selected at random from the sample, one at a time without replacement, what is the probability that both cards are red? A. $\frac{2}{9}$ B. $\frac{4}{81}$ C. $\frac{12}{35}$ D. $\frac{9}{25}$	80.	A survey was taken of the value of cars in a county, and it was found that the mean car value was $12,000 and the median car value was $10,000. Which of the following situations could explain the difference between the mean and median car values in the county? E. Some cars have value much less than the rest F. Some cars have value much more than the rest G. Most of the cars have value smaller than $12,000 H. Most of the cars have value greater than $12,000

Questions 81 – 86

81. Ella, Lucas and Sophia have $258 altogether. If Sophia has $82, what is the mean amount of money Ella and Lucas have altogether?

   A. $88
   B. $87
   C. $86
   D. $85

82. On the table are cards with images of animals. Among them, 17 are with cats, 14 – with dogs, 16 – with monkeys and 23 – with predators. Which animal card has exactly an 1 in 5 chance of being picked at random?

   E. Cat card
   F. Dog card
   G. Monkey card
   H. Predator card

83. In the parking lot of 40 cars, 18 are black and 10 have parking sensors. It is known that 4 black cars have parking sensors. If a car is selected at random, what is the probability that both of the following are true: the car is not black and does not have parking sensors?

   A. 0.5
   B. 0.4
   C. 0.25
   D. 0.2

84. The mean score of a team of 6 players in an online game was 12 e-points. If the player with the lowest score left the team, the mean score of the remaining players becomes 13 e-points. What was the lowest score?

   E. 5 e-points
   F. 6 e-points
   G. 7 e-points
   H. 8 e-points

85. The numbers 1, 2, 3, 4, and 5 are each written on separate cards. The five cards are put into a bag and two of them are drawn at random. What is the probability that the sum of the two cards drawn is no more than 4?

   A. 0.15
   B. 0.2
   C. 0.25
   D. 0.3

86. What is the median number of all two-digit perfect squares?

   E. 42.5
   F. 45.5
   G. 51.5
   H. 56.5

	Questions 87 – 92		
87.	A set of numbers contains exactly 12 odd numbers. The probability of choosing an odd number from the set is $\frac{2}{5}$. How many even numbers are in the set? A. 30 B. 24 C. 18 D. 15	90.	If the mean of numbers 11, x and $3x$ is $2y$, what is the value of $2x - 3y$? E. 5.5 F. −5.5 G. 11 H. −11
88.	There are 18 cans in the tourist's backpack. 5 of them are fish, $\frac{1}{3}$ are chicken and the rest are meat. Yesterday the tourist ate canned fish, today – canned chicken. What is the probability that tomorrow he will eat canned meat? E. $\frac{7}{18}$ F. $\frac{7}{17}$ G. $\frac{7}{16}$ H. $\frac{7}{15}$	91.	Mila surveys students at her school about the number of times they visit their grandparents during the summer. The table below shows Mila's results. | Number of times	Number of students
---	---
0	2
1	5
2	10
3 or more	18	 What is the probability that a student who participated in the survey visited his grandparents two or more times? A. 0.8 B. 0.2 C. 0.78 D. 0.22
89.	If the mean number of a and b is c, which of the following is the expression for b in terms of a and c? A. $c - 2a$ B. $2c - a$ C. $2a - c$ D. $a - 2c$	92.	This year, Mateo wants to earn an average of at least $1,800 a month. What should be the total annual amount earned for Mateo to achieve his goal? E. At least $21,000 F. At least $21,200 G. At least $21,400 H. At least $21,600

Questions 93 – 98

93. Aria scored a mean of 12 points per game in her first 4 basketball games. In her 5th game, she scored 17 points. What is Aria's mean score for the first five games?

   A. 12
   B. 12.5
   C. 13
   D. 13.5

94. A cooler contains four types of beverages: 6 bottles of lemonade, 8 bottles of cold tea, 7 bottles of apple juice and 3 bottles of carrot juice. What is the probability that a bottle chosen at random from this cooler is a juice bottle?

   E. $\frac{5}{12}$
   F. $\frac{7}{24}$
   G. $\frac{1}{3}$
   H. $\frac{1}{4}$

95. The mean weight of g girls in the class is 52 kg. If the mean weight of s students in the class is 54 kg, what is the mean weight of the boys in the class?

   A. $\frac{54s+52g}{s-g}$
   B. $\frac{54s-52g}{s-g}$
   C. $\frac{54s-52g}{s+g}$
   D. $\frac{54s+52g}{s+g}$

96. A set of 15 numbers has the mean of 7. What additional number must be included in this set to create a new set of numbers with the mean that is 2 more than the previous mean?

   E. 9
   F. 30
   G. 32
   H. 39

97. A bag contains 77 marbles that are red, blue, or yellow. The ratio of red to blue marbles is 1 : 2, and the ratio of red to yellow marbles is 2 : 1. If two red marbles are removed, what is the new probability of choosing a red marble?

   A. $\frac{3}{5}$
   B. $\frac{2}{7}$
   C. $\frac{4}{15}$
   D. $\frac{3}{25}$

98. Penelope has $3.75 in nickels, dimes and quarters. If the amount in nickels is half the amount in dimes and the amount in dimes is the same as the amount in quarters, what is the probability that a randomly selected coin will be nickel?

   E. $\frac{1}{6}$
   F. $\frac{5}{12}$
   G. $\frac{5}{6}$
   H. $\frac{7}{12}$

Questions 99 – 104

99. 5, 7, 9, 12, 17

A new number x is added to the list above so that the median number of the list becomes the same as the mean number of the list. What is the value of x?

A. 9
B. 10
C. 11
D. 13

100. If the mean of two numbers a and b is x, what is the mean number of three numbers a, b and $4x$ in terms of x?

E. x
F. $2x$
G. $3x$
H. $5x$

101. From 12 boys and 10 girls, the dance teacher must select a couple to participate in a dance competition. What is the probability that students will guess who the teacher will choose?

A. $\frac{1}{22}$
B. $\frac{1}{12}$
C. $\frac{1}{120}$
D. $\frac{1}{10}$

102. A bag contains 3 white, 4 red and 5 green balls. Two balls are drawn at random from the bag. What is the probability that the first ball is red and the second ball is white?

E. $\frac{1}{13}$
F. $\frac{1}{12}$
G. $\frac{1}{11}$
H. $\frac{1}{10}$

103. In a set A, the mean number of all five numbers is x. B is a set that is created by doubling each number from the set A. In terms of x, what is the mean number of the set B?

A. x
B. $2x$
C. $5x$
D. $10x$

104. A sports store has a container of 25 handballs: 8 white, 6 red, 3 yellow, 4 blue, and 4 green. If one ball is picked from the container at random, what is the probability that it will be neither red nor blue?

E. $\frac{2}{5}$
F. $\frac{6}{25}$
G. $\frac{3}{5}$
H. $\frac{11}{25}$

Questions 105 – 110

105. The table below shows the number of times that different desserts were ordered at a restaurant.

Dessert	Orders
Panna cotta	36
Brownie	28
Chocolate soufflé	22
Meringue	a

If the probability that a customer orders merengue as a dessert is 0.312, what is the value of a?

A. 33
B. 35
C. 37
D. 39

106. Among the city's population, 54% are female. 75% of the population drives a car. If 36% of the population are female who drive a car, what is the probability that a randomly selected city local is a male who does not drive a car?

E. 0.18
F. 0.25
G. 0.07
H. 0.39

107. The ratio of x to y is 2 : 3, the ratio of $x : z$ is 4 : 5. If the sum of $x, y,$ and z is between 40 and 50, what is the mean of these numbers?

A. 14
B. 15
C. 16
D. 17

108. The table below shows Adam's and Eva's mean scores on four subjects' tests.

	Math	Art	English	Science
Adam	88	86	88	90
Eva	83	91	89	85

Which of the following statements is true?

E. Adam's mean score on four tests is 88.25
F. Eva's mean score on four tests is 87.5
G. Their Math mean score is greater than English mean score
H. Their Art mean score is greater than Science mean score

109. The smallest score on Physics test in Mr. Kleberg's class is 25. When Mr. Kleberg rejected the smallest score, the range of the scores decreased by 2. Which of the following options could show two smallest scores in Mr. Kleberg's class?

A. 25, 26
B. 25, 27
C. 26, 28
D. 27, 29

110. If the mean number of a and 18 is x, what is the mean number of x and 18 in terms of a?

E. $0.25a + 9$
F. $0.5a + 18$
G. $0.5a + 27$
H. $0.25a + 13.5$

Questions 111 – 114

111.	There are 10 cookies on a plate: 6 with chocolate and 4 with strawberry jam. Alexander will choose two of these cookies to pack in his lunch. What is the probability that he will choose two different cookies? A. $\frac{8}{30}$ B. $\frac{6}{25}$ C. $\frac{1}{24}$ D. $\frac{1}{9}$	113.	A survey asked 50 students what pets they have. The following results are obtained: • 20 students have cats • 24 students have dogs • 4 students have both dogs and cats. What is the probability that a randomly selected student has neither cat nor dog? A. 0.02 B. 0.04 C. 0.1 D. 0.2
112.	Throwing two number dice, what is the probability of rolling two even numbers? E. $\frac{1}{2}$ F. $\frac{1}{4}$ G. $\frac{3}{4}$ H. $\frac{1}{3}$	114.	The candy box contains 36 orange and lemon candies. The probability of picking a lemon candy is $\frac{1}{3}$. How many lemon candies do you need to add so that the probability of picking out a lemon candy is the same as the probability of picking out an orange candy? E. 12 F. 15 G. 18 H. 24

Test 9: Geometry part 1

GRID-IN QUESTIONS

Questions 58 – 62

58.	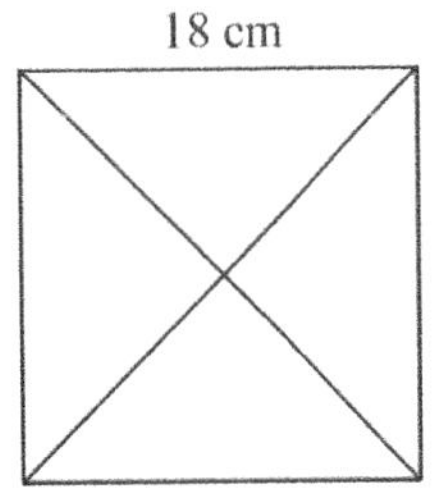 18 cm — What is the area of one of four triangles formed when the diagonals of the square above intersect?	61.	What is the area, in square units, of the parallelogram shown above?
59.	A rectangle has the perimeter of 18 in. If all four sides lengths are integers, how many possible different areas could this rectangle have?	62.	A regular heptagon has the side length of 3.2 in. A rhombus has the same perimeter as the heptagon. What is the side length of the rhombus?
60.	A box is 18 cm long, 15 cm wide, and 30 cm high. How many cubes with side length of 3 cm can fit in the box?		

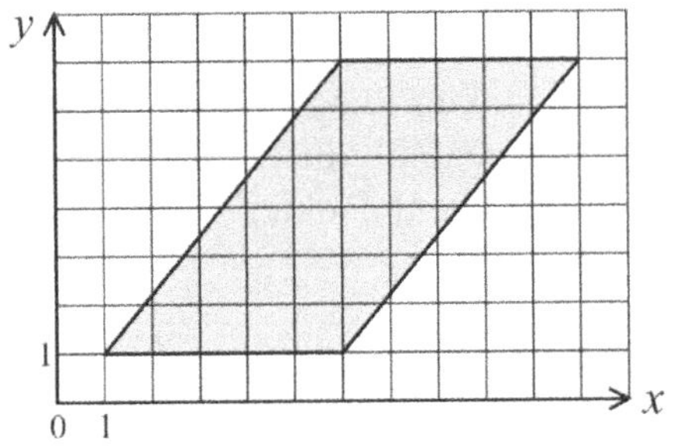

MULTIPLE CHOICE QUESTIONS

Questions 63 – 68

63. On the diagram above, the diameter of the smaller circle is the radius of the larger circle. If the radius of the smaller circle is 3 cm, what is the area of the larger circle?

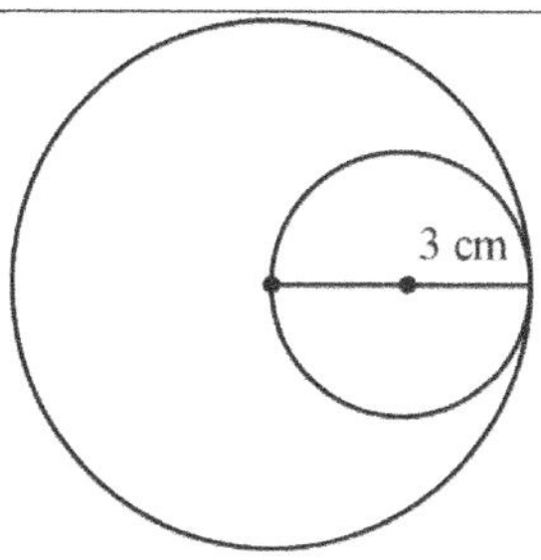

A. $6\pi\ cm^2$
B. $9\pi cm^2$
C. $36\pi\ cm^2$
D. $144\pi\ cm^2$

64. A rectangle has the perimeter of 46 cm. If one side of the rectangle is 3 cm longer than another side, what is the area of the rectangle?

E. $130\ cm^2$
F. $70\ cm^2$
G. $460\ cm^2$
H. $340\ cm^2$

65. What is the volume of the figure above?

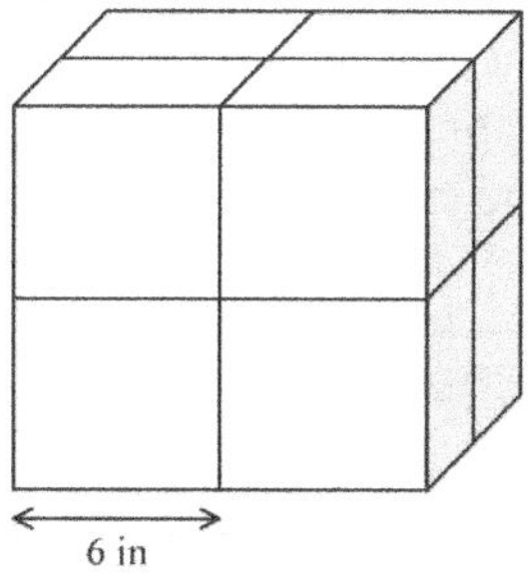

A. $216\ in^3$
B. $512\ in^3$
C. $1,240\ in^3$
D. $1,728\ in^3$

66. The figure above shows a rectangle, which is twice as long as wide. If the middle point of the longer side is the vertex of the triangle, what is the perimeter of the triangle?

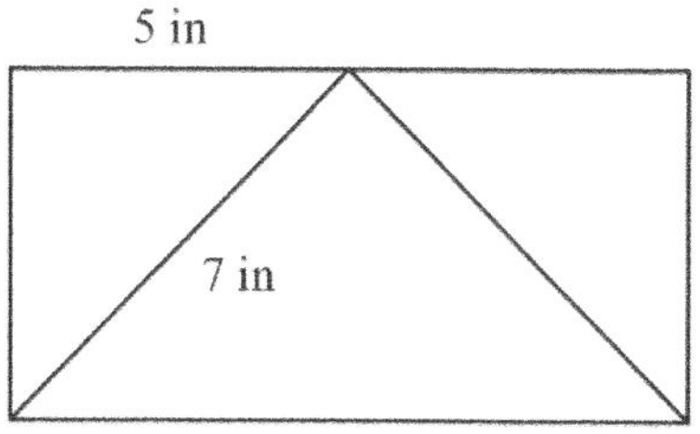

E. 17 in
F. 19 in
G. 24 in
H. 26 in

67. The bottom of the glass in the shape of a rectangular prism has an area of $36\ cm^2$. If a full glass holds $432\ cm^3$ of water, what is the height of the glass?

A. 8 cm
B. 9 cm
C. 11 cm
D. 12 cm

68. What is the area of the figure above?

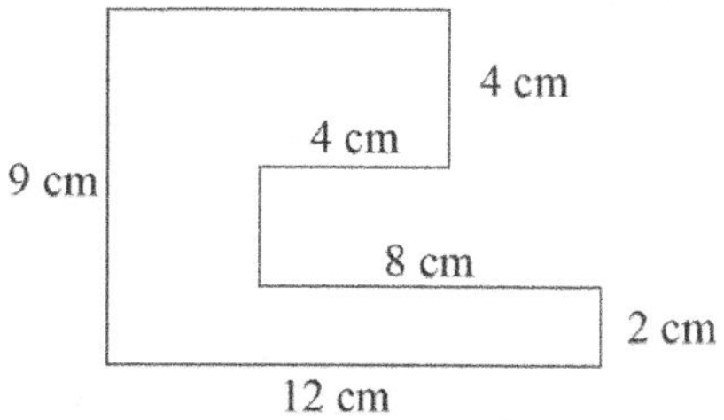

E. $61\ cm^2$
F. $65\ cm^2$
G. $68\ cm^2$
H. $72\ cm^2$

Questions 69 – 74

69. In the diagram above, O is the center of the circle. If the circumference of the circle is 28π in, what is the area of the right triangle AOB?

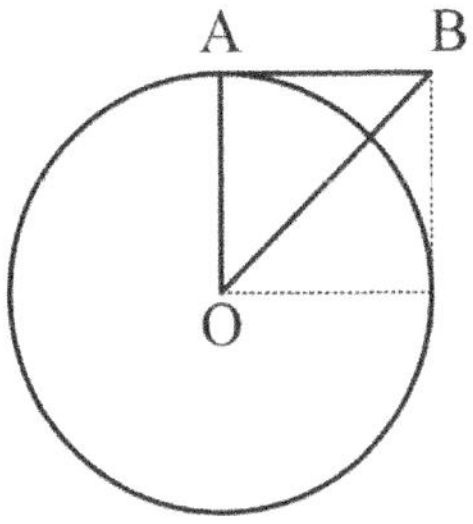

A. $98\pi\ in^2$
B. $98\ in^2$
C. $198\pi\ in^2$
D. $198\ in^2$

70. The base of a triangular pyramid has the area of $24\ ft^2$. If the height of the pyramid is $5\ ft$, what is the volume of the pyramid?

E. $40\ ft^3$
F. $60\ ft^3$
G. $80\ ft^3$
H. $120\ ft^3$

71. If two rectangular prisms have the same length, what is the ratio of their volumes in terms of x and y?

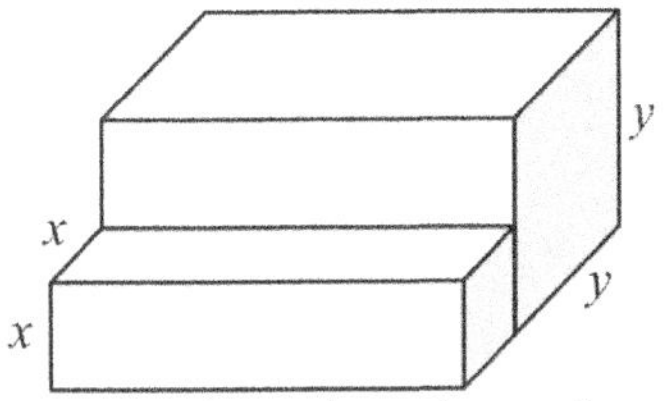

A. $x : y$
B. $x^3 : y^3$
C. $\sqrt{x} : \sqrt{y}$
D. $x^2 : y^2$

72. In the above figure, the area of the square is $64\ cm^2$, and the perimeter of each triangle is $24\ cm$. What is the perimeter of the isosceles trapezoid?

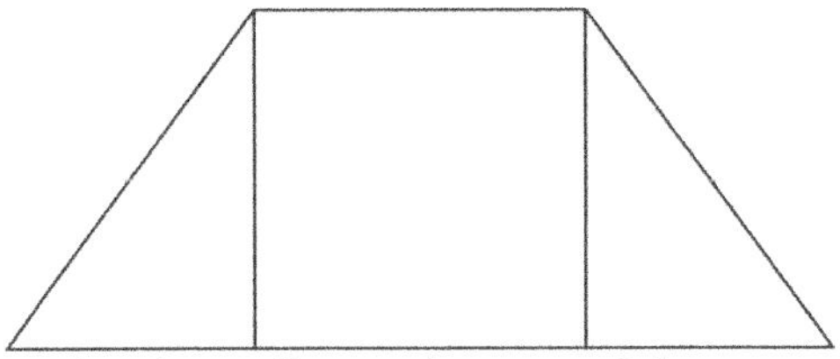

E. $48\ cm$
F. $64\ cm$
G. $80\ cm$
H. $112\ cm$

73. If the diagonal of a square and the diameter of a circle are equal in length, what is the ratio of the area of the square to the area of the circle?

A. $2 : \pi$
B. $1 : \pi$
C. $\pi : 1$
D. $\pi : 2$

74. The base of a cylinder is a circle with the diameter of $5\ in$. If the height of the cylinder is $12\ in$, what is the volume of the cylinder?

E. $120\pi\ in^3$
F. $60\pi\ in^3$
G. $75\pi\ in^3$
H. $300\pi\ in^3$

Questions 75 – 80

75.

y cm / *x* cm (parallelogram with right triangle)

If the area of the triangle is 12 cm^2, what is the area of the parallelogram in terms of *x* and *y*?

A. $\frac{6y}{x}$ cm^2

B. $\frac{24y}{x}$ cm^2

C. $\frac{6x}{y}$ cm^2

D. $\frac{24x}{y}$ cm^2

76. The diameter of larger circle is D, and the diameter of smaller circle is d. If the ratio of the area of the larger circle to the area of the smaller circle is 9 : 4, what is the ratio of their diameters?

E. $D : d = 9 : 4$
F. $D : d = 3 : 2$
G. $d : D = 9 : 4$
H. $d : D = 3 : 2$

77. Max ordered a pizza with a 24-cm diameter. Leon ordered a pizza with a 28-cm diameter. What is the difference in area of the two pizzas?

A. 2 cm
B. 4 cm
C. 16π cm^2
D. 52π cm^2

78. (cylinder: 3.2 cm radius, 4.5 cm height)

Which formula is correct in computing 25% of the volume of this shape?

E. $\frac{\pi}{4}(4.5)^2(3.2)$ cm^3
F. $\frac{\pi}{4}(3.2)^2(4.5)$ cm^3
G. $\frac{\pi}{4}(6.4)^2(4.5)$ cm^3
H. $\frac{\pi}{4}(4.5)^2(6.4)$ cm^3

79. Parking spaces surround a circular arena that is 63 ft wide. If a car drives around the whole arena looking for a parking space, how many feet would he have to drive to cover the whole circle? (Use approximation $\pi \approx \frac{22}{7}$)

A. 99 ft
B. 149 ft
C. 198 ft
D. 248 ft

80. A conical container has a radius of 10 cm and a volume of 60π cm^3. If the container is $\frac{3}{4}$ filled with water, how many centimeters deep does the water fill the container?

E. 1.35 cm
F. 1.45 cm
G. 1.5 cm
H. 1.8 cm

Questions 81 – 86

81. Region A and B are squares with the area of $64\ un^2$ and $36\ un^2$ respectively. What is the area of the region C?

A. $48\ un^2$.
B. $36\ un^2$.
C. $24\ un^2$.
D. $16\ un^2$.

82. In the parallelogram ABCD, the height BK is 15 cm long. What is the length of the height DH?

E. 25 cm
F. 18 cm
G. 9 cm
H. 16 cm

83. From the square with the area of $324\ in^2$ from the lower left corner, the square with the area of $64\ in^2$ was cut off. What is the perimeter of the shape formed?

A. 56 in
B. 64 in
C. 72 in
D. 80 in

84. The diagram shows a square with side length of a. If the diameter of a circle is half the side of the square, what is the area of the shaded region in terms of a?

E. $(1 - 0.5\pi)a^2$
F. $(1 - 0.25\pi)a^2$
G. $(1 - 0.125\pi)a^2$
H. $(1 - 0.0625\pi)a^2$

85. One vertex of a square is at the center of a circle and two vertices lie on the circle. If the radius of the circle is 2 in, what is the area of the figure above?

A. $4 + \pi\ in^2$
B. $4 + 2\pi\ in^2$
C. $4 + 3\pi\ in^2$
D. $4 + 4\pi\ in^2$

86. A square has the same perimeter as a rectangle with sides' lengths of 3 cm and 15 cm. What is the area of the square?

E. $81\ cm^2$
F. $45\ cm^2$
G. $9\ cm^2$
H. $36\ cm^2$

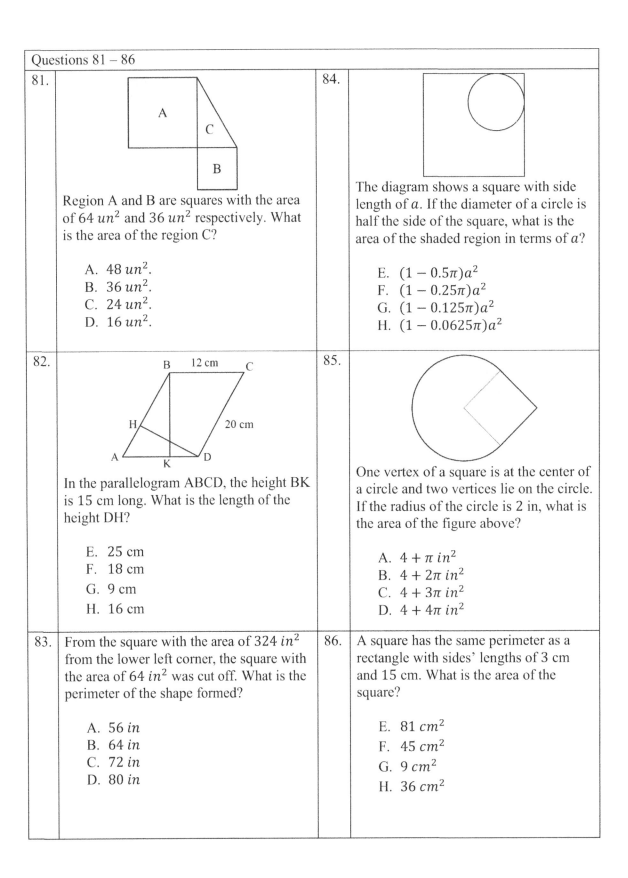

Questions 87 – 92

87. A certain polygon has 6 sides. One of the sides has a length of x, and three sides each have length $2x$. The lengths of the remaining two sides are 8 and 10. If the perimeter of the polygon is 60, what is the value of x?

   A. 6
   B. 7
   C. 8
   D. 9

88. In isosceles trapezoid above, the area of the square part is 196 cm^2. What is the area of the trapezoid?

   E. 784 cm^2
   F. 588 cm^2
   G. 444 cm^2
   H. 392 cm^2

89. Peter's lawn is in rectangular shape 30 feet wide and 120 feet long. If it takes Peter 2 minutes to mow 15 square feet, how many hours did it take Peter to finish mowing his lawn?

   A. 5 hours
   B. 6 hours
   C. 7 hours
   D. 8 hours

90. Alice and her brother both have square rooms. The ratio in size of Alice's room to Mathew's room is 5 : 4. The area of Alice's room is 225 square feet. What was the length of Mathew's room?

   E. 196 square feet
   F. 180 square feet
   G. 144 square feet
   H. 100 square feet

91. In the triangle ABC, points D and E are midpoints of the sides AB and BC. If BD = 5 cm, BE = 6 cm, and AC = 16 cm, what is the perimeter of quadrilateral ADEC?

   A. 35 cm
   B. 33 cm
   C. 31 cm
   D. 30 cm

92. What is the surface area of a shoebox that is 25 inches long, 14 inches wide, and 6 inches high?

   E. 1,168 in^2
   F. 876 in^2
   G. 2,100 in^2
   H. 584 in^2

Questions 93 – 98

93. What is the difference in the surface area of two cubes, one with edge 12 cm and one with an edge of 8 cm?

A. $120\ cm^2$
B. $240\ cm^2$
C. $360\ cm^2$
D. $480\ cm^2$

94.

Which of the following statements is true?

E. The perimeter of the triangle ABC is greater than the perimeter of the triangle ACD
F. AC is longer than AD
G. CD is longer than AB
H. The area of the triangle ABC is greater than the area of the triangle ACD

95. The area of a rectangle with sides a and b is A. The area of a parallelogram with sides a and b is B. Which of the following statements is true.

A. $A < B$
B. $A = B$
C. $A > B$
D. The relationship between A and B cannot be defined

96. A cube with an edge of length a has the same volume as a rectangular prism with dimensions 6 by 12 by 24. What is the value of a?

E. 6
F. 9
G. 12
H. 18

97.

In the rhombus ABCD, CO = 8 cm, BO = 6 cm. Which of the following statements is false?

A. The area of the rhombus is $96\ cm^2$
B. The perimeter of the rhombus is $40\ cm$
C. The perimeter of the triangle ACD is $36\ cm$
D. The area of the triangle ABD is $96\ cm^2$

98. In a square ABCD, M is the midpoint of AB and N is the midpoint of BC. If the area of the triangle BMN is $50\ cm^2$, what is the area of the square ABCD?

E. $200\ cm^2$
F. $400\ cm^2$
G. $600\ cm^2$
H. $800\ cm^2$

	Questions 99 – 104		
99.	Which cylinder would require the most paint to cover? A. A cylinder with radius of 1 unit and height of 6 units B. A cylinder with radius of 2 units and height of 3 units C. A cylinder with radius of 3 units and height of 2 units D. A cylinder with radius of 6 units and height of 1 unit	102.	Which cone would hold the most water? E. A cone with radius of 2 units and height of 10 units F. A cone with radius of 5 units and height of 5 units G. A cone with radius of 10 units and height of 2 units H. A cone with radius of 1 unit and height of 20 units
100.	In trapezoid ABCD, BM is parallel to CD and M is the midpoint of AD. If the area of the triangle ABM is 25 cm^2, what is the area of trapezoid ABCD? E. 50 cm^2 F. 75 cm^2 G. 100 cm^2 H. 125 cm^2	103.	Two rectangular prisms have square bases with side length of x units. The larger prism has length of y units, and the smaller prism's length is $\frac{3}{4}$ length of the larger prism. What is the combined volume, in square units, of both prisms? A. $0.75x^2y$ B. $1.25x^2y$ C. $1.5x^2y$ D. $1.75x^2y$
101.	In the square pyramid, each triangular face has the same area as the base. If the base area is 400 cm^2, what is the length of the height of each triangular face? A. 10 cm B. 20 cm C. 30 cm D. 40 cm	104.	Mr. Kelly has rectangular tiles with sizes 30 cm by 40 cm. What area will he not be able to cover with whole tiles? E. 120 cm by 200 cm F. 160 cm by 180 cm G. 240 cm by 140 cm H. 210 cm by 200 cm

Questions 105 – 110

105. The base of the triangular prism is A square units, the perimeter of the base is P units, and the lateral area of the prism is L square units. What is the volume, in cubic units, of the prism?

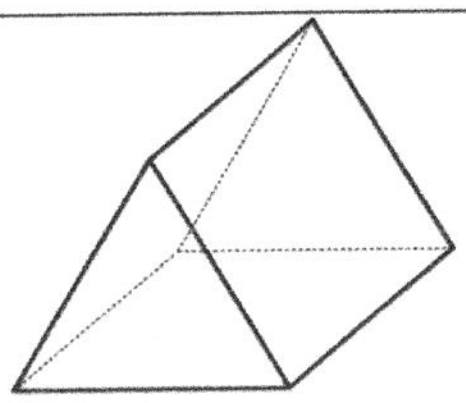

A. $A \times \frac{P}{L}$
B. $A \times \frac{L}{P}$
C. $P \times \frac{L}{A}$
D. $P \times \frac{A}{L}$

106. A ball with the circumference of the greatest circle of 18π inches is packed in a cubical box so that it touches each side of the interior of the box. What is the volume of the box?

E. $729\ in^3$
F. $2,916\ in^3$
G. $5,832\ in^3$
H. $6,561\ in^3$

107. The lengths of four sides of a quadrilateral are four consecutive integers. If the perimeter of the quadrilateral is 118 cm, what is the length of the longest side?

A. 28 cm
B. 29 cm
C. 30 cm
D. 31 cm

108. The diagram shows the shaded region in the square. What is the area of the shaded region?

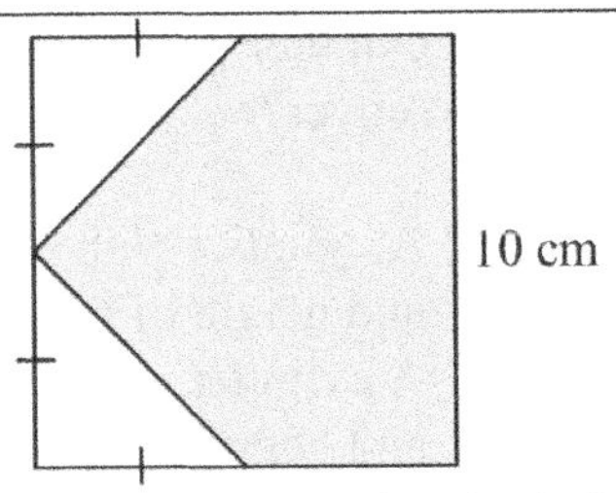

E. $25\ cm^2$
F. $50\ cm^2$
G. $60\ cm^2$
H. $75\ cm^2$

109. Ken has 64 feet of fencing to make a rectangular garden. Which dimensions will give Ken the garden with the greatest area?

A. 16 feet by 16 feet
B. 15 feet by 17 feet
C. 14 feet by 18 feet
D. 13 feet by 19 feet

110. If $Density = Mass \div Volume$, what is the $Mass$ of the cube with side length of 12 cm if its $Density$ is $1.5 \frac{g}{cm^3}$?

E. 2.592 kg
F. 25.92 kg
G. 1.152 kg
H. 11.52 kg

Questions 111 – 114

111.

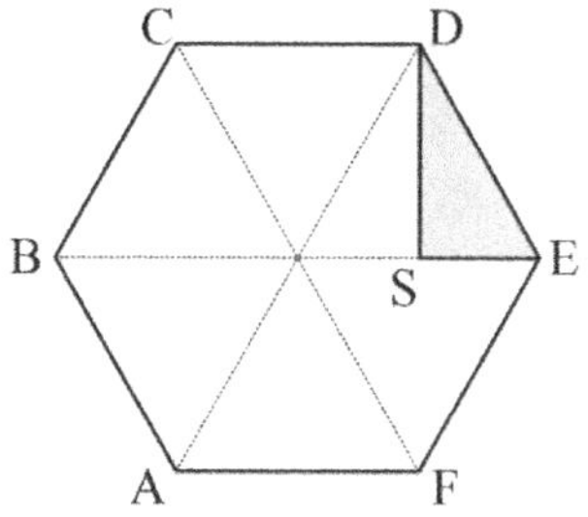

In regular hexagon ABCDEF, DS is perpendicular to SE. If the area of hexagon is 216 square units, what is the area of triangle SDE?

A. 12 square units
B. 14 square units
C. 16 square units
D. 18 square units

112.

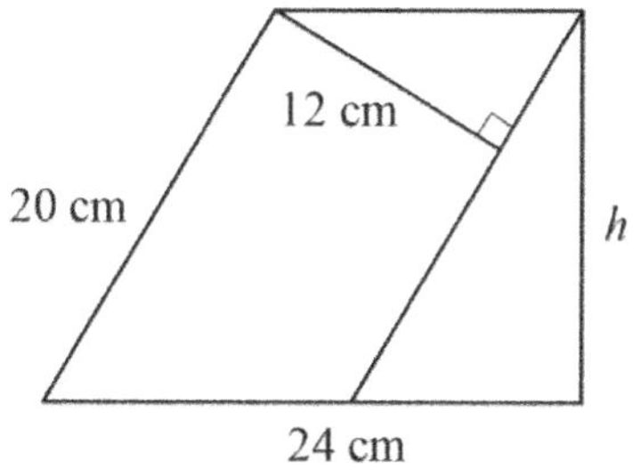

What is the area of trapezoid shown above in terms of h?

E. $120 + 12h$

F. $240 + 24h$

G. $\frac{120}{h} + 12$

H. $\frac{240}{h} + 24$

113.

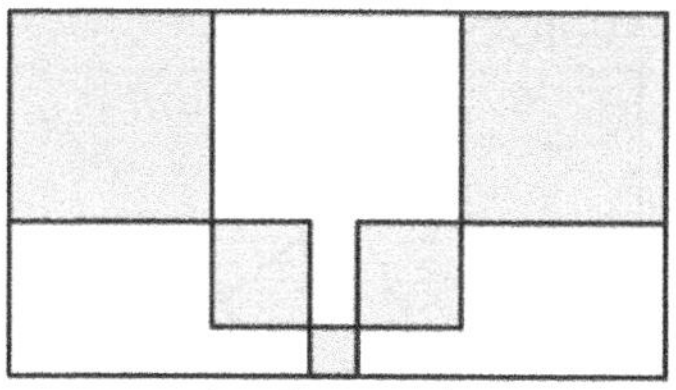

In the rectangle above, the side of each smaller shaded square is twice smaller than the side of the larger shaded square. What is the ratio of the area of the shaded region to the area of the rectangle?

A. $3:10$
B. $3:13$
C. $31:71$
D. $41:91$

114.

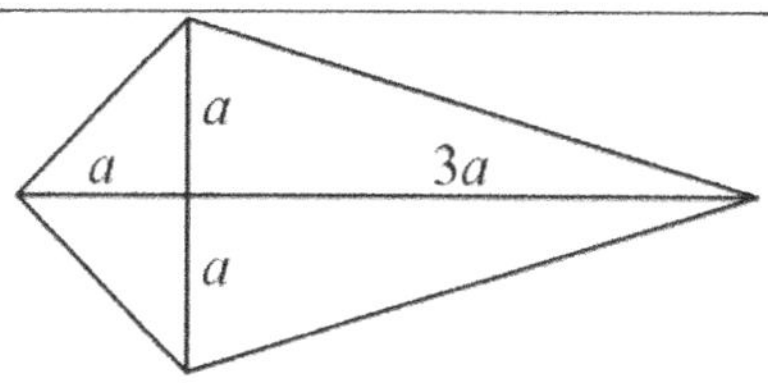

In terms of a, what is the area of the kite shown above?

E. $4a^2$
F. $3a^2$
G. $6a^2$
H. $8a^2$

Test 10: Geometry part 2

GRID-IN QUESTIONS		
Questions 58 – 62		
58. In the figure above, what is the value of $x + y$?	61.	In the figure above, what is the value of x?
59. The area of the circle is $49\pi\ cm^2$. What is the circumference of the circle? (Use approximation $\pi \approx \frac{22}{7}$)	62.	What is the measure of exterior angle of regular pentagon?
60. On the number line above, point A is located at -12, point B is located at 4. Where is the midpoint of BC located?		

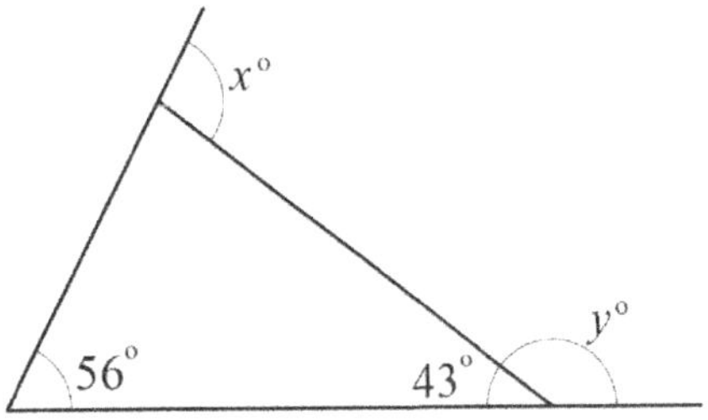

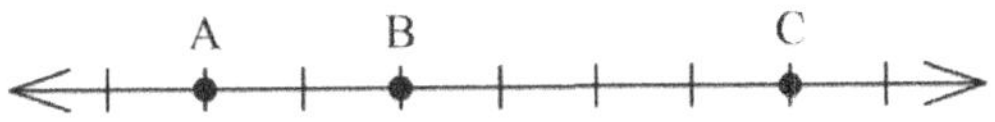

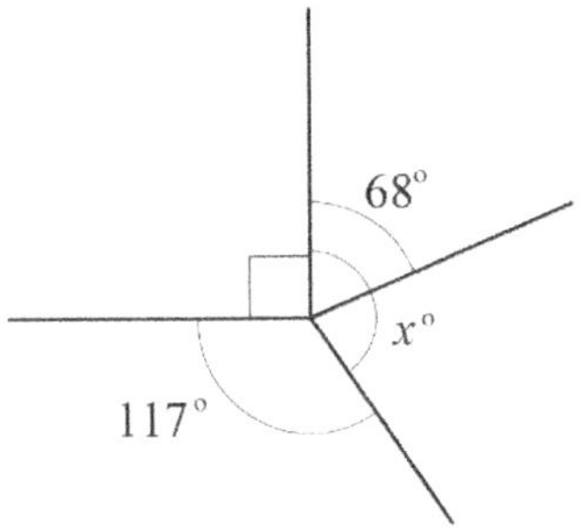

MULTIPLE CHOICE QUESTIONS

Questions 63 – 68

63.

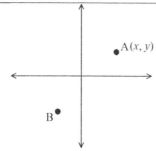

In the figure above, points A and B are equidistant from the origin. Which of the following could be the coordinates of the point B?

A. $(-x, -y)$
B. $(-y, x)$
C. $(-x, y)$
D. $(-y, -x)$

64.

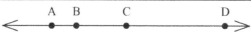

On the number line above, AB = $\frac{1}{2}$ BC, CD = 2 BC. If AC = 21 units, what is the length of BD?

E. 42 units
F. 49 units
G. 56 units
H. 63 units

65.

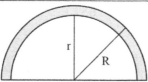

What is the area of the shaded region in terms of r and R?

A. $\pi(R^2 - r^2)$
B. $0.75\pi(R^2 - r^2)$
C. $0.5\pi(R^2 - r^2)$
D. $0.25\pi(R^2 - r^2)$

66.

  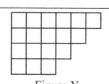

Figure X   Figure Y

The individual squares in figures X and Y are equally sized. If the area of the figure Y is 6 in^2 greater, what is the area of the figure X?

E. 54 in^2
F. 48 in^2
G. 96 in^2
H. 108 in^2

67. Point B lies outside the line a. How many lines passing through the point B and intersecting line a at the angle of 30° can be drawn?

A. 0
B. 1
C. 2
D. Infinitely many

68.

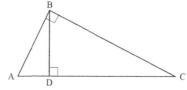

In the right triangle ABC, which of the following statements is always true?

E. $BD > AD$
F. $DC > BD$
G. $BD < AB$
H. $BC < BD$

283

Questions 69 – 74

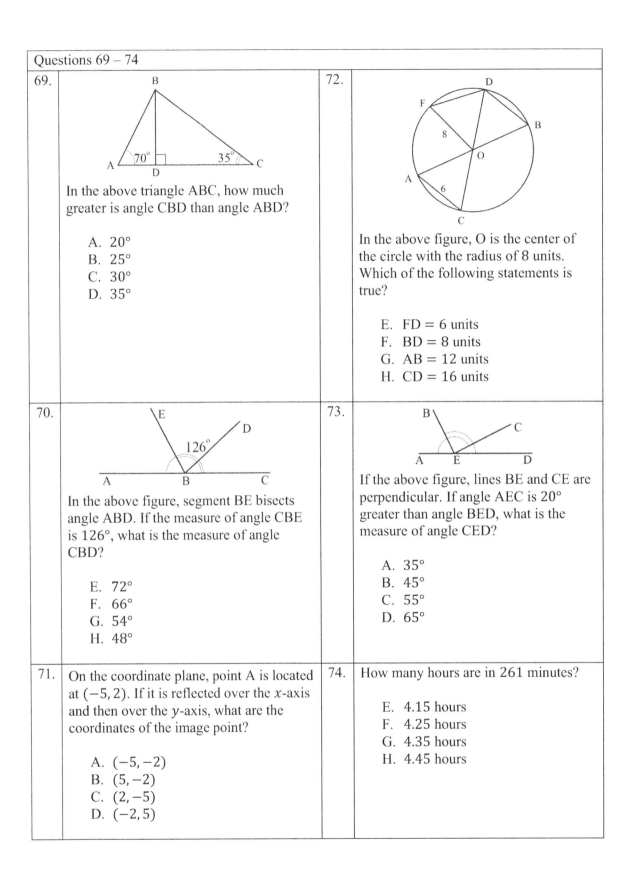

69. In the above triangle ABC, how much greater is angle CBD than angle ABD?

A. 20°
B. 25°
C. 30°
D. 35°

70. In the above figure, segment BE bisects angle ABD. If the measure of angle CBE is 126°, what is the measure of angle CBD?

E. 72°
F. 66°
G. 54°
H. 48°

71. On the coordinate plane, point A is located at $(-5, 2)$. If it is reflected over the x-axis and then over the y-axis, what are the coordinates of the image point?

A. $(-5, -2)$
B. $(5, -2)$
C. $(2, -5)$
D. $(-2, 5)$

72. In the above figure, O is the center of the circle with the radius of 8 units. Which of the following statements is true?

E. FD = 6 units
F. BD = 8 units
G. AB = 12 units
H. CD = 16 units

73. If the above figure, lines BE and CE are perpendicular. If angle AEC is 20° greater than angle BED, what is the measure of angle CED?

A. 35°
B. 45°
C. 55°
D. 65°

74. How many hours are in 261 minutes?

E. 4.15 hours
F. 4.25 hours
G. 4.35 hours
H. 4.45 hours

284

Questions 75 – 80

75.

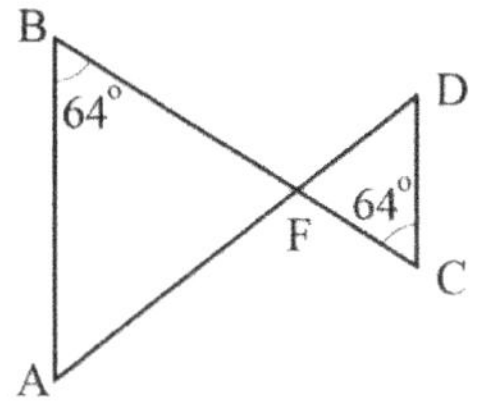

In the figure above, AB is parallel to DC. If angle FDC is 42°, and angle AFB is $(7x + 4)°$, what is the value of x?

A. 8
B. 9
C. 10
D. 11

76.

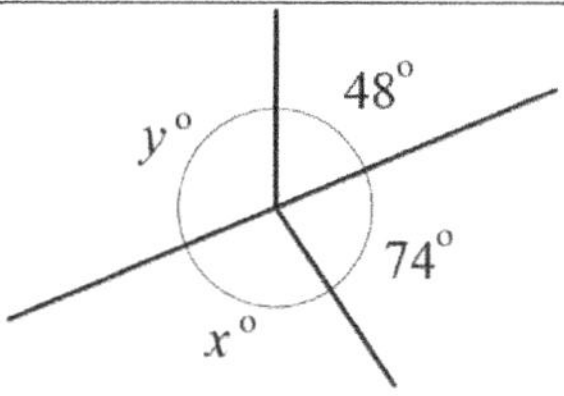

In the figure above, what is the value of $y - x$?

E. 24°
F. 26°
G. 28°
H. 30°

77. A circle has the area of a square inches. In terms of a, what is the circumference of the circle?

A. $2\pi a$ in
B. $2\pi\sqrt{a}$ in
C. $2\sqrt{\pi a}$ in
D. $2\sqrt{\dfrac{a}{\pi}}$ in

78.

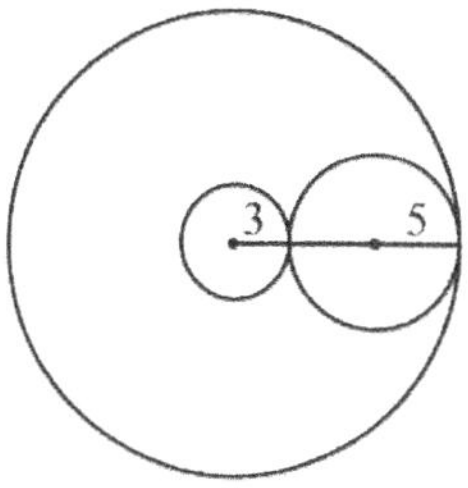

In the figure above, the radii of the smallest and medium circles are 3 and 5 units, respectively. What is the area of the greatest circle?

E. $13\pi\ un^2$.
F. $26\pi\ un^2$.
G. $64\pi\ un^2$.
H. $169\pi\ un^2$.

79.

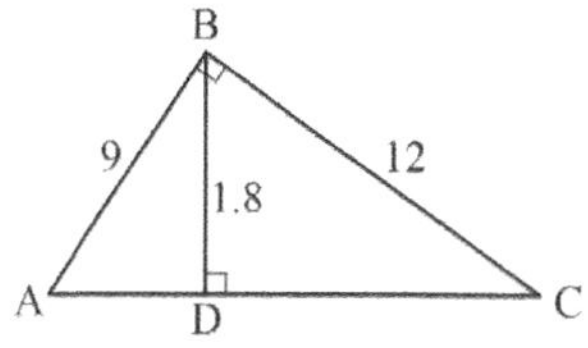

Angles ABC and BDC are right angles. Which of the following expressions represents AC?

A. $\dfrac{1.8}{9 \times 12}$
B. $\dfrac{9 \times 12}{1.8}$
C. $\dfrac{12 \times 1.8}{9}$
D. $\dfrac{12}{1.8 \times 9}$

80. In isosceles trapezoid, one angle is 138°. What is the sum of two smallest angles in trapezoid?

E. 78°
F. 80°
G. 82°
H. 84°

Questions 81 – 86

81.

Points A, B and C represents numbers as shown on the number line above. Which of the following expressions has the greatest value?

A. $A - B$
B. $C - B$
C. $B - A$
D. $C - A$

82. The filler for gift bags weighs 1.5 grams per cubic centimeter. If a gift box that measures 20 cm by 30 cm by 10 cm is packed with filler, how much filler, in kilograms, will be used?

E. 3 kg
F. 4.5 kg
G. 6 kg
H. 9 kg

83.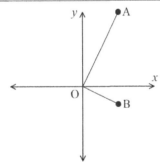

On the coordinate plane above, segments AO and BO are perpendicular and segment AO is twice as long as segment BO. If the coordinates of point A are $(4, 8)$, what are the coordinates of point B?

A. $(2, -4)$
B. $(-2, 4)$
C. $(4, -2)$
D. $(-4, 2)$

84.

Point B (not shown) is located between points A and C such that AB is 5 times as long as BC. What is the location of the midpoint of AB?

E. 5
F. 6
G. 7
H. 8

85. What time will it be 100 hours after 9 : 00 a.m. on Sunday?

A. 12 : 00 p.m on Thursday
B. 13 : 00 p.m on Thursday
C. 6 : 00 a.m on Thursday
D. 5 : 00 a.m on Thursday

86.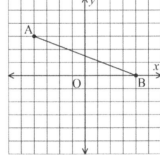

On the coordinate plane above, points A and B have coordinates $(-4, 3)$ and $(4, 0)$, respectively. Points A and C (not shown) are symmetric about the x-axis. What is the area of triangle ABC?

E. $48\ un^2$.
F. $64\ un^2$.
G. $32\ un^2$.
H. $24\ un^2$.

Questions 87 – 92

87.

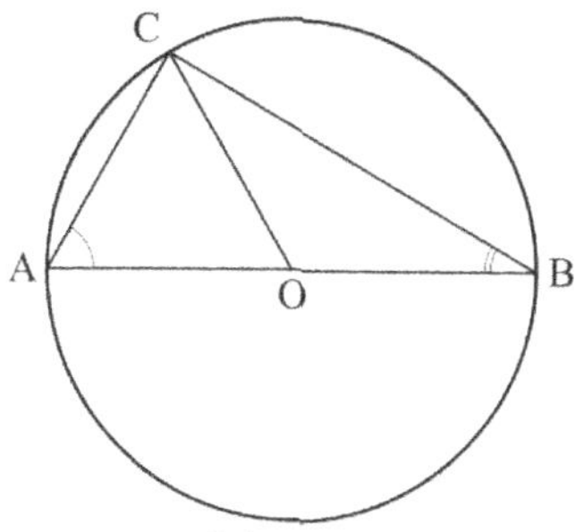

O is the center of the circle above, AB is its diameter. If angle OBC is 24°, what is angle OAC?

A. 48°
B. 54°
C. 66°
D. 72°

88. The measures of two complementary angles are in ratio 2 : 3. What is the measure of the supplement angle to the greater of these two angles?

E. 36°
F. 54°
G. 126°
H. 144°

89.

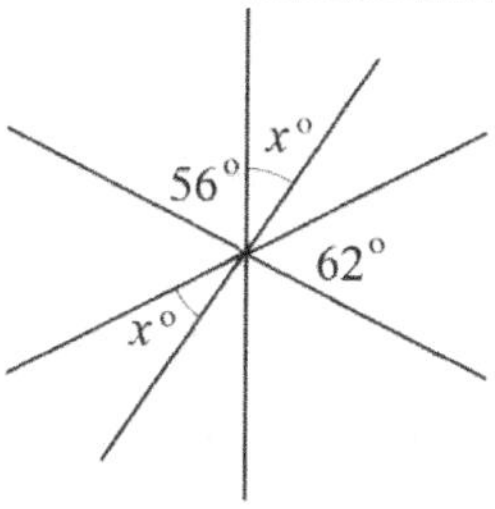

In the figure above, what is the value of x?

A. 30
B. 31
C. 32
D. 33

90.

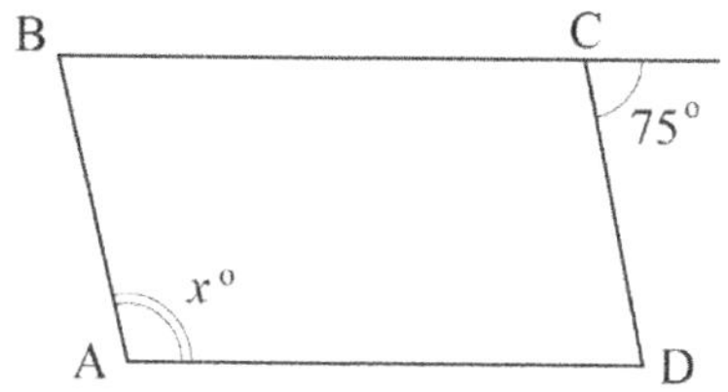

In the figure above, ABCD is a parallelogram. What is the value of x?

E. 75
F. 85
G. 95
H. 105

91. A square with side length of 6 cm has the same area as a circle with radius of r. What is the ratio of the perimeter of the square to the circumference of the circle?

A. $2 : \sqrt{\pi}$
B. $1 : \sqrt{\pi}$
C. $1 : 2\sqrt{\pi}$
D. $\sqrt{\pi} : 2$

92.

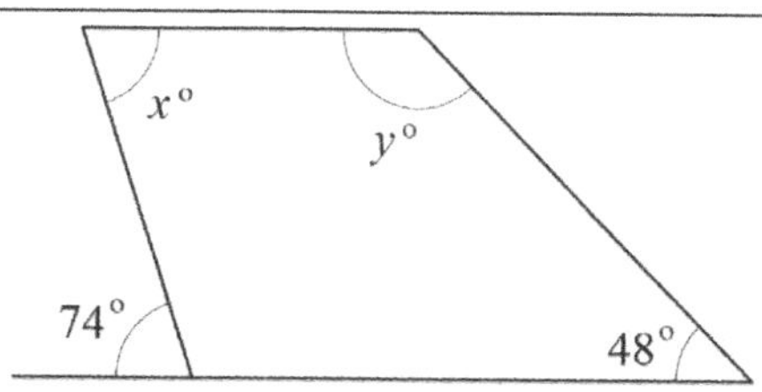

In the above figure, what is the value of $x + y$?

E. 180
F. 206
G. 220
H. 238

Questions 93 – 98			
93.	Nancy bikes 10 km in 30 minutes. Bryan bikes twice farther in 40 minutes. What is Bryan's average speed in kilometers per hour? A. 20 km/h B. 25 km/h C. 30 km/h D. 35 km/h	96.	Circle A has the radius of $\frac{2}{3}$ m. Circle B has the radius of $\frac{3}{2}$ m. What is the ratio of the area of circle A to circle B? E. 4 : 9 F. 16 : 81 G. 8 : 27 H. 2 : 3
94.	The diagram above shows one-fourth of the circle with radius of 16 in. What is the area of the shaded region? E. $64\pi - 128\ in^2$ F. $64\pi - 64\ in^2$ G. $128\pi - 64\ in^2$ H. $128\pi - 128\ in^2$	97.	In the figure above, what is the value of x? A. 30° B. 35° C. 45° D. 60°
95.	The diagram above shows segment AB lying on the line a. What is the y-intercept of line a? A. −1 B. 0 C. 1 D. 2	98.	What is the area of the triangle shown on the diagram above? E. $24\ un^2$. F. $32\ un^2$. G. $48\ un^2$. H. $64\ un^2$.

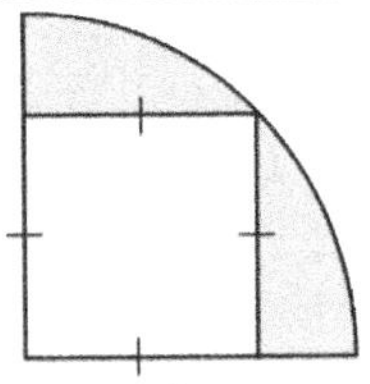

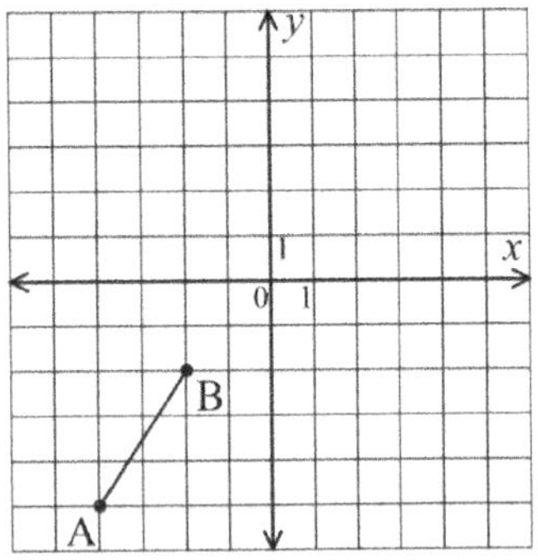

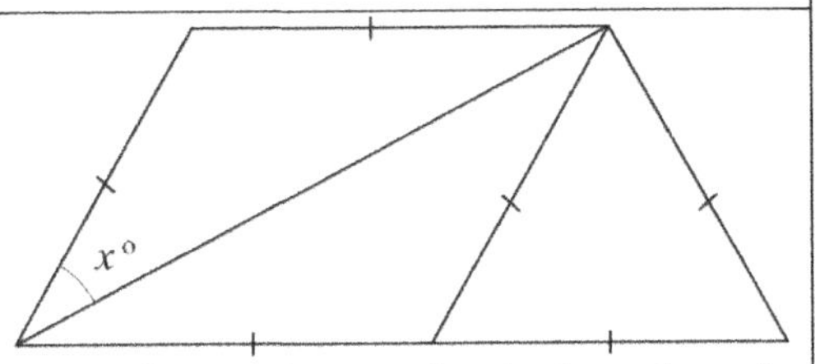

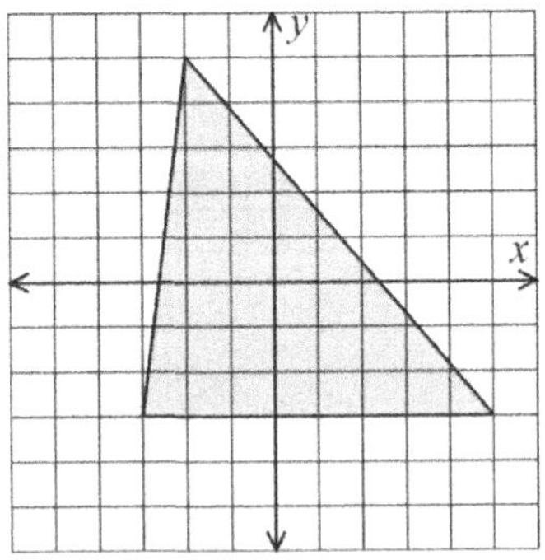

Questions 99 – 104

99.

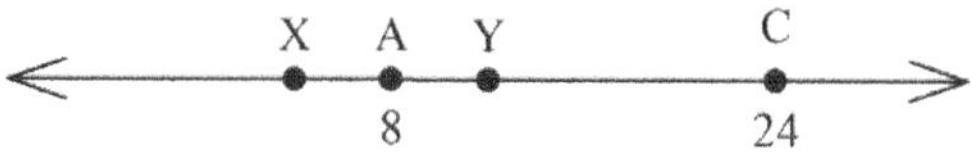

```
    X   A   Y           C
←───•───•───•───────────•───→
        8              24
```

On the number line above, point A is the midpoint of XY, point Y divides segment XC in the ratio 2 : 3. What is the lingth of YC?

A. 4 units
B. 8 units
C. 12 units
D. 16 units

100.

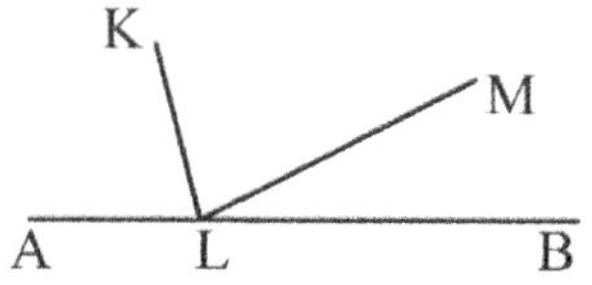

In the figure above, KL bisects angle ALM. Angle MLB is 36° less than angle ALK. What is angle KLM?

E. 48°
F. 54°
G. 72°
H. 76°

101. The interior angles of a six-sided polygon are in the ratio of 2 : 2 : 3 : 3 : 4 : 4. What is the measure of the greatest angle?

A. 160°
B. 140°
C. 130°
D. 120°

102.

```
    X   Y  Z        W
←───•───•──•────────•───→
```

On the number line above, point Z is the midpoint of XW, point Y divides segment XZ in the ratio 2 : 1. What is the ratio of YW to XW?

E. 2 : 3
F. 3 : 4
G. 1 : 3
H. 1 : 2

103.

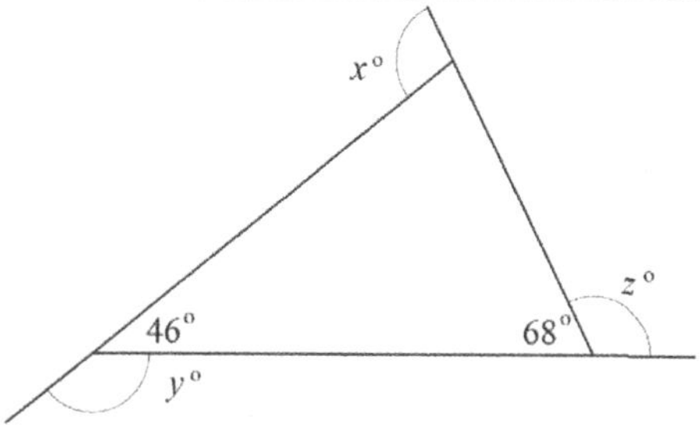

Which of the following statements is true about the above diagram?

A. $x° = 46° + 68°$
B. $y° = 46° + 68°$
C. $z° = 180° − 46°$
D. $x° = 180° − 68°$

104. XY is the diameter of a circle with center O and radius OZ is perpendicular to XY. What is angle XYZ?

E. 30°
F. 45°
G. 60°
H. 90°

Questions 105 – 110

105.

Figure X   Figure Y

The individual squares in figures X and Y are equally sized. If the perimeter of the figure X is 90 units, what is the perimeter of the figure Y?

A. 96 units
B. 99 units
C. 100 units
D. 102 units

106.

In the diagram above, what is the value of x?

E. 36°
F. 38°
G. 42°
H. 44°

107. The area of a sector of a circle of radius 18 cm is $27\pi \ cm^2$. What is the angle of the sector?

A. 30°
B. 36°
C. 45°
D. 48°

108.

In the above figure, what is the value of x?

E. 131°
F. 133°
G. 135°
H. 137°

109.

The above diagram shows a parallelogram. What is the value of x?

A. 30°
B. 40°
C. 50°
D. 60°

110. A square is inscribed in a circle of radius a and another square is circumscribing circle. What is the difference in area of two squares?

E. a^2
F. $2a^2$
G. $3a^2$
H. $4a^2$

Questions 111 – 114

111.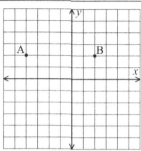

The coordinate plane above shows two vertices A(−5, 2) and B(2, 2) of a rectangle with area of 30 un^2. Which of the following points could be another two vertices of the rectangle?

A. (2, −3) and (−5, −3)
B. (2, −4) and (−5, −4)
C. (2, 5) and (−5, 5)
D. (2, 6) and (−5, 6)

112.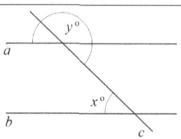

The diagram shows two parallel lines a and b cut by transversal c. Which of the following statements is true about x and y?

E. $y° = 360° − x°$
F. $y° = x°$
G. $y° = 180° + x°$
H. $y° + x° = 180°$

113.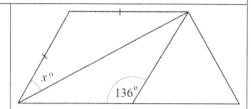

In the trapezoid above, parallel line to the leg of trapezoid intersects the greater base at angle of 136°. What is the value of x?

A. 11°
B. 22°
C. 33°
D. 44°

114.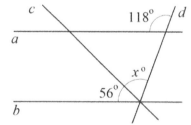

The figure above shows two parallel lines a and b cut by lines c and d. What is the value of x?

E. 62°
F. 61°
G. 60°
H. 59°

PRACTICE TEST 1

GRID-IN QUESTIONS		
Questions 58 – 62		
58. In the figure above, GRAP is a parallelogram. What is the value of x?	61.	A survey asked students what is their favorite color. In the class of 30 students, the following results are obtained. • 15 students like green. • 12 students like violet. • 5 students like neither green, nor violet. How many students like both colors?
59. The designer is painting walls in the room in two colors. The ratio of blue color to yellow color in the room must be 3 : 10. If the designer has already painted all blue parts using 210 mL of blue paint, how much yellow paint does he need?	62.	The sum of two consecutive integers is -27. If the smaller integer is increased by 5 and the larger integer is decreased by 2, what is the product of the two resulting integers?
60. For what value of g is $3g - 4 = 6 + 2g$?		

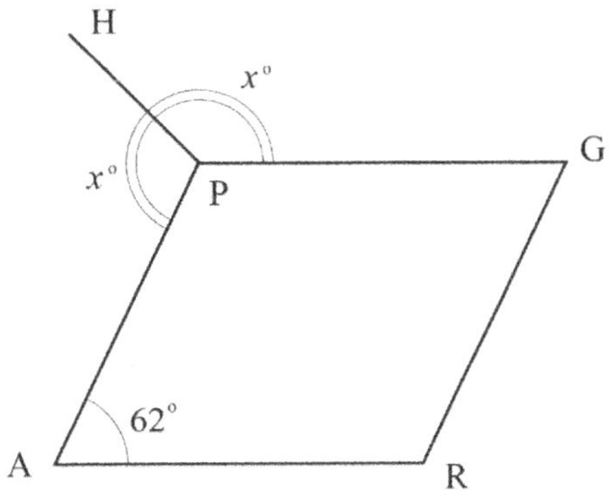

MULTIPLE CHOICE QUESTIONS

Questions 63 – 68

63. The set of possible values of a is $\{-2, 1, 7\}$. What is the set of possible values of b if $3b = a - 1$?

A. $\{-1, 0, 3\}$
B. $\{-1, 0, 2\}$
C. $\{-3, 0, 6\}$
D. $\{-3, 0, 9\}$

64. $2 - (3m + 4) + 2(5 - m) =$

E. $16 - 5m$
F. $12 - 5m$
G. $8 - 5m$
H. $4 - 5m$

65. Noah took 4 Math tests and 3 Science tests. All tests range from 0 to 100. Noah's mean in Math is 72. If all Science tests have the same sum as all Math tests, what was Noah's mean in Science?

A. 54
B. 66
C. 84
D. 96

66. Austin starts a game with half as many tokens as Emily. Emily gives Austin 6 tokens, but she still has 2 tokens more than Austin has. How many tokens does Austin have in the beginning?

E. 7
F. 14
G. 28
H. 56

67. In a scale diagram, $\frac{1}{8}$ cm represents 25 m. How many centimeters represent 1 meter?

A. 0.5
B. 0.05
C. 0.005
D. 0.0005

68. The perimeter of the rectangle is $48\ ft$. The ratio of the length to the width is $5 : 3$. What is the area of this rectangle?

E. $60\ ft^2$
F. $135\ ft^2$
G. $375\ ft^2$
H. $540\ ft^2$

Questions 69 – 74

69. PEOPLE GETTING TO WORK

Transport	Percent
On foot	11%
Bus	19%
Subway	44%
Car	26%

A researcher recorded the number of people using different types of transport when getting to work. The table above shows the percent distribution for 900 people taking part in the survey. How many people use public transport?

A. 171
B. 396
C. 405
D. 567

70.
$$1 \text{ dollar} = 12 \text{ tugriks}$$
$$4 \text{ dollars} = 25 \text{ ugriks}$$
Lisa has 60 tugriks and 75 ugriks. If she exchanges the tugriks and ugriks according to the rates above, how many dollars will she receive?

E. $17
F. $12
G. $8
H. $5

71. A box of colored marbles contains exactly 4 black marbles. The probability of choosing not a black marble is $\frac{7}{9}$. How many of the marbles are not black?

A. 12
B. 14
C. 16
D. 18

72. In the pyramid SABCD, each triangular face has the same area, and the base ABCD is a square with the area of $36\ cm^2$. If the length of SH is $4\ cm$, what is the surface area of the pyramid including the base?

E. $12\ cm^2$
F. $48\ cm^2$
G. $84\ cm^2$
H. $96\ cm^2$

73. In Math town, 60% of the population are males and 30% of them have brown eyes. Of the total Math town population, 28% have brown eyes. What percentage of the females in Math town have brown eyes?

A. 20%
B. 24%
C. 25%
D. 28%

74. The sum of the numbers $x, 2x$ and y is 42. The ratio of y to x is 5 : 3. What is the value of $2x$?

E. 9
F. 12
G. 15
H. 18

Questions 75 – 80

75. Which number line below shows the solution to the inequality $-2 \leq \frac{x}{3} < 1$?

A. 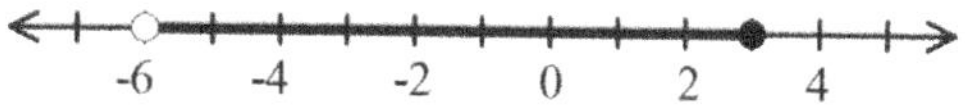
B. 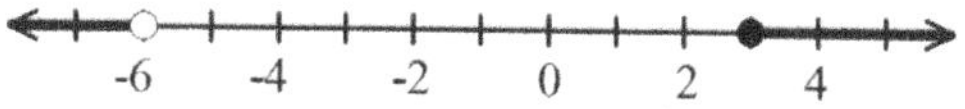
C. 
D.

76. Mr. Mortimer bought 4 melons for $3.20 each and a big watermelon weighing 7 kg. He paid $15.95 in total. What was the watermelon price per kilogram?

E. $0.15
F. $0.25
G. $0.35
H. $0.45

77. In a sample of 20 cards, 7 are red, 5 are blue and the rest are green. What is the probability that randomly selected card from the sample is not red?

A. $\frac{7}{20}$
B. $\frac{3}{5}$
C. $\frac{13}{20}$
D. $\frac{9}{10}$

78. What is the area of the shaded region in the graph above?

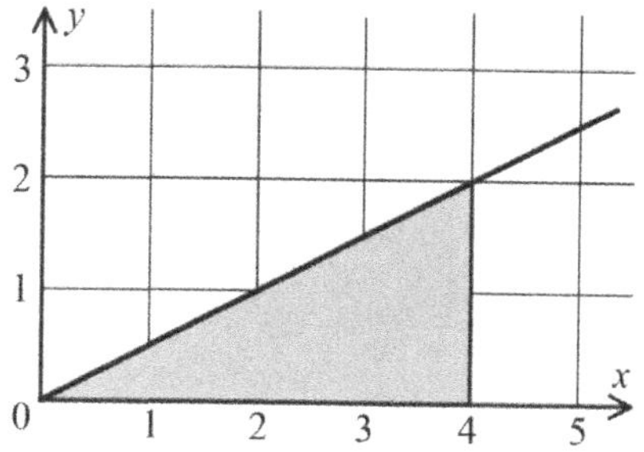

E. $2\ un^2$.
F. $4\ un^2$.
G. $6\ un^2$.
H. $8\ un^2$.

79.
10 tugriks = 1 rik
2 ugriks = 5 tugriks
4 ugriks = 5 griks

A tribe has four types of coins: tugriks, ugriks, griks and riks. The relationship between the coins is shown above. Which coin is most valuable?

A. Tugrik
B. Ugrik
C. Grik
D. Rik

80. In the Math test, 5 students get 78, 3 students get 86 and 2 students get 91. What is the mean score of all students?

E. 84
F. 83
G. 82
H. 81

Questions 81 – 86

81. PERCENT OF PEOPLE IN CARS

- 2, 25%
- 1, 6%
- 3, 38%
- 5, 12%
- 4, 19%

If 2,000 cars took part in the survey, how many more cars were with 3 people than with 5 people?

A. 500
B. 510
C. 520
D. 530

82. Which of the following numbers has factors that include the greatest factor of 119?

E. 42
F. 52
G. 68
H. 78

83. There are 280 boys in the kindergarten. There are 65 girls in the firs-year group. The ratio of girls to boys in the kindergarten is 8 : 7. How many girls are in the rest groups?

A. 255
B. 290
C. 215
D. 320

84. In a scale drawing of a triangular garden, sides measure 5 cm, 6.5 cm and 7 cm. The actual garden has the middle side measuring 13 m. What is the actual length of the longest side of the garden?

E. 10 m
F. 12 m
G. 14 m
H. 16 m

85. $1\frac{1}{3} + 2\frac{1}{6} - 3\frac{1}{2} + 4\frac{3}{4} =$

A. 4
B. 4.25
C. 4.5
D. 4.75

86. A car is travelling 48 miles per hour. Which of the following expressions would give the car's speed in feet per second? (1 mile = 5,280 feet)

E. $\frac{48 \cdot 5{,}280}{60}$

F. $\frac{48 \cdot 5{,}280}{3{,}600}$

G. $\frac{48 \cdot 60}{5{,}280}$

H. $\frac{48 \cdot 3{,}600}{5{,}280}$

I.

Questions 87 – 92

87. Now, Tia's age is $\frac{1}{3}$ of Mia's age. 9 years ago, Mia was 7.5 times older than Tia. How old is Tia now?

   A. 12 years old
   B. 13 years old
   C. 14 years old
   D. 15 years old

88. How many positive even factors does number 24 have?

   E. 8
   F. 6
   G. 4
   H. 2

89. The least of 7 consecutive natural numbers is a, and the greatest is b. Which of the following statements is not true?

   A. The sum of numbers is $7(a + 3)$
   B. The sum of numbers is $7b + 21$
   C. $a = b - 6$
   D. $b = a + 6$

90. Gwen is choosing one vegetable pizza from 4 possible vegetable pizzas and 2 meat pizzas from 6 possible meat pizzas. How many different ways can Gwen choose all needed pizzas?

   E. 19
   F. 34
   G. 60
   H. 96

91. Max bought a house worth $48,000 on credit. He paid an initial fee of $12,000 and paid $450 monthly for 5 years. How much more should Max pay for the house?

   A. $9,000
   B. $10,000
   C. $11,000
   D. $12,000

92. Working at a constant rate, Megan can solve 6 math problems in 20 minutes. Becky can solve 8 math problems in 24 minutes. How many math problems can they solve together in 30 minutes?

   E. 15
   F. 16
   G. 18
   H. 19

Questions 93 – 98

93. On the number line below, $QR = \frac{5}{6}$. Point P (not shown) is located between points Q and R. Which value is not a possible value for P?

Q at $3\frac{5}{12}$, R to the right.

A. 3.72
B. 4.21
C. 4.28
D. 3.76

94. In the set of consecutive integers from 10 to 36, inclusive, how many integers are multiples of 2, but not multiples of 3?

E. 8
F. 9
G. 12
H. 14

95. Perris must write a 350-word essay for school today. It took her 45 minutes to write 225 words. At this rate, how much time will it take her to write the whole essay?

A. $1\frac{1}{6}$ hours
B. $1\frac{1}{3}$ hours
C. $1\frac{1}{2}$ hours
D. $1\frac{2}{3}$ hours

96. Suppose $K = \frac{x}{y}$, $L = \frac{u}{v}$, and $x, y, u,$ and v do not equal to 0. What is $\frac{1}{KL}$ in terms of x, y, u and v?

E. $\frac{xu}{yv}$
F. $\frac{yv}{xu}$
G. $\frac{xv}{yu}$
H. $\frac{yu}{xv}$

97. A box contains 4 chocolate candies, 3 vanilla candies, and 8 almond candies. If Henry selects 2 candies at random from the box, without replacement, what is the probability that both candies are not almond?

A. 0.2
B. 0.25
C. 0.3
D. 0.45

98. Peter has two boards 20 inches and 32 inches long. He wants to cut them into parts of equal length without remains. What is the maximum possible length of each part?

E. 2 inches
F. 4 inches
G. 8 inches
H. 12 inches

Questions 99 – 104

99. NUMBER OF BUS ROUTES IN CITIES

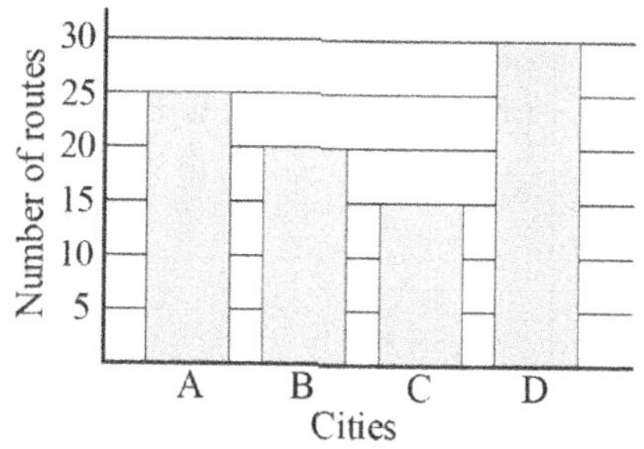

The graph above shows the number of different bus routes in 4 small cities. Cities A and C each have 3 drivers per bus route, city D has 2 drivers per bus route and city B has 4 drivers per bus route. Which of the cities has the greatest total number of drivers?
- A. City A
- B. City B
- C. City C
- D. City D

100. If $\frac{2}{k} = \frac{m}{6}$, which of the options represent k in terms of m?
- E. $\frac{m}{12}$
- F. $\frac{m}{3}$
- G. $\frac{12}{m}$
- H. $\frac{3}{m}$

101. $\frac{5}{13} = 0.\overline{384615}$

In the repeating decimal above, what is 153rd digit?
- A. 3
- B. 4
- C. 6
- D. 1

102. SCORES IN HISTORY TEST

Section	Highest Score	Range
I	92	34
II	95	33
III	97	36
IV	93	27

Ms. Tulip's history class is divided into three sections. The same test was given to each section. The table shows both the greatest score and the range of scores on this test for each section. What is the overall range of all four sections?
- E. 36
- F. 37
- G. 38
- H. 39

103. On the number line below, points A, B, C, and D are integers. If AB:BC:CD= 3 : 5 : 4, what is the length of BD?

A at -15, C at 1.

- A. 14
- B. 16
- C. 18
- D. 24

104. $200(2 - 0.4)^2 - 100 =$
- E. 220
- F. 156
- G. 412
- H. 512

	Questions 105 – 110		
105.	Styrofoam for facade insulation should be 0.6 cm thick. 2% error is allowed. What is the smallest allowable thickness of the Styrofoam? A. 0.588 cm B. 0.58 cm C. 0.589 cm D. 0.59 cm	108.	Allice has 3 red, 4 blue, 6 yellow, 5 green, and 12 pink strings. If she picks one string at random, what is the probability that it will be green? E. $\frac{1}{10}$ F. $\frac{1}{6}$ G. $\frac{2}{15}$ H. $\frac{1}{5}$
106.	If $5n$ is a positive even number, how many even numbers are in the range from $5n - 3$ to $5n + 4$? E. 2 F. 3 G. 4 H. 5	109.	Each month, Sergio has fixed expenses of $2,350 at his sewing studio. It costs him $32 to sew one dress, and he sells each dress for $48. What is Sergio's profit if he sews 1,000 dresses per month? A. $13,650 B. $24,650 C. $32,650 D. $45,650
107.	A bike travels 550 meters per minute. The radius of each tire on the bike is 1 meter. How many revolutions does one of these tires make per minute? (Use approximation $\pi \approx \frac{22}{7}$) A. 52.5 B. 63.5 C. 76.5 D. 87.5	110.	Using the approximation 1 inch = 2.54 centimeters, how many centimeters are in 8 feet 10 inches? E. 246.89 cm F. 269.24 cm G. 272.35 cm H. 281.13 cm

Questions 111 – 114

111. On the number line below, BD = 4.2, AD = 8.2, AC = 5.3. What is the position of point C?

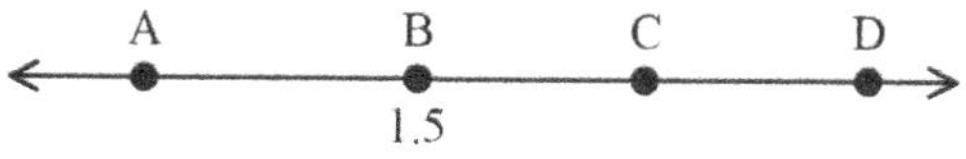

```
   A       B       C       D
←——•———————•———————•———————•——→
          1.5
```

A. 1.8
B. 2.3
C. 3.3
D. 3.8

112. If $2x - 5y = 18$, what is y in terms of x?

E. $y = 0.4x + 1.8$
F. $y = 0.4x - 1.8$
G. $y = 0.4x - 3.6$
H. $y = 0.4x + 3.6$

113. Bagels recipe calls for 3 parts of flour, 2 parts of sugar, 1 part of butter and $\frac{1}{8}$ part of vanilla. If you have 12 g of vanilla, how much flour do you need?

A. 96 g
B. 144 g
C. 192 g
D. 288 g

114.

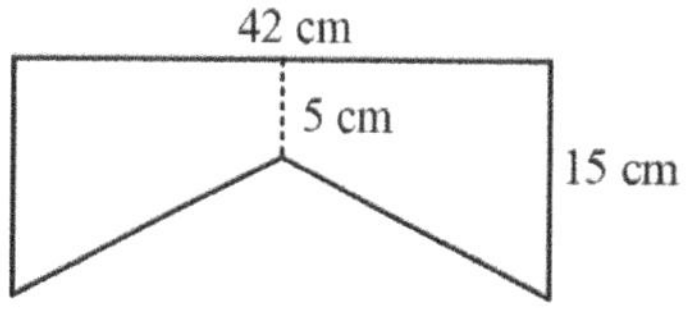

```
        42 cm
   ┌─────────────┐
   │    ┊5 cm     │
   │    /\       │ 15 cm
   │   /  \      │
```

Roger makes banner as shown above. How many square centimeters of fabric does he need?

E. $210\ cm^2$
F. $350\ cm^2$
G. $420\ cm^2$
H. $630\ cm^2$

PRACTICE TEST 2

GRID-IN QUESTIONS

Questions 58 – 62

58. In the figure above, GRAP is a parallelogram. What is the value of x?

59. The seller lays out cans of beans and corn on the shelves. The ratio of bean cans to corn cans on each shelf must be 6 : 7. If the seller has already put 35 corn cans, how many bean cans should he put to hold needed ratio?

60. For what value of u is $2u - 15 = -u$?

61. A survey asked students what is their favorite fast food. In the sample of 80 students, the following results are obtained.
- 37 students like pizza.
- 45 students like burgers.
- 8 students like both pizza and burgers.

How many students like neither pizza nor burgers?

62. The sum of two even consecutive integers is -46. If the smaller integer is divided by 4 and the larger integer is increased by 11, what is the product of the two resulting integers?

MULTIPLE CHOICE QUESTIONS

Questions 63 – 68

63. The set of possible values of x is $\{-1\frac{1}{4}, \frac{1}{4}, 2\frac{3}{4}\}$. What is the set of possible values of y if $\frac{y}{2} = x + \frac{1}{4}$?

  A. $\{-3, 1, 6\}$
  B. $\{-1, \frac{1}{2}, 3\}$
  C. $\{-2, 1, 6\}$
  D. $\{-\frac{1}{2}, \frac{1}{4}, \frac{3}{4}\}$

64. $2x - 3(5 - x) =$

  E. $-5(3 - x)$
  F. $-5(3 + x)$
  G. $5(x + 3)$
  H. $5(3 - x)$

65. Jeff took 3 Math tests and 2 History tests. All tests range from 0 to 100. Jeff's mean in Math is 82 and his mean in History is 87. What is Jeff's mean in all tests?

  A. 83
  B. 84
  C. 85
  D. 86

66. Brenda has three times more quarters than Lisa has. Brenda gives 20% of her quarters to Lisa, but she still has $1 more. How many quarters does Lisa have in the beginning?

  E. 5
  F. 10
  G. 15
  H. 20

67. In a scale diagram, $\frac{1}{4}$ cm represents 5 m. How many centimeters represent 12 meters?

  A. 0.006
  B. 0.06
  C. 0.6
  D. 6

68. The area of the rectangle is $48\,ft^2$. The ratio of the length to the width is 4 : 3. What is the perimeter of this rectangle?

  E. $14\,ft$
  F. $18\,ft$
  G. $24\,ft$
  H. $28\,ft$

Questions 69 – 74

69.
BUYERS FRUIT PREFERENCE

Fruit	Percent
Apple	35%
Pear	18%
Apricot	33%
Kiwi	14%

The market manager conducted a survey on which fruit buyers prefer. The table above shows the percent distribution for 200 buyers taking part in the survey. How many more buyers prefer apricots than pears?

A. 4
B. 8
C. 30
D. 34

70.
$$3 \text{ dollars} = 10 \text{ hams}$$
$$\frac{1}{2} \text{ dollar} = 6 \text{ bams}$$

Jeremy has 180 bams. If he exchanges the bams into dollars and dollars into hams, how many hams will he receive?

E. 15
F. 50
G. 30
H. 25

71. A box of colored marbles contains twice as many blue marbles as yellow marbles and 10 black marbles. The probability of choosing a black marble is $\frac{2}{5}$. How many of the marbles are in the box?

A. 15
B. 20
C. 25
D. 30

72. In the pyramid SABCD, each triangular face has the same area, and the base ABCD is a square. The surface area of the pyramid excluding the base is 64 cm^2. If the length of SH is 8 cm, what is the area of the base?

E. 12 cm^2
F. 16 cm^2
G. 20 cm^2
H. 25 cm^2

73. In a city, 30% of the population are wear glasses and 60% of them are males. It is known that 40% of the population are males. What percentage of the males in the city wear glasses?

A. 45%
B. 50%
C. 55%
D. 60%

74. The sum of the numbers $x, x - 2$ and $2y$ is 134. The ratio of x to y is 10 : 7. What is the value of y?

E. 28
F. 38
G. 40
H. 56

Questions 75 – 80

75. Which number line below shows the solution to the inequality $-3.5 \leq \frac{x-1}{2} < 1$?

   A. (number line with open circle at -6, closed circle at 3)
   B. (number line with open circle at -6, closed circle at 3)
   C. (number line with closed circle at -6, open circle at 3)
   D. (number line with closed circle at -6, open circle at 3)

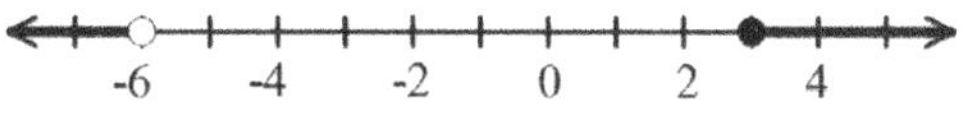

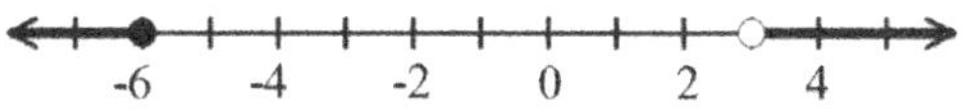

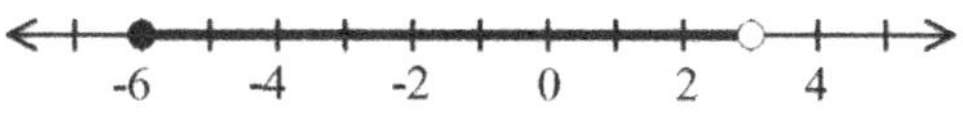

76. Asia bought 12 pencils for $0.85 each and 5 pens. She paid $17.20 in total. What was one pen price?

   E. $1.10
   F. $1.20
   G. $1.30
   H. $1.40

77. In a set of 36 tennis balls, 12 are orange, 4 are red and the rest are white. What is the probability that randomly selected tennis ball from the set is white?

   A. $\frac{1}{3}$
   B. $\frac{1}{9}$
   C. $\frac{5}{9}$
   D. $\frac{4}{9}$

78. What is the area of the shaded region in the graph above?

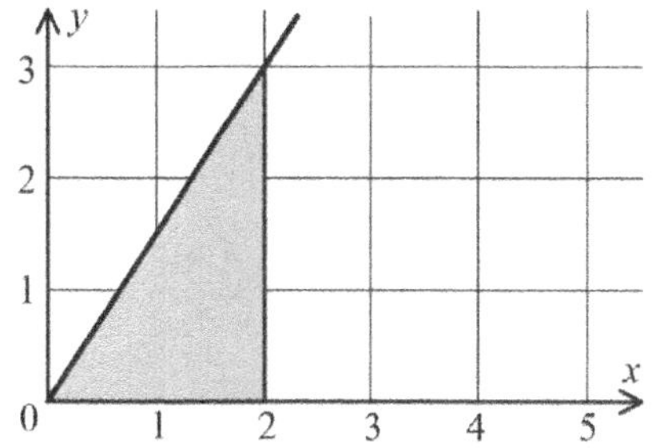

   E. $2\ un^2$.
   F. $3\ un^2$.
   G. $4\ un^2$.
   H. $6\ un^2$.

79. Three apples weigh as much as two pears. Three pears weigh as much as four avocados. Which of the following statements is true?

   A. 18 apples weigh as much as 16 avocados
   B. 1 apple weigh as much as 2 avocados
   C. 3 apples weigh as much as 6 avocados
   D. 12 apples weigh as much as 8 avocados

80. The mean of the numbers $x, x+1, 2x$ and 11 is 9. What is the mean of the numbers $x-1$ and 9?

   E. 4
   F. 5
   G. 6
   H. 7

\multicolumn{4}{l}{Questions 81 – 86}

81.	**NUMBER OF MEALS PER DAY** Pie chart: 1, 8%; 2, 16%; 3, 27%; 4, 34%; 5, 15% If 400 people took part in the survey, how many people take more than 3 meals per day? A. 108 B. 196 C. 200 D. 304	84.	The ratio of the sides of a certain triangle is 4 : 3 : 5. If the longest side of the triangle is 30 cm, what is the perimeter of the triangle? E. 72 *cm* F. 54 *cm* G. 48 *cm* H. 42 *cm*
82.	What is the greatest prime factor of 228? E. 11 F. 13 G. 17 H. 19	85.	$$\frac{4\frac{2}{5} - 2\frac{1}{10}}{23} \cdot 4 =$$ A. 40 B. 2.5 C. 0.4 D. 4
83.	A Math test has 40 questions. The first 15 questions are True-False questions and the rest are multiple-choice questions. What is the ratio of multiple-choice questions to all questions? A. 3 : 8 B. 3 : 5 C. 5 : 3 D. 5 : 8	86.	A taxi hurries with a constant speed of 84 *km/h*. Which of the following expressions would give the taxi's speed in meters per second? E. $\frac{84 \cdot 1{,}000}{60}$ F. $\frac{84 \cdot 1{,}000}{3{,}600}$ G. $\frac{84 \cdot 60}{1{,}000}$ H. $\frac{84 \cdot 3{,}600}{1{,}000}$

Questions 87 – 92

87. Leo is 32 years old. His son is 7 years old. In how many years will Leo double his son's age?

    A. 12 years
    B. 14 years
    C. 16 years
    D. 18 years

88. How many positive odd factors does number 42 have?

    E. 1
    F. 2
    G. 3
    H. 4

89. The sum of 6 consecutive natural numbers is a, and the greatest is b. Which of the following statements is true?

    A. Number b is greater than a
    B. $6b = a + 15$
    C. $a = 6b + 15$
    D. There is no dependence between a and b

90. The rental car company had 12 buses and 8 vans available to rent. How many different ways can customer choose 2 vans and 1 bus?

    E. 168
    F. 252
    G. 336
    H. 672

91. Susy has $124 in her savings account. She earns $28 a week babysitting. If Susy saves all of her earnings, after how many weeks will she have $432 saved?

    A. 9 weeks
    B. 11 weeks
    C. 13 weeks
    D. 15 weeks

92. Bill wants to use a cookie recipe that makes 48 cookies but he wants to reduce the number of cookies to 36. If the recipe specifies using 3 cups of sugar, how much sugar should he use?

    E. 4
    F. $\frac{3}{4}$
    G. 2
    H. $2\frac{1}{4}$

Questions 93 – 98

93. On the number line below, $UV = 1\frac{1}{3}$.
Point W (not shown) is located between points U and V. Which value is a possible value for W?

```
    U                V
<---•----------------•--------->
                    7 4/9
```

A. 6.01
B. 7.55
C. 6.11
D. 7.44

94. In the set of consecutive integers from 9 to 30, inclusive, how many integers are multiples of 3, but not multiples of 2?

E. 4
F. 5
G. 9
H. 11

95. Mila traveled 1,250 miles of her 3,125-mile trip in the first 3 days. At this rate, how long will it take her to finish the trip?

A. 4 days
B. $4\frac{1}{2}$ days
C. 5 days
D. $5\frac{1}{2}$ days

96. Suppose $M = \frac{a}{b}$, $N = \frac{c}{d}$, and a, b, c, and d do not equal to 0. What is $\frac{M}{N}$ in terms of $a, b, c,$ and d?

E. $\frac{ac}{bd}$

F. $\frac{ab}{cd}$

G. $\frac{bc}{ad}$

H. $\frac{ad}{bc}$

97. All 25 students in Audrey's class are going to run the 200-meter race. In how many different ways can the students finish in first and second places?

A. $25 \cdot 24$

B. $\frac{25 \cdot 24}{2}$

C. $25 \cdot 25$

D. $\frac{25+24}{2}$

98. Mr. Bran has 72 roses and 84 peons. He wants to plant the flowers in rows of equal width. What could be the maximum number of flowers that can be planted in a row if each row has only one type of flower?

E. 4
F. 6
G. 12
H. 14

Questions 99 – 104

99. FAVORITE TYPES OF PIZZA TOPPINGS

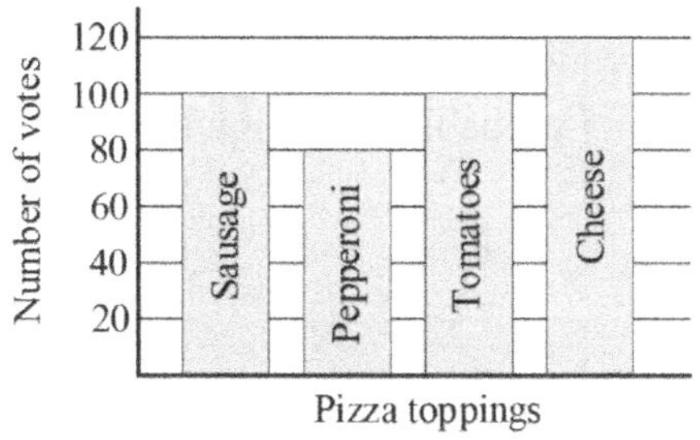

The graph above shows the number of votes for 4 most popular pizza toppings. Base on the bar diagram, which statement is not true?

A. Cheese got 20 more votes than Tomatoes
B. All toppings got 400 votes in total
C. Peperoni got 30 fewer votes than Cheese
D. Sausage and Tomatoes got in total as much as Cheese and Pepperoni

100. If $2 : x = 3 : (x - 1)$, what is the value of x?

E. -2
F. $-\frac{1}{2}$
G. 2
H. $\frac{1}{2}$

101. In the repeating decimal $\frac{7}{13} = 0.\overline{538461}$, what is 135th digit?

A. 5
B. 8
C. 6
D. 1

102. SCORES IN HISTORY TEST

Section	Max Score	Min Score
I	96	58
II	92	53
III	95	54
IV	89	61

Ms. Tulip's history class is divided into four sections. The same test was given to each section. The table shows both the greatest score and the smallest score on this test for each section. Which of the following statements is true?

E. The range of the II section is smaller than the range of the IV section
F. The range of the IV section is 27
G. The range of the I section is greater than the range of the III section
H. The greatest range is 41

103. On the number line below, points A, B, C, and D are integers. If $AB : BC : CD = 3 : 5 : 4$, what is the length of AD?

A   B   C   D
−15   1

A. 14
B. 16
C. 18
D. 24

104. $100 - 400(1 - 0.75)^2 =$

E. 75
F. 125
G. 0
H. 200

Questions 105 – 110

105. Utah's volleyball team played 40 games and won 28 of them. What percent did the team lose?

    A. 20%
    B. 30%
    C. 50%
    D. 70%

106. If $7n$ is a positive even number, how many even numbers are in the range from $7n + 2$ to $7n + 11$?

    E. 2
    F. 3
    G. 4
    H. 5

107. What is the circumference of the top surface of a circular manhole cover that has a diameter of 35 centimeters?

    A. 17.5π cm
    B. 35π cm
    C. 52.5π cm
    D. 70π cm

108. Allice has 3 red, 4 blue, 6 yellow, 5 green, and 12 pink strings. If she picks one string at random, what is the probability that it will be not pink?

    E. $\frac{2}{5}$
    F. $\frac{1}{5}$
    G. $\frac{1}{10}$
    H. $\frac{3}{5}$

109. The band wants to order T-shirts and caps. The T-shirts cost $17 each. The cap cost $9 each. Additionally, the band has to pay a shipping fee of $12. If the band orders t T-shirts and c caps, how much will it cost them?

    A. $\$(17(t + 12) + 9(c + 12))$
    B. $\$(17t + 9c + 12)$
    C. $\$(9t + 17c + 12)$
    D. $\$(9(t + 12) + 17(c + 12))$

110. Using the approximation 1 inch = 2.54 centimeters, how many centimeters are in 5 feet 4 inches?

    E. 153.42 cm
    F. 158.84 cm
    G. 162.56 cm
    H. 167.38 cm

Questions 111 – 114			
111.	On the number line below, BC = 3.1, AC = 6.7, AD = 9.9. What is the position of point D? A B C D ←●———●———●———●→ 1.5 A. 6.3 B. 6.8 C. 7.3 D. 7.8	113.	Garry is preparing for his college entrance exams. In a trial test, he answered 15 problems in 45 minutes. At this rate, how many questions can he expect to answer in $2\frac{1}{2}$ hours? A. 40 B. 45 C. 50 D. 55
112.	If $1 - 3x + 4y = 13$, what is x in terms of y? E. $x = 4 + \frac{4}{3}y$ F. $x = 4 - \frac{4}{3}y$ G. $x = -4 - \frac{4}{3}y$ H. $x = -4 + \frac{4}{3}y$	114.	(L-shaped figure with sides labeled 20 cm, 20 cm, 20 cm, 20 cm) A ceramics company wants to produce tiles in the shape shown above. What is the area of each tile? E. 400 cm^2 F. 800 cm^2 G. 1,200 cm^2 H. 1,600 cm^2

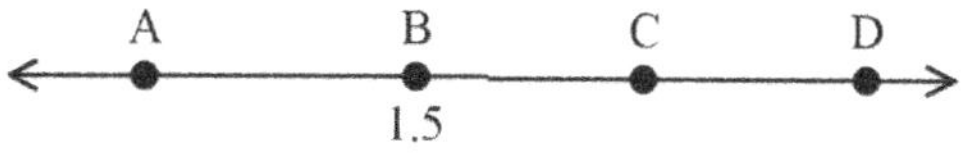

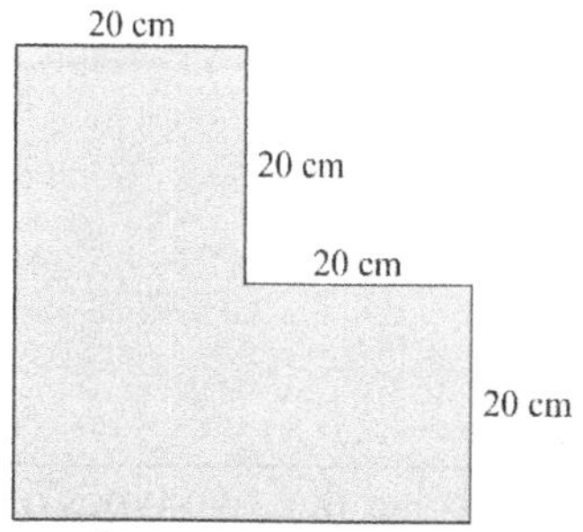

GRID-IN QUESTIONS

Questions 58 – 62

58.

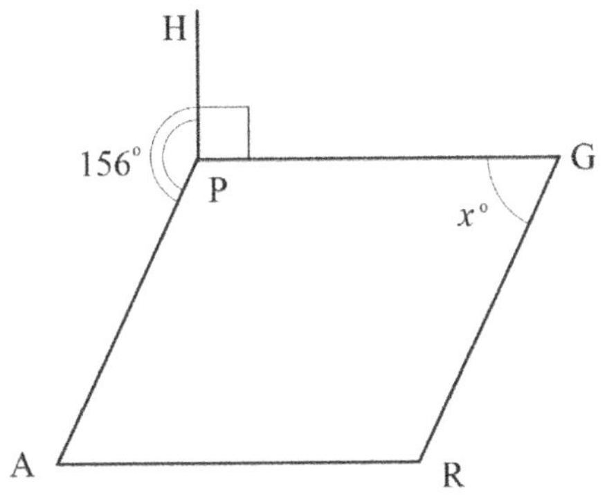

In the figure above, GRAP is a parallelogram. What is the value of x?

59. Ida feeds her dog two types of dog food: chicken-flavored and rabbit-flavored in the ratio 9 : 7. This month, Ida's dog eats 27 cans of chicken-flavored dog food. How many total cans of dog food does Ida's dog eat this month?

60. For what value of v is $12 - 3v = v$?

61. A survey asked students what additional language they learn. In the sample of 60 students, the following results are obtained.
- 37 students learn French.
- 35 students learn German.
- 13 students do not learn French and German.

How many students learn both French and German?

62. The product of two negative consecutive integers is 63. If the smaller integer is divided by 3 and the larger integer is increased by 5, what is the product of the two resulting integers?

MULTIPLE CHOICE QUESTIONS

Questions 63 – 68

63. The set of possible values of t is $\{-6, -2, 8\}$. What is the set of possible values of s if $t = 2s - 2$?

   A. $\{-1, 0, \frac{5}{2}\}$

   B. $\{-4, 0, 10\}$

   C. $\{-2, 0, \frac{5}{2}\}$

   D. $\{-2, 0, 5\}$

64. $3 - 4(1 - x) + x =$

   E. $-1 - 3x$
   F. $-1 + 3x$
   G. $5x - 1$
   H. $5x + 1$

65. The mean weight of four men is 81.5 kg. The heaviest man weighs 89 kg and the lightest weighs 73 kg. What is the mean weight of two remaining men?

   A. 82 kg
   B. 83 kg
   C. 84 kg
   D. 85 kg

66. On the farm, the number of chicken is 4 times the number of horses. In total, all chicken and all horses have 228 legs. Now many more chicken than horses are on the farm?

   E. 19
   F. 38
   G. 57
   H. 76

67. Lionel wants to build a model of a 150-meter tall building. He will be using a scale of 0.6 centimeters = 4 meters. How tall will the model be?

   A. 18 cm
   B. 22.5 cm
   C. 36 cm
   D. 62.5 cm

68. The ratio of Jude's money and Roger's money was 4 : 5. After they each spent $20, the ratio became 11 : 15. How much money did Jude have at first?

   E. $60
   F. $64
   G. $72
   H. $80

Questions 69 – 74

69.

BUYERS FRUIT PREFERENCE

Fruit	Percent
Apple	37%
Pear	18%
Apricot	34%
Kiwi	11%

The market manager conducted a survey on which fruit buyers prefer. The table above shows the percent distribution for 300 buyers taking part in the survey. How many fewer buyers prefer kiwis than pears?

A. 9
B. 21
C. 48
D. 69

70.

5 dollars = 9 hams
$\frac{1}{2}$ dollar = 4 bams

Carla has 126 hams. If she exchanges the hams into dollars and dollars into bams, how many bams will she receive?

E. 560
F. 540
G. 520
H. 500

71. A box of colored marbles contains twice as many blue marbles as yellow marbles and 15 white marbles. The probability of choosing a white marble is $\frac{5}{9}$. How many blue marbles are in the box?

A. 4
B. 8
C. 12
D. 27

72. In the pyramid SABCD, each triangular face has the same area, and the base ABCD is a square. The surface area of the pyramid including the base is $132\ cm^2$. If the length of AD is $6\ cm$, what is the length of SH?

E. $4\ cm$
F. $8\ cm$
G. $11\ cm$
H. $16\ cm$

73. If a house is sold for $90,000 there is a loss of 20% on the cost price. For how much should it be sold to make a gain of 20% on the cost price?

A. $100,000
B. $120,000
C. $125,000
D. $135,000

74. The sum of the numbers $3x, x+1$ and y is 85. The ratio of x to y is 1 : 2. What is the value of $2y$?

E. 14
F. 28
G. 42
H. 56

Questions 75 – 80

75. Which number line below shows the solution to the inequality
$$-2 < 2x - 4 \leq 2?$$

A.

B.

C.

D.

76. Janelle buys 3 boxes of popcorn and 6 colas at the movies for herself and her two friends. Each box of popcorn costs $1.95. If Janelle pays $13.29 in total, how much does one cola cost?

E. $1.24
F. $1.22
G. $1.21
H. $1.18

77. In a set of 60 tennis balls, there twice as many orange balls as red balls and 7 times more white balls than red balls. What is the probability that randomly selected tennis ball from the set is orange?

A. $\frac{1}{5}$

B. $\frac{1}{10}$

C. $\frac{2}{5}$

D. $\frac{3}{10}$

78.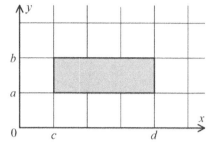

What is the area of the shaded region in the graph above?

E. $ab + cd \ un^2$.
F. $(b - a)(d - c) \ un^2$.
G. $(a - b)(d - c) \ un^2$.
H. $ab - cd \ un^2$.

79. 5 apples weigh as much as 4 pears. 3 pears weigh as much as 2 avocados. Which of the following statements is true?

A. 12 apples weigh as much as 6 avocados
B. 10 apples weigh as much as 4 avocados
C. 15 apples weigh as much as 8 avocados
D. 8 apples weigh as much as 5 avocados

80. The mean of the numbers $x, x - 2, 3x$ and 13 is 24. What is the mean of the numbers x and $x - 2$?

E. 14
F. 15
G. 16
H. 17

Questions 81 – 86			
81.	NUMBER OF MEALS PER DAY 5, 15% 1, 8% 4, 34% 2, 16% 3, 27% If 600 people took part in the survey, how many people take less than 3 meals per day? A. 144 B. 162 C. 258 D. 306	84.	The ratio of the sides of a certain triangle is 2 : 6 : 7. If the shortest side of the triangle is 8 cm, what is the perimeter of the triangle? E. 60 cm F. 52 cm G. 36 cm H. 28 cm
82.	Mathew is arranging his baseball cards in a frame. If he has 36 cards, in how many different numbers of rows and columns can he display them if each row has the same number of cards greater than one but less than 36? E. 4 F. 5 G. 6 H. 7	85.	$$\frac{4\frac{2}{5} + 2\frac{1}{10}}{13} \div \frac{1}{4} =$$ A. 0.125 B. 0.5 C. 2 D. 8
83.	A Math test has 35 questions. The first 14 questions are True-False questions and the rest are multiple-choice questions. What is the ratio of multiple-choice questions to True-False questions? A. 3 : 2 B. 3 : 5 C. 2 : 3 D. 2 : 5	86.	A taxi hurries with a constant speed of 26 m/s. Which of the following expressions would give the taxi's speed in kilometers per hour? E. $\frac{26 \cdot 1{,}000}{60}$ F. $\frac{26 \cdot 1{,}000}{3{,}600}$ G. $\frac{26 \cdot 60}{1{,}000}$ H. $\frac{26 \cdot 3{,}600}{1{,}000}$

	Questions 87 – 92		
87.	Martin is 36 years old. His son is 11 years old. In how many years will Martin double his son's age? A. 12 years B. 14 years C. 16 years D. 18 years	90.	The rental car company had 10 buses and 6 vans available to rent. How many different ways can customer choose 2 buses and 3 vans? E. $C_2^{10} \cdot C_3^6$ F. C_5^{16} G. $C_2^{10} + C_3^6$ H. $C_3^{10} \cdot C_2^6$
88.	In the list of numbers below, how many of them have prime factors greater than 10? 22, 24, 26, 28, 30, 32, 34, 36, 38 E. 2 F. 3 G. 4 H. 5	91.	Asia has $256 in her savings account. She earns $36 a week babysitting. If Asia saves all of her earnings, after how many weeks will she have $508 saved? A. 7 weeks B. 6 weeks C. 5 weeks D. 4 weeks
89.	The sum of 4 consecutive natural numbers is a, and the smallest is b. Which of the following statements is not true? A. Number a is greater than b B. $4b = a - 6$ C. The greatest number is $b + 4$ D. The mean number of these numbers is $b + 1.5$	92.	Ross wants to use a cookie recipe that makes 24 cookies but he wants to increase the number of cookies to 32. If the recipe specifies using $2\frac{1}{2}$ cups of sugar, how much sugar should he use? E. $3\frac{1}{3}$ F. $3\frac{1}{6}$ G. 3 H. $2\frac{5}{6}$

Questions 93 – 98

93. On the number line below, $UV = 3\frac{1}{9}$. Point W (not shown) is located between points U and V. Which value is not a possible value for W?

   U ————————•——————— V
                        $7\frac{4}{9}$

   A. 4.66
   B. 4.33
   C. 7.11
   D. 7.44

94. In the set of consecutive integers from 6 to 30, inclusive, how many integers are multiples of 2, but not multiples of 4?

   E. 6
   F. 7
   G. 11
   H. 13

95. An 8-ounce can of tomatoes costs $1.12. At this rate, how much will cost a 18-ounce can of tomatoes?

   A. $2.52
   B. $2.48
   C. $2.44
   D. $2.42

96. Suppose $A = \frac{a}{b}$, $B = \frac{b}{a}$, and a, b do not equal to 0. What is $\frac{1}{A} \div \frac{1}{B}$ in terms of a and b?

   E. $\frac{a^2}{b^2}$
   F. $\frac{b^2}{a^2}$
   G. $\frac{1}{ab}$
   H. 1

97. All 20 students in Audrey's class are going to run the 200-meter race. In how many different ways can the students finish in first, second, and third places?

   A. $20 \cdot 20 \cdot 20$
   B. $\frac{20 \cdot 19 \cdot 18}{2}$
   C. $20 \cdot 19 \cdot 18$
   D. $\frac{20 \cdot 19 \cdot 18}{2 \cdot 3}$

98. Mr. Johansson has 112 irises and 196 daises. He wants to plant the flowers in rows of equal width. What could be the maximum number of flowers that can be planted in a row if each row has only one type of flower?

   E. 4
   F. 7
   G. 14
   H. 28

Questions 99 – 104

99. FAVORITE TYPES OF PIZZA TOPPINGS

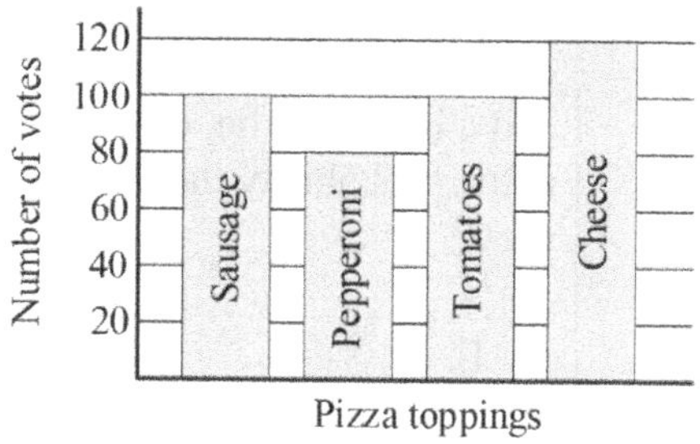

The graph above shows the number of votes for 4 most popular pizza toppings. Base on the bar diagram, which statement is true?

A. On average, 90 people voted for Sausage, Pepperoni and Tomatoes
B. On average, 90 people voted for Sausage and Pepperoni
C. On average, 105 people voted for Tomatoes and Cheese
D. On average, 95 people voted for each topping

100. If $3 : (x + 1) = 4 : (2x - 1)$, what is the value of x?

E. $-2\frac{1}{2}$
F. $-3\frac{1}{2}$
G. $2\frac{1}{2}$
H. $3\frac{1}{2}$

101. In the repeating decimal $\frac{3}{7} = 0.\overline{428571}$, what is 211th digit?

A. 4
B. 8
C. 7
D. 1

102. SCORES IN HISTORY TEST

Section	Min Score	Max Score
I	62	94
II	61	92
III	64	91

Ms. Edward's chemistry class is divided into three sections. The same test was given to each section. The table shows both the greatest score and the smallest score on this test for each section. What is the overall range of all scores in all three sections?

E. 30
F. 31
G. 32
H. 33

103. On the number line below, points A, B, C, and D are integers. If AB : BC : AD = 2 : 3 : 7, what is the length of AC?

A, B (-8), C (1), D

A. 14
B. 15
C. 16
D. 17

104. $100(1 + 0.5)^2 - 200(1 - 0.5)^2 =$

E. 0
F. 75
G. 125
H. 175

Questions 105 – 110

105. Paula got a puppy 4 weeks ago. In this time, the puppy's weight increased to 185% of its initial weight. If initially puppy weighed 14 ounces, what was puppy's increase in weight, in ounces?

   A. 8.5 ounces
   B. 10.7 ounces
   C. 11.9 ounces
   D. 25.9 ounces

106. If $5n$ is a positive odd number, how many even numbers are in the range from $5n - 3$ to $5n + 7$?

   E. 6
   F. 5
   G. 4
   H. 3

107. A porcelain factory is producing dinner plates with a diameter of 28 cm. They plan to put a blue edge on each plate. How much blue edging they need for 200 plates? (Use approximation $\pi \approx \frac{22}{7}$)

   A. 176 m
   B. 112 m
   C. 88 m
   D. 352 m

108. Jordan's basketball team must decide on a new uniform. The team has a choice of silver shorts or white shorts and a black, white, or grey shirt. What is the probability the shirt will not be grey?

   E. $\frac{2}{3}$
   F. $\frac{1}{3}$
   G. $\frac{1}{6}$
   H. $\frac{5}{6}$

109. The cost of a car tire is $65 plus $20 per order regardless of the number of tires purchased. If Mrs. Kyoto order is for $325, which of the following equations can be used to find the number of ordered tires, x?

   A. $65 + 20x = 325$
   B. $20 + 65x = 325$
   C. $20x = 325 + 65$
   D. $65x = 325 + 20$

110. The ceilings of most classrooms are about 8 feet 6 inches above the floor. How many centimeters high is the ceiling? (Use the approximation 1 inch = 2.54 centimeters)

   E. 259.08 cm
   F. 256.54 cm
   G. 245.36 cm
   H. 241.22 cm

Questions 111 – 114

111. On the number line below, AC = 7.4, AD = 10.1, BD = 5.2. What is the position of point B?

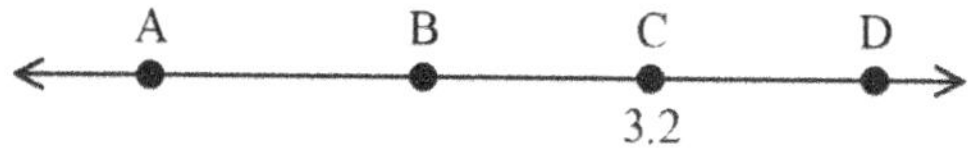

```
  A       B       C       D
←—●———————●———————●———————●—→
                  3.2
```

A. 0.7
B. 0.4
C. −0.4
D. −0.7

112. If $5 - 2x - 6y = 11$, what is x in terms of y?

E. $x = 3 - 3y$

F. $x = 3 + 3y$

G. $x = -3 - 3y$

H. $x = -3 + 3y$

113. A scientists estimate that the human body contains 40 kg of water for every 50 kg of body weight. At this rate, what is the number of kilograms of water in a child who weighs 30 kg?

A. 22
B. 23
C. 24
D. 25

114.

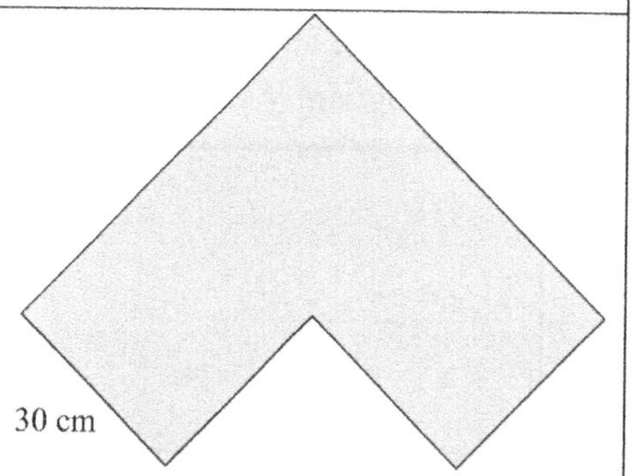

30 cm

A ceramics company wants to produce tiles in the shape shown above consisting of three identical squares. What is the perimeter of each tile?

E. 210 cm
F. 240 cm
G. 270 cm
H. 300 cm

PRACTICE TEST 4

GRID-IN QUESTIONS

Questions 58 – 62

58. In the figure above, GRAP is a parallelogram. What is the value of x?

59. Melanie feeds her cat two types of cat food: fish-flavored and liver-flavored in the ratio 9 : 13. This month, Melanie's cat eats 66 bags of cat food. How many more liver-favored than fish-favored bags does Melanie's cat eat this month?

60. For what value of t is $7 - 4t = t - 23$?

61. A survey was taken of 300 university students. It was reported that 176 were taking math, 135 were taking chemistry, and 36 were taking math and chemistry. How many students took only math and only chemistry?

62. The product of two negative consecutive integers is 168. If the smaller integer is divided by 7 and the larger integer is increased by 4, what is the product of the two resulting integers?

MULTIPLE CHOICE QUESTIONS		
Questions 63 – 68		
63.	The set of possible values of t is $\{-6, -2, 8\}$. The set of all possible values of s is $\{-1, 1, 6\}$. Which of the following options shows the relationship between t and s? A. $s = 2t + 4$ B. $2t = s + 4$ C. $t = 2s + 4$ D. $2s = t + 4$	66.	On the farm, the number of ducks is 3 times the number of cows. In total, all ducks and all cows have 300 legs. Now many ducks are on the farm? E. 30 F. 60 G. 90 H. 120
64.	$-6 - (1 - 3(2 - x)) =$ E. $-1 - 3x$ F. $-1 + 3x$ G. $-12 - 3x$ H. $-12 + 3x$	67.	Cristiano wants to build a model of a 2.4-meter tall football gates. He will be using a scale of 1.2 centimeters = 0.6 meters. How tall will the model be? A. 4.8 cm B. 1.2 cm C. 0.48 cm D. 12 cm
65.	The mean weight of five men is 82 kg. The heaviest man weighs 94 kg and the lightest weighs 70 kg. What is the mean weight of three remaining men? A. 81 kg B. 82 kg C. 83 kg D. 84 kg	68.	The ratio of Benny's money and Danny's money was 6 : 5. After Benny spent \$30 and Danny spent \$20, the amounts of money they had left are the same. How much money did Danny have at first? E. \$60 F. \$55 G. \$50 H. \$45

Questions 69 – 74

69. FAVORITE SPORT

Sport	Percent or fraction
Football	$\frac{1}{4}$
Basketball	35%
Baseball	30%
Tennis	$\frac{1}{10}$

The teacher conducted a survey among 120 students about what kind of sports they would like to do. How many more students prefer baseball to tennis?

A. 20
B. 24
C. 25
D. 30

70.
4 dollars = 30 coli
5 loci = 2 dollars

Petra has 12 dollars and 150 coli. If she exchanges the coli into dollars and dollars into loci, how many loci will she receive?

E. 40
F. 50
G. 60
H. 80

71. A box of 80 colored marbles contains twice as many blue marbles as yellow marbles and 26 white marbles. What is the probability of choosing blue marble from the box?

A. 0.45
B. 0.35
C. 0.325
D. 0.225

72. In the right triangular prism CATDOG, each triangular face is in the shape of equilateral triangle. The lateral area of the prism (excluding the bases) is $312\ cm^2$. If the length of CD is 13 cm, what is the side length of each triangular face?

E. 7 cm
F. 8 cm
G. 11 cm
H. 12 cm

73. If a house is sold for $119,000 there is a loss of 15% on the cost price. For how much should it be sold to make a gain of 15% on the cost price?

A. $153,000
B. $156,000
C. $161,000
D. $168,000

74. The sum of the numbers $2x + 5$ and $y - 4$ is 61. The ratio of x to y is 4 : 7. What is the value of $y - x$?

E. 12
F. 16
G. 24
H. 28

Questions 75 – 80

75. Which number line below shows the solution to the inequality
$2 \leq \frac{1}{2}x + 1 < 4$?

A.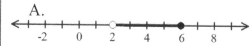

B.

C.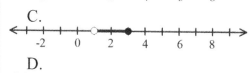

D.

76. Margaret buys 4 boxes of popcorn and 8 colas at the movies for herself and her three friends. Each box of popcorn costs $1.75. If Margaret pays $16.20 in total, how much does one cola cost?

E. $1.05
F. $1.10
G. $1.15
H. $1.20

77. In a set of 40 tennis balls, there are twice as many red balls as orange balls and 5 times more white balls than orange balls. What is the probability that randomly selected tennis ball from the set is not red?

A. 0.125
B. 0.375
C. 0.625
D. 0.825

78.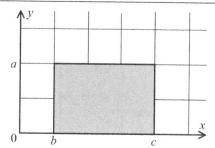

What is the area of the shaded region in the graph above?

E. $ab + ac\ un^2$.
F. $bc - ac\ un^2$.
G. $ac - bc\ un^2$.
H. $ac - ab\ un^2$.

79. 5 jars contain as much as 6 bottles. 2 bottles contain as much as 3 cups. How many cups are in 4 jars?

A. 2.5
B. 5.6
C. 7.2
D. 10

80. The range of three numbers is 12. The mean of these numbers is 14. What is the greatest of these numbers if the median is 12?

E. 9
F. 12
G. 18
H. 21

Questions 81 – 86

81. The pie chart above represents data collected in a survey of the favorite sports of a sample of 600 people. How many more people prefer football than baseball?

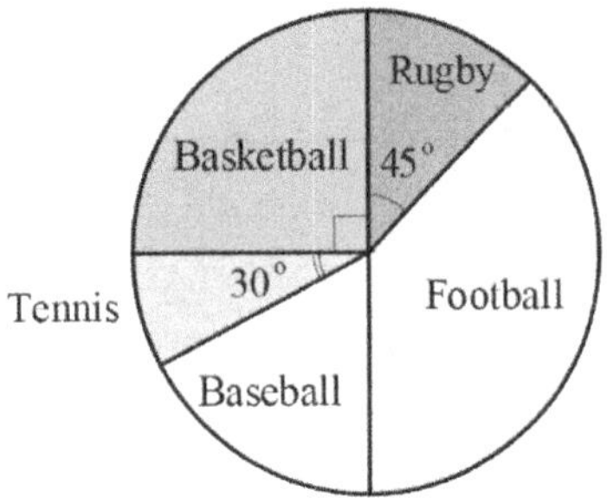

A. 124
B. 125
C. 126
D. 127

82. Jan is arranging his toy soldiers in a rectangle. If he has 28 soldiers, in how many different numbers of rectangles can he display them if each row has the same number of soldiers greater than one but less than 28?

E. 4
F. 5
G. 6
H. 7

83. Math book has 240 pages. The chapter "Rates and Proportions" runs from page 127 to page 151. What is the ratio of the number of pages of this chapter to the total number of pages in the book?

A. 13 : 120
B. 1 : 10
C. 5 : 48
D. 8 : 63

84. The ratio of the sides of a certain triangle is 5 : 7 : 9. If the perimeter of the triangle is 105 cm, how much longer is the longest side than the shortest side?

E. 45 cm
F. 35 cm
G. 25 cm
H. 20 cm

85. $\dfrac{5}{8} \div \left(2\dfrac{1}{3} - 1\dfrac{5}{6}\right) =$

A. 0.75
B. 0.5
C. 1
D. 1.25

86. A plane flies with a constant speed of 270 m/s. Which of the following is the plane's speed in kilometers per hour?

E. 75 km/h
F. 150 km/h
G. 972 km/h
H. 844 km/h

	Questions 87 – 92		
87.	In 2010, Anna was 4 times as old as her daughter was. In 2018, Anna was 2.8 times as old as her daughter was. What will be Anna's age in 2025? A. 48 years B. 54 years C. 56 years D. 63 years	90.	You and a group of friends are at amusement park planning your route around the park. You are all interested in 7 rides and 5 games. How many different routes consisting of two rides or two games could you take? E. $C_2^{12} \cdot C_2^{10}$ F. C_4^{12} G. $C_2^7 + C_2^5$ H. $C_2^7 \cdot C_2^5$
88.	In the list of numbers below, how many of them have prime factors greater than 10? 32, 33, 34, 35, 36, 37, 38, 39, 40, 41, 42 E. 4 F. 5 G. 6 H. 7	91.	A local theater has parterre and balcony seating. The theater contains 800 seats with 550 seats in the balcony. The parterre ticket is worth $17.50. If at the premiere the whole hall was full and the theater raised $10,975, what was the cost of the balcony seating ticket? A. $10.50 B. $11 C. $11.50 D. $12
89.	The sum of 3 consecutive natural numbers is a, and the greatest is b. Which of the following statements is true? A. $b = a - 3$ B. $3b = a - 3$ C. The middle number is $b + 1$ D. The smallest number is $b - 2$	92.	Matt wants to use a cookie recipe that makes 20 cookies but he wants to increase the number of cookies to 36. If the recipe specifies using $1\frac{1}{4}$ cups of sugar, how much sugar should he use? E. 2 F. $2\frac{1}{4}$ G. $2\frac{1}{2}$ H. $2\frac{3}{4}$

Questions 93 – 98

93. On the number line below, position of point A is −2.4. The distance BC is three times greater than the distance AB. If AC = 5.6, what is the position of point B?

```
  C           A    B
<─●───────────●────●──>
```

A. −0.4
B. −0.2
C. 0.2
D. 0.4

94. In the set of consecutive integers from 8 to 44, inclusive, how many integers are multiples of 2, but not multiples of 6?

E. 11
F. 12
G. 13
H. 14

95. An 6-ounce can of corn costs $1.50. At this rate, how much will cost a 16-ounce can of corn?

A. $4
B. $3.75
C. $3.50
D. $3.25

96. Suppose $A = \frac{a}{b}$, $B = \frac{b}{a}$, and a, b do not equal to 0. What is $(A + 1) \times B$ in terms of a and b?

E. $\frac{a+1}{a}$

F. $\frac{a+b}{a}$

G. $\frac{a+1}{b}$

H. $\frac{a+b}{b}$

97. There are 15 students on your school's student committee and there are 2 available executive positions: head and secretary. How many different ways can 2 students be elected from the student committee?

A. 105

B. 29

C. 210

D. 30

98. Cornet is pasting square pieces of colored paper of equal size onto a board 60 cm by 42 cm. If only whole square pieces are used, and the board is to be completely covered, what is the smallest possible number of square pieces Corned should use?

E. 40
F. 50
G. 70
H. 90

Questions 99 – 104

99. NUMBER OF BOOKS SOLD

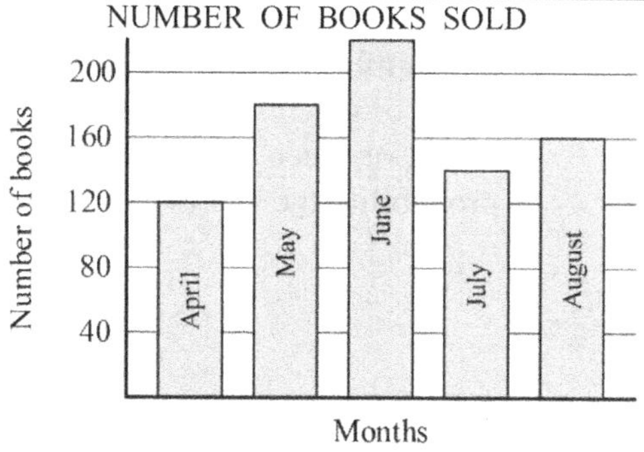

The graph above shows the number (in hundreds) of books sold during five months. Base on the bar diagram, which statement is true?

A. In July, 140 books were sold
B. In June, 2,200 books were sold
C. 400 more books were sold in July than in August
D. 6,000 fewer books were sold in April than in May

100. If $12 : 5 = 9 : (x + 3)$, what is the value of x?

E. $\frac{1}{4}$
F. $\frac{3}{4}$
G. $1\frac{1}{4}$
H. $1\frac{1}{2}$

101. Which of the following numbers is not a repeating decimal?

A. $4.\overline{102}$
B. $\frac{40}{7}$
C. $3.2\overline{41}$
D. $\frac{7}{40}$

102. SCORES IN MATH TESTS

	Test 1	Test 2	Test 3	Test 4
Joe	87	84	91	88
Ron	92	86	85	77

The table above shows the scores Joe and Ron received on 4 tests. Which of the following statements is true?

E. Ron's mean score is greater than Joe's mean score
F. Joe's range in scores is greater than Ron's range in scores
G. Ron's mean score on tests 1 and 4 is less than Joe's mean score on these tests
H. Joe's maximum score is greater than Ron's maximum score

103. The marks on the number line below are evenly spaced. At which point is 0 located?

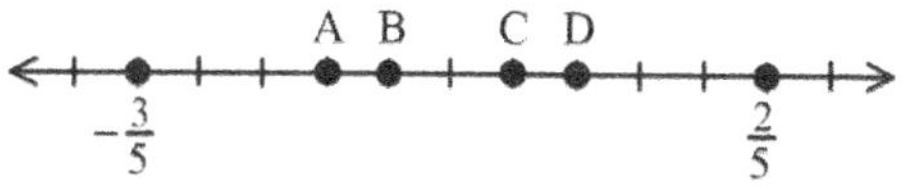

A. A
B. B
C. C
D. D

104. $200(0.75 - 1) + 100(1 - 0.5)^2 =$

E. 0
F. 25
G. -25
H. -50

329

Questions 105 – 110

105. A container is half filled with water. If 4 L of water is added to the container, the container becomes 70% filled with water. How many more liters of water should be added to the container to fill it completely?

   A. 4.5 L
   B. 5 L
   C. 5.5 L
   D. 6 L

106. If $11n$ is a positive even number, which of the following statements is always true?

   E. $11n - 1$ is divisible by 3
   F. $11n + 7$ is an even number
   G. $11n - 5$ is an odd number
   H. $11n + 3$ is divisible by 6

107. A trail in the shape of a circle has a diameter of 3.5 miles. Terry biked around the trail twice. How far did Terry bike? (Use approximation $\pi \approx \frac{22}{7}$)

   A. 5.5 miles
   B. 11 miles
   C. 16.5 miles
   D. 22 miles

108. Carry's football team must decide on a new uniform. The team has a choice of white or green shorts and a black, white, or green shirt. What is the probability the shorts will be white?

   E. $\frac{1}{3}$
   F. $\frac{1}{2}$
   G. $\frac{2}{3}$
   H. $\frac{5}{6}$

109. Henry and his sister collected 200 stamps in total. If Henry collected 14 fewer stamps than twice his sister's number of stamps, which of the following equations could be used to find x, the number of sister's stamps?

   A. $200 = x + 2(x + 14)$
   B. $200 = x + 2(x - 14)$
   C. $200 = x + 14 + 2x$
   D. $200 = x + 2x - 14$

110. The football field measures 360 feet by 270 feet. What is the perimeter of the field in meters? (Use the approximation 1 foot = 0.3 meter)

   E. 378 m
   F. 376 m
   G. 189 m
   H. 188 m

Questions 111 – 114

111. Points T, U, V, and W are located at −5, −1, 3, and 7, respectively, on a number line. What is the distance between midpoints of segments TU and VW?

A. 5
B. 6
C. 7
D. 8

112. If $22 = 7 - 3k + 5m$, what is m in terms of k?

E. $m = 3 + 0.6k$

F. $m = 75 + 15k$

G. $m = 3 - 0.6k$

H. $m = 75 - 15k$

113. The decimal 0.08 can be represented as fraction $\frac{x}{75}$. What is the value of x?

A. 6
B. 3
C. 12
D. 4

114.

10 cm

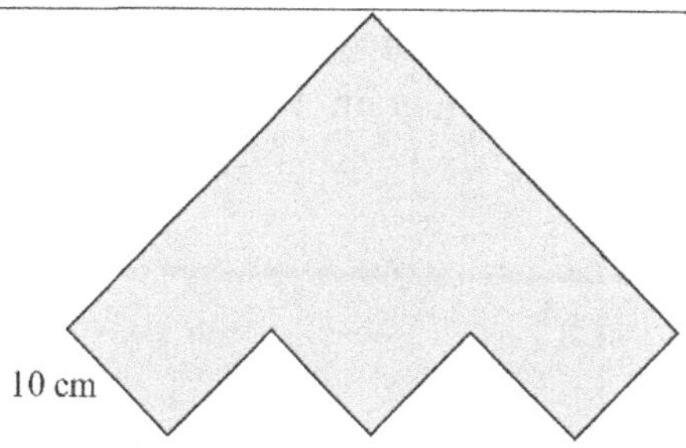

A ceramics company wants to produce tiles in the shape shown above consisting of six identical squares. What is the perimeter of each tile?

E. 60 cm
F. 80 cm
G. 100 cm
H. 120 cm

PRACTICE TEST 5

GRID-IN QUESTIONS

Questions 58 – 62

58.

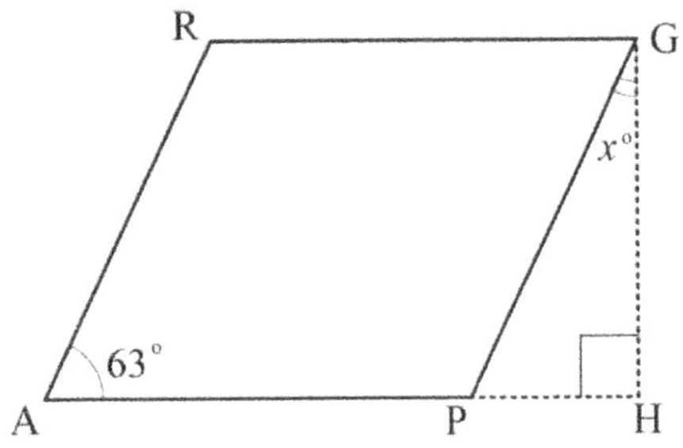

In the figure above, GRAP is a parallelogram. What is the value of x?

59. There are 2 roads going through a village. The ratio of the width of the first road to the width of the second road is 8 : 5. If the first road is 120 cm wider than the second road, how wide is the second road, in centimeters?

60. For what value of y is $5y - 13 = 3y - 7$?

61. At a buffet, 56 people chose coffee and 35 people chose juice. 17 people chose both coffee and juice. If 12 people chose neither coffee nor juice, how many people visited the buffet?

62. The sum of two negative consecutive integers is -145. If the greater integer is divided by 9 and the smaller integer is increased by 50, what is the product of the two resulting integers?

332

MULTIPLE CHOICE QUESTIONS

Questions 63 – 68

63. The set of possible values of a is $\{-4, -1, 5\}$. The set of all possible values of b is $\{-5, 1, 13\}$. Which of the following options shows the relationship between a and b?

A. $b = 3 - 2a$
B. $2b = 3 - a$
C. $b = 3 + 2a$
D. $2b = 3 + a$

64. $12 - (2(x+1) - 1) =$

E. $9 - 2x$
F. $11 + 2x$
G. $9 + 2x$
H. $11 - 2x$

65. A student scored 74, 65, 76, 82, 78 on the first five math tests he took. After he took his 6th math test, the mean is now 77. What was his score on the 6th test?

A. 88
B. 87
C. 86
D. 85

66. Mila earns money each week by tutoring and by babysitting. She charges twice as much per hour of tutoring as per hour of babysitting. This week, she works 8 hours. If she charges $13 per hour of tutoring and earns $84.50 this week, how many hours does she tutor?

E. 3
F. 4
G. 5
H. 6

67. Naomi wants to draw a model of a 7.2-meter long playground. She will be using a scale of 3 centimeters = 1.5 meters. How long will Naomi's model be?

A. 3.6 cm
B. 9.6 cm
C. 12.8 cm
D. 14.4 cm

68. The ratio of George's money and Tia's money was 9 : 4. After George spent $24 and Tia collected $11, the amounts of money they had are the same. How much money did Tia have at first?

E. $7
F. $28
G. $36
H. $64

Questions 69 – 74

69. FAVORITE SPORT

Sport	Percent or fraction
Football	28%
Basketball	$\frac{1}{3}$
Baseball	x%
Tennis	$\frac{1}{6}$

The teacher conducted a survey among students about what kind of sports they would like to do. What is the value of x?

A. 20
B. 21
C. 22
D. 23

70.
3 dollars = 16 bots
7 dots = 2 dollars

Sergio has 80 bots and 140 dots. If he exchanges the bots and dots to dollars, how many dollars will he receive?

E. $25
F. $40
G. $55
H. $60

71. A box of 60 colored marbles contains three times as many blue marbles as yellow marbles and 12 white marbles. What is the probability of choosing not blue marble from the box?

A. $\frac{7}{15}$
B. $\frac{1}{5}$
C. $\frac{8}{15}$
D. $\frac{2}{5}$

72. In the right triangular prism CATDOG, each triangular face is in the shape of equilateral triangle. The perimeter of each triangular face is 33 cm and the length of AO is 15 cm. What is the lateral area of the prism?

E. 165 cm^2
F. 345 cm^2
G. 495 cm^2
H. 515 cm^2

73. Initially, a store had 2,000 books for selling. 60% of them were detectives and the rest were thrillers. In a week, 20% of the detectives and 10% of thrillers were sold. What was the new percentage of remaining detectives?

A. Nearly 40%
B. Nearly 48%
C. Nearly 51%
D. Nearly 57%

74. The sum of the first and third of five consecutive odd integers is 78. What is the sum of remaining three integers?

E. 127
F. 117
G. 107
H. 97

Questions 75 – 80

75. Which number line below shows the solution to the inequality
$$-4 < 8 - 2x \leq 4?$$

A.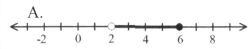

B.

C.

D.

78.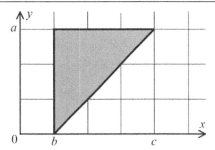

What is the area of the shaded region in the graph above?

E. $\frac{1}{2}(ac - bc)\ un^2$.

F. $\frac{1}{2}(bc - ac)\ un^2$.

G. $\frac{1}{2}(ac - ab)\ un^2$.

H. $\frac{1}{2}(ab - ac)\ un^2$.

76.
PRICE LIST

Lamp	Skate	Cap	Belt	Bag
$18.20	$35.50	$9.99	$6.75	$16.40

To buy a bag, a lamp, and a cap, Boris has to borrow $16 more dollars. How much money does Boris have?

E. $63.69
F. $60.59
G. $28.59
H. $44.59

79. 6 agents can sell 333 cars in 3 months. At this rate, how many cars can 3 agents sell in 6 months?

A. 222
B. 333
C. 666
D. 999

77. In a set of 100 tennis balls, there are 15 more red balls than orange balls and 17 white balls. What is the probability that randomly selected tennis ball from the set is not red?

A. 0.49
B. 0.51
C. 0.34
D. 0.17

80. Jordan read a total of 630 pages in a week. He read 320 pages during the weekend. What was the average number of pages he read during the weekdays?

E. 90
F. 74
G. 62
H. 126

Questions 81 – 86

81. **FAVORITE SPORT**

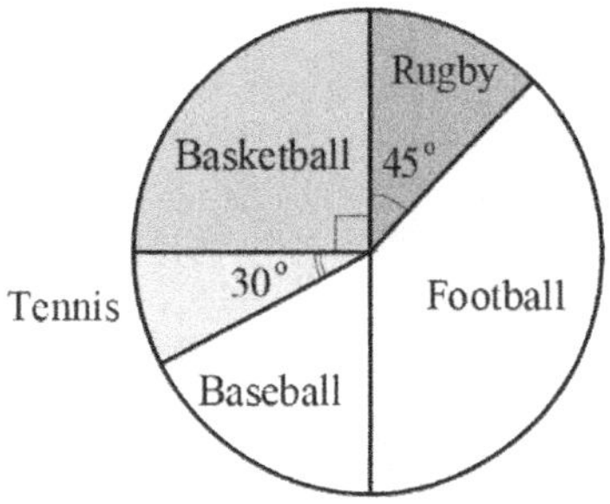

The pie chart above represents data collected in a survey of the favorite sports of a sample of 480 people. How many more people prefer baseball than rugby?

A. 20
B. 40
C. 60
D. 80

82. A new moon occurs every 30 days. If the last new moon occurred on a Tuesday, how many days will pass before a new moon occurs again on a Tuesday?

E. 30
F. 140
G. 210
H. 280

83. Math book has 350 pages. The chapter "Percent" runs from page 243 to page 291. What is the ratio of the number of pages of this chapter to the total number of pages in the book?

A. 25 : 181
B. 24 : 175
C. 12 : 85
D. 7 : 50

84. The ratio of the number of marbles in Jar A to Jar B to Jar C is 2 : 5 : 4. There are 12 more marbles in Jar C than there are in Jar A. How many marbles should be replaced from Jar B to Jar A so that jars A and B have the same number of marbles?

E. 9 marbles
F. 8 marbles
G. 7 marbles
H. 6 marbles

85. $\left(1\dfrac{1}{8} - \dfrac{7}{16}\right) \div \dfrac{11}{32} =$

A. $\dfrac{1}{2}$
B. 2
C. $\dfrac{2}{11}$
D. $5\dfrac{1}{2}$

86. Audrey is planning to visit Library, which is 960 meters away from the school. If Audrey walks 6 kilometers per hour, how long, in minutes, will it take her to get to Library?

E. 4
F. 5
G. 5.6
H. 9.6

	Questions 87 – 92			
87.	In 2010, Dora was 3 times as old as her son was. In 2019, Dora was 2.25 times as old as her son was. What will be Dora's age in 2030? A. 45 years B. 54 years C. 56 years D. 65 years	90.	You and a group of friends are at amusement park planning your route around the park. You are all interested in 9 rides and 7 games. How many different routes consisting of three rides and two games could you take? E. $C_3^9 \cdot C_2^7$ F. $C_3^7 + C_2^9$ G. $C_2^7 + C_3^9$ H. $C_3^7 \cdot C_2^9$
88.	In the list of numbers below, how many of them are multiples of 12? 36, 40, 44, 48, 52, 56, 60, 64, 68, 72 E. 4 F. 5 G. 6 H. 7	91.	Josh is raising money for a charity. Someone made a fixed donation of $250. Then, Josh asks each participant to make a contribution of $15. If Josh raises $580 in total, how many participants make their contribution? A. 18 B. 20 C. 22 D. 24
89.	The sum of 4 consecutive even natural numbers is a, and the smallest is b. Which of the following statements is true? A. $a = 4b + 6$ B. $a = 4b + 8$ C. $a = 4b + 12$ D. $a = 4b + 16$	92.	A restaurant offers a daily menu consisting of a first dish, main dish and dessert. On Saturday, the ratio of sold first dishes to second dishes was 2 : 3 and the ratio of second dishes to desserts was 4 : 5. What was the ratio of the first dishes to desserts? E. 1 : 4 F. 2 : 5 G. 4 : 9 H. 8 : 15

	Questions 93 – 98		

93.	On the number line below, position of point C is -5.6. The distance BC is three times greater than the distance AB. If $AC = 8.4$, what is the position of point B?
	
	    C A B
	←——●——————●——●——→
	
	    A. 7
	    B. 6.4
	    C. 6
	    D. 5.6
		96.	Suppose $A = \frac{a}{b}$, where a, b do not equal to 0. What is $A + \frac{1}{A}$ in terms of a and b?
			
			    E. $\frac{a^2+b^2}{ab}$
			
			    F. $\frac{ab}{a^2+b^2}$
			
			    G. $\frac{a+b}{ab}$
			
			    H. $\frac{ab}{a+b}$

94.	How many 2-digit numbers are multiples of 5 but not multiples of 10?
	
	    E. 8
	    F. 9
	    G. 10
	    H. 11
		97.	There are 12 students on your school's student committee and there are 3 available executive positions: chairman, vice-chairman and secretary. How many different ways can 3 students be elected from the student committee?
			
			    A. 1,728
			
			    B. 1,452
			
			    C. 1,440
			
			    D. 1,320

95.	A supermarket had 450 kiwi bags in stock. It sold out 90 kiwi bags in 2 days. At the same rate, how many more days is needed to sell all remaining kiwi bags?
	
	    A. 4
	    B. 6
	    C. 8
	    D. 10
		98.	Max is pasting square pieces of colored paper of equal size onto a board 66 cm by 48 cm. If only whole square pieces are used, and the board is to be completely covered, what is the greatest possible side length of square pieces Max should use?
			
			    E. 2
			    F. 3
			    G. 6
			    H. 12

Questions 99 – 104

99. NUMBER OF BOOKS SOLD

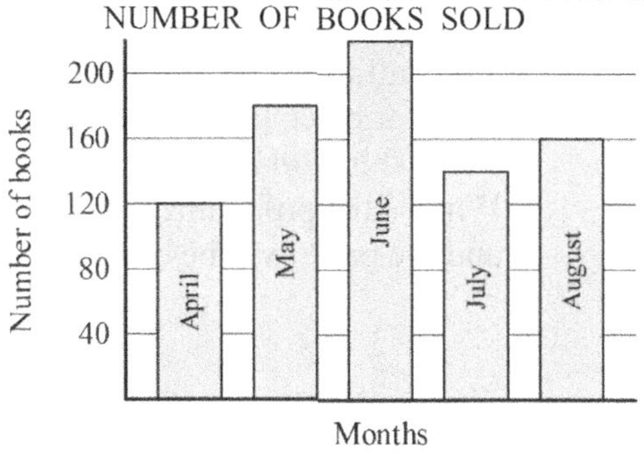

The graph above shows the number (in hundreds) of books sold during five months. Base on the bar diagram, which statement is not true?

A. In May, 18,000 books were sold
B. In July, 14,000 books were sold
C. In April, 400 fewer books were sold than in August
D. In June, 4,000 more books were sold than in May

100. If $18 : 7 = 6 : (2 - x)$, what is the value of x?

E. $\frac{1}{3}$
F. $-\frac{1}{3}$
G. $\frac{2}{3}$
H. $-\frac{2}{3}$

101. Which of the following numbers is a repeating decimal?

A. $\frac{4}{25}$
B. $\frac{7}{125}$
C. $\frac{8}{15}$
D. $\frac{9}{150}$

102. SCORES IN MATH TESTS

	Test 1	Test 2	Test 3	Test 4
Steve	68	64	59	73
Luis	72	76	80	78

The table above shows the scores Steve and Luis received on 4 tests. Which of the following statements is true?

E. Steve's mean score is 10 points less than Luis's mean score
F. Steve's range in scores is 6 points greater than Luis's range in scores
G. Steve's maximum score is 8 points less than Luis's maximum score
H. Steve's minimum score is 12 points less than Luis's minimum score

103. The marks on the number line below are evenly spaced. At which point is 0 located?

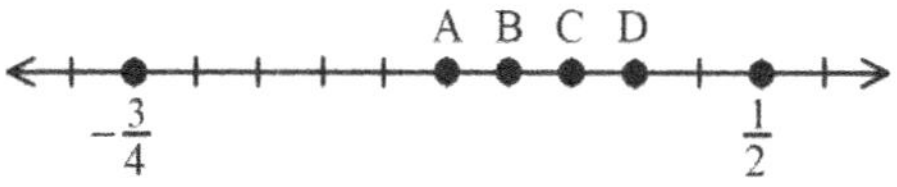

A. A
B. B
C. C
D. D

104. $400\left(2 - 1\frac{3}{4}\right)^2 - 200\left(2 - 2\frac{1}{4}\right)^2 =$

E. 12.5
F. 25
G. 37.5
H. 50

Questions 105 – 110

105. A container is one-fourth filled with water. If 7 L of water is added to the container, the container becomes 60% filled with water. What is the capacity of the container?

   A. 5 L
   B. 12 L
   C. 15 L
   D. 20 L

106. If $9n$ is a positive even number, which of the following statements is always true?

   E. $9n - 2$ is an odd number
   F. $9n + 4$ is an even number
   G. $9n - 5$ is an even number
   H. $9n + 3$ is divisible by 6

107. A trail in the shape of a circle has a diameter of 3.5 miles. Ronny biked around the trail a total of 44 miles. How many trails did Ronny bike? (Use approximation $\pi \approx \frac{22}{7}$)

   A. 2
   B. 3
   C. 4
   D. 5

108. Daniel's soccer team must decide on a new uniform. The team has a choice of white or black pants, red, white, or silver shirt and black or white helmets. What is the probability the helmets and the pants will be black?

   E. $\frac{1}{3}$
   F. $\frac{1}{4}$
   G. $\frac{1}{6}$
   H. $\frac{2}{3}$

109. Bill and his brother collected 300 baseball cards in total. If Bill collected 10 more stamps than 4 times his brother's number of cards, which of the following equations could be used to find x, the number of brother's cards?

   A. $300 = x + 4x + 10$
   B. $300 = x + 4x - 10$
   C. $300 = x + 4(x + 10)$
   D. $300 = x + 4(x - 10)$

110. The playground measures 62 feet by 43 feet. What is the perimeter of the playground in meters? (Use the approximation 1 foot = 0.3 meter)

   E. 29 m
   F. 31.5 m
   G. 45.5 m
   H. 63 m

	Questions 111 – 114			
111.	Points U, V, and W are located at −6, −2, and 12, respectively, on a number line. What is the distance between midpoints of segments UV and VW? A. 6 B. 7 C. 8 D. 9	113.	The decimal 0.15 can be represented as fraction $\frac{x}{60}$. What is the value of x? A. 9 B. 6 C. 5 D. 3	
112.	If $2(1 - x) + 3y = 12 - x$, what is x in terms of y? E. $x = 10 - 3y$ F. $x = \frac{10}{3} - y$ G. $x = y = \frac{10}{3}$ H. $x = 3y - 10$	114.	A shape consists of 9 small squares, and each square has an area of $9\ cm^2$. What is the perimeter of the shape? E. 16 cm F. 32 cm G. 48 cm H. 432 cm	

PRACTICE TEST 6

GRID-IN QUESTIONS

Questions 58 – 62

58.
Mr. Douglas opened an account with a deposit of $5,400. This account earns 6% simple interest annually. How many years will it take him to earn $1,620 on his $5,400 deposit?

59.
$$25 - 15 \div |3 - 6| - (-3)^3 \times \frac{5}{3}$$

What is the value of the expression above?

60.
Solve for x:

$$4(1 - 2x) + 5(3x + 2) = 28$$

61.

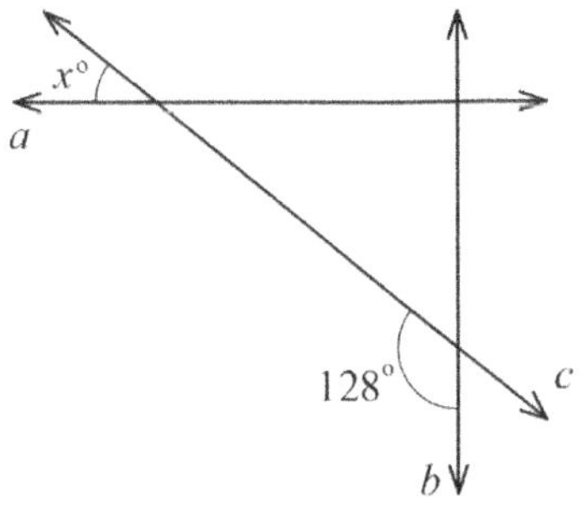

In the figure above, line a is perpendicular to the line b. What is the value of x?

62.
The mean value of seven number is 35. Three of these numbers with the mean of 31 were discarded. What is the mean of the remaining four numbers?

Questions 63 – 66

63.
$$3^3 + 5^3 =$$

A. 512

B. 34

C. 152

D. 706

64.
Last week, $1\frac{1}{4}$ inches of snow fell on Sunday, $1\frac{1}{3}$ inches fell on Monday, and $2\frac{1}{8}$ inches fell on Tuesday. How many inches of snow fell during thise three days?

E. $4\frac{1}{24}$ inches

F. $4\frac{7}{12}$ inches

G. $4\frac{5}{12}$ inches

H. $4\frac{17}{24}$ inches

65.
An alarm bell will ring when the electrical voltage will increase to 140% of the maximum allowable level. If the maximum allowable voltage is 220 V, at what voltage will the alarm bell ring?

A. 308 V

B. 132 V

C. 528 V

D. 416 V

66.
A gear of a large mechanism makes one complete revolution every 75 minutes. If the gear ends moving at 10 : 45, at what time will the gear start to complete 5 revolutions?

E. 04 : 45

F. 04 : 30

G. 04 : 15

H. 04 : 00

Questions 67 – 70

67.

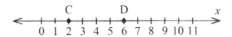

Points A and B are not shown on the number line above. If D is the midpoint of AB and A is the midpoint of CD, where on the number line would point B be located?

A. 4

B. 6

C. 8

D. 10

68.

$$\frac{24}{16} = \frac{5}{n}$$

What value of n makes the equation above true?

E. $7\frac{1}{2}$

F. $1\frac{1}{5}$

G. $5\frac{1}{6}$

H. $3\frac{1}{3}$

69. If m is an integer and $5m + 5$ is an even number, which expression must also represent an even number?

A. $5m$

B. $3m + 1$

C. $4m + 3$

D. $2m - 1$

70. The product of two positive integers is 91. Which number could be the difference of the two integers?

E. 6

F. 7

G. 8

H. 9

Questions 71 – 74

71.
If *n* is an even integer that is greater than −14.15, what is the smallest possible value of *n*?

A. −14

B. −16

C. −10

D. −12

72.
Noah's literature assignment is to read 390 pages. He planned to do the assignment in 5 hours. He read the first 180 pages in 2 hours. What is the mean number of pages he must read per hour during the next 3 hours in order to complete the assignment according to the plan?

E. 65

F. 70

G. 75

H. 78

73.
Between which two consecutive integers is the fraction $\frac{33}{9}$?

A. 2 and 3

B. 3 and 4

C. 4 and 5

D. 5 and 6

74.
Emily is 4 feet 11 inches tall, and Megan is 5 feet 3 inches tall. What is the difference in height between Megan and Emily?

E. 1 feet 8 inches

F. 4 inches

G. 8 inches

H. 1 feet 4 inches

Questions 75 – 78

75.

PAINT SOLD

Paint	Number of cans	Percentage of total
Green	15	18.75%
Blue	17	21.25%
Yellow	13	16.25%
Red	11	13.75%
White	24	29.50%
Total	**80**	**99.50%**

One number in the percentage column is incorrect. Which change needs to be made?

A. Change "Green" to 18.25%

B. Change "Blue" to 21.75%

C. Change "Yellow" to 16.75%

D. Change "White" to 30%

76.
$$x \div 32 = 21 \div 24$$

For what value of x is the proportion shown above true?

E. 16

F. 24

G. 28

H. 36

77.
$$\frac{6^2 + (-9)^2 + 4^2}{(6 - 9 + 4)^2} =$$

A. 133

B. −29

C. −133

D. 29

78.
Tia contributed $480 toward the purchase of a $1,600 computer. Her sister contributed $620 toward the same computer. Their parents provided the rest of the money for the computer. What percentage of the total cost of the computer did Tia's parents pay?

E. 29.25%

F. 31.25%

G. 33.75%

H. 37.5%

Questions 79 – 82

79. The numbers $a, b, c,$ and d are different, and each is equal to 2, 4, 8, 12, or 16. If $4a = c$, $2c = b$ and $d = \frac{3}{4}b$, what is the value of d?

A. 4

B. 8

C. 12

D. 16

80. $\{0.2, 0.02, 0.002, 0.0002, 0.00002\}$

If person chooses a number from the set above, what is the probability that this number is greater than 0.001?

E. $\frac{1}{5}$

F. $\frac{2}{5}$

G. $\frac{3}{5}$

H. $\frac{4}{5}$

81. Bethany answered 12 out of 30 questions on a Science test correctly. What percentage of the questions did she answer incorrectly?

A. 40%

B. 45%

C. 55%

D. 60%

82.

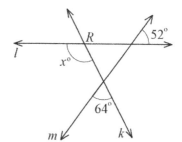

Lines k and l intersect at point R, and m is a straight line. What is the value of x?

E. 64°

F. 116°

G. 52°

H. 122°

Questions 83 – 86

83.
If x is a whole number, which of the following statements must be true?

A. $\frac{1}{x} < \frac{1}{x+1}$

B. $\frac{1}{x} > \frac{1}{x-1} + 1$

C. $\frac{1}{x} < \frac{1}{x-1}$

D. $\frac{1}{x} > \frac{1}{x+1} + 1$

84.
A bag contains black balls, red balls, and white balls. There are 18 white balls in the bag. The probability of randomly choosing a white ball is $\frac{1}{5}$. If the probability of randomly choosing a black ball is thrice the probability of choosing a red ball, how many black balls are in the basket?

E. 18

F. 36

G. 54

H. 72

85.
It took Lucas 1.5 hours to cover 9 kilometers. What was his average speed in miles per hour? (Use approximation 1 mile = 1.6 kilometers)

A. 5.625

B. 9.6

C. 14.4

D. 3.75

86.
Integer y is evenly divisible by 6. Which expression below is also evenly divisible by 6?

E. $2y + 9$

F. $3y - 9$

G. $5y + 12$

H. $4y - 15$

348

Questions 87-90

87. Molly has 5 nickels, 12 dimes and 13 quarters in her wallet. If she removes one coin randomly, what is the probability that it will not be a dime?

A. $\frac{3}{5}$

B. $\frac{2}{5}$

C. $\frac{5}{6}$

D. $\frac{1}{6}$

88.

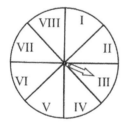

The arrow starts on Space III and moves anticlockwise around the circle. It moves through one space each second. What space will the arrow point to in 1 minute?

E. VII

F. VIII

G. I

H. V

89. Juan is one of the 5 members of a jury. If 2 members of that jury are selected to be the head and its secretary, how many of the possible pairs would include Juan?

A. 4

B. 6

C. 8

D. 10

90. If $t = 6$ and $s = -2$, what is the value of $\dfrac{12 - 3(t - 1)}{5s + 2(t - s)}$?

E. $\frac{1}{2}$

F. 2

G. -2

H. $-\frac{1}{2}$

Questions 91 – 94

91.

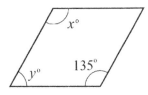

In the parallelogram above, what is the value of $x - y$?

A. 90°

B. 95°

C. 100°

D. 105°

92.

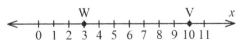

On the number line above, point X (not shown) is located on line segment WV so that $WX = \frac{2}{5} XV$. What is the position of point X?

E. 4

F. 5

G. 7

H. 8

93. Rosie and Anna divided some cards between themselves. Anna got 45% of all cards. If Rosie received 20 more cards than Anna, how many cards did Rosie receive?

A. 90

B. 100

C. 200

D. 120

94.

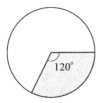

The shaded sector of the circle shown above has an area of $3\pi \; in^2$. What is the diameter of the circle?

E. 4.5 in

F. 6 in

G. 7.5 in

H. 9 in

Questions 95 – 98

95. Which graph represents the solution to the inequality $-2x + 5 < -3$?

A.

B.
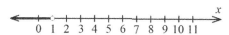

C.
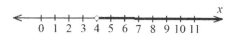

D.

96. A chemist mixed three solutions, I, II, and III, in a glass container. The amount of the solution I is twice the amount of the solution II, and the amount of the solution III is $\frac{3}{4}$ the amount of the solution I. What is the ratio of the amounts of all three solutions I, II and III?

E. $2 : 1 : 3$

F. $1 : 2 : 3$

G. $2 : 4 : 3$

H. $4 : 2 : 3$

97. Jim has a baseball cards, and Bill has b baseball cards. If Bill gives 4 baseball cards to Jim, Jim will have 3 times as many cards as Bill. Which equation shows this relationship?

A. $a + 4 = 3(b - 4)$

B. $a - 4 = 3(b + 4)$

C. $b + 4 = 3(a - 4)$

D. $b - 4 = 3(a + 4)$

98. On Saturday, Sophia read 24% of her entire book. On Sunday, she read another 32% of the book. In lowest terms, what fraction of the book is left for her to read?

E. $\frac{17}{50}$

F. $\frac{11}{25}$

G. $\frac{14}{25}$

H. $\frac{33}{50}$

Questions 99 – 102

99.

$\{11, 12, 13, \ldots, 99, 100\}$

How many numbers of the set shown above are multiples of 2 but not multiples of 6?

A. 15
B. 30
C. 29
D. 45

100.

Kerry runs 12 kilometers in 1 hour 20 minutes. At this rate, how many meters does she run per minute?

E. 140
F. 144
G. 148
H. 150

101.

For what value of x is the equation $\frac{x}{4} - 3 = 2(1 - x) + 6$ true?

A. $\frac{26}{9}$
B. $\frac{35}{9}$
C. $\frac{28}{9}$
D. $\frac{44}{9}$

102.

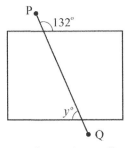

The diagram above shows line segment PQ intersecting a rectangle. What is the measure of angle y?

E. 78°
F. 68°
G. 58°
H. 48°

352

Questions 103 – 106

103.

TEST SCORES

Scores	Number of Students
21 – 40	4
41 – 60	15
61 – 80	24
81 – 100	7

All 200 students in Grade 8 at a school are assigned to pass the Math test. A teacher records the scores in a random sample of the tests. Based on this sample, how many students in the entire grade would be expected to pass the test with score no less than 41 points?

A. 16

B. 32

C. 168

D. 184

104.
Which percentage is closest in value to 0.00319?

E. 32%

F. 3.2%

G. 0.32%

H. 0.032%

105.
Mary passes three Math tests with a mean score of 88 and two Science tests with a mean score of 86. What was the mean score for all five tests?

A. 87

B. 87.2

C. 87.4

D. 87.6

106.
A box in the shape of rectangular prism is 12 cm long, 5 cm wide and 4 cm high. What is the volume of the box?

E. $128\ cm^3$

F. $240\ cm^3$

G. $256\ cm^3$

H. $480\ cm^3$

Questions 107 – 110

107.

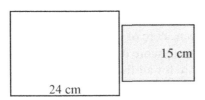

The figure above shows two similar rectangles. If the perimeter of the shaded rectangle is 70 cm, what is the perimeter of the unshaded rectangle?

A. 84 cm

B. 82 cm

C. 80 cm

D. 78 cm

108.
The greatest common factor of 48 and x is 6. Which option shows possible values for x?

E. 18, 30, 42

F. 18, 36, 42

G. 12, 24, 30

H. 30, 42, 60

109.
Donkey and Tiger each had the same jar of honey. They started to eat honey at the same moment. Tiger ate honey 2.5 times faster than Donkey. If Tiger ate his honey in 12 minutes, how many more minutes did Donkey eat his honey?

A. 30 minutes

B. 24 minutes

C. 18 minutes

D. 12 minutes

110.
There are 15 red balls and 25 black balls in the first hat, and 12 blue balls and 18 green balls in the second hat. A student selects one ball from the fist hat and one ball from the second hat. What is the probability that he will chose a red and a blue ball?

E. 0.15

F. 0.12

G. 0.1

H. 0.09

Questions 111 – 114

111.

A family drives 270 miles from city A to city B. They cover the first 120 miles in 2 hours. If they continue to drive at the same rate, how many more hours they will spend on the trip?

A. 2.25 hours

B. 2.5 hours

C. 2.75 hours

D. 3 hours

112.

What is the least of six consecutive integers whose sum is 273?

E. 41

F. 42

G. 43

H. 44

113.

If all possible values of x are indicated by the shaded part on the number line above, which inequality best describes all possible values of $\frac{1}{x}$?

A. $\frac{1}{5} \leq x \leq 1\frac{1}{2}$

B. $\frac{1}{5} \leq x \leq 1\frac{1}{3}$

C. $\frac{1}{5} \leq x \leq 1\frac{2}{3}$

D. $\frac{1}{5} \leq x \leq \frac{2}{3}$

114.

Sonya selects an arbitrary card from 10 cards numbered 1, 2, 3, ..., 10, writes its value, and returns it back. Then she selects another card, writes its value next to the written one. What is the probability that Sonya's 2-digit number consists of the same digits?

E. $\frac{1}{100}$

F. $\frac{1}{10}$

G. $\frac{9}{100}$

H. $\frac{3}{10}$

PRACTICE TEST 7

GRID-IN QUESTIONS

Questions 58 – 62

58.	Simplify: $-2.5 + 1.24 - (-2.36)$	61.	An ornamental bush grows $1\frac{1}{6}$ inches every 5 days. A gardener cuts off the top $\frac{2}{3}$ inch of the bush every 5 days. If the bush was 15 inches tall at the beginning, how many inches tall is the bush after 60 days?
59.	Angles A and B are supplementary. The measure of angle A is 4 times the measure of angle B. What is the measure of angle A?	62.	SURVEY OF 150 EMPLOYEES 	Number of family members	Number of employees	 |---|---| | 1	9	 | 2	15	 | 3	38	 | 4	57	 | 5	25	 | 6	6	 The table above shows the number of family members in each of 150 employees' families. What is the median number of members in these families?
60.	A juice mixture contains $\frac{3}{8}$ gallon of apple juice and $\frac{1}{12}$ gallon of grape juice. How many gallons of apple juice per gallon of grape juice does the mixture contain? (Express your answer as a decimal)		

MULTIPLE CHOICE QUESTIONS

Questions 63 – 68

63. This year, ranger Johnson caught 336 criminals, which is 5% more than ranger Reeks caught. How many more criminals did ranger Johnson catch?

    A. 16
    B. 32
    C. 304
    D. 320

64. If $\dfrac{3a}{b} - \dfrac{a}{3b} = \dfrac{\Box a}{3b}$ and $b \neq 0$, what number is represented by $\Box$?

    E. 2
    F. 4
    G. 6
    H. 8

65.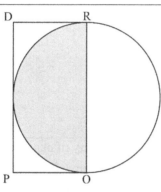

    In figure above, DROP is a rectangle. Points O and R are on the circle. If the area of the rectangle is $72\ cm^2$, what is the area of the shaded semicircle?

    A. $6\pi\ cm^2$
    B. $12\pi\ cm^2$
    C. $18\pi\ cm^2$
    D. $36\pi\ cm^2$

66. A list of consecutive integers begins with x and ends with y. If $x - y = -24$, how many integers are in the list?

    E. 23
    F. 24
    G. 25
    H. 26

67. Simplify:
    $$\dfrac{\dfrac{44(x+5)}{4} - 66}{11}$$

    A. $x - 1$
    B. x
    C. $x + 1$
    D. $x + 2$

68. Two glasses each are half-full. If one-third of the water from the first glass is poured into the second glass, how much water is still needed to completely fill the second glass with water?

    E. $\frac{1}{6}$ glass
    F. $\frac{1}{3}$ glass
    G. $\frac{1}{2}$ glass
    H. $\frac{2}{3}$ glass

Questions 69 – 74

69.
$$1 < 16 - 5n < 7$$
If n is a whole solution to the inequality above, what is the value of $\frac{1}{n}$?

A. 0.2
B. 0.25
C. 0.5
D. 0.75

70. 64% of people pooled like peaches. If 522 people do not like peaches, how many people like peaches?

E. 1,660
F. 1,450
G. 1,044
H. 928

71. A library-reading hall is in the shape of square. The area of the floor is $784\ ft^2$. In a scale drawing of the library, 1 inch $= 14$ feet. What is the area of the floor in the scale drawing?

A. $2\ in^2$
B. $4\ in^2$
C. $14\ in^2$
D. $49\ in^2$

72. A computer program randomly generates a sequence of whole numbers from 1 to 15, inclusive. If the computer generates a sequence of 500 numbers, what is the best prediction of the number of even numbers in the sequence?

E. 210
F. 233
G. 250
H. 267

73. A bicycle rental company charges a one-time fee of $12 plus $0.45 per mile biked. Kira rented a bicycle and used a coupon for 20% off the total rental cost. After the coupon was applied, Kira spent a total of $16.08. How many miles did she bike?

A. 14
B. 16
C. 18
D. 20

74. The probability of choosing a blue ball at random from a bag of 40 balls is $\frac{1}{8}$. After 3 blue balls are replaced with 3 red balls, what is the probability of randomly choosing a blue ball from the bag?

E. 0.02
F. 0.04
G. 0.05
H. 0.08

Questions 75 – 80

75. Each number in a sequence is formed by multiplying the previous number by 3 and then adding 2. If the 8th number in the sequence is 74, what is the 7th number?

   A. 24
   B. 26
   C. 216
   D. 224

76. 1st group of judges: 9.6; 9.4; 8.9; 9.3
    2nd group of judges: 8.8; 9.1; 8.6; 8.3

   Two groups of judges award each gymnast. Each judge can put at most 10 points. Then the gymnast's score is the sum of two groups' means. If judges awarded the gymnast as shown above, what was the gymnast score?

   E. 9
   F. 17.8
   G. 18
   H. 18.4

77. A 1.8-m board was cut into two pieces of different lengths. The longer piece has a length of x m. Which inequality represents all possible values of x?

   A. $0 < x \leq 0.9$
   B. $0 < x < 0.9$
   C. $0.9 \leq x < 1.8$
   D. $0.9 < x < 1.8$

78. What is the area of the shaded region shown in the figure above?

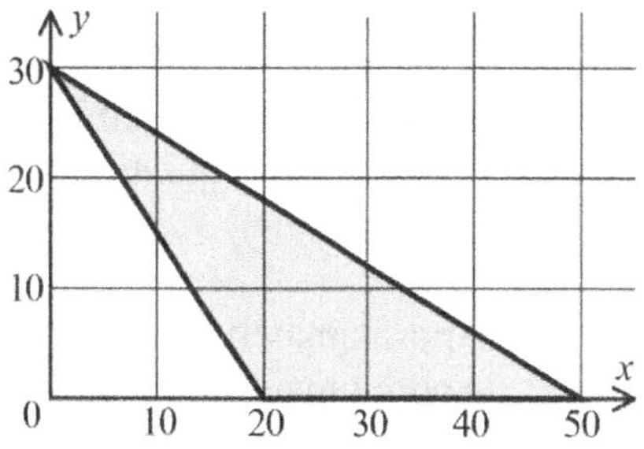

   E. $900 \; un^2$.
   F. $600 \; un^2$.
   G. $450 \; un^2$.
   H. $250 \; un^2$.

79. $$C = \frac{5}{9}(F - 32)$$

   Yesterday in Mathtown, the highest Celsius temperature, C, was 34°, and the lowest temperature was 29°. What was the difference between these temperatures, in degrees Fahrenheit, F?

   A. 15°F
   B. 12°F
   C. 10°F
   D. 9°F

80. Let x be an even number. In terms of x, what is the sum of the two odd numbers closest to x?

   E. $2x + 3$
   F. $2x$
   G. $2x - 1$
   H. $2x - 3$

Questions 81 – 86

81. In 2019, the grain harvest was 900 thousand tons, which was collected from 175 thousand hectares. What is the average grain yield in quintals per hectare? (1 ton = 10 quintals)

    A. Approximately 0.51
    B. Approximately 5.1
    C. Approximately 51
    D. Approximately 510

82.

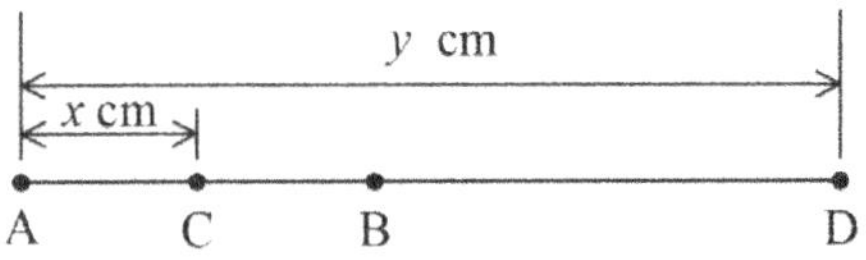

    In the figure above, C is the midpoint of AB. Which segment has length $y - 2x$ cm?

    E. AB
    F. BC
    G. BD
    H. CD

83.

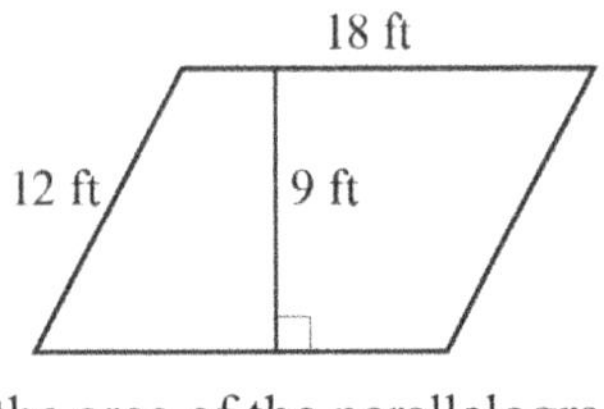

    What is the area of the parallelogram shown above?

    A. 108 ft^2
    B. 162 ft^2
    C. 184 ft^2
    D. 216 ft^2

84. Peter earns money washing cars. On Thursday, he washed 6 more cars than on Friday. On Saturday, he washed 4 fewer cars than on Thursday. If Peter washed 71 cars in total, how many cars did he wash on Saturday?

    E. 21
    F. 23
    G. 25
    H. 27

85. TEST SCORES IN Mr. Pili CLASS

Test Score	Number of Students
50	2
60	4
70	5
80	4
90	3
100	2

    What is the mean score in Mr. Pili's class?

    A. 70
    B. 72
    C. 74
    D. 75

86. Which inequality has the solution represented on the number line below?

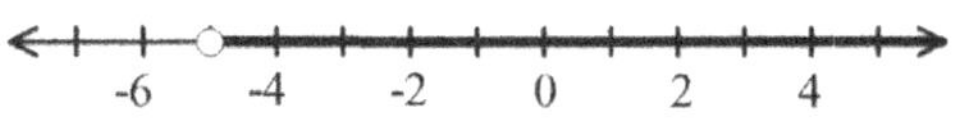

    E. $9 - 2x > 18$
    F. $9 - 2x > 19$
    G. $9 - 2x < 18$
    H. $9 - 2x < 19$

Questions 87 – 92

87. The reciprocal of $\frac{1}{5}$ is added to the reciprocal of 4. What is the reciprocal of the sum?

A. $\frac{4}{21}$

B. $\frac{21}{4}$

C. $\frac{21}{5}$

D. $\frac{5}{21}$

88. Mia sewed the square flag with side length of 35 cm. Tia sewed the square flag with side length of 36 cm. What is the difference between the area of Tia's flag and the area of Mia's flag?

E. $4\ cm^2$
F. $16\ cm^2$
G. $1\ cm^2$
H. $71\ cm^2$

89. PUNCAKE RECIPE (4 SERVINGS)

Ingredients	Amount
Wheat flour	1 cup
Milk	$\frac{3}{4}$ cup
Sugar	$\frac{1}{2}$ cup
Baking Powder	2 teaspoons

The table shows the amounts of ingredients needed to make 4 servings of cupcakes. What is the unit rate for cups of milk per cup of sugar?

A. 0.375
B. 1.5
C. 0.25
D. 1.25

90. $\left(\frac{4}{7} - \frac{1}{2}\right)x = \frac{1}{3} + \frac{3}{4}$

In the equation above, what is the value of x?

E. $12\frac{1}{3}$

F. 8

G. $15\frac{1}{6}$

H. 16

91. In a certain state, the states tax rate increased from 6% to 6.5%. If the increase in the state tax on $x item was $1.80, what is the value of x?

A. 300
B. 320
C. 350
D. 360

92. Evaluate:

$|(-12 - (-7)) - 15| + |-22|$

E. -42
F. -2
G. 2
H. 42

Questions 93 – 98

93.

COLOR BALLS IN ILLUSIONIST'S HAT

Color	Percent
White	$p + 2$
Red	$3p + 4$
Blue	$5p - 5$
Green	$p - 1$
Total	100

The table above shows the percent of color balls in illusionist's hat. What percent of the balls are red?

A. 10%
B. 24%
C. 34%
D. 45%

94.

P ———4——— Q ———7——— R

On the number line above, the distance between P and Q is 4 units, and the distance between Q and R is 7 units. What is the distance between R and the midpoint of P and Q?

E. 5.5
F. 9
G. 3
H. 7.5

95. By what percent did the price of a suit increase if its price was increased from $36 to $45?

A. 15%
B. 20%
C. 25%
D. 30%

96.

8 cm
12 cm
10 cm   10 cm

The net above shows the dimensions of four identical triangles and square base of the pyramid. What is the surface area of the pyramid?

E. $336\ cm^2$
F. $384\ cm^2$
G. $192\ cm^2$
H. $528\ cm^2$

97. Derek's mean number of scored points in 6 basketball games is 18. If his mean number in last 5 games was 17, how many points did Derek score in the first game?

A. 19
B. 21
C. 23
D. 25

98. The price of a hot-dog is decreased by 16%. If initially the hot-dog costs $2.50, what is the final price of the hot-dog?

E. $0.40
F. $1.20
G. $2.10
H. $2.90

	Questions 99 – 104		
99.	Grace bought 5 packs of chips for $14. Each pack of chips contains 350 grams of chips. At this rate, how much would Grace pay for 3 packs of chips weighing 250 grams each? A. $5 B. $6 C. $7 D. $9	102.	Melanie wants to use string to make 3 brindles for her kite. The string costs $3 a yard. If each brindle requires $2\frac{1}{3}$ yards of string, how much will Melanie pay for the string? E. $7 F. $12 G. $14 H. $21
100.	$10.8 \div 0.012 =$ E. 9,000 F. 900 G. 90 H. 9	103.	A graph shows the proportional relationship between number of minutes, x, spent on a test and the student's score, y. The ordered pair $(15, 8)$ is on the graph. Which of the following statements is true? A. Student scored 1 point in 7 minutes B. Student scored 15 points in 8 minutes C. Student scored 7 points per minute D. Student scored 8 points in 15 minutes
101.	A tank with a 400-liter capacity is currently half filled with water. A water drops out of the tank at a rate of 2.5 liters per minute. In how many minutes will the tank be one-fourth filled with water? A. 4 B. 10 C. 40 D. 100	104.	In a school survey, 60 out of 90 students said they read books. If there are 850 students at this school, which of the following numbers is the best estimate of the number of students reading books? E. 567 F. 576 G. 613 H. 1,275

	Questions 105 – 110		
105.	A driver plans to drive 500 miles in 8 hours. Which equation describes the relationship between the time, t, in hours, and the distance travelled, d, in miles? A. $d = \frac{2}{125}t$ B. $d = 125t$ C. $d = \frac{125}{2}t$ D. $d = 2t$	108.	$12(0.008) - 8(0.12) =$ E. -0.864 F. 0 G. 0.864 H. 1.056
106.	A tourist hiked $3\frac{1}{2}$ miles before afternoon and $2\frac{1}{4}$ miles after afternoon. He stopped for a night and the next day returned by the same route. He walked $2\frac{1}{3}$ miles before dinner. How many more miles did the tourist have to walk? E. $2\frac{5}{12}$ F. $3\frac{5}{6}$ G. $3\frac{5}{12}$ H. $2\frac{5}{6}$	109.	What is the value of $11\frac{4}{5} + \left(-6\frac{3}{10}\right) - \left(-1\frac{1}{2}\right)?$ A. $16\frac{3}{5}$ B. 4 C. $19\frac{3}{5}$ D. 7
107.	A child grows $2\frac{1}{3}$ cm in $\frac{1}{2}$ of a year. What is his yearly growth rate in centimeters per year? A. $2\frac{2}{3}$ B. $1\frac{1}{6}$ C. $4\frac{1}{6}$ D. $4\frac{2}{3}$	110.	Mr. Donahue has $1,800 in a saving account that earns 6% simple interest per year. How much will he have in the account in 2 years, if there is no money withdrawn? E. $3,816 F. $4,045 G. $2,016 H. $2,145

Questions 111 – 114

111. The probability of an event occurring is 0.04. What is the chance that the event will not occur?

A. Likely
B. Unlikely
C. Either likely or unlikely
D. Neither likely nor unlikely

112. GREEN PAINT

Cups of yellow paint	Cups of blue paint
2.5	1.5
5	3
x	7.5

The table above shows the number of cups of yellow paint and blue paint used to make a green paint.
Based on the relationship between the numbers of cups of yellow and blue paints, what is the value of x?

E. 10
F. 11.5
G. 12
H. 12.5

113.
```
 A           C              B
←●─┼─┼─┼─┼─┼─●─┼─┼─┼─┼─●─┼→
 -6 -5 -4 -3 -2 -1  0  1  2  3  4  5  6
```
On the number line above, what is the distance, in units, between the midpoint of AB and midpoint of AC?

A. 3
B. 4
C. 5
D. 6

114. Melissa uses 28 beads for every 4 cm of the necklace. There is a proportional relationship between the number of beads and the length of the necklace. What is the constant of proportionality for this relationship?

E. 6 beads per centimeter
F. 7 centimeters per bead
G. 7 beads per centimeter
H. 6 centimeters per bead

PRACTICE TEST 8

	GRID-IN QUESTIONS		
	Questions 58 – 62		
58.	Simplify: $$-3.82 + 2.6 - (-1.42)$$	61.	In a week, the cat's claws grow by 1 mm and then the cat's mistress trims $\frac{7}{8}$ mm of the claws. What will be the length of a cat's claws in 5 weeks, if in the last 5th week the cat's mistress has not cut its claws? (Express your answer as decimal)
59.	Angles A and B are complementary. The measure of angle A is 5 times the measure of angle B. What is the measure of angle A?	62.	SURVEY OF 240 CAR OWNERS | Number of passengers	Number of employees
---	---
0	36
1	72
2	83
3	31
4	18	 The table above shows the results of a survey of 240 car owners about the most comfortable number of passengers in their car. What is the median number of passengers in the cars?
60.	In the tea mixture, $\frac{1}{6}$ is green tea and $\frac{3}{4}$ is black tea. What fraction is black tea from green tea? (Express your answer as a decimal)		

MULTIPLE CHOICE QUESTIONS

Questions 63 – 68

63. In the burger-eating competition, Max ate 45 burgers, which is 10% less than Roger ate. How many burgers did they eat together?

A. 50
B. 5
C. 90
D. 95

64. If $\dfrac{5a}{b} - \dfrac{a}{2b} = \dfrac{\Box a}{4b}$ and $b \neq 0$, what number is represented by $\Box$?

E. 4
F. 8
G. 9
H. 18

65.

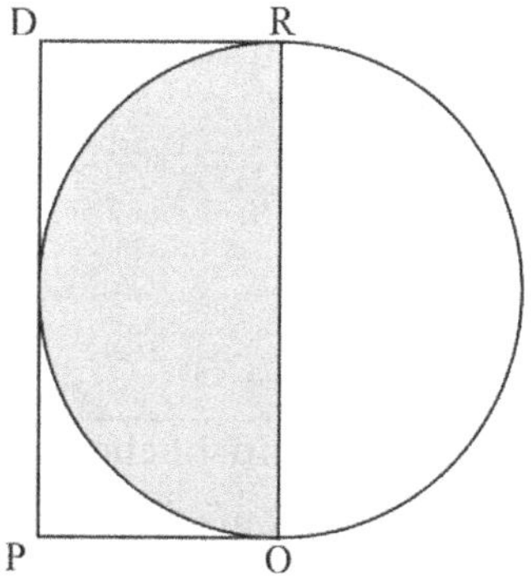

In figure above, DROP is a rectangle. Points O, and R are on the circle. If the area of the shaded region is $8\pi\ cm^2$, what is the area of the rectangle DROP?

A. $8\ cm^2$
B. $16\ cm^2$
C. $24\ cm^2$
D. $32\ cm^2$

66. A list of consecutive integers begins with x and ends with y. If there are 37 numbers in the list, what is the value of $y - x$?

E. 35
F. 36
G. 37
H. 38

67. Simplify:

$$\dfrac{\dfrac{51(3-x)}{3} + 34}{17}$$

A. $5 - x$
B. $4 - x$
C. $3 - x$
D. $1 - x$

68. Two glasses each are $\dfrac{2}{3}$-full. If one-third of the water from the first glass is poured into the second glass, how much water is still needed to completely fill the second glass with water?

E. $\dfrac{1}{9}$ glass
F. $\dfrac{1}{6}$ glass
G. $\dfrac{1}{3}$ glass
H. $\dfrac{2}{9}$ glass

Questions 69 – 74

69.
$$-10 \leq 11 - 7n < -3$$
If n is a whole solution to the inequality above, what is the value of $\frac{1}{n}$?

A. $\frac{1}{2}$

B. $\frac{1}{3}$

C. $\frac{1}{4}$

D. $\frac{1}{5}$

70. 58% of people pooled have a driver's license. If 1,449 people do not have a driver's license, how many people have a driver's license?

E. 3,450
F. 2,560
G. 2,001
H. 1,983

71. A gym is in the shape of square. The area of the floor is $2,025\ m^2$. In a scale drawing of the gym, 1 cm = 15 m. What is the area of the floor in the scale drawing?

A. $3\ cm^2$
B. $9\ cm^2$
C. $15\ cm^2$
D. $25\ cm^2$

72. A computer program randomly generates a sequence of whole numbers from 1 to 19, inclusive. If the computer generates a sequence of 1,000 numbers, what is the best prediction of the number of odd numbers in the sequence?

E. 474
F. 493
G. 526
H. 532

73. Health insurance for travel abroad costs $44 plus $3.50 per day. Luna bought the insurance and used a coupon for 10% off the total cost. After the coupon was applied, Luna spent a total of $74.25. How many days will her insurance be valid?

A. 9
B. 10
C. 11
D. 12

74. The probability of choosing a green ball at random from a bag is $\frac{1}{5}$. After 4 green balls are removed from the bag, the probability of randomly choosing a green ball from the bag is $\frac{1}{6}$. How many green balls were initially in the bag?

E. 16
F. 20
G. 96
H. 100

Questions 75 – 80

75. Each number in a sequence is formed by dividing the previous number by 2 and then adding 5. If the 9th number in the sequence is 82, what is the 10th number?

    A. 169
    B. 159
    C. 36
    D. 46

76. 1st group of judges: 9.2; 9.1; 8.7; 8.5; 8.7
    2nd group of judges: 8.6; 9.0; 8.7; 8.6; 8.9

    Two groups of judges award synchronized swimmers. Each judge can put at most 10 points. Then the swimmers' score is the sum of two groups' means. If judges awarded the swimmers as shown above, what was their score?

    E. 17.5
    F. 17.6
    G. 17.8
    H. 17.9

77. A 3.6-m board was cut into three pieces of different lengths. The shortest piece has a length of x m. Which inequality represents all possible values of x?

    A. $0 < x \leq 1.2$
    B. $0 < x < 1.2$
    C. $0 < x < 1.8$
    D. $1.2 < x < 1.8$

78. What is the area of the shaded region shown in the figure above?

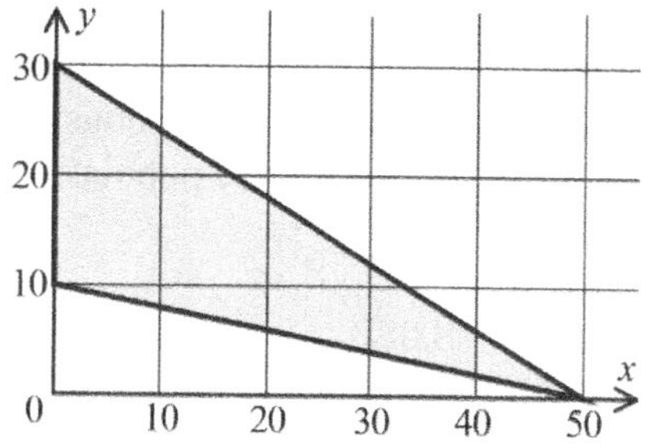

    E. $250\ un^2$.
    F. $500\ un^2$.
    G. $750\ un^2$.
    H. $1{,}000\ un^2$.

79. $$C = \frac{5}{9}(F - 32)$$

    Yesterday in Mathtown, the highest Fahrenheit temperature, F, was 59°, and the lowest temperature was 41°. What was the difference between these temperatures, in degrees Celsius, C?

    A. 1°C
    B. 2°C
    C. 10°C
    D. 5°C

80. Let x be an even number. In terms of x, what is the sum of the two even numbers closest to x?

    E. $2x - 6$
    F. $2x - 4$
    G. $2x$
    H. $2x + 6$

Questions 81 – 86

81. In 2019, the population density of France was 122 people per square kilometer. If the area of France is 640 thousand square kilometers, what is the population of France?

A. 78,080
B. 780,800
C. 7,808,000
D. 78,080,000

82.

```
        |← y cm →|
|←x cm→|
●───────●───────●───────────●
A       C       B           D
```

In the figure above, C is the midpoint of AB. In terms of x and y, what is the length of BD?

E. $y - x$
F. $y + x$
G. $y + 2x$
H. $y - 2x$

83.

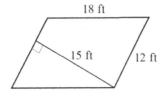

What is the area of the parallelogram shown above?

A. $180\ ft^2$
B. $216\ ft^2$
C. $244\ ft^2$
D. $270\ ft^2$

84. Grant earns money mowing lawns. On Tuesday, he mowed 3 fewer lawns than on Monday. On Wednesday, he mowed 5 more lawns than on Tuesday. If Grant mowed 20 lawns in total, how many lawns did he mow on Wednesday?

E. 4
F. 6
G. 7
H. 9

85. TEST SCORES IN Mr. Vegan's CLASS

Test Score	Number of Students
50	1
60	4
70	6
80	5
90	3
100	1

What is the mean score in Mr. Vegan's class?

A. 70
B. 72
C. 74
D. 75

86. Which inequality has the solution represented on the number line below?

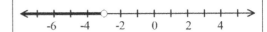

E. $10 - 3x > 19$
F. $10 - 3x > 18$
G. $10 - 3x > 17$
H. $10 - 3x > 16$

Questions 87 – 92

87. The reciprocal of $\frac{2}{3}$ is subtracted from the reciprocal of 3. What is the reciprocal of the difference?

A. $\frac{7}{6}$

B. $\frac{7}{3}$

C. $\frac{6}{7}$

D. $\frac{3}{7}$

88. Gloria cut the square flag with side length of 30 cm. Jude cut the square flag with side length of 32 cm. What is the difference between the area of Gloria's flag and the area of Jude's flag?

E. $2\ cm^2$
F. $4\ cm^2$
G. $62\ cm^2$
H. $124\ cm^2$

89. PUNCAKE RECIPE (4 SERVINGS)

Ingredients	Amount
Wheat flour	1 cup
Milk	$1\frac{1}{3}$ cups
Sugar	$\frac{1}{2}$ cup
Baking Powder	2 teaspoons

The table shows the amounts of ingredients needed to make 4 servings of cupcakes. What is the unit rate for cups of wheat flour per cup of milk?

A. 0.25
B. 0.5
C. 0.75
D. $1\frac{1}{3}$

90. $$\left(\frac{3}{8} - \frac{1}{3}\right)x = \frac{1}{2} + \frac{5}{6}$$

In the equation above, what is the value of x?

E. 32
F. 16
G. 8
H. 4

91. In a certain state, the states tax rate increased from 4.5% to 5%. What was the increase in the state tax on $150 item?

A. $7.50
B. $0.75
C. $157.50
D. $150.75

92. Evaluate:

$$|(-3.6 - (-0.6)) - 11| + |-18|$$

E. -4
F. -32
G. 4
H. 32

Questions 93 – 98

93. COLOR BALLS IN ILLUSIONIST'S HAT

Color	Percent
White	$x + 3$
Red	$2x - 6$
Blue	$2x + 1$
Green	$x + 12$
Total	100

The table above shows the percent of color balls in illusionist's hat. What percent of the balls are green?

A. 18%
B. 24%
C. 27%
D. 31%

94. On the number line above, the distance between P and Q is 5 units, and the distance between P and R is 12 units. What is the distance between P and the midpoint of Q and R?

E. 6
F. 8
G. 8.5
H. 9.5

95. By what percent did the price of trainers decrease if its price was decreased from $85 to $68?

A. 20%
B. 25%
C. 75%
D. 80%

96. The net above shows the dimensions of four identical triangles and square base of the pyramid. What is the lateral area of the pyramid?

E. 60 cm^2
F. 240 cm^2
G. 340 cm^2
H. 480 cm^2

97. Otis's mean number of scored points in 5 basketball games is 13. If his mean number in first 4 games was 11, how many points did Otis score in the last game?

A. 19
B. 21
C. 23
D. 25

98. The price of a French fries is increased by 8%. If initially a portion of French fries costs $3.50, what is the final price of one portion of French fries?

E. $3.60
F. $3.68
G. $3.80
H. $3.78

	Questions 99 – 104		
99.	Ezra bought 4 packs of crackers for $12. Each pack of crackers contains 450 grams of crackers. At this rate, how much would Ezra pay for 3 packs of crackers weighing 200 grams each? A. $4 B. $5 C. $6 D. $7	102.	Hazel wants to use rope to make 2 strops for her backpack. The rope costs $4.50 a yard. If each strop requires $1\frac{5}{6}$ yards of rope, how much will Hazel pay for the rope? E. $8.25 F. $16.50 G. $33 H. $49.50
100.	$0.07 \div 1.4 =$ E. 0.0005 F. 0.005 G. 0.05 H. 0.5	103.	A graph shows the proportional relationship between number of points, x, a player scored in online game and the time, y, in minutes, he spent on this game. The ordered pair (12.5, 4.5) is on the graph. Which of the following statements is true? A. A player scored 12.5 points in 4.5 minutes B. A player scored 4.5 points in 12.5 minutes C. A player scored 12.5 points per minute D. A player scored 4.5 points in per minute
101.	A tank with a 600-liter capacity is currently 50% filled with water. A water pours into the tank at a rate of 3 liters per minute. In how many minutes will the tank be three-fourths filled with water? A. 5 B. 10 C. 50 D. 100	104.	In a school survey, 55 out of 80 students said they like Math. If there are 600 students at this school, which of the following numbers is the best estimate of the number of students, which like Math? E. 187 F. 365 G. 413 H. 873

Questions 105 – 110

105. A swimmer plans to swim 1,200 meters in 6.4 minutes. Which equation describes the relationship between the time, t, in minutes, and the distance, d, in meters?

   A. $d = \frac{2}{375}t$

   B. $d = 375t$

   C. $d = 2t$

   D. $d = \frac{375}{2}t$

106. A chocolate lover bought $2\frac{3}{8}$ kg of chocolates. He ate $\frac{3}{4}$ kg of chocolates the first day, $\frac{5}{8}$ kg of chocolates the second day, $\frac{2}{3}$ kg of the chocolate the third day and left the rest for the fourth day. What day did he eat the most chocolate?

   E. 1st
   F. 2nd
   G. 3rd
   H. 4th

107. A newborn child triples his weight during the first year. If the child is born weighing 3,500 g, what is the average monthly weight gain during the first year of life?

   A. 292 g
   B. 583 g
   C. 875 g
   D. 924 g

108. $100(10^2 - 0.1^2) =$

   E. 9,999
   F. 999.9
   G. 990
   H. 99

109. What is the value of
   $\left(-3\frac{1}{5}\right) \div \left(2 - \left(-\frac{7}{10}\right)\right)?$

   A. $-2\frac{6}{13}$

   B. $-1\frac{5}{27}$

   C. $-\frac{27}{32}$

   D. $2\frac{6}{13}$

110. Mr. Morten has $2,400 in a saving account that earns 7.5% simple interest per year. In how many years will he have $3,120 in his account, if there is no money withdrawn?

   E. 2
   F. 3
   G. 4
   H. 5

	Questions 111 – 114		
111.	Your boss randomly assigns everyone an extra hour work on workdays' evenings (between 18 : 00 and 22 : 00). What are the chances you get Wednesday between 20 : 00 and 22 : 00? A. 7.5% B. 10% C. 12.5% D. 15%	113.	A number line from -6 to 6, with A at -6, C at -1, B at 5. On the number line above, what is the distance, in units, between the midpoint of BC and midpoint of AB? A. 1.5 B. 2 C. 2.5 D. 3
112.	VIOLET PAINT 	Cups of blue paint	Cups of red paint
---	---
3	2
x	3
5	y | The table above shows the number of cups of blue paint and red paint used to make a violet paint. Based on the proportional relationship between the numbers of cups of blue and red paints, what is the value of xy? E. 10 F. 15 G. $\frac{3}{5}$ H. $\frac{5}{3}$	114.	Renata uses 24 beads for every 4 cm of the necklace. There is a proportional relationship between the number of beads and the length of the necklace. Which of the following statements is true? E. Renata uses 6 beads for every 2 cm of necklace F. Renata uses 4 beads per centimeter of necklace G. Renata uses 6 beads per centimeter of necklace H. Renata uses 4 beads for every 2 cm of necklace

PRACTICE TEST 9

GRID-IN QUESTIONS

Questions 58 – 62

58.
$$-\frac{1}{2}x(1 + 3x) + \frac{2}{3}(6x - 9)$$
After the expression above is simplified, what is the coefficient of x expressed as a decimal?

59. Two number cubes have sides labeled 1 through 6. Both number cubes are rolled. How many different outcomes will have a sum of 7?

60.

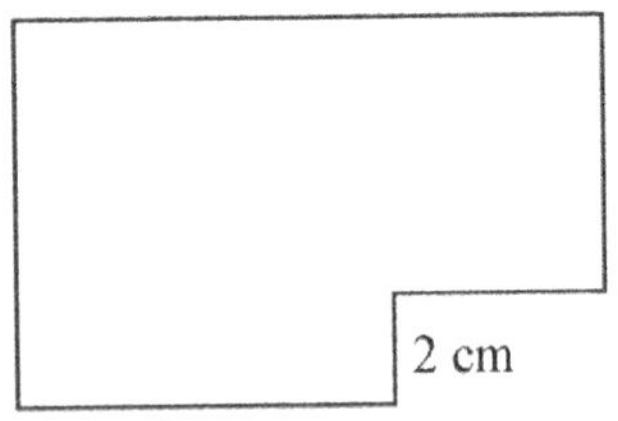

14 cm

6 cm

2 cm

9 cm

The figure above shows a scale drawing of a garden, where 1 centimeter represents 1.5 meters. What is the perimeter of the actual garden in meters?

61. At a city, the temperature increased from −2°C to 1°C between 6 : 00 a.m. and 10 : 00 a.m. By 14 : 00 p.m., the temperature was 4.5 times greater than the 10 : 00 a.m. temperature. What was the total increase in temperature between 6 : 00 a.m. and 14 : 00 p.m., in degrees Celsius?

62.

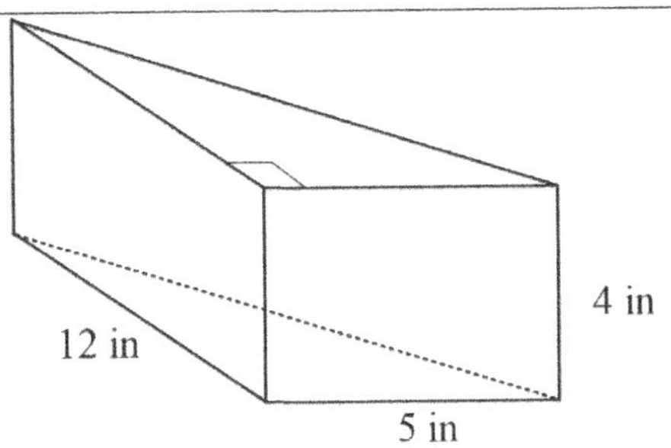

12 in
4 in
5 in

The figure above is a triangular prism. The lateral sides are rectangles and bases are right triangles. What is the volume of the figure, in cubic inches?

MULTIPLE CHOICE QUESTIONS

Questions 63 – 68

63. The graph above shows the height of a plant, y, in inches, after x weeks of growth. What is represented by the point with coordinates $(4, 36)$?

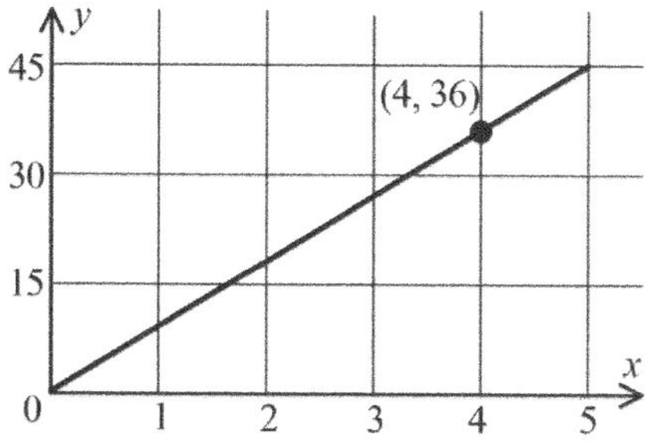

A. In 36 weeks, a plant grew to 4 inches
B. A unit rate of growth is 9 inches per week
C. The x-intercept is 4
D. The y-intercept is 36

64. The number line shows points A, B, C and D. Which point represents the sum
$$-3.5 - (-8.5)?$$

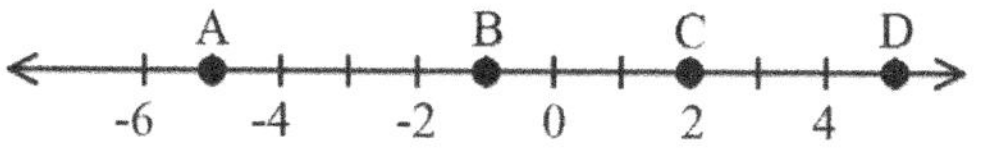

E. A
F. B
G. C
H. D

65. If $\frac{12x}{8} = \frac{15}{2y}$, where $x \neq 0$ and $y \neq 0$, what is the product of x and y?

A. 5
B. 10
C. 15
D. 20

66. Unfolding the tent, Dan uses 8-inch pegs. He drives this peg into the ground by $2\frac{1}{2}$ in. What is the length of the peg left above the ground?

E. 6.5 in
F. 6 in
G. 5.5 in
H. 5 in

67. A house is on sale with 8% discount. What is the discounted price of the house that originally costs $125,000?

A. $135,000
B. $130,000
C. $115,000
D. $110,000

68.
$$8\frac{1}{4} \div 5\frac{1}{2} =$$

E. $\frac{2}{3}$
F. $1\frac{1}{2}$
G. 3
H. 2

Questions 69 – 74

69. In a football, each team has 24 players and 3 coaches. There are also a number of team assistants. The ratio of team assistants to coaches is 2 : 1. What is the ratio of team assistants to players?

   A. 1 : 3
   B. 1 : 4
   C. 1 : 5
   D. 1 : 6

70. $$2n(5 - m) + 3mn = 20$$
   In the equation above, if $n = 4$, what is the value of m?

   E. 5
   F. −5
   G. 15
   H. −15

71. Olivia types at the rate of 180 symbols per minute. Clarissa types 25% more symbols per minute than Olivia. If they both type 36,000-symbol assignments on the same day, how many more minutes will Olivia type than Clarissa?

   A. 20 minutes
   B. 30 minutes
   C. 40 minutes
   D. 50 minutes

72. Ben is running on a circular athletic stadium. He has already run 1 km. Each lap around the track is a distance of 400 meters. His goal is to run at least 3 km in total. How many more laps does he need to complete in order to reach his goal?

   E. 2
   F. 3
   G. 4
   H. 5

73. There are 15 mint candies, 8 vanilla candies, and some chocolate candies. The probability of choosing a mint candy at random is thrice as great as the probability of choosing a chocolate candy at random. What is the probability of choosing a vanilla candy at random?

   A. $\frac{1}{7}$
   B. $\frac{2}{7}$
   C. $\frac{3}{7}$
   D. $\frac{4}{7}$

74. In 1990, the university had 4,000 students. In 2010, the number of students increased by 15% with respect to 1990. In 2020, the number of students increased by 10% with respect to 2010. What was the number of students in 2020?

   E. 5,000
   F. 5,060
   G. 5,100
   H. 5,160

Questions 75 – 80

75. Advertising says that the use of whitening toothpaste gives 98.6% effect. Based on the advertising statement, what fraction of the users will not feel the effect?

A. $\frac{7}{500}$

B. $\frac{3}{125}$

C. $\frac{7}{493}$

D. $\frac{3}{493}$

78. What decimal is equivalent to $-\frac{15}{11}$?

E. $-1.\overline{63}$
F. $-1.6\overline{3}$
G. $-1.\overline{36}$
H. $-1.3\overline{6}$

76. Leanna records the number of pages she notes during her class. The table below shows the data she collected.

Number of pages	Time (in hours)
4.5	1.5
6	2
7.5	2.5

Which equation represents the relationship between the number of pages, y, and the time, x, in hours?

E. $y = 3x$
F. $y = 1.5x$
G. $y = \frac{2}{3}x$
H. $y = \frac{1}{3}x$

79. Mathtown will hold a vote on whether to build a new Mathland park. The town council surveyed a random sample of 300 residents to determine whether they would be in favor of building this park. 165 people said "yes", 56 people said "No" and the rest answered "Not decided yet". Based on the survey results, how many of the 36,000 voters will be in favor of building the park?

A. 19,800
B. 20,100
C. 20,300
D. 20,500

77. $$-2\frac{3}{5}, -\frac{13}{10}, -2\frac{3}{10}, -2$$

Which number above is the greatest?

A. $-2\frac{3}{5}$
B. $-\frac{13}{10}$
C. $-2\frac{3}{10}$
D. -2

80. Each slice of pizza requires $\frac{2}{5}$ ounce of yeast. How many slices can be made if 30 ounces of yeast are used?

E. 12
F. 15
G. 75
H. 100

Questions 81 – 86

81. $$\frac{3\left(2\frac{5}{6} - 3\frac{1}{6}\right)}{2\left(3\frac{1}{3} - 2\frac{2}{3}\right)} =$$

   A. $-1\frac{1}{3}$
   B. $-\frac{3}{4}$
   C. $-\frac{1}{3}$
   D. -3

82. $$-7 \leq 2 - 3x < 8$$
    Which number line represents the values of x that satisfy the inequality above?

    E. <number line from -2 (open) to 3 (closed)>
    F. <number line from -2 (closed) to 3 (open)>
    G. <number line from -3 (closed) to 2 (open)>
    H. <number line from -3 (open) to 3 (closed)>

83. If 1 plumb = 0.8 gear, how many gears are equivalent to 12 plumbs?

    A. 15
    B. 10.4
    C. 10
    D. 9.6

84. Simplify:
    $$-6x + (-8)(3 - 2.5x) =$$

    E. $4x - 24$
    F. $-8x - 24$
    G. $14x - 24$
    H. $-26x - 24$

85. Box A contains 24 pencils, and box B contains 36 pencils. The probability of drawing a grey pencil at random from box A is $\frac{1}{3}$. The probability of drawing a grey pencil at random from box B is $\frac{1}{6}$. All the pencils are mixed in box C. What is the probability of drawing a grey pencil at random from box C?

    A. $\frac{1}{9}$
    B. $\frac{1}{18}$
    C. $\frac{7}{30}$
    D. $\frac{7}{15}$

86. Vinnie-the-Pooh can eat 3 jars with honey in 5 hours. At this rate, how long will it take him to eat 8 jars with honey?

    E. 13 hours
    F. 13 hours 15 minutes
    G. 13 hours 20 minutes
    H. 13 hours 30 minutes

Questions 87 – 92

87. Grace and her friends counted the numbers of dried apricots and prunes in their bags of dried fruit mix. The table below shows these numbers. Which other dried fruit mix bag has a ratio of dried apricots to prunes in the same proportional relationship as Grace's bag?

	Grace	Ronald	Vicky	Susy	Max
Apricots	6	5	4	3	2
Prunes	9	10	8	5	3

A. Ronald
B. Vicky
C. Susy
D. Max

88. If $y = 3.5x$, what is the value of $4y(y - 1.5x) + 5x$ in terms of x?

E. $28x^2 + 5x$
F. $33x$
G. $33x^2$
H. $14x^2 + 5x$

89. If $x = -6$, what is the difference of x and 25% of $|x|$?

A. -4.5
B. -7.5
C. 4.5
D. 7.5

90.

What is the area of the shaded region, in square inches?

E. 3π
F. 6π
G. 9π
H. 39π

91. The volume of a cube is 343 cubic feet. What is the length, in feet, of one side of this cube?

A. 5
B. 6
C. 7
D. 9

92. The integers $n - 2$, $n - 1$, and n are factors of 504. What is the greatest possible value of n?

E. 6
F. 7
G. 8
H. 9

Questions 93 – 98

93. In May, an item was on sale for x. In June, this item was on sale for $65.10, which was a 5% increase from price. In July, the price of the item was 10% lower than it was in June. How much higher was the May's price than the July's price?

   A. $1.71
   B. $2.41
   C. $3.41
   D. $3.71

94. The popular rock band conducted a 66-day tour. If their tour started on Tuesday, on what day did this tour end?

   E. Tuesday
   F. Wednesday
   G. Thursday
   H. Friday

95. Adrian received a check for $55.08 for working 9 hours at his part-time job. The amount on the check was his total pay after 15% in taxes was deducted. What was Adrian's hourly pay rate before taxes were deducted?

   A. $7
   B. $7.10
   C. $7.20
   D. $7.30

96. What is the total surface area, in square centimeters, of the closed box shown above?

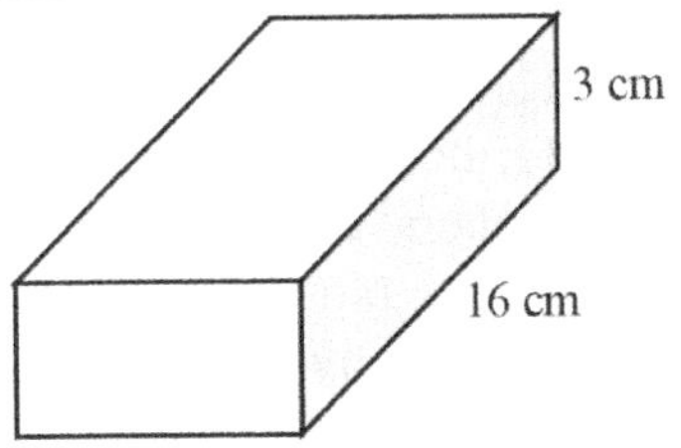

   E. 120
   F. 143
   G. 240
   H. 286

97. The value of a smartphone decreases at a constant rate. If the smartphone is worth $775 six months after its original purchase date and $650 eleven months after its original purchase date, what was the value of the smartphone on its original purchase date?

   A. $925
   B. $900
   C. $875
   D. $400

98. A bag contains 5 green, 4 blue, and 3 yellow balls. Mila selects 3 balls from the bag at random, one at a time, without replacing them. What is the probability that she selects all three yellow balls?

   E. $\frac{1}{1,728}$
   F. $\frac{1}{1,320}$
   G. $\frac{1}{288}$
   H. $\frac{1}{220}$

	Questions 99 – 104		
99.	Aisha earns $\frac{3}{4}$% per year on the money in her savings account. Which expression is not another way to write $\frac{3}{4}$%? A. $\frac{0.75}{100}$ B. $\frac{75}{10,000}$ C. $\frac{3}{400}$ D. 0.075	102.	A box contains a total of 20 color stickers with colors in the ratio $Green : Blue : Red = 3 : 5 : 2$. Suppose that one sticker of each color is removed from the box and not replaced. What is the probability that the next sticker chosen will not be blue? E. $\frac{9}{17}$ F. $\frac{8}{17}$ G. $\frac{9}{20}$ H. $\frac{2}{5}$
100.	Initially, in a lake, there were 120 frogs. In each of the next four years, the number of frogs increased by 20% over the number of frogs from the previous year. How many frogs were there in 4 years? (Round to the nearest whole number.) E. 249 F. 236 G. 207 H. 204	103.	What is the least positive integer evenly divisible by the first 5 positive integers? A. 50 B. 60 C. 80 D. 120
101.	$4x - 7 \geq 12 - 2(6x - 3)$ What is the solution set to the inequality above? A. $x \leq \frac{25}{16}$ B. $x \geq \frac{25}{16}$ C. $x \leq \frac{13}{16}$ D. $x \geq \frac{13}{16}$	104.	Suppose that x, y, and z are non-zero integers. Under which set of conditions would the product $-x^3 y^4 z^5$ always be positive? E. x and z are both negative F. The product xz is negative G. x, y and z are positive H. x, y and z are negative

Questions 105 – 110

105.	Three different colors of paint are available to paint the entrance threshold, the door, and the doorframe. How many different ways are there to paint the three parts of the door? A. 3 B. 6 C. 9 D. 27	108.	A factory planned to use 15 machines to fill an order of chocolates in 10 days. After working for 4 days, 5 more machines were added. How many days did it take in total to finish? E. 6.5 F. 7.5 G. 8.5 H. 9.5
106.	Isosceles triangle ABC is similar to isosceles triangle EFG. What is the perimeter of triangle EFG? (12 cm, 18 cm, 6 cm shown on figures) E. 42 cm F. 32 cm G. 28 cm H. 26 cm	109.	Jill has a rectangular tank, measuring 24 inches in length, 10 inches in width, and 8 inches in height. The tank is holding 1,080 in^3 of liquid. What fraction of the height is the height of the water? A. $\frac{4}{5}$ B. $\frac{9}{10}$ C. $\frac{7}{10}$ D. $\frac{9}{16}$
107.	Charlie has 3 pairs of socks: black, white and grey. All socks were mixed in a box. Charlie chooses one sock and without putting the first sock back, he picks a second sock at random. What is the probability that he chooses two socks of one color? A. $\frac{1}{5}$ B. $\frac{1}{30}$ C. $\frac{1}{10}$ D. $\frac{1}{6}$	110.	$\|x - 3\| \geq 5$ What is the solution to the inequality above? E. $-2 \leq x \leq 8$ F. $x \leq -2$ or $x \geq 8$ G. $-8 \leq x \leq 2$ H. $x \leq -8$ or $x \geq 2$

Questions 111 – 114

111. A rectangular kitchen floor is 5 m long and 4 m wide. It will be covered completely with new square tiles measuring 25 cm on each side. How many tiles will cover the floor?

A. 36
B. 160
C. 240
D. 320

112. An aqua park sells twice as many tickets on Sunday as on any weekday, and thrice as many tickets on Saturday as on any weekday. If the number of tickets sold this week totaled 15,000, how many tickets are expected to be sold on the following Sunday?

E. 1,500
F. 3,000
G. 4,500
H. 6,000

113. A rectangular football field had a length of 100 meters and a width of 80 meters. The field was recently enlarged, with the length increased by 10 meters and the width increased by 10%. By what percentage was the area of the field increased?

A. 19%
B. 20%
C. 21%
D. 22%

114. If x and y are both negative integers with $x < y - 1$, which expression has the least value?

E. $x - 1$
F. $y - 1$
G. $x + 1$
H. $y + 1$

PRACTICE TEST 10

0GRID-IN QUESTIONS			
Questions 58 – 62			
58.	$-\frac{1}{3}x(6 - 3x) + \frac{5}{6}(6x - 12)$ After the expression above is simplified, what is the coefficient of x expressed as a decimal?	61.	At a city, the temperature increased from $-12°C$ to $-5°C$ between 5 : 00 a.m. and 8 : 00 a.m. By 11 : 00 a.m., the temperature was 4°C greater than the 8 : 00 a.m. temperature. What was the total increase in temperature between 5 : 00 a.m. and 11 : 00 a.m., in degrees Celsius?
59.	Two number cubes have sides labeled 1 through 6. Both number cubes are rolled. How many different outcomes will have a sum of 5 or 8?	62.	[Figure: triangular prism with dimensions 12 in, 5 in, 4 in] The figure above is a triangular prism. The lateral sides are rectangles and bases are right triangles. What is the surface area of the figure, in square inches?
60.	[Figure: L-shaped garden with dimensions 14 cm, 6 cm, 2 cm, 9 cm] The figure above shows a scale drawing of a garden, where 1 centimeter represents 1.5 meters. What is the area of the actual garden, in square meters?		

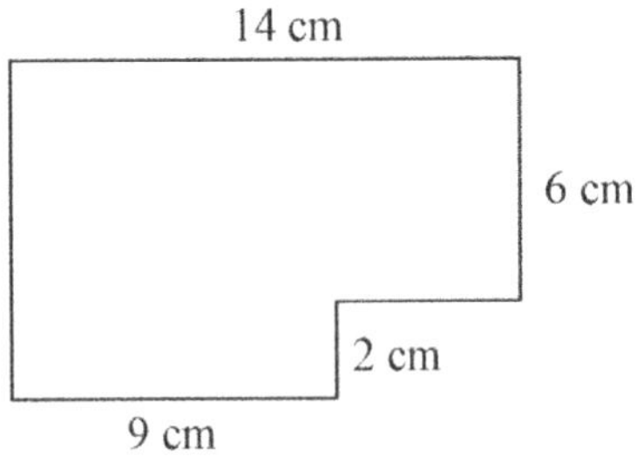

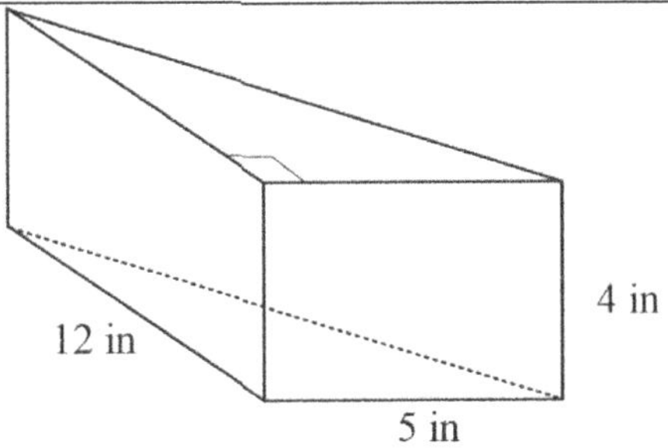

386

MULTIPLE CHOICE QUESTIONS

Questions 63 – 68

63. The graph above shows the height of a plant, y, in millimeters, after x days of growth. If in 20 days, the plant is 40 mm tall, which point on the graph represents this situation?

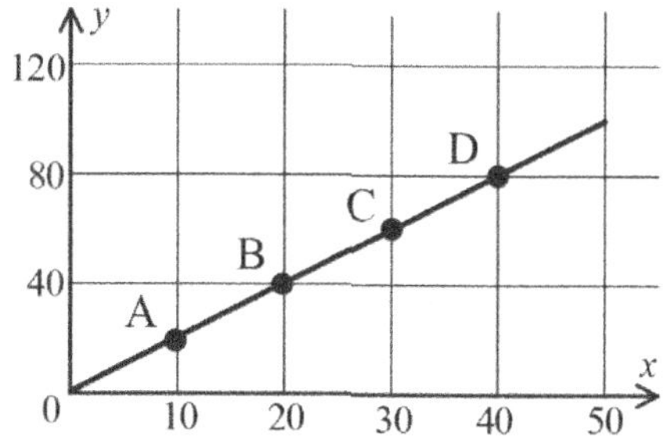

A. A
B. B
C. C
D. D

64. The number line shows points A, B, C and D. Which point represents the expression
$$-2(-1.5 - (-2))?$$

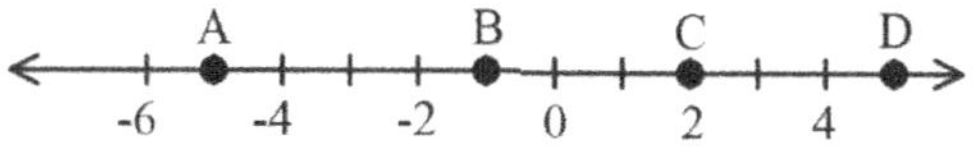

E. A
F. B
G. C
H. D

65. If $\frac{14}{49x} = \frac{9y}{21}$, where $x \neq 0$ and $y \neq 0$, what is the product of x and y?

A. 1.5
B. 3
C. 2
D. $\frac{2}{3}$

66. Sam played with a folding 1.5-meter roulette. From the left edge he folded four parts of 10 cm each, from the right edge – five parts of 10 cm each. What fraction of the roulette left unfolded?

E. $\frac{1}{5}$
F. $\frac{2}{5}$
G. $\frac{3}{5}$
H. $\frac{4}{5}$

67. A pair of branded jeans is on sale with 12% discount. What is the discounted price of the jeans that originally costs $80?

A. $68
B. $70
C. $70.40
D. $70.80

68. $3\frac{1}{4} \div \left(2\frac{1}{2} \div 5\right) =$

E. $3\frac{1}{2}$
F. $\frac{13}{50}$
G. $6\frac{1}{2}$
H. $1\frac{3}{10}$

	Questions 69 – 74		
69.	In the school league, 18 teams take part. They are judged by 6 judges. There are also a number of judges' assistants. The ratio of judges' assistants to judges is 3 : 2. What is the ratio of judges' assistants to teams? A. 1 : 2 B. 2 : 1 C. 1 : 9 D. 9 : 1	72.	Lucas is running on a circular athletic stadium. He has already run $\frac{1}{3}$ of what he planned to run. Each lap around the track is a distance of 400 meters. His goal is to run 3.6 km in total. How many more laps does he need to complete in order to reach his goal? E. 3 F. 4 G. 5 H. 6
70.	$$2mn - \frac{1}{2}n(m-n) = -16$$ In the equation above, if $n = -2$, what is the value of m? E. 2 F. −2 G. 6 H. −6	73.	In the basket, here are 8 apples, 6 pears, and some apricots. The probability of choosing an apple at random is twice as great as the probability of choosing an apricot at random. What is the probability of choosing a pear at random? A. $\frac{1}{6}$ B. $\frac{1}{5}$ C. $\frac{1}{4}$ D. $\frac{1}{3}$
71.	Olivia types at the rate of 180 symbols per minute. Clarissa types 25% fewer symbols per minute than Olivia. If they both type 21,600-symbol assignments on the same day, how many minutes will Clarissa type her assignment? A. 120 minutes B. 160 minutes C. 200 minutes D. 240 minutes	74.	In 1980, the university had 2,000 students. In 2000, the number of students increased by 40% with respect to 1980. In 2020, the number of students increased by 18% with respect to 2000. How many more students were in the university in 2020 than in 2000? E. 500 F. 504 G. 440 H. 144

Questions 75 – 80

75. Statistics say that 72.4% of accidents are covered by insurance. Based on the statistics statement, what fraction of accidents are not covered by insurance?

A. $\frac{69}{500}$

B. $\frac{69}{25}$

C. $\frac{69}{50}$

D. $\frac{69}{250}$

76. Megan records the number of pages she notes during her classes. The table below shows the data she collected.

Number of pages	Time (in hours)
4.5	1.2
5.25	x
y	1.8

What is the value of $x \cdot y$?

E. $\frac{35}{18}$

F. $\frac{18}{35}$

G. 9.45

H. 8.35

77. $|-2.4|, \quad -2.3, \quad 2.5, \quad \frac{1}{-2.4}$

Which number above is the smallest?

A. $|-2.4|$
B. -2.3
C. 2.5
D. $\frac{1}{-2.4}$

78. What decimal is equivalent to $\frac{23}{11}$?

E. $2.\overline{90}$
F. $2.9\overline{0}$
G. $2.\overline{09}$
H. $2.0\overline{9}$

79. The mean of a set of 12 numbers is 84. When a number 82 is removed from the set, and the number x is added to the set, the mean is changed to 85. What is the value of x?

A. 85
B. 86
C. 90
D. 94

80. Each cupcake requires 0.05 g of powder. How many cupcakes can be made if 4 grams of powder are used?

E. 60
F. 70
G. 80
H. 90

389

Questions 81 – 86

81.
$$\frac{4\left(3\frac{2}{3} - 4\frac{1}{3}\right)}{5\left(2\frac{1}{6} - 1\frac{5}{6}\right)} =$$

A. $-\frac{5}{8}$

B. $-2\frac{1}{2}$

C. $-1\frac{3}{5}$

D. $-\frac{2}{5}$

82.
$$-4 < 6 - 5x \leq 21$$
Which number line represents the values of x that satisfy the inequality above?

E. [number line from -2 (open) to 4 (closed)]

F. [number line from -2 (closed) to 2 (open)]

G. [number line from -3 (closed) to 2 (open)]

H. [number line from -3 (open) to 2 (closed)]

83. If 1.5 plumbs = 0.4 gear, how many gears are equivalent to 24 plumbs?

A. 16
B. 6.4
C. 90
D. 60

84. Simplify:
$$-3.4x + (-4.5)(2 - 8x) =$$

E. $33.6x - 9$
F. $-39.4x - 9$
G. $-37.4x - 9$
H. $32.6x - 9$

85. Box A contains 16 grey pencils, and box B contains 24 grey pencils. The probability of drawing a grey pencil at random from box A is $\frac{1}{4}$. The probability of drawing a grey pencil at random from box B is $\frac{1}{5}$. All the pencils are mixed in box C. What is the probability of drawing a grey pencil at random from box C?

A. $\frac{5}{23}$

B. $\frac{1}{40}$

C. $\frac{1}{20}$

D. $\frac{1}{9}$

86. Vinnie-the-Pooh can eat 3 jars with honey in 5 hours. At this rate, what fraction of a jar with honey will he eat in 50 minutes?

E. $\frac{1}{3}$

F. $\frac{1}{2}$

G. $\frac{2}{3}$

H. $\frac{3}{4}$

Questions 87 – 92

87. Mila and her friends counted the numbers of dried apricots and prunes in their bags of dried fruit mix. The table below shows these numbers. If the ratio of dried apricots to prunes is the same in all bags, what is the value of y?

	Mila	Alice	Henry
Apricots	12	4	$4x$
Prunes	15	x	y

A. 20
B. 24
C. 25
D. 28

88. If $y = -0.05x$, what is the value of $10y(y - 0.45x) - 0.25x$ in terms of x?

E. x
F. $0.25x$
G. 0
H. $0.5x$

89. If $x = -8$, what is the difference of x and 75% of $|2x|$?

A. -4
B. -20
C. 4
D. 20

90. If the area of the shaded region is $36\pi \ in^2$, what is the value of x?

E. 8
F. 16
G. 6
H. 12

91. The volume of a cube is 512 cubic feet. What is the surface area, in square feet, of this cube?

A. 64
B. 256
C. 324
D. 384

92. The integers n, $n + 1$, and $n + 2$ are factors of 720. What is the greatest possible value of n?

E. 6
F. 7
G. 8
H. 9

Questions 93 – 98

93. In June, an item was on sale for $x. In July, this item was on sale for $91.20, which was a 5% decrease from price. In August, the price of the item was 10% lower than it was in July. How much higher was the June's price than the August's price?

    A. $13.92
    B. $14.18
    C. $14.40
    D. $14.86

94. The popular rock band conducted a 50-day tour. If their tour ended on Friday, on what day did this tour start?

    E. Wednesday
    F. Thursday
    G. Friday
    H. Saturday

95. Bill received a check for $81.64 for working 13 hours at his part-time job. The amount on the check was his total pay after 20% in taxes was deducted. What was Bill's hourly pay rate before taxes were deducted?

    A. $7.55
    B. $7.65
    C. $7.75
    D. $7.85

96. If the total surface area of the box shown is $222\ cm^2$, what is the value of x?

    E. 11
    F. 12
    G. 13
    H. 14

97. The value of a TV decreases at a constant rate. If the TV is worth $1,190 five months after its original purchase date and $1,142 nine months after its original purchase date, what was the value of the TV on its original purchase date?

    A. $1,240
    B. $1,250
    C. $1,260
    D. $1,280

98. A bag contains 10 green, 8 blue, and 2 white balls. Naomi selects 2 balls from the bag at random, one at a time, without replacing them. What is the probability that she selects all two white balls?

    E. $\frac{2}{95}$
    F. $\frac{1}{95}$
    G. $\frac{1}{190}$
    H. $\frac{1}{380}$

Questions 99 – 104

99. Which expression is not another way to write 0.2%?

A. 0.002

B. $\dfrac{1}{50}$

C. $\dfrac{2}{1{,}000}$

D. $\dfrac{0.2}{100}$

100. The scientists began their experiment on 40 mice. Six months later, the number of mice increased by 15%. At this rate, how many mice would be there in 2 years? (Round to the nearest whole number.)

E. 53
F. 61
G. 69
H. 70

101. $8 - 3x \geq 20 - 5(x - 1)$
What is the solution set to the inequality above?

A. $x \leq 8.5$
B. $x \geq 8.5$
C. $x \leq 3.5$
D. $x \geq 3.5$

102. The colored paper package contains 200 color sheets in the ratio of colors $Green : Blue : Yellow = 4 : 3 : 1$. Suppose that 10 sheets of each color are removed from the box and not replaced. What is the probability that the next sheet chosen will be yellow?

E. $\dfrac{3}{34}$

F. $\dfrac{3}{40}$

G. $\dfrac{13}{40}$

H. $\dfrac{13}{34}$

103. What is the least positive integer evenly divisible by numbers 4, 5, 6 and 9?

A. 60
B. 90
C. 120
D. 180

104. Suppose that x, and y are non-zero integers. Under which set of conditions would the expression $-\dfrac{x^4 y^2}{y^3 x^2}$ always be positive?

E. x and y are both positive
F. x is negative
G. y is negative
H. xy is negative

Questions 105 – 110

105. Martina has to make a morning choice of uniform. She has a choice of three white shirts and two black skirts. In how many different ways can Martina make her choice?

   A. 3
   B. 5
   C. 6
   D. 12

106.

   Isosceles triangle ABC is similar to isosceles triangle EFG. Which of the following statements is false?

   E. $\frac{GF}{CB} = \frac{12}{18}$
   F. $\frac{EF}{AB} = \frac{2}{3}$
   G. $\frac{GE}{EF} = \frac{AC}{AB}$
   H. $\frac{EG}{AB} = \frac{EF}{AC}$

107. The shooter hits the target with a probability of 0.8. What is the probability that the shooter will miss on the first shot and hit the target with the second?

   A. 0.64
   B. 0.32
   C. 0.16
   D. 0.8

108. A factory planned to use 40 machines to fill an order of chocolates in 10 days. After working for 2 days, 10 more machines were added. How many days did it take in total to finish?

   E. 6.4
   F. 7.4
   G. 8.4
   H. 9.4

109. Pit has a rectangular tank, measuring 20 inches in length, 8 inches in width, and 12 inches in height. The tank is holding 1,440 in^3 of liquid. What fraction of the height is the height of the water?

   A. $\frac{2}{3}$
   B. $\frac{3}{4}$
   C. $\frac{4}{5}$
   D. $\frac{5}{6}$

110. $|2 - x| \leq 6$

   What is the solution to the inequality above?

   E. $-4 \leq x \leq 8$
   F. $x \leq -4$ or $x \geq 8$
   G. $-8 \leq x \leq 4$
   H. $x \leq -8$ or $x \geq 4$

	Questions 111 – 114		
111.	A rectangular bathroom floor is 3.5 m long and 2.5 m wide. It will be covered completely with new square tiles measuring 25 cm on each side. How many tiles will cover the floor? A. 120 B. 140 C. 160 D. 180	113.	A rectangular football field had a length of 110 meters and a width of 90 meters. The field was recently reduced, with the length decreased by 10% and the width decreased by 5 m. By what percentage was the area of the field decreased? A. 15% B. 16% C. 17% D. 18%
112.	Miranda has 12 fewer dimes than 4 times the number of nickels. If Miranda has $17.20 in dimes, how much does she have in total? E. $19 F. $19.20 G. $19.40 H. $19.50	114.	If x and y are both negative integers with $x < y$, which expression has the greatest value? E. $1 - x$ F. $1 - y$ G. $-x$ H. $-y$

PRACTICE TEST 11

GRID-IN QUESTIONS

Questions 58 – 62

58. $-2.2(x + 5) + 4.8(10 - x)$

If $x = -6$, what is the value of the expression above?

59. Angles A and B are supplementary. The ratio of the measure of angle A to the measure of angle B is 2 : 3. What is the measure of the greater angle?

60.

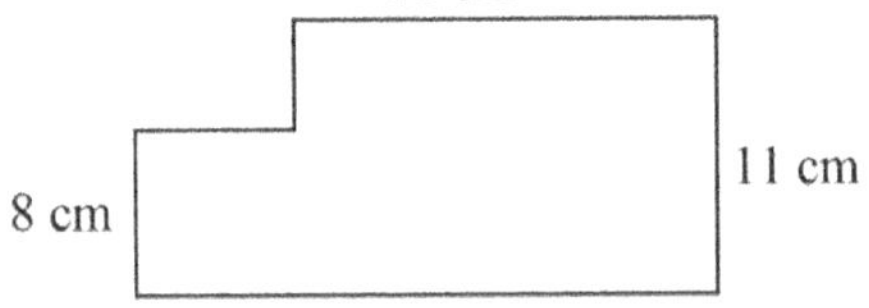

16 cm

8 cm   11 cm

20 cm

The figure above shows a scale drawing of a garden, where 1 centimeter represents 1.5 meters. What is the perimeter of the actual garden, in meters?

61. SURVEY OF 50 EMPLOYEES

Number of family members	Number of employees
1	4
2	8
3	16
4	18
5	4
6	0

The table above shows the number of family members in each of 50 employees' families. What is the mean number of members in these families?

62.

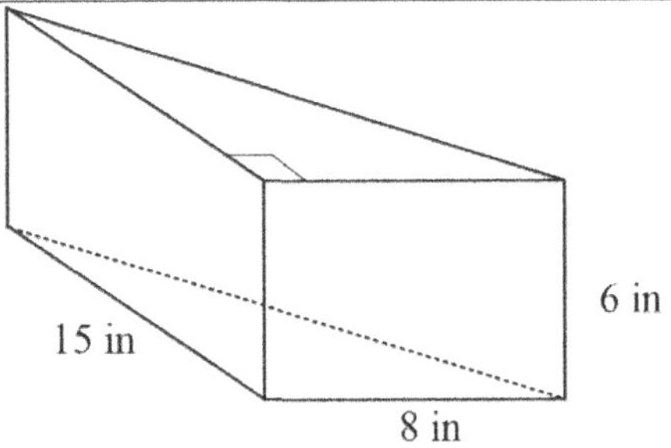

15 in   6 in   8 in

The figure above is a triangular prism. The lateral sides are rectangles and bases are right triangles. What is the lateral area of the figure, in square inches?

396

MULTIPLE CHOICE QUESTIONS

Questions 63 – 68

63.

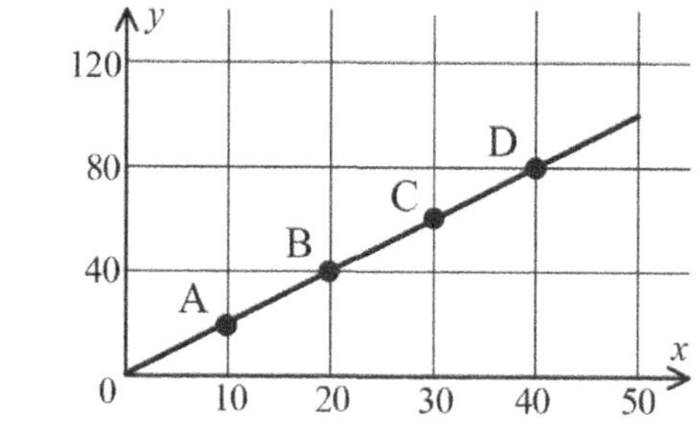

The graph above shows the number of points, y, scored in a game, after x minutes passed. If a player scored 20 points in 10 minutes, which point on the graph represents this situation?

A. A
B. B
C. C
D. D

64.

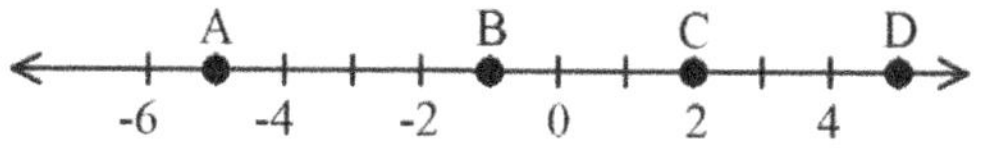

The number line shows points A, B, C and D. Which point represents the expression $-3\frac{1}{8}(0.6 - (-1))$?

E. A
F. B
G. C
H. D

65. If $\frac{15}{25x} = \frac{6y}{10}$, where $x \neq 0$ and $y \neq 0$, what is the product of x and y?

A. 1.5
B. 3
C. 2
D. 1

66. A list of consecutive integers begins with a and ends with b. If $\frac{a-b}{2} = -18$, how many integers are in the list?

E. 35
F. 36
G. 37
H. 38

67. This year, dealer Mike sold 28 more cars than last year. If the number of cars sold by Mike last year is 96% of the number of cars he sold this year, how many cars did he sell this year?

A. 644
B. 672
C. 700
D. 728

68. $5\frac{1}{3} \div \left(1\frac{1}{4} \div 10\right) =$

E. $\frac{2}{3}$
F. $\frac{32}{75}$
G. $66\frac{2}{3}$
H. $42\frac{2}{3}$

Questions 69 – 74			
69.	$19 < 40 - 3n < 25$ If n is a whole solution to the inequality above, what is the value of $\frac{n-1}{n}$? A. $\frac{4}{5}$ B. $\frac{5}{6}$ C. $\frac{6}{7}$ D. $\frac{7}{8}$	72.	A computer program randomly generates a sequence of multiples of 3 from 1 to 21, inclusive. If the computer generates a sequence of 200 numbers, what is the best prediction of the number of even multiples in the sequence? E. 114 F. 100 G. 105 H. 86
70.	35% of people pooled like driving at a high speeds. Among those who do not like to drive at high speeds, 44% believe that riding at high speeds is dangerous. What percentage of people do not drive at high speeds and do not consider driving at high speeds dangerous? E. 15.4% F. 19.6% G. 36.4% H. 56%	73.	In the basket, there are 12 apples, 10 pears, and some apricots. The probability of choosing an apricot at random is four times as small as the probability of choosing an apple at random. What is the probability of choosing a pear at random? A. $\frac{1}{5}$ B. $\frac{2}{5}$ C. $\frac{3}{5}$ D. $\frac{4}{5}$
71.	The 1st runner runs 1 km in 4 minutes. The 2nd runner spends 12.5% more time per kilometer than the 1st runner. How much longer will the second runner spend than the first to run the 5-km distance? A. 2 minutes B. 2.25 minutes C. 2.5 minutes D. 2.75 minutes	74.	Each number in a sequence is formed by dividing the previous number by 2 and then subtracting 2. If the 3rd number in the sequence is 5.5, what is the first number in this sequence? E. 30 F. 32 G. 34 H. 36

Questions 75 – 80			
75.	Statistics say that 72.8% of India's population is vegetarian. Based on the statistics statement, what fraction of India's population is not vegetarian? A. $\frac{69}{250}$ B. $\frac{17}{75}$ C. $\frac{34}{125}$ D. $\frac{69}{500}$	78.	What is the area of the shaded region shown in the figure above? E. $200 \; un^2$. F. $400 \; un^2$. G. $500 \; un^2$. H. $600 \; un^2$.
76.	Rita records the number of pages read each day she reads. The table below shows the data she collected. 	Number of pages	Time (in hours)
---	---
120	1.5
200	2.5
240	x | What is the value of x? E. 2.75 F. 3 G. 3.25 H. 3.5	79.	The mean of a set of 10 numbers is 111. When a number 119 is removed from the set, and the number x is added to the set, the mean is changed to 109. What is the value of x? A. 99 B. 100 C. 101 D. 107
77.	$-|-7.1|; \; |-6.9|; \; -6.8; \; -(-7.2)$ Which number above is the smallest? A. $-|-7.1|$ B. $|-6.9|$ C. -6.8 D. $-(-7.2)$	80.	Let x be an odd number. In terms of x, what is the sum of the two even numbers closest to x and greater than x? E. $2x + 2$ F. $2x + 3$ G. $2x + 4$ H. $2x + 6$

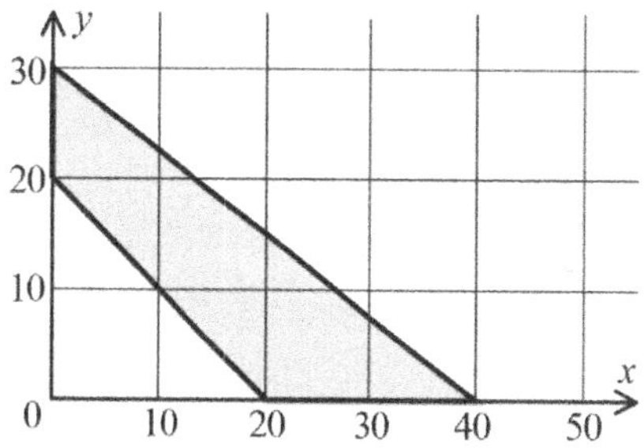

Questions 81 – 86

81. $1.\overline{18} + \dfrac{9}{11} =$

   A. $1\dfrac{8}{11}$
   B. $1\dfrac{10}{11}$
   C. 2
   D. $2\dfrac{1}{11}$

82.

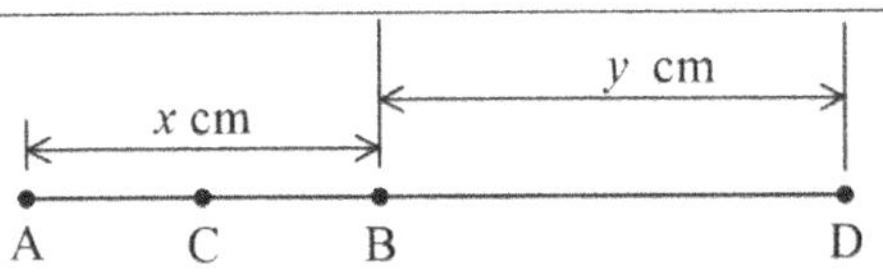

   A————C————B————————D
   $\underbrace{}_{x\text{ cm}}$ $\underbrace{}_{y\text{ cm}}$

   In the figure above, C is the midpoint of AB. What is the length of the segment CD in terms of x and y?

   E. $\dfrac{y+x}{2}$
   F. $y + \dfrac{x}{2}$
   G. $\dfrac{y-x}{2}$
   H. $y - \dfrac{x}{2}$

83. If 3 plumbs = 0.2 gear, and 2 gears = 0.4 whip, how many whips are equivalent to 36 plumbs?

   A. 6
   B. 7.5
   C. 0.72
   D. 0.48

84. Simplify:
   $$-(3 - 2(x+5)) - 4x =$$

   E. $-13 - 6x$
   F. $7 - 2x$
   G. $7 - 6x$
   H. $-13 - 2x$

85. Box A contains 10 grey pencils. Box B contains 50 pencils. The probability of drawing a grey pencil at random from box A is $\dfrac{2}{5}$. The probability of drawing a grey pencil at random from box B is $\dfrac{1}{10}$. All the pencils are mixed in box C. What is the probability of drawing a grey pencil at random from box C?

   A. $\dfrac{1}{5}$
   B. $\dfrac{1}{15}$
   C. $\dfrac{1}{2}$
   D. $\dfrac{1}{25}$

86.

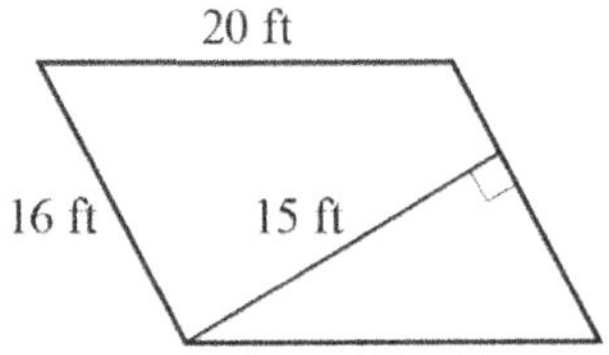

   (parallelogram with sides 20 ft and 16 ft, with a height of 15 ft drawn to the side of length 20 ft)

   What is the area of the parallelogram shown above?

   E. $320\ ft^2$
   F. $300\ ft^2$
   G. $240\ ft^2$
   H. $210\ ft^2$

Questions 87 – 92

87. The reciprocal of $1\frac{1}{5}$ is multiplied by reciprocal of $\frac{1}{12}$. What is the reciprocal of the product?

   A. 10
   B. $\frac{72}{5}$
   C. $\frac{1}{10}$
   D. $\frac{5}{72}$

88. A recipe calls for 1.5 kg of potatoes, and 0.4 kg of mushrooms. The costs of potatoes and mushrooms are $0.50, and $2.40 per kg respectively. What is the cost of 9.5 kg of this recipe?

   E. $14.50
   F. $11.55
   G. $9.50
   H. $8.55

89. If $x = 12$, what is the difference of x and $\frac{1}{6}$ of $|-3x|$?

   A. 6
   B. −6
   C. 12
   D. −12

90. What is the area of the shaded region? (outer 18 in, inner 5 in)

   E. $299\pi \ in^2$
   F. $224\pi \ in^2$
   G. $56\pi \ in^2$
   H. $4\pi \ in^2$

91. The surface area of a cube is $96 \ ft^2$. What is the volume, in cubic feet, of this cube?

   A. 64
   B. 128
   C. 216
   D. 324

92. Two consecutive integers are factors of 528. What is the quotient when 528 is divided by product of these integers?

   E. 2
   F. 3
   G. 4
   H. 6

Questions 93 – 98

93. COLOR BALLS IN THE BOX

Color	Percent
Blue	$p+2$
Red	$3p+4$
Green	$p-1$
Total	100

The table above shows the percent of color balls in the box. What percent of the balls are not green?

A. 18%
B. 21%
C. 61%
D. 82%

94.

On the number line above, the distance between P and Q is 6 units, and the distance between P and R is 19 units. What is the distance between P and the midpoint of Q and R?

E. 6.5
F. 9.5
G. 12.5
H. 13.5

95. The price of a school uniform increases from $25 to $28. By what percent does the price increase?

A. 3%
B. 6%
C. 9%
D. 12%

96.

If the base area of the box shown is $90\ cm^2$, what is the surface area of the box?

E. $159\ cm^2$
F. $180\ cm^2$
G. $318\ cm^2$
H. $360\ cm^2$

97. Melanie bought 6 bags of dog food for $14.40. Each bag of dog food contains 240 grams. At this rate, how much would Melanie pay for 4 bags of dog food weighing 300 grams each?

A. $10
B. $11
C. $12
D. $13

98. A bag contains 10 green and 5 blue balls. Naomi selects 2 balls from the bag at random, one at a time, without replacing them. What is the probability that she selects first ball green and second ball blue?

E. $\frac{5}{21}$
F. $\frac{2}{15}$
G. $\frac{1}{50}$
H. $\frac{2}{9}$

	Questions 99 – 104		
99.	If A = 15 and B = 9, which of the following numbers represents repeating decimal? A. $\frac{B}{A}$ B. $\frac{B}{A^2}$ C. $\frac{A}{B}$ D. $\frac{A^2}{B}$	102.	In a school survey, 125 out of 150 students said they use smartphones more than 1 hour per day. If there are 700 students at this school, which of the following numbers is the best estimate of the number of students not using smartphones more than 1 hour per day? E. 596 F. 104 G. 117 H. 583
100.	The scientists began their experiment on 100 mice. Six months later, the number of mice decreased by 5%. At this rate, how many mice would be there in 2 years? (Round to the nearest whole number.) E. 80 F. 81 G. 86 H. 90	103.	A train started from Denver to Kansas City at 8 : 23 a.m. The train travelled at an average speed of 70 miles per hour. If the distance between Denver and Kansas City is 595 miles, at what time did the train arrive at Kansas City? A. 16 : 23 p.m. B. 16 : 35 p.m. C. 16 : 53 p.m. D. 17 : 05 p.m.
101.	The 45-liter tank of the car is half filled with gasoline. On average, the car travels 100 km consuming 6 liters of gasoline. At this rate, how far can the car travel? A. 300 km B. 325 km C. 350 km D. 375 km	104.	Suppose that x, and y are non-zero integers. If $(-x)^4(-y)^5$ is positive, which of the following statements is <u>always</u> true? E. x and y are both positive F. x is negative and y is positive G. x is negative H. y is negative

Questions 105 – 110

105. There are 8 performers in a talent show. If they were lined up in a queue in such a way, that anyone could be the first and the rest in alphabetical order, how many such queues could there be?

A. 8
B. 8^8
C. 8!
D. 7!

106. Isosceles triangle ABC is similar to isosceles triangle EFG. What is EF in terms of x?

(Triangle EFG with sides 16 cm; triangle ABC with side 20 cm and base x cm)

E. $\frac{5}{4}x$

F. $\frac{4}{5}x$

G. $4x$

H. $5x$

107. The shooter hits the target with a probability of 0.7. What is the probability that the shooter will miss one of two shots?

A. 0.09
B. 0.21
C. 0.42
D. 0.49

108. Luis biked from home to school. For the first 10 minutes, he biked at an average speed of 8 km/h. For the next 15 minutes, he biked at an average speed of 6 km/h. What was the average speed for the whole route?

E. 6.8 km/h
F. 7 km/h
G. 7.2 km/h
H. 7.4 km/h

109. What is the value of

$$10^2(12 - 3^2) - 200\left(\frac{1}{2}\right)^4 ?$$

A. 275
B. 278.5
C. 287.5
D. 295

110. Mr. Kruger has $3,800 in a saving account that earns 4.5% simple interest per year. How much will he have in the account in 4 years, if there is no money withdrawn?

E. $4,484
F. $6,840
G. $7,280
H. $15,884

Questions 111 – 114			
111.	A is at -5, C is at -1, B is at 4 on a number line from -6 to 6. On the number line above, point D is not shown. Point D divides the segment BA in the same ratio as point C divides the segment AB. Where could be point D located? A. 1 B. 0.5 C. 0 D. −0.5	113.	A rectangular handball field had a length of 130 feet and a width of 65 feet. A rectangular volleyball field had a length of 60 feet and a width of 30 feet. By what percentage is the area of the handball field greater than the area of volleyball field? A. ≈ 21% B. ≈ 121% C. ≈ 370% D. ≈ 470%
112.	Lester has 8 more dimes than 3 times the number of nickels. If Lester has $4.70 in dimes, how much does he have in total? E. $5.15 F. $5.25 G. $5.35 H. $5.45	114.	If $x < y < 0$, which expression has the smallest value? E. $2 - x$ F. $y - 2$ G. $x - 2$ H. $2 - y$

PRACTICE TEST 12

GRID-IN QUESTIONS

Questions 58 – 62

58.

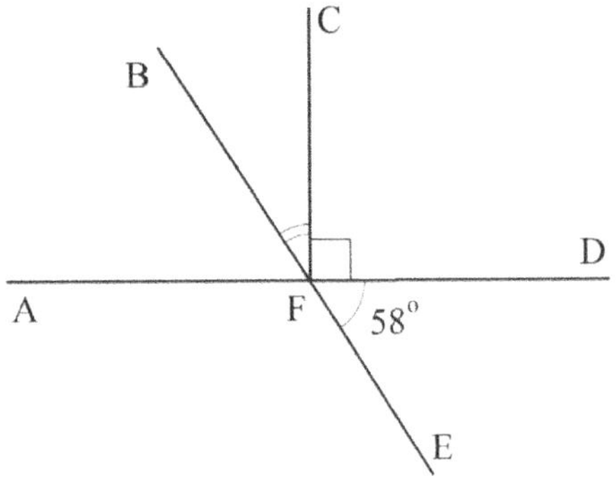

In the figure above, CF is perpendicular to FD, $m\angle EFD = 58°$. What is the measure of angle BFC?

59. A grocery store is selling apples and pears in the ratio $\frac{1}{2} : \frac{2}{3}$. On Monday, the store sells 39 kg of apples. How many kilograms of fruit does the store sell in total?

60. If $5w + 9 = 13 - 3w$, what is the value of w?

61.

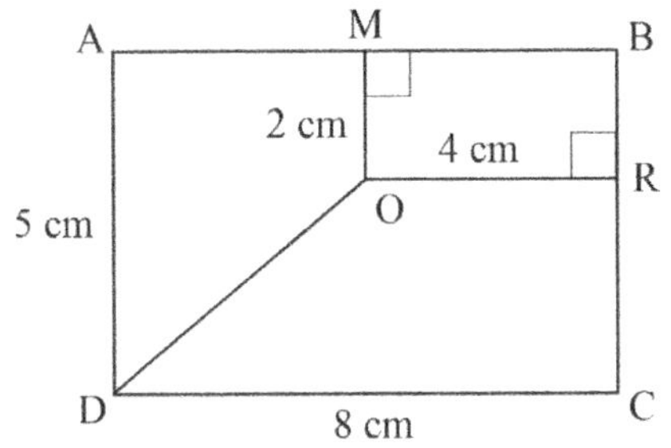

In rectangle ABCD, MO is perpendicular to AB and RO is perpendicular to BC. What is the length of DO?

62. A teacher wants to create a schedule for Tuesday. There are four subjects: Math, Art, Sports, and English. The only term is that Math cannot go straight away after Sports. How many different combinations of the schedule are possible?

406

	MULTIPLE CHOICE QUESTIONS		
	Questions 63 – 68		
63.	Gabriela cut a piece of tape 4 inches long from the 2-foot tape. What part of the tape was left? A. $\frac{1}{3}$ B. $\frac{1}{6}$ C. $\frac{2}{3}$ D. $\frac{5}{6}$	66.	The Denver Sports Store sells leggings, T-shirts and caps in the ratio 6 : 3 : 2. This season, they sold 200 more leggings than caps and T-shirts altogether. How many T-shirts did they sell this season? E. 600 F. 800 G. 1,000 H. 1,200
64.	If $a = -3$, $b = 4$ and $c = 10$, what is the value of the expression below? $$\frac{2(b^2 - a^2)}{c} + \frac{1}{2}$$ E. 1.4 F. 1.9 G. 0.9 H. 1.2	67.	A basket contain 5 red balls, 4 blue balls and 2 black balls. What is the probability that when you randomly choose two balls you will choose the 2 black balls? A. $\frac{1}{55}$ B. $\frac{2}{55}$ C. $\frac{1}{110}$ D. $\frac{2}{50}$
65.	Blake is 21 years old now. 3 years ago, his sister was as old as he will be in five years. How old will Blake's sister be in 4 years? A. 18 B. 26 C. 30 D. 33	68.	If $4x - 7y = 14$, what is y in terms of x? E. $y = \frac{4}{7}x - 14$ F. $y = 4x - 2$ G. $y = \frac{4}{7}x - 2$ H. $y = 4x - 14$

	Questions 69 – 74		
69.	Which of the following list shows only factors of both numbers 24 and 32? A. 1, 2, 3, 8 B. 1, 2, 4, 6 C. 1, 2, 4, 8 D. 1, 2, 4, 12	72.	Melanie has a fair coin and a number die. What is the probability that Melanie will flip a head and roll an even number? E. $\frac{1}{4}$ F. $\frac{1}{2}$ G. $\frac{3}{4}$ H. 1
70.	It took Brian 10 days to read a novel of 210 pages, while Sandra read the same book at a rate 17 pages per day. At these rates, how many more days will it take Sandra than Brian to read 357-page book? E. 3 F. 4 G. 5 H. 6	73.	If the radius of each circle is 6.5 cm, what is the area of the outer rectangle? A. 84.5 cm^2 B. 169 cm^2 C. 253.5 cm^2 D. 338 cm^2
71.	Maggie needed to perform 6 experiments for her biology project. For the first 5 experiments, she spent on average a 20 minutes per experiment. If she wants to decrease her average spent time to 18 minutes per experiment, how long should her 6th experiment be? A. 14 minutes B. 12 minutes C. 10 minutes D. 8 minutes	74.	On the above number line, 0.4 is the midpoint between y and z. If y is located at -0.1 and $xy : yz = 2 : 5$, where is point x located? E. -0.5 F. -0.4 G. -0.3 H. -0.2

Questions 75 – 80

75. At first, Alexia has $13. To encourage her to do her homework, her parents pay her $6 daily. After some days passed, Alexia has collected $P. Write an expression representing the number of days Alexia was doing her homework.

   A. $P - 6 \times 13$
   B. $\frac{P-13}{6}$
   C. $6P - 13$
   D. $\frac{P-6}{13}$

76. If $\frac{a}{b} = \frac{b+1}{2}$, what is the value of $2a - b$?

   E. b^2
   F. $b^2 + b$
   G. $b^2 + 2b$
   H. $b^2 + 2$

77. Karen has 4 fewer dimes than thrice the number of quarters Aidan has. If they have the same amounts in cents, how many quarters does Aidan have?

   A. 6
   B. 7
   C. 8
   D. 9

78. The pharmaceutical company lacks 8% of all their products. Of the rest of the products that enter the market, 80% are sold, and the rest are returned back. What is the total percentage of products sold?

   E. 80%
   F. 92%
   G. 85.6%
   H. 73.6%

79. Vernon draws a map on which 1.5 cm represents 240 km. If the distance between two points on the map is 2.4 cm, what is the actual distance between these points?

   A. 324 km
   B. 384 km
   C. 280 km
   D. 150 km

80.

   In right trapezoid MATH, diagonal MT divides the trapezoid into two isosceles right triangles. If the area of the triangle MTH is 36 cm^2, what is the area of the trapezoid MATH?

   E. 54 cm^2
   F. 60 cm^2
   G. 66 cm^2
   H. 72 cm^2

Questions 81 – 86

81. HOW STUDENTS GET TO SCHOOL

By bus / 135° / On foot / Biking

What percent of students prefer biking as the way to get to school?

A. 12.5%
B. 18%
C. 24.5%
D. 25%

82. Mr. Tulip has two boxes with candy. In the 1st box, he has 10 dark chocolate and 15 milk chocolate candy. In the 2nd box, he has 8 dark chocolate and 12 milk chocolate candy. If he chooses one candy from each box, what is the probability that one of them will be milk and other – chocolate?

E. 0.50
F. 0.48
G. 0.36
H. 0.24

83. If x is an even negative integer and $12 - 7x > 56$, what is greatest possible even value of x?

A. -6
B. -7
C. -8
D. -10

84. The table below shows the average temperature in two cities over the week.

	Mon	Tue	Wed	Thu	Fri	Sat	Sun
A	12°C	14°C	15°C	14°C	16°C	15°C	12°C
B	8°C	6°C	9°C	11°C	10°C	8°C	11°C

What is the difference between the mean temperatures in cities B and A?

E. 3°C
F. 4°C
G. 5°C
H. 6°C

85. $2\frac{5}{8}\left(5\frac{1}{3} - x\right) + \frac{5}{2}\left(x - \frac{4}{5}\right) =$

A. $16 + \frac{1}{8}x$
B. $16 - \frac{1}{8}x$
C. $12 + \frac{1}{8}x$
D. $12 - \frac{1}{8}x$

86. What is $\frac{1}{144}$ of 648?

E. $\frac{3^2}{2^2}$
F. $\frac{3}{2^2}$
G. $\frac{3^2}{2}$
H. $\frac{3}{2}$

	Questions 87 – 92		
87.	Among the 50 men on the street, 18 wore hats and 35 wore gloves. If 11 men had both hat and gloves, how many men wore neither hat nor gloves? A. 3 B. 8 C. 9 D. 12	90.	There are 60 people in a bus. The number of 43.75% of adults in the bus is equal to 50% of the children. How many adults are there? E. 32 F. 30 G. 28 H. 26
88.	If $x = -4$ and $y = 5$, what is the greatest number in the set below? $$\frac{x^2}{y}, \frac{x}{y^2}, \frac{x}{y}, \frac{x^2}{y^2}$$ E. $\frac{x^2}{y}$ F. $\frac{x}{y^2}$ G. $\frac{x}{y}$ H. $\frac{x^2}{y^2}$	91.	If $M - 1 = \frac{1}{K}$, what is $K + 1$ in terms of M? A. $\frac{1}{M}$ B. $\frac{M}{M+1}$ C. $\frac{M}{M-1}$ D. $\frac{1}{M+1}$
89.	How many multiples of 10 are in between -63 and 38? A. 3 B. 7 C. 9 D. 10	92.	A fruit juicer was sold with a profit of 12% for $50.40. What was the old selling price of the fruit juicer? E. $42 F. $44 G. $45 H. $48

	Questions 93 – 98		
93.	What is the surface area of 3D shape represented by its net below? 8 ft 1.5 ft 3 ft A. $36\ ft^2$ B. $40.5\ ft^2$ C. $64\ ft^2$ D. $81\ ft^2$	96.	Clarence and Bruce start climbing stairs on the 1st floor. When Clarence is on the 5th floor, Bruce is on the 4th floor. Which floor will Bruce be on when Clarence is on the 17th floor? E. 13th F. 14th G. 15th H. 16th
94.	Which of the following statements is false? E. $0.8 \times 10^4 = 8{,}000$ F. $0.03 \times 10^3 = 300$ G. $0.002 \times 10^3 = 2$ H. $0.05 \times 10^4 = 500$	97.	A 24 cm O 7 cm T G C 18 cm D 6 cm Triangles CAT and DOG are similar. Which of the following statements is false? A. The perimeter of the triangle CAT is 64 cm B. Side AT is 21 cm long C. Side DO is 8 cm long D. The perimeter of the triangle DOG is 21 cm
95.	Point $(-5, 7)$ was reflected across one of the axes. Which of the following could be the coordinates of image point? A. $(5, -7)$ B. $(5, 7)$ C. $(7, -5)$ D. $(-7, -5)$	98.	By using digits 0, 1, 2, 3 exactly once, what is the difference between the greatest 4-digit number and the smallest 4-digit number? E. 2,187 F. 2,178 G. 1,980 H. 1,890

Questions 99 – 104

99. FAVORITE PETS OF GRADE 8 STUDENTS

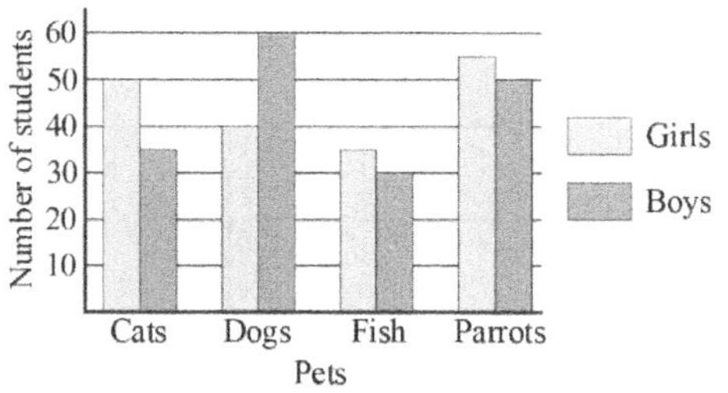

The graph above shows which pets girls and boys prefer. Which pets students like the most?

A. Cats
B. Dogs
C. Fish
D. Parrots

100. Eli has 16 coins, all of which are dimes and nickels. If her nickels were dimes and her dimes were nickels, her coins would total 20 cents more. How many dimes does Eli have?

E. 6
F. 8
G. 10
H. 12

101. If $A = \frac{5}{2}$ and $B = 6$, which of the following options represents a repeating decimal?

A. AB
B. $\frac{B}{A}$
C. $\frac{A}{B}$
D. $A + B$

102. NUMBER OF STUDENTS

Class	Number of students
Ms. Ruiz	31
Mr. Judd	28
Mrs. Kinsley	27
Mr. Harp	29
Mrs. Lee	x

If the mean number of students in all classes is 28, how many students are in Mrs. Lee class?

E. 28
F. 25
G. 24
H. 30

103. On the number line below, $zw = 1.2$, $xw = 6.5$ and $xy = 11.9$. What is zy?

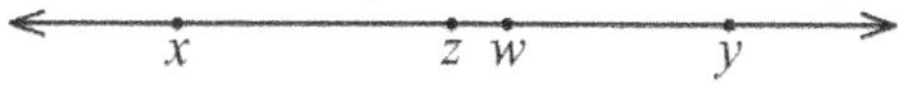

A. 5.4
B. 6.4
C. 6.6
D. 7.2

104. In a 4 L mixture, the ratio of juice to water is 1 : 4. You want the ratio of juice to all mixture be 1 : 3. Which of the following statements is true?

E. You should add 0.8 L of water
F. You should add 0.8 L of juice
G. You should add 0.4 L of water
H. You should add 0.4 L of juice

413

Questions 105 – 110

105. If $a \nabla b = \frac{1}{2}b - \frac{1}{3}a$, what is the value of $6 \nabla 9$?

A. 0
B. 1
C. −1.5
D. 2.5

106. It took Mrs. Adams 1 hour 20 minutes to bake 40 cookies. If she started baking cookies at 8 : 15 a.m., at what time will she finish baking 56 cookies?

E. At 10 : 07 a.m
F. At 10 : 02 a.m
G. At 9 : 57 a.m
H. At 9 : 52 a.m.

107. Edwin has 4 apples and 5 pears at his house. If he wants to take 2 apples or 2 pears outside, in how many different ways could he choose fruit?

A. 16
B. 32
C. 60
D. 240

108. What fraction of the rectangle is shaded?

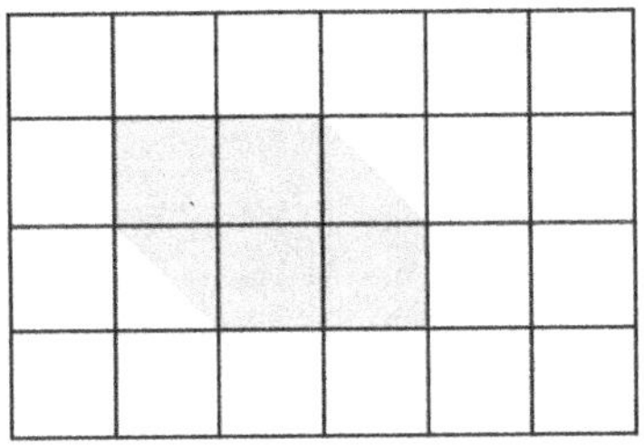

E. $\frac{1}{4}$

F. $\frac{1}{6}$

G. $\frac{5}{12}$

H. $\frac{5}{24}$

109. Nicholas has a new system of currency using tokens, marbles, and stars. The values are shown below.
2 tokens = 5 marbles
4 stars = 3 tokens
Nicholas is paying his brother 8 stars and 10 marbles. How many tokens is this payment worth?

A. 10 tokens
B. 8 tokens
C. 6 tokens
D. 5 tokens

110. A population of 75 slugs has increased by 120%. What is the total number of slugs after the increase?

E. 165
F. 150
G. 135
H. 90

Questions 111 – 114			
111.	$y = 5 - 2x$ Value 1: The value of x when $y = 17$ Value 2: The value of y when $x = 6$ Which of the following statements is true? A. Both values are equal B. The value 1 is greater C. The value 2 is greater D. Too little information to compare values 1 and 2	113.	The expression $\frac{a}{b}\left(\frac{b}{c} - \frac{b}{a}\right)$ is equivalent to… A. $\frac{c}{a} - 1$ B. $\frac{a}{c} + 1$ C. $\frac{c}{a} + 1$ D. $\frac{a}{c} - 1$
112.	 The graph below shows the temperature measurements during 12-hour period. What was the difference between the highest and lowest temperatures from 3 : 00 a.m. till 12 : 00 a.m.? E. 14°C F. 16°C G. 12°C H. 8°C	114.	Dean is going to order some pairs of socks on a website. The price of order depends on the number of pairs of socks ordered and a shipping fee for delivering the order. The amount of money, y, paid for x pairs of socks ordered on the website is given by the formula $y = 3.25x + 12$. What is the meaning of 3.25 in this formula? E. The price of one pair of socks on a website F. The price of 12 pair of socks on a website G. The shipping fee of 12 pairs of socks H. The shipping fee of one pair of socks

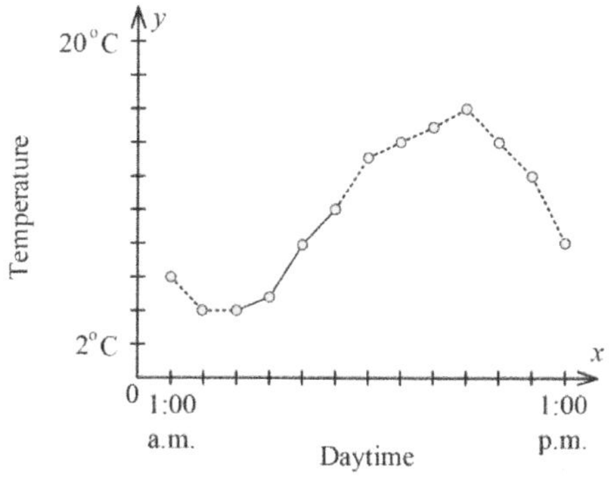

PRACTICE TEST 13

GRID-IN QUESTIONS

Questions 58 – 62

58. In the figure above, CF is perpendicular to FD, $m\angle BFC = 33°$. What is the measure of angle AFE?

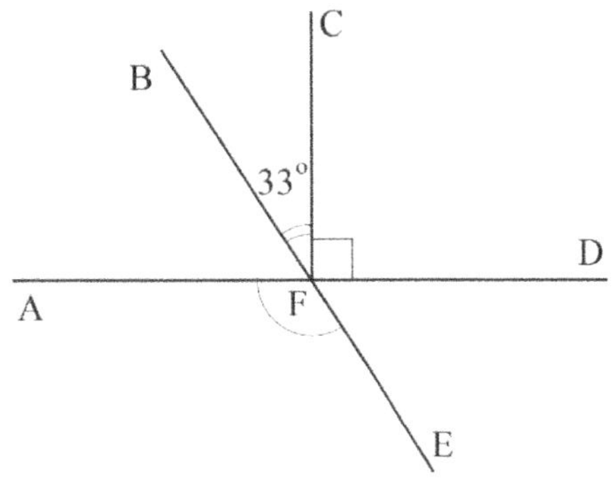

59. A grocery store is selling mangos and avocados in the ratio $\frac{2}{3} : \frac{3}{4}$. On Sunday, the store sells 126 kg of avocados. How many kilograms of mangos does the store sell on Sunday?

60. If $4u - 13 = 6u - 21$, what is the value of u?

61. In rectangle ABCD, point M is the midpoint of side AB, point R divides side BC in the ratio 2 : 3, MO is perpendicular to AB and RO is perpendicular to BC. What is the length of DO?

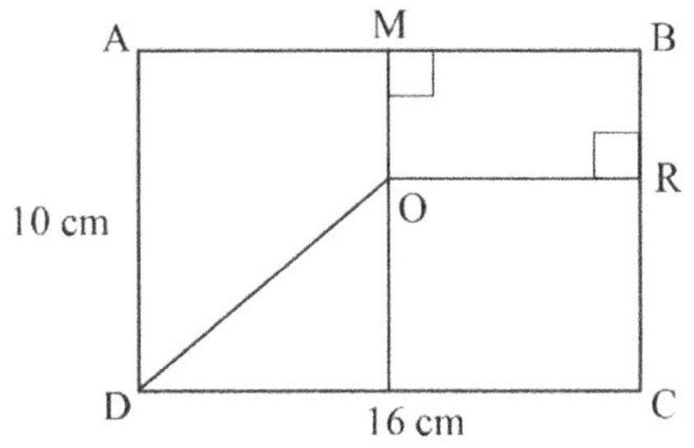

62. A teacher wants to create a schedule for Friday. There are five subjects: Math, Art, Sports, History and English. The only term is that Math cannot go straight away after Sports. How many different combinations of the schedule are possible?

	MULTIPLE CHOICE QUESTIONS		
	Questions 63 – 68		
63.	Ted cut a piece of wire 8 inches long from the 3-foot wire. What part of the wire was left? A. $\frac{5}{9}$ B. $\frac{2}{3}$ C. $\frac{7}{9}$ D. $\frac{4}{9}$	66.	The Chess Club sells banners, timers and chess in the ratio 4 : 6 : 5. This season, they sold 120 more timers than banners. How many timers and chess did they sell this season? E. 300 F. 360 G. 600 H. 660
64.	If $a = -2$, $b = 4$ and $c = -5$, what is the value of the expression below? $$\frac{1}{2} - \frac{b^2 - a^2}{2c}$$ E. 1.7 F. -0.7 G. 2.9 H. -1.9	67.	A basket contain 3 red balls, 8 blue balls and 9 black balls. What is the probability that when you randomly choose two balls you will choose the 2 red balls? A. $\frac{1}{190}$ B. $\frac{2}{190}$ C. $\frac{3}{190}$ D. $\frac{4}{190}$
65.	Isaac is 34 years old now. 6 years ago, his brother was as old as he was three years ago. How old will Isaac's brother be in 3 years? A. 31 B. 37 C. 40 D. 43	68.	If $2 - 8x + 3y = 7$, what is x in terms of y? E. $x = 3y - 5$ F. $x = 5 - 3y$ G. $x = \frac{3}{8}y - \frac{5}{8}$ H. $x = \frac{5}{8} - \frac{3}{8}y$

Questions 69 – 74

69. Which of the following list shows only factors of both numbers 40 and 48?

A. 1, 2, 4, 6
B. 1, 2, 4, 8
C. 1, 3, 4, 6
D. 1, 4, 5, 8

70. It took Ralph 8 days to read a novel of 360 pages, while Diana read the same book at a rate 50 pages per day. At these rates, how many more days will it take Ralph than Diana to read 450-page book?

E. 1
F. 2
G. 3
H. 4

71. Hanna needed to perform 5 experiments for her chemistry project. For the first 4 experiments, she spent on average a 16 minutes per experiment. If she wants to decrease her average spent time to 15 minutes per experiment, how long should her 5th experiment be?

A. 15 minutes
B. 13 minutes
C. 11 minutes
D. 9 minutes

72. Daisy has a fair coin and a number die. What is the probability that Daisy will flip a head and roll a number greater than 4?

E. $\frac{1}{6}$
F. $\frac{1}{2}$
G. $\frac{1}{3}$
H. $\frac{5}{6}$

73. If the circumference of each circle is 17π cm, what is the area of the outer rectangle?

A. $289\ cm^2$
B. $426\ cm^2$
C. $578\ cm^2$
D. $1{,}156\ cm^2$

74. On the above number line, the distance between 0.4 and x is the same as distance between y and z. If $yz = 1.5$, where could point y be located?

E. -1.3
F. -1.2
G. -1.1
H. -0.9

Questions 75 – 80

75. At first, Nicole has $24. To encourage her to help her parents, they pay her $4.50 daily. After some days passed, Nicole has collected $S. Write an expression representing the number of days Alexia was helping her parents.

   A. $\frac{24-S}{4.50}$

   B. $\frac{4.50}{24-S}$

   C. $\frac{4.50}{S-24}$

   D. $\frac{S-24}{4.50}$

76. If $\frac{a-1}{2b} = \frac{b+1}{3}$, what is the value of $2b - 3a$?

   E. $3 + 2b^2$
   F. $-3 - 2b^2$
   G. $3 - 2b^2$
   H. $-3 + 2b^2$

77. Marsha has 5 more nickels than 4 times the number of quarters Charlie has. If they have the same amounts in cents, how many nickels does Marsha have?

   A. 5
   B. 15
   C. 20
   D. 25

78. A factory that makes glasses lacks 14% of all their products. Of the rest of the products that enter the market, 90% are sold, and the rest are returned back. What is the total percentage of glasses sold?

   E. 86%
   F. 82.6%
   G. 78%
   H. 77.4%

79. Mario draws a map on which 1.8 in represents 72 miles. If the actual distance between two cities is 153 miles, what is the distance on the map between these cities?

   A. 3.825 in
   B. 3.875 in
   C. 3.915 in
   D. 3.935 in

80.

In right trapezoid MATH, diagonal MT divides the trapezoid into two isosceles right triangles. If the area of the trapezoid MATH is 48 cm^2, what is the area of the triangle MTH?

   E. 16 cm^2
   F. 20 cm^2
   G. 24 cm^2
   H. 32 cm^2

Questions 81 – 86

81. HOW STUDENTS GET TO SCHOOL

    (pie chart: By bus, On foot, Biking 60°)

    What fraction of students prefer getting by bus to school?

    A. $\frac{1}{6}$
    B. $\frac{1}{3}$
    C. $\frac{1}{2}$
    D. $\frac{2}{3}$

82. Mr. Bertram has two boxes with candy. In the 1st box, he has 4 dark chocolate and 6 milk chocolate candy. In the 2nd box, he has 3 dark chocolate and 7 milk chocolate candy. If he chooses one candy from each box, what is the probability that one of them will be milk and other – chocolate?

    E. 0.46
    F. 0.36
    G. 0.28
    H. 0.18

83. If x is an even negative integer and $15 - 5x > 28$, what is greatest possible even value of x?

    A. -2
    B. -3
    C. -4
    D. -6

84. The table below shows the average temperature in two cities over the week.

	Mon	Tue	Wed	Thu	Fri	Sat	Sun
A	22°C	25°C	24°C	24°C	25°C	26°C	22°C
B	18°C	17°C	16°C	14°C	15°C	15°C	17°C

    What is the difference between the mean temperatures in cities A and B?

    E. 4°C
    F. 6°C
    G. 8°C
    H. 10°C

85. $1\frac{3}{7}\left(2\frac{1}{3} - x\right) - \left(\frac{1}{3} + \frac{4}{7}x\right) =$

    A. $3 - \frac{6}{7}x$
    B. $3 - 2x$
    C. $3 + \frac{6}{7}x$
    D. $3 + 2x$

86. What is $\frac{1}{96}$ of 72?

    E. $\frac{3^2}{2^2}$
    F. $\frac{3}{2^2}$
    G. $\frac{3^2}{2}$
    H. $\frac{3}{2}$

Questions 87 – 92

87. Among the 80 women on the street, 37 wore skirt and 59 wore trainers. If 18 women had both skirt and trainers, how many women wore neither skirt nor trainers?

    A. 1
    B. 2
    C. 3
    D. 4

88. If $x = -3$ and $y = 4$, what is the greatest number in the set below?
    $$xy, x^2y, xy^2, x+y$$

    E. xy
    F. x^2y
    G. xy^2
    H. $x+y$

89. How many multiples of 5 are in between -22 and 16?

    A. 7
    B. 8
    C. 9
    D. 10

90. There are 45 people in a café. The number of 28% of adults in the café is equal to 35% of the children. How many children are there?

    E. 18
    F. 20
    G. 24
    H. 25

91. If $M + 1 = \frac{1}{K}$, what is $K - 1$ in terms of M?

    A. $\frac{1}{M}$
    B. $\frac{M}{M-1}$
    C. $-\frac{1}{M+1}$
    D. $-\frac{M}{M+1}$

92. A coffee machine was sold with a loss of 22% for $191.10. What was the old selling price of the coffee machine?

    E. $245
    F. $240
    G. $235
    H. $230

Questions 93 – 98			
93.	What is the surface area of 3D shape represented by its net below? 4.5 ft 2 ft 10 ft A. 74 ft^2 B. 119 ft^2 C. 139 ft^2 D. 148 ft^2	96.	Luka and Eric start climbing stairs on the 2nd floor. When Luka is on the 5th floor, Eric is on the 4th floor. Which floor will Luka be on when Eric is on the 10th floor? E. 13th F. 14th G. 15th H. 16th
94.	Which of the following statements is true? E. $1.02 \times 10^3 = 10,200$ F. $2.53 \times 10^4 = 25,030$ G. $0.304 \times 10^4 = 3,040$ H. $0.051 \times 10^3 = 5.1$	97.	A 15 cm O 14.4 cm T 2.5 cm C D 2.2 cm G Triangles CAT and DOG are similar. What is the length of the side CT? A. 11 cm B. 12.1 cm C. 12.21 cm D. 13.2 cm
95.	Point $(2, -11)$ was reflected across one of the axes. Which of the following could be the coordinates of image point? A. $(11, -2)$ B. $(-11, 2)$ C. $(-2, 11)$ D. $(-2, -11)$	98.	By using digits 0, 4, 6, 7 exactly once, what is the difference between the greatest 4-digit number and the smallest 4-digit number? E. 2,970 F. 3,537 G. 2,790 H. 3,573

Questions 99 – 104

99. FAVORITE PETS OF GRADE 8 STUDENTS

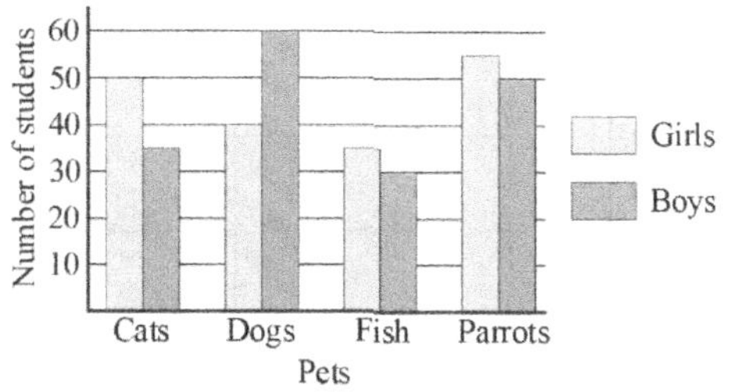

The graph above shows which pets girls and boys prefer. How many more boys prefer parrots than girls prefer fish?

A. 5
B. 10
C. 15
D. 20

100. Liam has 35 coins, all of which are pennies and nickels. If his nickels were pennies and his pennies were nickels, his coins would total 60 cents more. How many nickels does Liam have?

E. 6
F. 8
G. 10
H. 12

101. If $A = \frac{4}{3}$ and $B = 4\frac{1}{2}$, which of the following options represents a repeating decimal?

A. AB

B. $\frac{B}{A}$

C. $\frac{A}{B}$

D. $3A + B$

102. NUMBER OF STUDENTS

Class	Number of girls	Number of boys
Ms. Ruiz	13	x
Mr. Judd	16	11
Mrs. Kinsley	14	17
Mr. Harp	12	16
Mrs. Lee	15	14

If the mean numbers of girls and boys are the same, how many boys are in Mrs. Ruiz class?

E. 11
F. 12
G. 13
H. 14

103. On the number line below, $zw = 0.9$, $xw = 5.6$ and $xy = 10.1$. What is zy?

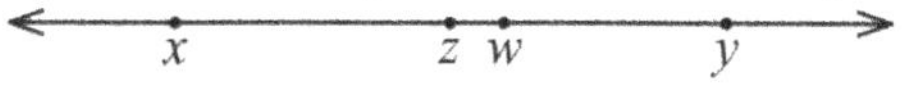

A. 4.5
B. 5.4
C. 6.3
D. 7.2

104. In a 5 L mixture, the ratio of juice to water is 2 : 3. You want the ratio of juice to water be 3 : 4. How much juice should you add?

E. 0.25 L
F. 0.5 L
G. 0.75 L
H. 1 L

Questions 105 – 110

105. If $a \nabla b = \frac{1}{3}b - \frac{1}{4}a$, what is the value of $12\nabla 24$?

A. 12
B. −2
C. −1
D. 5

106. It took Mrs. Lucas 1 hour 40 minutes to bake 50 cookies. If she started baking cookies at 9 : 25 a.m., at what time will she finish baking 40 cookies?

E. At 10 : 25 a.m
F. At 10 : 35 a.m
G. At 10 : 45 a.m
H. At 10 : 55 a.m.

107. Seth has 4 apples and 5 pears at his house. If he wants to take 2 apples and 2 pears outside, in how many different ways could he choose fruit?

A. 16
B. 32
C. 60
D. 240

108. What fraction of the rectangle is shaded?

E. $\frac{1}{4}$

F. $\frac{1}{6}$

G. $\frac{7}{24}$

H. $\frac{5}{24}$

109. Jose has a new system of currency using tokens, marbles, and stars. The values are shown below.

3 tokens = 5 marbles
7 stars = 2 tokens

Jose is paying his sister 21 stars and 15 marbles. How many tokens is this payment worth?

A. 15 tokens
B. 12 tokens
C. 9 tokens
D. 6 tokens

110. A population of 120 blue rats has decreased by 15%. What is the final number of blue rats after the decrease?

E. 108
F. 102
G. 98
H. 92

Questions 111 – 114

111.
$y = 3x + 1$
Value 1: The value of x when $y = -11$
Value 2: The value of y when $x = -2$
Which of the following statements is true?

A. Both values are equal
B. The value 1 is greater
C. The value 2 is greater
D. Too little information to compare values 1 and 2

112.

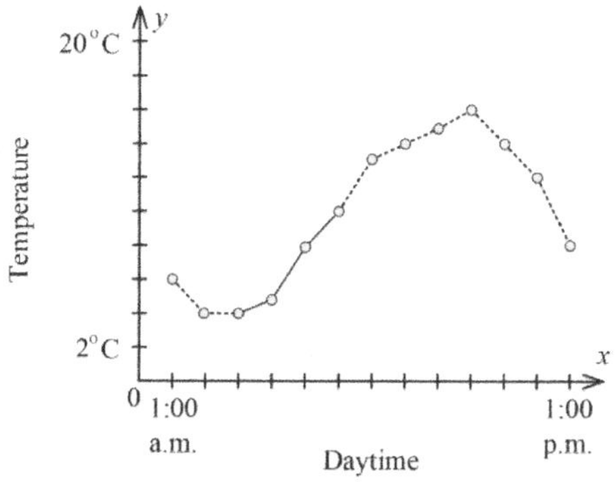

The graph below shows the temperature measurements during 12-hour period. What was the highest temperature from 1 : 00 a.m. till 8 : 00 a.m.?

E. 18°C
F. 16°C
G. 14°C
H. 12°C

113. The expression $\frac{2}{a}\left(\frac{2a}{b} - \frac{b}{2a}\right)$ is equivalent to…

A. $\frac{4a^2}{b} - b$

B. $\frac{4}{b} - \frac{b}{a^2}$

C. $\frac{4a}{b} - \frac{b}{a}$

D. $4a - \frac{b}{a^2}$

114. Cedric is going to order some number of tennis balls on a website. The price of order depends on the number of balls ordered and a shipping fee for delivering the order. The amount of money, y, paid for x tennis balls ordered on the website is given by the formula $y = 0.32x + 13$. What is the meaning of 13 in this formula?

E. The price of one ball on a website
F. The price of 13 balls on a website
G. The shipping fee of order
H. The shipping fee of delivering order of 13 balls

PRACTICE TEST 14

GRID-IN QUESTIONS

Questions 58 – 62

58.

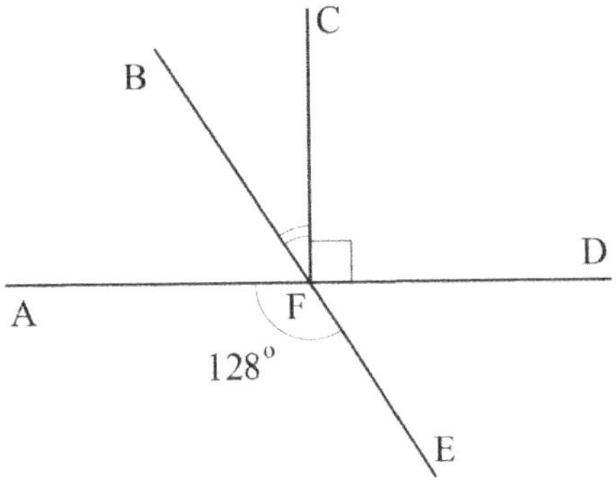

In the figure above, CF is perpendicular to FD, $m\angle AFE = 128°$. What is the measure of angle BFC?

59. In the restaurant, the ratio of meat dishes to fish dishes sold is $\frac{3}{4} : \frac{1}{3}$. On Saturday, the restaurant sells 84 fish dishes. How many meat dishes does the restaurant sell on Saturday?

60. If $5 - 3v = 4v - 23$, what is the value of v?

61.

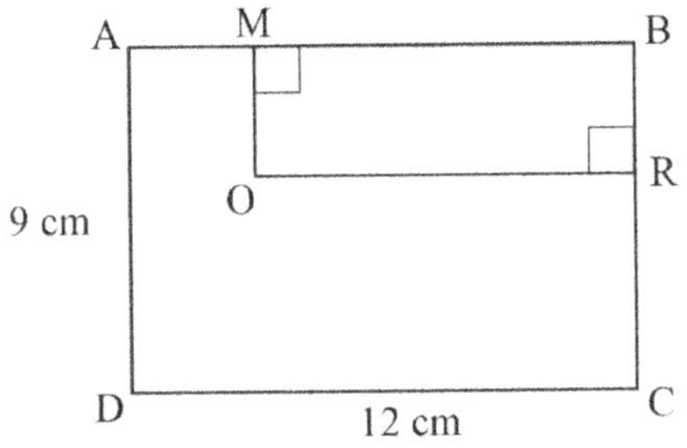

In rectangle ABCD, point M divides the side AB in the ratio 1 : 3, point R divides side BC in the ratio 1 : 2, MO is perpendicular to AB and RO is perpendicular to BC. What is the perimeter of quadrilateral BROM?

62. There are 6 paratroopers on the board of the plane, 2 of which have to jump one after another. In how many different ways it can be done?

MULTIPLE CHOICE QUESTIONS

Questions 63 – 68

63. 1 gram = 0.035 ounce
How many ounces are in 35 grams?

A. 0.001
B. 1,225
C. 1.225
D. 1,000

64. If $a = -5$, $b = 2$ and $c = -4$, what is the value of the expression below?

$$\frac{a^2c}{b^2} - \frac{1}{2}$$

E. 24.5
F. −25.5
G. −24.5
H. 25.5

65. Craig is 8 years old and Albert is 3 years older than Craig. In how many years will the sum of their ages be 31?

A. 12
B. 10
C. 8
D. 6

66. In the pizzeria, the ratio of children to men is 4 : 1 and the ratio of children to women is 3 : 2. What is the ratio of men to women in the pizzeria?

E. 4 : 3
F. 3 : 4
G. 3 : 2
H. 2 : 3

67. In the school, approximately 60% of students went to school on foot. 2 students of this school were chosen at random. What is the probability that these two students went to school on foot?

A. 0.6
B. 0.36
C. 0.12
D. 0.06

68. If $5 - 10x + y = 7$, what is x in terms of y?

E. $x = 0.2 + 0.1y$
F. $x = -0.2 + 0.1y$
G. $x = 0.2 - 0.1y$
H. $x = -0.2 - 0.1y$

Questions 69 – 74

69.	Which of the following numbers is not a multiple of 12? A. 528 B. 576 C. 624 D. 644	72.	The spinner has three equal sections painted in red, green and blue. Chase spins this spinner twice. What is the sample space for this event? (Use notation R = Red, G = Green, B = Blue) E. $\{R, G, B\}$ F. $\{RR, GG, BB\}$ G. $\{RG, GR, RB, BR, GB, BG\}$ H. $\{RR, GG, BB, RB, BR, RG, GR, GB, BG\}$
70.	A group of 6 students took 18 days to finish a scientific project. After 4 days, 2 students left the group. How many more days did it take the remaining students to finish the project? E. 4 F. 5 G. 6 H. 7	73.	If the radius of each semicircle is 9 cm, what is the area of the outer rectangle? A. $324\ cm^2$ B. $243\ cm^2$ C. $162\ cm^2$ D. $81\ cm^2$
71.	The average height of 4 maples and 6 pines is 4.5 m. If the average height of 6 pines is 5.8 m, what is the average height of 4 maples? A. 2.55 m B. 2.85 m C. 3.15 m D. 3.45 m	74.	On the above number line, the distance between -1.2 and y is the same as the distance between x and z. If x is located at -0.3, what is yz? E. 0.9 F. 1.2 G. 1.8 H. 2.4

Questions 75 – 80

75. On Monday, a jacket costed $P and a shirt costed $S. On Saturday, the jacket was discounted by 25%, and the shirt was discounted by $\frac{1}{3}$. What is the total price of the jacket and shirt on Saturday?

    A. $\frac{1}{4}P + \frac{1}{3}S$

    B. $\frac{3}{4}P + \frac{1}{3}S$

    C. $\frac{1}{4}P + \frac{2}{3}S$

    D. $\frac{3}{4}P + \frac{2}{3}S$

76. If $\frac{a}{b+2} = \frac{a+2}{b}$, what is the value of $a + b$?

    E. −4
    F. −2
    G. 2
    H. 4

77. In total, Marlin has 30 five-dollar and ten-dollar bills. If he has $205, how many five-dollar bills does Marlin have?

    A. 21
    B. 19
    C. 11
    D. 9

78. At the end of 2018 year, Beverly received $1,600 bonus. At the end of the 2019 year, she received $2,000 bonus. By what percent did her bonus increase from 2018 to 2019?

    E. 20%
    F. 25%
    G. 120%
    H. 125%

79. Teo draws a map on which 2 in represents 45 miles. If the distance on the map between two cities is 9 in, what is the actual distance between these cities?

    A. 100 miles
    B. 150.5 miles
    C. 202.5 miles
    D. 210 miles

80.

    In right trapezoid MATH, diagonal MT divides the trapezoid into two isosceles right triangles. If the area of the trapezoid MATH is 84 cm^2, what is the area of the triangle MAT?

    E. 28 cm^2
    F. 35 cm^2
    G. 42 cm^2
    H. 56 cm^2

Questions 81 – 86

81. FAVORITE FRUIT

Pie chart: Apricots 130°, Peaches 80°, Nectarines (remaining)

What fraction of students prefer nectarines?

A. $\frac{2}{9}$
B. $\frac{7}{12}$
C. $\frac{5}{9}$
D. $\frac{5}{12}$

82. Mr. Nijman has two boxes with marbles. In the 1st box, he has 12 red marbles and 28 black marbles. In the 2nd box, he has 21 red marbles and 29 black marbles. If he chooses one marble from each box, what is the probability that both marbles will be red?

E. 0.126
F. 0.294
G. 0.406
H. 0.72

83. How many negative integers are the solutions to the inequality $5 - 3x < 12$?

A. 1
B. 2
C. 3
D. 4

84. The table below shows the number of pages Kerry reads per week.

Mon	Tue	Wed	Thu	Fri	Sat	Sun
32	35	48	42	58	x	64

If the mean number of pages read on weekend is 15 more than the mean number of pages read from Monday till Friday, what is the value of x?

E. 52
F. 54
G. 56
H. 58

85. $2\frac{2}{5}\left(8\frac{3}{4} + x\right) + \frac{3}{5}x =$

A. $21 + x$
B. $3(7 - x)$
C. $3(7 + x)$
D. $21 - x$

86. What is $\frac{1}{2^5}$ of 432?

E. $\frac{3^4}{2}$
F. $\frac{3^3}{2}$
G. $\frac{3^2}{2}$
H. $\frac{3}{2}$

Questions 87 – 92

87. 28 students wrote a math test. 9 students gave wrong answers to the 1st problem and 12 gave wrong answers to the 2nd problem. If 14 students solve the two problems correctly, how many students solve both problems incorrectly?

    A. 5
    B. 7
    C. 11
    D. 14

88. If $x = \frac{1}{2}$ and $y = -4$, what is the smallest number in the set below?
    $$xy, x^2y, xy^2, x + y$$

    E. xy
    F. x^2y
    G. xy^2
    H. $x + y$

89. How many multiples of 3 are in between -11 and 13?

    A. 7
    B. 8
    C. 9
    D. 10

90. In the theatre, 40% of visitors have opera glasses. 12% of the remaining have monocles. What percent of all visitors have monocles?

    E. 7.2%
    F. 14.4%
    G. 28%
    H. 48%

91. If $M - 2 = \frac{1}{K}$, what is $\frac{K}{2}$ in terms of M?

    A. $\frac{2}{M-2}$

    B. $\frac{1}{2(M-2)}$

    C. $\frac{1}{2M} - 2$

    D. $\frac{2}{M} - 2$

92. Mr. King and his wife together earn $4,128 per month. If Mr. King earns 8% less money than his wife per month does, how much does Mrs. King earn per month?

    E. $2,050
    F. $2,100
    G. $2,150
    H. $2,200

431

Questions 93 – 98

93. What is the surface area of the regular square pyramid represented by its net below?

   4 cm
   6 cm

   A. 48 cm^2
   B. 84 cm^2
   C. 96 cm^2
   D. 132 cm^2

94. In Winslow, there are 2.9×10^2 people per square kilometer. The area of the city is 3.2×10^1 km^2. What is total population in Winslow?

   E. 92
   F. 928
   G. 9,280
   H. 92,800

95. Point $(-5, -6)$ was translated along one of the axes to form point $(-5, -1)$. Which of the following statements is true?

   A. It was translated 5 units to the left
   B. It was translated 5 units to the right
   C. It was translated 5 units up
   D. It was translated 5 units down

96. Matthew goes up from the 2nd to the 10th floor in 40 seconds. In how many seconds will Matthew go up from the 3rd to the 7th floor?

   E. 20 seconds
   F. 25 seconds
   G. 28 seconds
   H. 32 seconds

97.

   A
   15 cm
   14.4 cm
   C   T
              D
   O
   2.5 cm
   2.2 cm
   G

   Triangles CAT and DOG are similar. What is the length of the side OD?

   A. 2.3 cm
   B. 2.35 cm
   C. 2.4 cm
   D. 2.45 cm

98. The product of two positive integers is 36. What is smallest possible sum of these two numbers?

   E. 12
   F. 13
   G. 20
   H. 37

Questions 99 – 104

99. **FAVORITE STUDENTS' SUBJECTS**

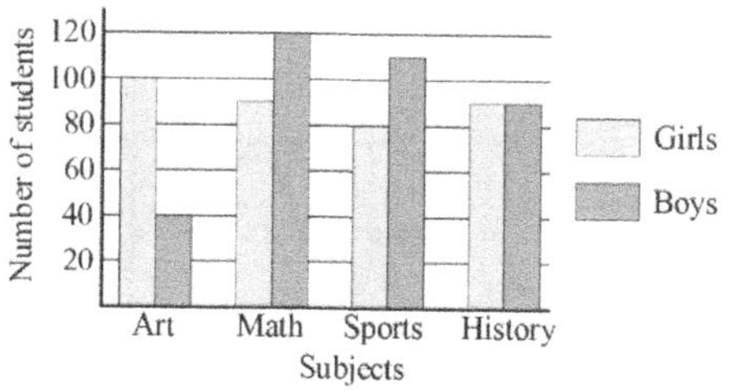

The graph above shows, which school subjects girls and boys prefer. What is the most preferred school subject?

A. Art
B. Math
C. Sports
D. History

100. Perris had 17 more nickels than dimes. In total, she had $3.55 in nickels and dimes. How many nickels did she have?

E. 18
F. 25
G. 28
H. 35

101. If $A = 0.2$ and $B = 1.1$, which of the following options represents a repeating decimal?

A. AB
B. $\frac{B}{A}$
C. $\frac{A}{B}$
D. $A + B$

102. **NUMBER OF STUDENTS**

Class	Number of girls	Number of boys
Ms. Ruiz	9	22
Mr. Judd	17	14
Mrs. Kinsley	13	18
Mr. Harp	16	15
Mrs. Lee	a	11

If the mean numbers of girls and boys are the same, how many girls are in Mrs. Lee class?

E. 15
F. 16
G. 20
H. 25

103. On the number line below, $zw = 2xy$, $yz = 3xy$. What is the ratio of $xz : yw$?

A. 3 : 4
B. 4 : 5
C. 5 : 6
D. 6 : 7

104. In a 2 L mixture, there are 200 ml less juice than water. If you want the ratio of juice to water be 3 : 5, how much water should you add?

E. 0.3 L
F. 0.4 L
G. 0.5 L
H. 0.6 L

Questions 105 – 110

105. If $a \nabla b = \frac{1}{3}(b - a) + 1$, what is the value of $6 \nabla 12$?

A. −1
B. 1
C. 2
D. 3

106. Blanche reached the shopping center at 10 : 15 a.m. She shopped for 160 minutes and arrived at home at 1 : 30 p.m. How long did it take Blanche to go home from the market?

E. 30 minutes
F. 35 minutes
G. 40 minutes
H. 45 minutes

107. Lincoln has 3 apples, 4 pears and 5 peaches at his house. He wants to take 2 different fruit to school. In how many different ways could he choose them?

A. 47
B. 59
C. 66
D. 73

108. What fraction of the rectangle is shaded?

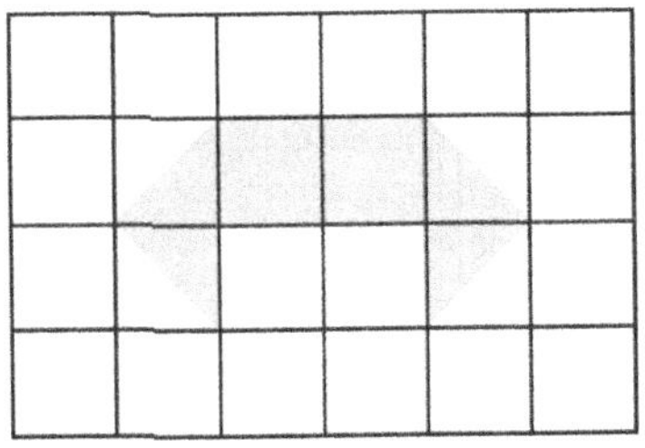

E. $\frac{1}{4}$
F. $\frac{1}{6}$
G. $\frac{7}{24}$
H. $\frac{5}{24}$

109. Owen has a new system of currency using tokens, marbles, stars, and cards. The values are shown below.
    4 tokens = 3 marbles = 2 cards
    4 stars = 6 tokens = 1 card
Owen has 12 stars, 9 marbles and 10 tokens. How many cards does Owen have?

A. 9 cards
B. 10 cards
C. 11 cards
D. 12 cards

110. In the triangle, 1st angle is 150% of the 2nd angle and 75% of the 3rd angle. What is the measure of the greatest angle in the triangle?

E. 100°
F. 90°
G. 80°
H. 70°

434

	Questions 111 – 114		
111.	$12x + 10y = 1$ Value 1: The value of x when $y = \frac{1}{5}$ Value 2: The value of y when $x = \frac{1}{6}$ Which of the following statements is true? A. Both values are equal B. The value 1 is greater C. The value 2 is greater D. Too little information to compare values 1 and 2	113.	The expression $\left(\frac{1}{a} - \frac{1}{b}\right) \div \frac{a+b}{ab}$ is equivalent to… A. $\frac{a+b}{a-b}$ B. $\frac{a+b}{b-a}$ C. $\frac{b-a}{a+b}$ D. $\frac{a-b}{a+b}$
112.	The graph below shows the distance Rowan travelled during 12-hour period. How many kilometers did he travel from 11 : 00 a.m. till 6 : 00 p.m.? E. 3.5 km F. 4 km G. 4.5 km H. 5 km	114.	Every morning you take a bus and travels to school. The distance to your school can be modeled by the equation $d = 10 - 50h$, where d is the distance travelled in kilometers and h is the number of hours the bus have travelled. What is the meaning of 50 in this formula? E. The distance from school to house F. The distance travelled in 50 minutes G. The distance travelled per hour H. The distance left to travel

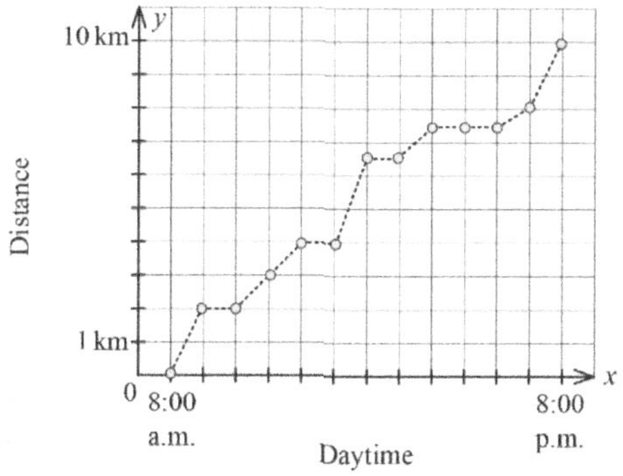

PRACTICE TEST 15

GRID-IN QUESTIONS

Questions 58 – 62

58.

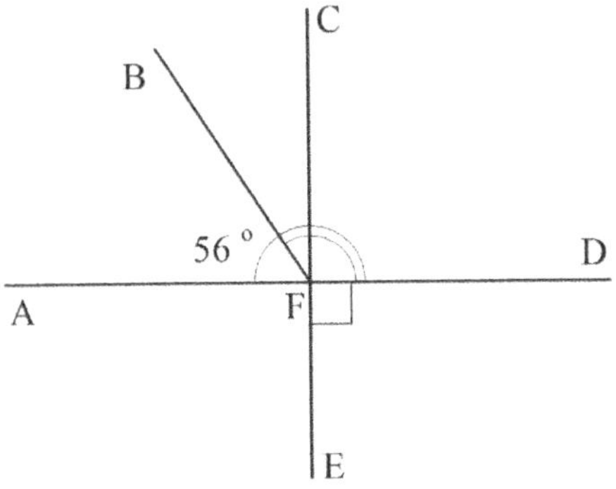

In the figure above, FE is perpendicular to FD, $m\angle AFB = 56°$. What is the measure of angle BFD?

59. In the restaurant, the ratio of meat dishes to fish dishes sold is $\frac{4}{5} : \frac{1}{2}$. On Sunday, the restaurant sells 156 meat and fish dishes. How many fish dishes does the restaurant sell on Sunday?

60. If $\frac{1}{2}a - 4 = -\frac{1}{4}a - 1$, what is the value of a?

61.

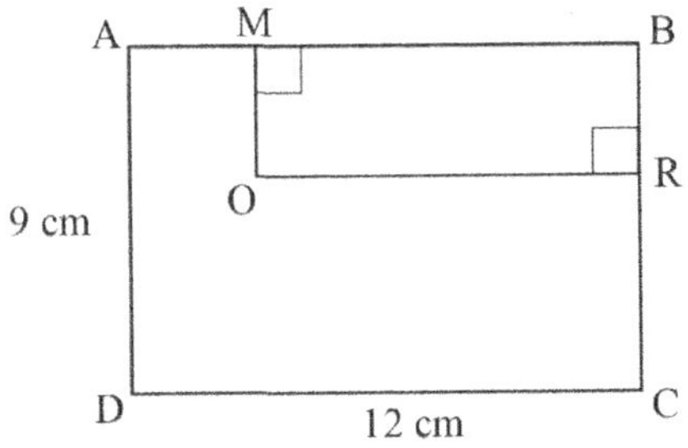

In rectangle ABCD, point M divides the side AB in the ratio 1 : 3, point R divides side BC in the ratio 1 : 2, MO is perpendicular to AB and RO is perpendicular to BC. What is the area of AMORCD?

62. There are 7 paratroopers on the board of the plane, 3 of which have to jump one after another. In how many different ways it can be done?

MULTIPLE CHOICE QUESTIONS
Questions 63 – 68

63.
$$1 \text{ inch} = 2.54 \text{ cm}$$
How many inches are in 12.7 centimeters?

A. 0.2
B. 2
C. 0.5
D. 5

64. If $a = -2$, $b = 3$ and $c = -5$, what is the value of the expression below?
$$\frac{a-b}{c^2} + 1\frac{1}{5}$$

E. 1
F. 1.2
G. 1.4
H. 1.6

65. Cliff is 11 years old and Melanie is 2 years younger than Cliff. In how many years will the sum of their ages be 32?

A. 12
B. 10
C. 8
D. 6

66. In the pizzeria, the ratio of children to men is 3 : 1 and the ratio of children to women is 4 : 3. What is the ratio of women to men in the pizzeria?

E. 4 : 9
F. 3 : 8
G. 9 : 4
H. 8 : 3

67. In the school, approximately 20% of students went to school on foot. 2 students of this school were chosen at random. What is the probability that these two students didn't go to school on foot?

A. 0.04
B. 0.16
C. 0.64
D. 0.8

68. If $8 = 1 - 2x + 4y$, what is x in terms of y?

E. $x = 2y + 3.5$
F. $x = -2y + 3.5$
G. $x = -2y - 3.5$
H. $x = 2y - 3.5$

Questions 69 – 74

69.	Which of the following numbers is not a multiple of 15? A. 570 B. 630 C. 725 D. 765	72.	The spinner has seven equal sections among which three are painted in red, two – in green, one – in blue and one – in yellow. Teo spins this spinner once. What is the sample space for this event? (Use notation R = Red, G = Green, B = Blue, Y = Yellow) E. $\{R, G, B, Y\}$ F. $\{R, R, R, G, G, B, Y\}$ G. $\{R, G, B\}$ H. $\{R, R, G, G, G, B, Y\}$
70.	A group of 5 students took 15 days to finish a project. After 9 days, 3 students left the group. How many days did it take the students to finish the project in this case? E. 15 F. 18 G. 22 H. 24	73.	If the perimeter of the outer rectangle is 18 cm, what is the radius of each semicircle? A. 3.6 cm B. 3 cm C. 2.4 cm D. 1.8 cm
71.	The average height of 3 bushes and 5 trees is 3.5 m. If the average height of 5 trees is 4.4 m, what is the average height of 3 bushes? A. 2 m B. 2.1 m C. 2.2 m D. 2.3 m	74.	On the above number line, points x and y divide the segment wz into three equal parts. If $xz = 2.8$ and point w is located at -1.2, what is the location of point z? E. 2.4 F. 2.8 G. 3 H. 3.2

Questions 75 – 80

75. At the sale, there was a 40% discount on a T-shirts worth $T each and 30% on caps worth $C each. What is the discount price of m T-shirts and n caps?

   A. $0.4nT + 0.3mC$
   B. $0.4mT + 0.3nC$
   C. $0.6nT + 0.7mC$
   D. $0.6mT + 0.7nC$

76. If $\frac{2a}{b} = \frac{b-1}{2}$, what is the value of $\frac{1}{a}$?

   E. $\frac{b^2-b}{4}$
   F. $\frac{4}{b^2-b}$
   G. $b^2 - b$
   H. $\frac{1}{b^2-b}$

77. In total, Penelope has 36 five-dollar and ten-dollar bills. She has 4 more five-dollar bills than ten-dollar bills. How much does Penelope have in total?

   A. $290
   B. $280
   C. $270
   D. $260

78. At the end of November, Marcus received $120 bonus. At the end of December, he received $390 bonus. By what percent did his bonus increase from November to December?

   E. 120%
   F. 125%
   G. 220%
   H. 225%

79. Phil draws a map on which 0.5 in represents 10 miles. If the distance on the map between two cities is 8 in, what is the actual distance between these cities?

   A. 40 miles
   B. 80 miles
   C. 120 miles
   D. 160 miles

80. In isosceles trapezoid MATH, which triangle has the same area as triangle RAT?

   E. MAR
   F. HAT
   G. RTH
   H. MAH

Questions 81 – 86

81. FAVORITE FRUIT

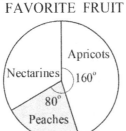

What fraction of students prefer nectarines or peaches?

A. $\frac{2}{9}$
B. $\frac{4}{9}$
C. $\frac{5}{9}$
D. $\frac{7}{9}$

82. Mr. Palmer has two boxes with marbles. In the 1st box, he has 32 red marbles and 18 black marbles. In the 2nd box, he has 7 red marbles and 13 black marbles. If he chooses one marble from each box, what is the probability that both marbles will be black?

E. 0.182
F. 0.234
G. 0.36
H. 0.91

83. How many positive integers are the solutions to the inequality $7 > -11 + 3x$?

A. 6
B. 5
C. 4
D. 3

84. The table below shows the time (in minutes) Dylan usually spent on homework.

Mon	Tue	Wed	Thu	Fri	Sat	Sun
45	50	80	75	25	0	x

If the mean time spent is 45 minutes, what is the value of x?

E. 40 minutes
F. 45 minutes
G. 50 minutes
H. 55 minutes

85. $\dfrac{\left(3\frac{1}{4} - \frac{13}{2}\right)}{1\frac{5}{8}} \times 2^3 =$

A. -4
B. 4
C. -16
D. 16

86. What is the lowest common multiple of $2^3 \times 3^2$ and $2^2 \times 3^3$?

E. $2^2 \times 3^2$
F. $2^3 \times 3^3$
G. $2^4 \times 3^4$
H. $2^5 \times 3^5$

	Questions 87 – 92		
87.	45 students wrote a science test. 17 students gave wrong answers to the 1st problem and 21 gave wrong answers to the 2nd problem. If 8 students solve the two problems incorrectly, how many students solve both problems correctly? A. 15 B. 13 C. 11 D. 9	90.	In the theatre, 55% of visitors are female. 24% of males read theatrical booklet. What percent of all visitors are males, which read theatrical booklet? E. 10.8% F. 13.2% G. 24% H. 45%
88.	If $x = -5$ and $y = 0.4$, which of the following statements is true? E. $x + y$ is a positive number F. xy is a positive number G. $y^2 + x$ is a negative number H. $x^2 + y$ is a negative number	91.	If $A + B = 2A - 5B$, what is $\frac{A}{B}$? A. $\frac{1}{6}$ B. 2 C. $\frac{1}{2}$ D. 6
89.	A school club has 24 girls and x boys. The president of the club wants to divide students into groups with each group containing 6 girls and 5 boys. If no one left over, what could be the value of x? A. 12 B. 18 C. 20 D. 30	92.	Mrs. Helm and her husband together earn $68,880 per year. If Mrs. Helm earns 5% more money than her husband per year does, how much does Mr. Helm earn per year? E. $32,860 F. $33,600 G. $35,280 H. $36,020

Questions 93 – 98

93. If the lateral area of the regular square pyramid represented by its net below is 90 cm^2, what is the base area?

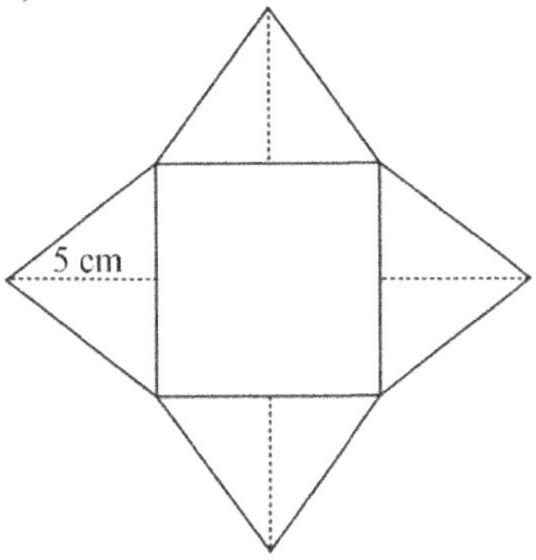

    A. 36 cm^2
    B. 49 cm^2
    C. 64 cm^2
    D. 81 cm^2

94. In Sacramento, there are 5.3×10^3 people per square mile. The area of the city is $10^2 \ mi^2$. What is total population in Sacramento?

    E. 5,300,000
    F. 530,000
    G. 53,000
    H. 5,300

95. Point $(x, -4)$ was translated 6 units to the left to get point $(-4, -4)$. What is the value of x?

    A. -10
    B. -6
    C. -2
    D. 2

96. Using only two-cent coins and five-cent coins, how many price values between 10 cents and 20 cents inclusive can you form?

    E. 6
    F. 7
    G. 10
    H. 11

97. On the above diagram, AD = 35 cm. What is the length of the side OD?

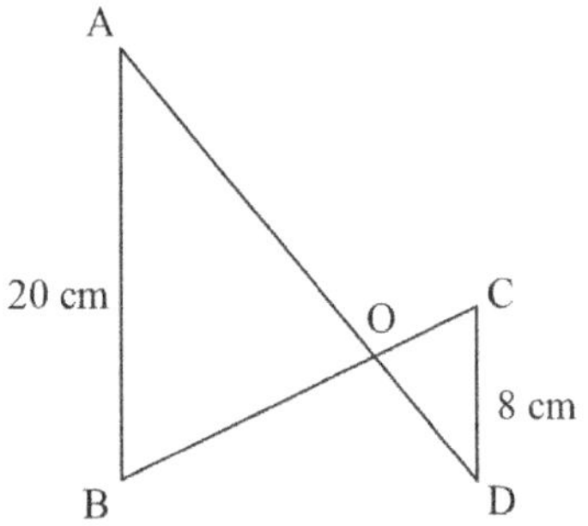

    A. 12 cm
    B. 11 cm
    C. 10 cm
    D. 9 cm

98. The product of two positive integers is 40. What is greatest possible sum of these two numbers?

    E. 13
    F. 14
    G. 22
    H. 41

Questions 99 – 104

99. **FAVORITE STUDENTS' SUBJECTS**

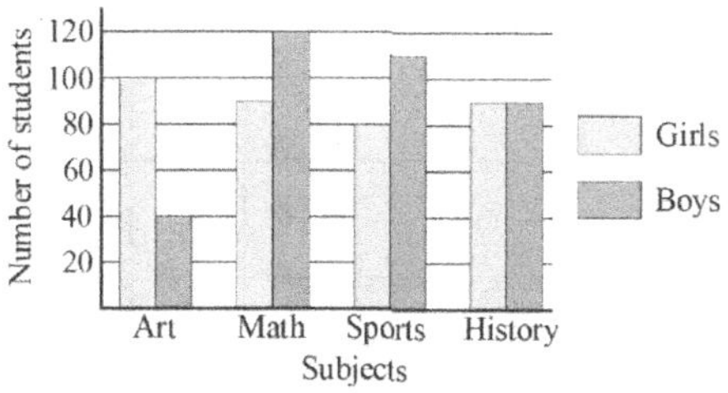

The graph above shows, which school subjects girls and boys prefer. How many more boys, which prefer Math than girls, which prefer Sports?

A. 10
B. 20
C. 30
D. 40

100. Emma had 12 more nickels than dimes and 4 less dimes than quarters. In total, she had $4.80. How many quarters did she have?

E. 8
F. 12
G. 16
H. 20

101. If $A = -3.5$ and $B = \frac{1}{7}$, which of the following options does not represent a terminating decimal?

A. AB

B. $\frac{1}{AB}$

C. $\frac{A}{B}$

D. $\frac{B}{A}$

102. **NUMBER OF STUDENTS**

Class	Number of girls	Number of boys
Ms. Ruiz	11	19
Mr. Judd	a	13
Mrs. Kinsley	14	12
Mr. Harp	15	b
Mrs. Lee	17	16

If the mean numbers of girls and boys are the same, how many more girls are in Mr. Judd's class than boys in Mr. Harp's class?

E. 2
F. 3
G. 4
H. 5

103. On the number line below, $zw = 1.5xy$, $yz = 2.5xy$. What is the ratio of $xw : yw$?

$\xleftarrow{\hspace{3cm}} \overset{\bullet}{x} \quad \overset{\bullet}{y} \qquad \overset{\bullet}{z} \quad \overset{\bullet}{w} \xrightarrow{\hspace{3cm}}$

A. 3 : 4
B. 4 : 5
C. 5 : 4
D. 4 : 3

104. In a 2.5 L mixture, there are 400 ml less juice than water. If you want the ratio of juice to water be 1 : 1, how much juice should you add?

E. 0.3 L
F. 0.4 L
G. 0.5 L
H. 0.6 L

Questions 105 – 110

105. If $a\nabla b = \frac{1}{2}(-b - (-a))$, what is the value of $10\nabla(-6)$?

  A. 8
  B. 2
  C. −2
  D. −8

106. A boat travels for 2 hours with a current of 2 mph and then returns the same distance upstream in 150 minutes. What is the boat's speed in calm water?

  E. 20 mph
  F. 19 mph
  G. 18 mph
  H. 17 mph

107. Lincoln has 7 apples, and 5 peaches at his house. He wants to take two fruit to school. In how many different ways could he choose it?

  A. 12
  B. 35
  C. 66
  D. 132

108. What percent of the rectangle is shaded?

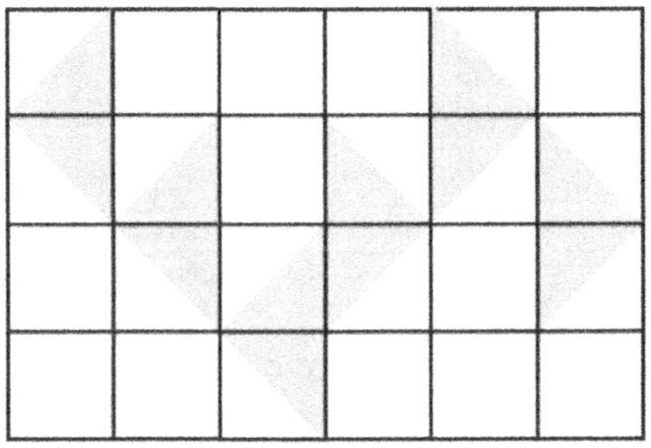

  E. 12%
  F. 18%
  G. 20%
  H. 25%

109. Diana has a new system of currency using tokens, marbles, stars, and cards. The values are shown below.
  3 tokens = 2 marbles = 4 cards
  5 stars = 2 tokens = 3 cards
Diana has 14 cards. Which of the following statements is false about Diana's collection?

  A. Diana has 10 tokens
  B. Diana has 4 marbles and 10 stars
  C. Diana has 4 tokens and 5 marbles
  D. Diana has 8 tokens and 1 marble

110. In the triangle, 1st angle is 300% of the 2nd angle and 60% of the 3rd angle. What is the measure of the smallest angle in the triangle?

  E. 100°
  F. 60°
  G. 40°
  H. 20°

Questions 111 – 114

111.
$$5x - 6y = 1$$
<u>Value 1:</u> The value of x when $y = 1\frac{1}{2}$
<u>Value 2:</u> The value of y when $x = 2\frac{3}{5}$
Which of the following statements is true?

A. Both values are equal
B. The value 2 is greater
C. The value 1 is greater
D. Too little information to compare values 1 and 2

113. The expression $\frac{2}{a} \div \frac{1}{b} - \frac{2}{b} \div \frac{1}{a}$ is equivalent to…

A. $2\left(\frac{b}{a} - \frac{a}{b}\right)$

B. $\frac{2}{ab}$

C. 0

D. $2\left(\frac{a}{b} - \frac{b}{a}\right)$

112.

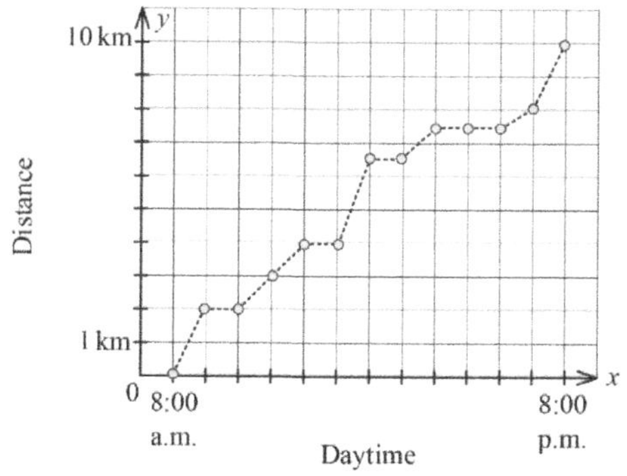

The graph below shows the distance Harper travelled during 12-hour period. During this period, how long did he not move?

E. 3 hours
F. 4 hours
G. 5 hours
H. 6 hours

114. Jakub wants to organize a party. If each of the 20 guests contributes $12, Jakub must add $60. He wants to reduce everyone's contribution to no more than $10. If Jakub adds the same amount as before, what is the minimum number of additional guests he should invite?

E. 2
F. 3
G. 4
H. 5

PRACTICE TEST 16

GRID-IN QUESTIONS

Questions 58 – 62

58. In the figure above, line a is perpendicular to line b. What is the value of x?

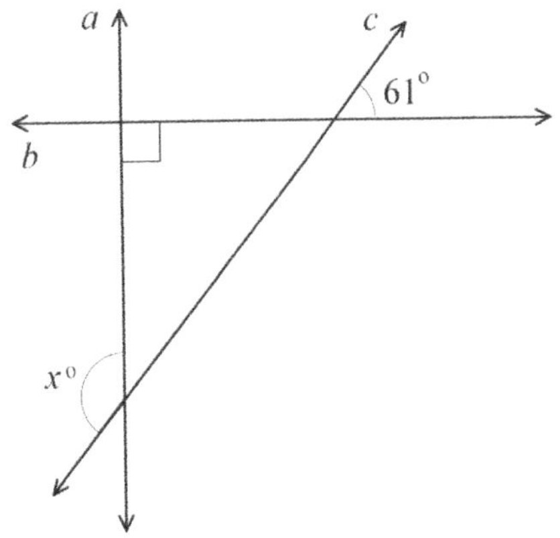

59. Mr. Owen opened an account with deposit of $4,400. This account earns 5% simple interest annually. How many years will it take Mr. Owen to earn $660 on his deposit?

60. If $2x - 2(5 - x) = 1$, what is the value of x?

61. The mean number of 7 numbers is 112. Two of these numbers have the mean of 107. What is the mean of remaining 5 numbers?

62. $$5 + 16 \div |-4| - 3\frac{1}{2} \times (-2)^3$$

What is the value of the expression shown above?

MULTIPLE CHOICE QUESTIONS		
Questions 63 – 68		
63.	$(-3)^3 + 4^2 - (-5)^0 =$ A. -10 B. 42 C. -12 D. 44	66. A water mill wheel makes one full revolution in 6 minutes. If the water mill wheel starts moving at 9 : 45 a.m., at what time will the wheel complete 14 full revolutions? E. 10 : 24 a.m. F. 10 : 48 a.m. G. 11 : 05 a.m. H. 11 : 09 a.m.
64.	On Tuesday, Nina bought $1\frac{1}{3}$ kg of apples. On Wednesday, she bought $\frac{7}{4}$ kg of pears. On Thursday, she bought $1\frac{1}{2}$ kg of peaches. How much fruit did Nina buy in total? E. $3\frac{7}{12}$ kg F. $4\frac{7}{12}$ kg G. $3\frac{1}{4}$ kg H. $4\frac{1}{4}$ kg	67. (number line shown with points B at 2 and A at 7, marks 0 through 14) Points C and D are not shown on the number line above. If A is the midpoint of BC, and D is the midpoint of AB, what is the distance between points C and D? A. 6 B. 7 C. 8 D. 9
65.	70% of the children playing football are boys. 35% of boys are wearing T-shirts. What percent of all children are boys wearing T-shirts? A. 24.5% B. 35% C. 40.5% D. 50%	68. $$\frac{72}{15} = \frac{48}{m}$$ What value of m makes the equation above true? E. 10 F. 12 G. 8 H. 5

Questions 69 – 74

69. Between which two consecutive integers is the fraction $-\frac{48}{13}$?

   A. -6 and -5
   B. -5 and -4
   C. -4 and -3
   D. -3 and -2

70. If n is an integer and $3n + 2$ is an even number, which of the following numbers must be even too?

   E. $n - 1$
   F. $2n + 1$
   G. $3n + 3$
   H. $5n + 4$

71. The product of two integers is 119. Which of the following numbers could be the sum of these two integers?

   A. 17
   B. 27
   C. -24
   D. -27

72. If x is an odd negative integer solution to the inequality $2x < -12.4$, what is the greatest possible value of x?

   E. -5
   F. -7
   G. -11
   H. -13

73. Malik has to write a 2,500-word essay. He planned to write the essay in 4 hours. Malik writes the first 400 words in 1 hour. What is the mean number of words he must write per hour during the remaining time in order to finish the essay according to his plan?

   A. 500 pages per hour
   B. 600 pages per hour
   C. 700 pages per hour
   D. 800 pages per hour

74. An elephant is 10 feet 5 inches tall. A giraffe is 17 feet 2 inches tall. Which of the following statements is true?

   E. The elephant is 7 feet 3 inches taller than the giraffe
   F. The elephant is 6 feet 9 inches taller than the giraffe
   G. The giraffe is 7 feet 3 inches taller than the elephant
   H. The giraffe is 6 feet 9 inches taller than the elephant

Questions 75 – 80

75. NUMBER OF STUDENTS WEARING GLASSES

	Number of students	Percentage
Grade 5	3 out of 24	12.5%
Grade 6	4 out of 25	16%
Grade 7	4 out of 20	20%
Grade 8	5 out of 25	25%

One number in the percentage column is incorrect. Which change needs to be made?

A. Change Grade 5 to 12%
B. Change Grade 6 to 20%
C. Change Grade 7 to 25%
D. Change Grade 8 to 20%

76. If $\frac{x+1}{14} = \frac{3}{49}$, what is the value of $7x$?

E. 6
F. 7
G. -1
H. $-\frac{1}{7}$

77. $\left(-5\frac{1}{3}\right) \times \left(-\frac{1}{2}\right)^3 + 3\frac{1}{3} =$

A. 4
B. $2\frac{1}{3}$
C. $4\frac{2}{3}$
D. 2

78. The number of students at a high school was increased by 18% to 413 after the promotion company. How many students were there at the high school before the increase?

E. 300
F. 320
G. 340
H. 350

79. The numbers a, b, and c are selected from the set $\{-4, -2, 2, 8\}$. It is known that $a = -\frac{c}{2} = -2b$. Which number from the set was not used?

A. -4
B. -2
C. 2
D. 8

80. $\{0.02 \times 10^2, 0.02 \times 10^1, 0.02, 0.02 \times 10^{-1}, 0.02 \times 10^{-2}\}$

If a person chooses a number at random from the set above, what is the probability that the number is less than 0.05?

E. 0.8
F. 0.6
G. 0.5
H. 0.4

Questions 81 – 86

81. There are 50 color marbles in a box. 20% of them are red. If 40% of the red marbles were taken out of the box, what will be the percentage of red marbles in the box?

A. About 13%
B. About 15%
C. About 17%
D. About 18%

82.

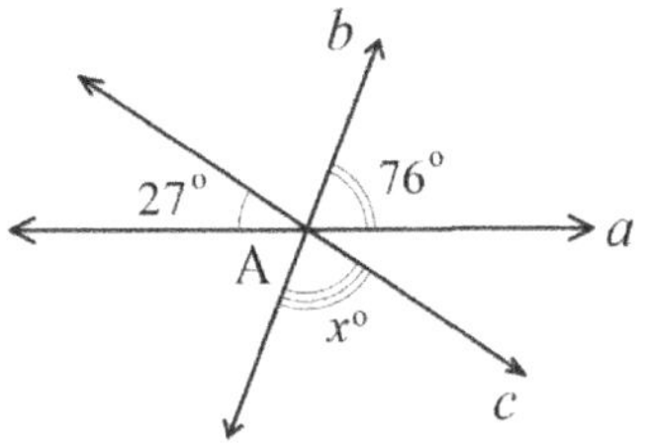

Lines a, b, and c intersect at point A. What is the value of x?

(Diagram shows lines a, b, c intersecting at A with angles $27°$, $76°$, and $x°$)

E. 77
F. 89
G. 95
H. 103

83. Which statement must be true if x is a decimal greater than 0 but less than 1?

A. $\frac{1}{x} < 1$
B. $-\frac{1}{x} > -1$
C. $\frac{1}{x} > 1$
D. $-1 < -\frac{1}{x} < 0$

84. A basket contains red, green and blue balls. There are 25 red balls in the basket. The probability of randomly choosing a green ball is $\frac{1}{15}$. The probability of randomly choosing a red ball is $\frac{1}{3}$. How many blue balls are in the basket?

E. 30
F. 35
G. 40
H. 45

85.
$$1 \text{ mile} = 1.6 \text{ kilometers}$$
It took Chloe 80 minutes to ride her bicycle 10 miles. What was Chloe's rate at kilometers per hour?

A. 16 km/h
B. 12.5 km/h
C. 12 km/h
D. 7.5 km/h

86. What is the greatest common factor of $2^5 \times 3^3$ and $2^3 \times 3^5$?

E. $2^2 \times 3^2$
F. $2^3 \times 3^3$
G. $2^4 \times 3^4$
H. $2^5 \times 3^5$

Questions 87 – 92

87. Mr. Lumen gives two math problems to 25 students as homework. 11 students give wrong answers to the 2nd problem and 8 students solve the 2nd problem correctly but give wrong answers to the 1st problem. How many students solve both problems correctly?

    A. 5
    B. 6
    C. 7
    D. 8

88. If $x = -\frac{4}{5}$ and $y = 2$, which of the following statements is false?

    E. $x + y$ is a positive number
    F. xy is a negative number
    G. $y^2 + x$ is a negative number
    H. $x^2 + y$ is a positive number

89. Mr. Tracy is one of the 7 members of the scientific group. If 2 members of that scientific group are selected to go to a conference, which fraction of the possible pairs of members would include Mr. Tracy?

    A. $\frac{2}{7}$

    B. $\frac{3}{7}$

    C. $\frac{1}{7}$

    D. $\frac{6}{7}$

90.

In the parallelogram above, what is the value of $x + y$?

    E. 132
    F. 148
    G. 94
    H. 96

91. If $3A - 2B = 3B + 2A$, what is $\frac{2B}{A}$?

    A. $\frac{1}{5}$

    B. $\frac{2}{5}$

    C. $\frac{1}{10}$

    D. $\frac{5}{2}$

92.

On the number line above, point K (not shown) is located such that point M divides the line segment KN in the ratio 2 : 1. What is the position of the point K?

    E. 3
    F. 2
    G. 1
    H. 0

Questions 93 – 98

93. Larry and Kim divided their coins between themselves. Kim got 45% of all coins. If Larry got 28 coins more than Kim, how many coins did Kim get?

A. 126
B. 252
C. 154
D. 308

94. The shaded sector of the circle shown above has the area of $45\pi\ cm^2$. What is the circumference of the circle?

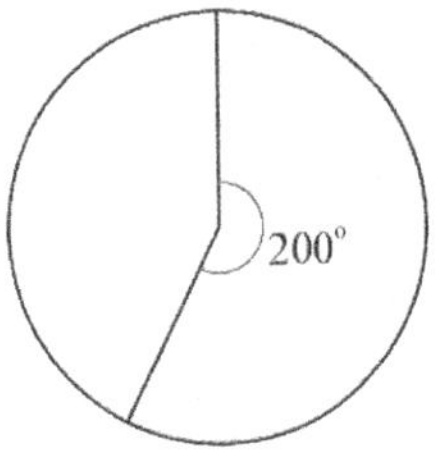

E. $9\pi\ cm$
F. $12\pi\ cm$
G. $15\pi\ cm$
H. $18\pi\ cm$

(Circle with sector marked 200°)

95. How many natural solutions does the inequality $-11 < 3 - 2x \leq 9$ have?

A. 9
B. 10
C. 6
D. 7

96. A student mixed three liquids A, B and C in the jar. He took twice as much liquid A as liquid B and five times as much liquid C as liquid A. What is the ratio of the amount of liquid A to the amount of liquid B to the amount of liquid C in the mixture?

E. $2 : 1 : 5$
F. $2 : 5 : 1$
G. $2 : 1 : 10$
H. $2 : 10 : 1$

97. Melanie has a comics and Jordan has b comics. If Jordan gives 3 comics to Melanie, then Melanie will have 1.5 times as many comics as Jordan has. Which equation shows the relationship between a and b?

A. $1.5(a + 3) = b - 3$
B. $1.5(b - 3) = a + 3$
C. $1.5(b + 3) = a - 3$
D. $1.5(a - 3) = b + 3$

98. Yesterday, Marissa read 20% of her book. Today, Marissa read 60% of what she read yesterday. In lowest terms, what fraction of the book is left for her to read?

E. $\frac{17}{25}$
F. $\frac{4}{5}$
G. $\frac{18}{25}$
H. $\frac{1}{5}$

Questions 99 – 104

99.

NUMBER OF PAGES READ

Number of pages	Number of students
< 25	3
25 – 50	4
50 – 75	6
75 – 100	3

All 80 students in Grade 8 at a school are assigned to read the same 100-page book. A teacher records the number of pages read in a random sample of the students, as shown in the table above. Based on this sample, how many students in the entire grade would be expected to read at least 50 pages?

A. 15
B. 20
C. 30
D. 45

100. Emma runs 9 kilometers in 1 hour 15 minutes. At this rate, how many meters does she run per second?

E. 1.5
F. 2
G. 2.5
H. 3

101. $$\frac{x+3}{2} - \frac{x+2}{3} + \frac{x+1}{6} = 2$$

For what value of x is the equation above true?

A. 1
B. 2
C. 3
D. 6

102.

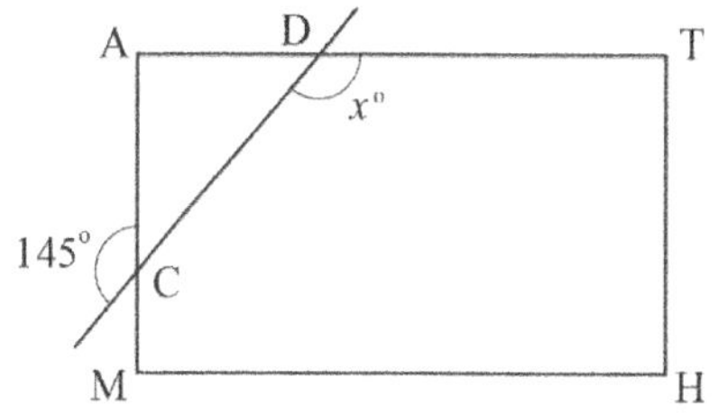

The diagram above shows line segment CD intersecting a rectangle MATH. What is the measure of angle x?

E. 55°
F. 35°
G. 125°
H. 155°

103. $\{1, 2, 3, \ldots, 48, 49, 50\}$

How many members of the set shown above are multiples of 2 but not multiples of 5?

A. 10
B. 15
C. 20
D. 25

104. Which percentage is closest to the decimal 0.0048?

E. 5%
F. 0.5%
G. 50%
H. 0.05%

453

Questions 105 – 110

105.	Iola passed 4 Math tests with a mean score of 81.5 and 3 History tests with a mean score of 85. What was the mean of the scores for all tests Iola passed? A. 82 B. 82.5 C. 83 D. 83.5	108.	*[Figure: outer rectangle with length 15 cm containing inner rectangle with width 2.5 cm]* In the figure above, the inner rectangle is similar to the outer rectangle. The length of the outer rectangle is 15 cm, and the width of the inner rectangle is 2.5 cm. If the perimeter of the inner rectangle is 20 cm, what is the width of the outer rectangle? E. 4.5 cm F. 5 cm G. 6 cm H. 7.5 cm
106.	A rectangular prism has the volume of 280 in^3. The base of the rectangular prism is 7 inches wide and 5 inches long. What is the height of the prism? E. 2 inches F. 4 inches G. 8 inches H. 16 inches	109.	The greatest common factor of 48 and x is 8. Which of the following numbers could be x? A. 32 B. 36 C. 40 D. 44
107.	Malcolm has 6 apples, and 8 peaches at his house. He wants to take three fruit to school. In how many different ways could he choose them? A. 182 B. 2,184 C. 1,092 D. 364	110.	In the triangle, 1st angle is 60% of the 2nd angle and 7° greater than the 3rd angle. What is the measure of the smallest angle in the triangle? E. 36° F. 44° G. 51° H. 85°

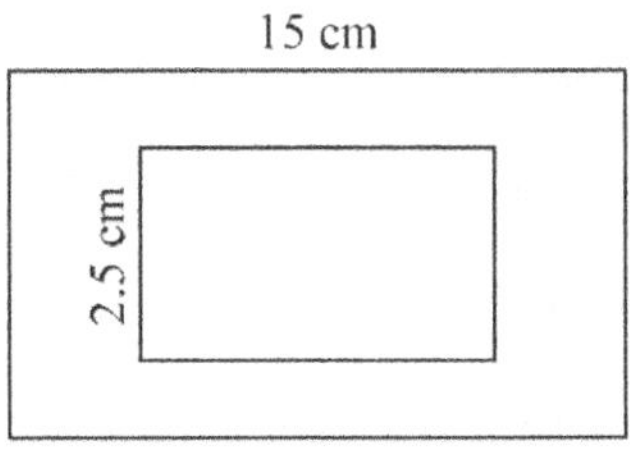

	Questions 111 – 114		
111.	$4x + 3y = 12$ Value 1: The value of x when $y = -\frac{5}{3}$ Value 2: The value of y when $x = -\frac{7}{4}$ Which of the following statements is true? A. Both values are equal B. The value 2 is greater C. The value 1 is greater D. Too little information to compare values 1 and 2	113.	The expression $\left(\frac{a}{b} - \frac{1}{2b}\right) \div \frac{2}{b}$ is equivalent to… A. $2a - 1$ B. $\frac{2a-1}{2}$ C. $\frac{2a-1}{4}$ D. $\frac{2a-1}{8}$
112.	What is the least of five consecutive integers whose sum is -190? E. -36 F. -40 G. -35 H. -39	114.	Tia has $5 in quarters. Nola has $3 in nickels. Which of the following statements is true? E. Tia has 5 more coins than Nola has F. Tia has 10 more coins than Nola has G. Nola has 5 more coins than Tia has H. Nola has 10 more coins than Tia has